The American Enco   with

Buddhism

1 8 4 4 – 1 9 1 2

Victorian Culture & the Limits of Dissent

THOMAS A. TWEED

With a New Preface by the Author

THE UNIVERSITY OF NORTH CAROLINA PRESS

Chapel Hill & London

Originally published by Indiana University Press in 1992.
Paperback edition published by the University of
North Carolina Press in 2000.

The paper in this book meets the guidelines for permanence
and durability of the Committee on Production Guidelines
for Book Longevity of the Council on Library Resources.

Library of Congress Cataloging-in-Publication Data
Tweed, Thomas A.
The American encounter with Buddhism, 1844–1912:
Victorian culture and the limits of dissent /
Thomas A. Tweed; with a new preface by the author.
p. cm.
Originally published: Bloomington,
Indiana University Press, c1992.
Includes bibliographical references.
ISBN 0-8078-4906-5 (pbk.: alk. paper)
1. Buddhism—United States—History. 2. Buddhism—
Study and teaching—United States—History. 3. United
States—Intellectual life—1865–1918. 4. United States—
Civilization—Buddhist influences. I. Title.
BQ734.T84 2000 294.3'0973'09034—dc21 00-060725

Chapter 1 of this book is a revised and expanded version of
my article, "'The Seeming Anomaly of Buddhist Negation':
American Encounters with Buddhist Distinctiveness,
1858–1877," *Harvard Theological Review* 83 (January 1990):
65–92. Copyright 1990 by the President and Fellows of
Harvard College. Reprinted by permission.

04 03 02 01 00 5 4 3 2 1

The American Encounter with
Buddhism
1 8 4 4 – 1 9 1 2

For My Wife,
Margaret L. McNamee

Contents

Foreword

In this volume Thomas A. Tweed invites readers to enter a sophisticated universe of American discourse among later Victorians who criticized Buddhism, sympathized with it, or even converted to it. He explores with care and thoroughness a conversation which, if over now, is still of more than antiquarian interest. Tweed's American Buddhists and Buddhist sympathizers tell us significant things about the late Victorian culture they shared with mainline Protestants and others. For the Americans who turned to Buddhism make it clear that, even in the nineteenth century, turning east did not signal complete alienation.

In a study that concentrates our attention on processes of cultural contact more than on complexities of the Buddhist tradition, Tweed's protagonists are Euro-American Buddhists and others attracted by this Asian religion. The chronological focus is the second half of the nineteenth century. There Tweed documents a case that illuminates the limits of religious dissent and the extent of cultural consent in American society. In doing so, he refines the argument of R. Laurence Moore (*Religious Outsiders and the Making of Americans*) regarding outsiders and insiders in American religious and cultural history—giving us a picture of "outsiders" who are not really that at all. Tweed shows us people with a family quarrel about aspects of American culture. These people turn to an "exotic" Eastern religion only insofar as it affirms certain basic American values. Thus, by looking at the values these Buddhists and kindred spirits affirm—theism, individualism, optimism, activism—Tweed's study casts indirect light on the cultural mainstream. In fact, it thereby confirms what others have told us about American society in the Victorian era. Tweed's close analysis of one discourse community (to use his language), despite the small numbers involved in it, provides insights about the dominant concerns and assumptions of the time.

More than that, Tweed improves our understanding of the contact process between Eastern and Western thought, demonstrating clearly that it was not simply New England intellectuals or romantics who were attracted to Buddhism in America. In his examination of the reception accorded this Asian religion by Americans, we encounter critics, scholars, travelers, and converts scattered throughout the United States and representing more than one class of people. Tweed makes creative use of diverse evidence to substantiate this fact, sifting through old journals to gain a sense of audience, reading Victorian Buddhist periodicals for names, and examining private correspondence. By these means he is able to establish the existence of a flourishing religiocultural network.

To aid his analysis, Tweed constructs a typology of Buddhist adherents and sympathizers that comprises three categories—esoterics, rationalists, and romantics. He shows the diverse ways in which these different groups of dissenting Victorians embodied American values and the prevailing assumptions of Anglo-Protestant Victorian culture. Some Americans, for example, were primarily impressed with what they saw as Buddhism's compatibility with science and with its relative tolerance as compared with Western faiths. Others expressed sympathy for the "intellectual land-scape" of the Eastern worldview, found meaningful parallels between the Buddha and Jesus, or pointed to the ethical dimensions in both Buddhism and Christianity. Still others recognized a "Protestant" quality to both faiths. These varying responses to and interpretations of Buddhism reveal the complexity of cultural contact; they suggest both why some Americans were attracted to Buddhism and why the actual adherents were so few in number.

Among those drawn to Buddhism in the late nineteenth century were the spiritually disillusioned as well as the curious. Many adherents and sympathizers also explored other religious options available at the time, including Theosophy and Spiritualism. Although dissenters of various stripes, these Americans were unable to reject completely the dominant cultural beliefs and values. According to Tweed, the individuals who were part of this complex pattern of dissent and consent were able to give up more easily the ideas of a personal creator and of a substantial, immortal self than their commitments to individualism, optimism, and activism. Tweed's discovery of this significant fact challenges us to examine other dissenting American religious communities to see to what extent they, too, involve reciprocal relations with or mirror the values of the dominant culture.

Catherine L. Albanese
Stephen J. Stein

Preface to the Paperback Edition

A reporter for *Atlantic Monthly* notes that "of the religions of the East, Buddhism is the best known and most popularly appreciated." A book reviewer observes that Buddhism has "numerous enthusiastic admirers" in the United States. A newspaper in New York reports swelling interest in the religion: "It is no uncommon thing to hear a New Yorker say he is a Buddhist nowadays." And another media story about Boston suggests that "the term 'American Buddhist' is not an uncommon one at date." At a time when Buddhism has never been more visible in American culture, when a 1997 cover story in *Time* celebrated "America's Fascination with Buddhism," all this media trumpeting of a Buddhist vogue might not seem noteworthy. Except that these observations about Buddhism's widespread appeal were written a century ago—in 1900, not 2000. And the nation's "fascination" with this Asian religion, I suggest in *The American Encounter with Buddhism*, has a long and intriguing history.[1]

The vast majority of Buddhists in the United States have been Asian immigrants or the descendants of immigrants, and the first Asians to carry their inherited faith with them to American shores came from China. The Chinese started arriving in large numbers in the 1850s, and other Buddhist immigrants from East Asia—Japanese and Korean—docked in Hawaii and along the Pacific Coast during the 1890s. A series of racist laws—starting with the 1882 Chinese Exclusion Act and culminating in the 1924 Immigration Act—blocked entry to the nation's borders for most Asians, although tens of thousands of Asian American Buddhists who were already in the United States continued to practice their faith at home altars and public temples during the first half of the twentieth century. And during World War II, when President Roosevelt ordered Japanese Americans to internment camps, some U.S. Buddhists even worshiped behind barbed wire. In 1965, Congress abandoned the unfair national quota system when it passed the Hart-Celler Immigration Act, which allowed more Asians to gain admission to the United States. Since then, almost four of every ten migrants entering the country have come from Asia—Vietnam, China, Thailand, Laos, Kampuchea, Myanmar, or Sri Lanka. Asian Americans now number more than 10.5 million, and many of these newest Americans are cradle Buddhists.[2]

But if most of the Buddhists in the United States claim Asian descent, that isn't the whole story. Converts and sympathizers have been important too. As I show in this book, Americans of European ancestry began calling themselves Buddhists in the late nineteenth century, not the late twentieth. Some professing converts were isolated seekers who remained obscure to their contemporaries. Consider, for example, one of the most compelling characters I discovered: Frank Graeme Davis was a student at the University of South Dakota who wrote to Japanese Buddhist priests, subscribed to Buddhist magazines, and met every Friday night in his dorm room with four friends "for the purpose of studying Buddhism." Other Buddhist converts were minor celebrities around the turn of the twentieth century. Marie deSouza Canavarro, whom the press called "Sister Sanghamitta," became the first woman to formally convert to Buddhism on U.S. soil in 1897. She also lectured as a Buddhist authority in Asia and the West, wrote books and articles about the religion, and even ran a Buddhist school for girls in Sri Lanka. And Buddhist sympathizers—those who had interest in the religion but did not formally or fully affiliate with it—also played a role in the nineteenth-century encounter with Buddhism. For example, Abby Ann Judson, the daughter of a famous Baptist missionary to Burma, saw herself as a Spiritualist, but she dabbled in Buddhism and came to believe that "the religion of Buddha is far superior to what is known as Christianity." Paul Carus, the philosopher and magazine editor, defended Buddhist ideas, composed Buddhist hymns, and encouraged Buddhist missionaries, even though he was never willing to call himself a Buddhist. Some European American converts and sympathizers—for instance, Dwight Goddard and L. Adams Beck—maintained their interest in Buddhism after the late Victorian vogue had passed. But not many. It was only after World War II, and especially during the 1960s and 1970s, that thousands of Americans again turned east.

We are now in the midst of a second Buddhist vogue, more intense and widespread than the late Victorian "fascination" with the religion of the Buddha. All informed observers agree that there are more American Buddhists than ever, cradle and convert Buddhists, but because the U.S. Census no longer records religious affiliation, no one knows how many. Martin Baumann, a respected scholar of Western Buddhism, has estimated that there are between 3 and 4 million U.S. Buddhists. Of those, Baumann suggests, 800,000 are converts, European Americans and African Americans who were raised as Catholics, Jews, or Protestants but have embraced Buddhism as adults. Even if Baumann's estimate is high, it seems certain that converts are an important part of the story of Buddhism after 1965. More than 1,500 Buddhist temples mark the contemporary American landscape, and converts meditate and chant at Zen, Vipassana, Soka Gakkai, and Tibetan centers all across the country. High-profile converts—including Richard Gere, Steven Segal, Adam Yauch, and Tina Turner—bring the religion public visibility and cultural clout. So do Paul Carus's and Graeme Davis's spiritual descendants—the contemporary nightstand Buddhists, sympathizers who read popular manuals like Philip Kapleau's *Three Pillars of Zen* at night and then rise in the morning to sit almost cross-legged on a pillow facing their bedroom wall. Some of those contemporary sympathizers are as isolated and obscure as Davis; others enjoy the cultural spotlight. Moviegoers who follow director Martin Scorsese's career know of his appreciation of Buddhist values, which was evident in his 1997 film *Kundun*. And most sports fans know that Phil Jackson, successful NBA coach, self-consciously draws inspiration from Zen Buddhism.

Through the influence of celebrity converts and sympathizers—as well as the impact of more Asian teachers, transnational connections, textual translations, and flourishing institutions—Buddhism had profoundly shaped American culture by the turn of the twenty-first century. That influence has been especially notable in the years since 1991, when I sent the original manuscript of this book to the publisher. A lot can happen in less than a decade. Buddhism's cultural impact now is everywhere—in medicine, painting, music, poetry, publishing, psychotherapy, film, fashion, advertising, and television.

Consider some examples. Mindfulness and meditation practices popularized by Vipassana Buddhist centers and the Vietnamese Buddhist teacher Thich Nhat Hanh have influenced American medicine and psychotherapy. Duke, one of the nation's leading medical centers, offers an eight-week class in "Mindfulness-Based Stress Reduction." The program uses meditation to teach participants "to cultivate awareness and reduce stress." "With practice," the program promises, "you can apply these skills to everyday situations and connect more fully with yourself, your loved ones, and the life you are living." Similar programs flourish at medical centers and mental heath clinics across the country.[3]

Influence appears also in the fashion industry. Vivienne Tam's spring 1997 collection showed Asian influences, including wispy brown blouses with a serene Buddha gazing out toward the viewer, holding his palms together to signal gratitude and respect. Tam, who was born in China and raised in Hong Kong, explained that she designed her line to help promote a "spiritually balanced life." "The Buddhas represent," Tam revealed in one interview, "the highest power in the universe, and I would like the clothes to achieve a very peaceful and calm feeling. And not just for you wearing it, but also for the person looking at you." As often happens in the fashion industry, three years later copies of Tam's Buddha designs, and similar representations on cotton T-shirts, could be found in ready-to-wear collections for children and youth at stores such as Limited Too and Sears. In one department store's spring 2000 catalog, a young boy in green shorts and brown sandals models a yellow cotton T-shirt with an image of a round-bellied Buddha. Below the image are three Chinese characters; above the Buddha is the translation, a printed petition or proclamation: "Good Fortune." By the turn of the millennium, you could find the Buddha at the mall.[4]

Observers could notice a similar movement from high culture design to popular culture fad in the Buddhist-inspired "power beads" that millions of Americans were wearing in 2000. Zoe Metro (née Heather Aponick), a thirty-year-old New York designer, saw the Tibetan spiritual leader, the Dalai Lama, wearing the traditional Buddhist prayer beads on his wrist. And she was inspired to create her own line. Metro began selling wooden beads in Chinese take-out containers at $25 to $30 each and grossed $1 million by the end of 1999. She switched from wooden beads to semiprecious stones, each with its own spiritual significance, and soon the bracelets were "flying off shelves at many big department stores and pricey boutiques." Metro, and the manufacturers who jumped on the trend, were self-consciously reproducing traditional Buddhist artifacts: *juzu*, or Buddhist prayer beads, which Asian monks and laity wear to signal Buddhist identity and count the recitations of mantras, such as the Pure Land Buddhist sacred phrase *Namu Amida Butsu* (I take refuge in Amida Buddha). But American marketers added a New Age twist by linking different colored beads with different moral qualities, spiritual benefits, or secular advantages. So, for example, in the line sold at the accessory store Claire's, purple is for truth, pink is for love, and black is for courage. As Sarah Lessen, a thirty-year-old New Yorker who wears a rock quartz power bead bracelet representing strength explained: "I look down at my wrist, and I remember I need to be strong. It's a great inspiration." These bracelets, which vendors market under multiple names (including "power beads", "spiritual bracelets," and "karma beads"), have been exceptionally popular, among young as well as old, men as well as women. "Everyone is buying these powerbeads, all ages, all sexes, across the country," said Jennifer De Winter, associate general merchandise manager at Saks Fifth Avenue. "Rarely do you get a trend that appeals to so many people. It's incredible." And it's incredible that a traditional Buddhist ritual artifact could circulate so widely in American culture, even if many Americans who wear the beads—including countless schoolgirls—do not know their Buddhist origin or traditional function.[5]

Other instances of Buddhist cultural influence are even more obvious, as in the movie *Little Buddha*, the TV sitcom *Dharma and Greg*, and the RE/MAX television advertisement that uses red-robed Tibetan monks to sell real estate. And Buddhist themes were central in a 2000 episode of Fox's animated series *King of the Hill*. That episode, "Won't You Pimai Neighbor?," playfully recalls the plot of *Little Buddha* as it also humorously documents America's changing religious landscape. Bobby, the pudgy son of a racist Texas Methodist, dates the daughter of his Laotian Buddhist neighbors, Kahn and Minh, and struggles to know what to do when Buddhist monks identify him as the reincarnation of their deceased Tibetan spiritual leader, Lama Sanglug. During the course of the episode, millions of prime-time viewers see Buddhist immigrants celebrate Pimai, the Laotian New Year, in Kahn and Minh's suburban backyard. Americans hear three Buddhist monks (two Tibetans and a Western convert) explain the doctrine of rebirth and watch Bobby sit in the lotus position on his bedroom floor, chanting *Om mani padme hum* (Hail to the jewel in the lotus), a Tibetan Buddhist mantra that invokes the power of Avalokiteshvara, the bodhisattva of compassion.[6]

Of course, cartoon chanting, stress workshops, *Time* covers, Buddha

T-shirts, celebrity converts, *Little Buddha*, Zen basketball, and power beads, don't, by themselves, amount to much. The producers of *King of the Hill* parody many American cultural patterns, and most power bead wearers couldn't recite Buddhism's Four Noble Truths. Hollywood films deal with myriad current issues, celebrities dabble with all sorts of spiritual fads, NBA coaches will do anything to motivate high-priced players, and *Time* celebrates any "fascination" that sells magazines. Yet when we consider these and many other signs of interest—including the media omnipresence of the Dalai Lama, the Zen-inspired installations of video artist Bill Viola, and the music of Buddhist convert Adam Yauch of the Beastie Boys—Buddhism's contemporary cultural influence seems indisputable.[7]

I don't know anyone who predicted the swelling popularity of Buddhism during the 1990s—I certainly didn't see it coming—and the concomitant boom in scholarship about American Buddhism has been just as surprising and just as notable. When I wrote *The American Encounter with Buddhism*, there was little scholarship on the topic. Three comprehensive volumes dealt directly and fully with U.S. Buddhism, but only one of those was authored by a scholar: *American Buddhism* by Charles S. Prebish, a Buddhist studies specialist. To confess to a colleague at a scholarly conference that you researched Buddhism in America elicited a befuddled stare. It just was not an area of study. Scholars specialized in (Asian) Buddhism and American (Christian) religion, but no one studied American Buddhism. By 2000 that had changed, as lively new subfields emerged in Buddhist studies and American studies.[8]

As evidence of this shift, consider two edited volumes that arose from conferences, *The Faces of Buddhism in America* (1998) and *American Buddhism: Methods and Findings in Recent Scholarship* (1999). Taken together, these two books offered contributions from thirty-two different authors—historians, sociologists, philosophers, anthropologists, and Buddhist studies specialists. By 2000, several dozen scholars, and many more graduate students laboring in the archives or the field, studied Buddhism in America as a primary or secondary research interest. Conference sessions, and even several-day meetings, addressed the topic. A new journal, the *Journal of Global Buddhism*, appeared, and there were more and more Ph.D. dissertations all the time—for example, fourteen between 1993 and 1997 analyzed American Buddhism.[9]

And since 1992, specialists have filled the shelves with books and articles. Several helpful surveys of this growing scholarly literature have appeared, and one of those lists 193 books and articles and 34 web pages, films, and CD-ROMs. Several broader works that deal with Asian religions in America contain helpful material on U.S. Buddhism, including *World Religions in America: An Introduction* (1994), *On Common Ground: World Religions in Amer-*

ica (1997), and *Asian Religions in America: A Documentary History* (1999). Three single-author books—by a sociologist, a Buddhologist, and a U.S. religious historian—provide overviews of American Buddhism: Joseph B. Tamney's *American Society in the Buddhist Mirror* (1992), Charles Prebish's *Luminous Passage: The Practice and Study of Buddhism in America* (1999) and Richard Hughes Seager's *Buddhism in America* (1999). A number of books have focused on particular Buddhist groups, including several studies by sociologists and anthropologists. Before 1992, a few social scientists had studied Asian American Buddhists and North American converts, but in the past decade several scholars trained in sociology or anthropology have offered models of how to study Buddhist groups in the United States and Canada. Among those important works are Penny Van Esterik's *Taking Refuge: Lao Buddhists in North America* (1992), Paul David Numrich's *Old Wisdom in the New World: Americanization in Two Theravada Buddhist Temples* (1996), Janet McLellan's *Many Petals of the Lotus: Asian Buddhist Communities in Toronto* (1999), and Phillip Hammond and David Machacek's *Soka Gakkai in America: Accommodation and Conversion* (1999). And other social scientific studies of convert and cradle Buddhists are now under way.[10]

Since *The American Encounter with Buddhism* first appeared, several other scholars have contributed to the conversation about the early history of Buddhism in the United States. Historians Martin Verhoeven and Harold Henderson have studied Paul Carus, who plays an important role in my narrative. Buddhist studies specialist Tessa Bartholomeusz has written a fine study of Buddhist nuns in Sri Lanka, and that book offers important new information about Marie deSouza Canavarro. Richard Seager has published an engaging overview of the World's Parliament of Religions of 1893, where Asian Buddhist speakers, including Anagarika Dharmapala and Soyen Shaku, made such an impact. And Stephen Prothero wrote an award-winning biography of Henry Steel Olcott, the first American Buddhist convert and a major character in the story I tell in this book.[11]

This enlivened scholarly conversation has led to new discoveries about the Victorian encounter with Buddhism. Most important, it has helped me uncover the only error—corrected in this edition—that I have found in my original text: I perpetuated a long scholarly lineage of misidentifying the translator of "The Preaching of the Buddha" (xix, 2, 7). I suggested the appearance of that piece was one of two events that opened the U.S. conversation about Buddhism, and I claimed that Henry David Thoreau translated it from a French edition of a Buddhist sacred text, the Lotus Sutra. In doing so, I continued an interpretive tradition that stretches back to 1885, when an article in the *Journal of Speculative Philosophy* by George Willis Cooke identified Thoreau as the translator. In 1993, Wendell Piez, a literary scholar and special collections librarian who had repeated the same mistake in print, began wondering. He did more digging and uncovered the error. Elizabeth Palmer Peabody (1804–94), not the author of *Walden*, edited and translated that important selection from Buddhist scriptures in 1844. Peabody, one of the leading female intellectuals of her day, was an educator, reformer, author, editor, and publisher. She might be best remembered for founding the first English-speaking kindergarten in the United States in 1861, but she also was one of two female charter members of the Transcendental Club. Peabody associated herself with the Transcendentalist movement and its social and intellectual innovations. She taught at Bronson Alcott's Temple School from 1834 to 1836. By 1840, she had opened a bookstore, a place where Boston intellectuals gathered and plans for the Brook Farm experiment formed. Ralph Waldo Emerson, a lifelong friend, tutored her in Greek, and at his urging, in 1841 she assumed the editorship of *The Dial*, the Transcendentalist periodical. It was in that magazine that the groundbreaking excerpt from Buddhist scripture appeared in 1844.[12]

The discovery of Peabody's role adds another colorful character to the story of the American encounter with Buddhism, while not dislodging Thoreau, whose importance remains undiminished. Abundant evidence of his personal engagement with Buddhism—for example in *Walden* and *A Week on the Concord and Merrimack Rivers*—assures Thoreau a place of prominence. And while I misidentified the translator, I was right about the original text: it was a selection from Eugene Bournouf's French edition of the Lotus Sutra. So it is still correct to claim that the American encounter with Buddhism began in 1844, when Edward Elbridge Salisbury lectured on Buddhist history to the American Oriental Society and *The Dial* published an excerpt from an important Buddhist text. But knowing that Peabody was responsible for the excerpt provides new angles of vision on the Victorian encounter, while adding another name to the lineage of liberal female interpreters of Asian religions in nineteenth-century Massachusetts: from Hannah Adams to Lydia Maria Child to Elizabeth Peabody. Most important, it encourages us to look again at the complex network of personal relations that sustained the early conversation about Buddhism. Peabody, a Unitarian and Transcendentalist who never disassociated herself from liberal Christianity, was not as smitten by Asian religions as the most radical of her generation—for example, Dyer Lum, who publicly announced his preference for Buddhism in 1875. But she befriended and corresponded with many who make an appearance in this story, including Sir Edwin Arnold, Ralph Waldo Emerson, Lydia Maria Child, Thomas Wentworth Higginson, James Freeman Clarke, and Samuel Johnson.[13]

Consider one letter that Peabody mailed to Johnson in the 1850s. Penned two decades before Johnson published the first volume of his *Oriental Religions and Their Relation to Universal Religion*, the missive acknowledges her continuing allegiance to liberal Christianity but praises lectures that Johnson recently delivered in Boston. "I could not say to you when I saw you," she wrote, "all that I felt of the very great value of your lectures on Eastern religions. They seem to me to be the most adequate and useful statements that have been made." Peabody then encourages Johnson to submit his interpretations of Asian religions to a wider audience: "But do publish them and soon. . . . They seem to me as truly so many floods of inspiration." Johnson, an important interpreter of Buddhism, did not take her suggestion immediately, but he did eventually. Because of her interactions with Johnson and others and—even more important—her translation of the Lotus Sutra, Peabody makes a claim to enter the story of Buddhism in the United States. And we can only hope that future archival excavations and creative reinterpretations will force us to revise that narrative again and again.[14]

Even if we need to expand the story to include Peabody, no new historical evidence or scholarly interpretations have challenged the basic argument I made in this book, and in recent years some scholars have even extended that argument by applying it to Buddhist converts in other periods and cultures. In *The American Encounter with Buddhism* I argue that a lively public discussion about Buddhism emerged between 1844 and 1912. And, to the astonishment and horror of some Christian observers, by the 1880s—and especially between 1893 and 1906—thousands of Americans began to identify themselves as converts or show signs of sympathy for that Asian religion. Those sympathizers and converts, I propose, tended to be one of three types—esoteric, rationalist, or romantic. Most important, this wider public conversation reveals much about Victorian culture in America. Christian missionaries who worried about the Buddhist vogue and American converts who celebrated it disagreed about much, but they shared several basic Victorian values that Buddhism, as it was then interpreted, seemed to contradict: theism, individualism, optimism, and activism. And if some American Buddhist sympathizers could reject the idea of a personal creator and the belief in a substantial self, very few late Victorians—even Buddhist advocates—could abandon their deep-seated commitments to optimism (a belief in the basic goodness and inevitable progress of individual persons, human life, and cosmic history) and activism (the centering of moral action and the concern to uplift individuals, enter politics, and reform societies). This—and the paucity of Asian teachers, translations, and institutions—helps to explain why convert Buddhism as an organized movement didn't flourish in the United States until later in the twentieth century.[15]

But by the start of the twenty-first century it was flourishing, and a new and even more far-reaching Buddhist vogue had set in. More and more Americans were turning east—and, thereby, changing the religious landscape, sparking a scholarly boom, and shaping popular culture. This historical study traces the roots of this second Buddhist vogue. And it offers clues about why contemporary converts champion socially active or "engaged" Buddhism, why women lead so many Zen and Vipassana centers, and why lay followers play so prominent a role in American Buddhism today. As this historical study informs our analysis of contemporary convert Buddhism we can see more clearly the enduring cultural significance of activism, individualism, and optimism.We can begin to explain why Buddhism is taking on new forms as Americans try to make it their own.

Thomas A. Tweed
Chapel Hill, North Carolina
1 June 2000

NOTES

1. William Davies, "The Religion of Gotama Buddha," *Atlantic Monthly* 74 (Sept. 1894): 335. Anonymous review of *Buddha's Tooth Worshipped by the Buddhists of Ceylon in the Pagoda called "Dalada-Maligawa" at Kandy, American Ecclesiastical Review*, n.s., 9 (Dec. 1898): 659–61. The excerpt from the *New York Journal* was quoted in *The Buddhist Ray*, 6 (May–June 1893): 4. The story about Boston is Lilian Whiting, "Boston Days," *New Orleans Times Democrat*, 19 Dec. 1894 and 28 Apr. 1895. The cover of the 13 Oct. 1997 issue of *Time* offered an image of Brad Pitt surrounded by Tibetans in traditional dress, a scene from the film *Seven Years in Tibet*. The same issue contained three stories on "The Americanization of Buddhism": David Van Biema, "Buddhism in America," 72–81; Richard Corliss, "Zen and the Art of Moviemaking," 82–83; and Bruce Handy, "A Conversation Runs through It: Brad Pitt on Buddhism, Fame, and Argentine Girls," 84.

2. The statistics on immigration and the Asian American population are taken from the U.S. Bureau of the Census, and the estimate of Asian and Pacific Islanders in the United States is for 1998 (10,507,000), which was the latest information available when this book went to press. U.S. Bureau of the Census, *Statistical Abstract of the United States: 1999*, Table 18. That information can be found at www.census.gov/statab/freq/99s0022.txt.

3. The Duke Center for Integrative Medicine, Duke University Medical Center, "Mindfulness-Based Stress Reduction Class," June–Aug. 2000. The description of the program goals appeared in a newspaper advertisement in the *Chapel Hill News*, 28 May 2000, A7.

4. Elsa Klensch, "Asian Influences Add Serenity to Tam's Spring Line," CNN Style, 27 Feb. 1997, www.cnn.com/STYLE/9702/28/vivienne.tam. For a glimpse at the Buddha images in her spring 1997 collection, see www.firstview.com/WRTWspring97/Vivienne_Tam. The children's cotton T-shirt with the Buddha image can be found in *Spring Sale*, Hudson Belk, Spring 2000, p. 13. I am grateful to my student, Holton Wilkerson, for alerting me to the influence of Vivienne Tam's fashion designs. See also the brief account in Jeff Yang et al., *Eastern Standard Time: A Guide to Asian Influences on American Culture from Astro Boy to Zen Buddhism* (New York: Mariner Books, 1997), 285.

5. The most helpful account of the origin and popularity of power beads is Rachel Beck's Associated Press story, which appeared in newspapers around the country: "Powerbead Bracelets Attracting Eager Masses," *Sun Sentinel*, 11 Oct. 1999, www.sunsentinel.com. All of the statistics and quotations in the text are from this article. See also "Let It Bead," *People*, 11 Oct. 1999, 82; and Melissa Weinberger, "Suddenly in Style: Powerbeads," 29 Jan. 1999, http://sacramento.sidewalk.citysearch.com/E/G/SACCA/0000/01/29/cs1.html.

6. "Won't You Pimai Neighbor," episode #4ABE18, *King of the Hill*, 20th Century Fox Television, written by John Altschuler and Dave Krinsky, final draft, 17 Aug. 1999. For the Buddhist influences on Chuck Lorre, *Dharma and Greg*'s executive producer and co-creator, see his "vanity cards." They are flashed on the screen at the end

of each episode and collected at the web page, http://abc.go.com. On these vanity cards, Lorre offers spiritual reflections, including many that highlight Buddhism, especially Zen. I am grateful to my student Tricia McCauley for her research on *Dharma and Greg.*

7. On the media presence of the Dalai Lama, and Asian monks more generally, see Jane Naomi Iwamura, "The Oriental Monk in American Popular Culture," in *Religion and Popular Culture in America*, ed. Bruce David Forbes and Jeffrey H. Mahan (Berkeley: University of California Press, 2000), 25–43. For Phil Jackson's account of the influence of Zen on his life and coaching, see Phil Jackson and Hugh Delehanty, *Sacred Hoops: Spiritual Lessons of a Hardwood Warrior* (New York: Hyperion, 1995), 43–58. On Adam Yauch's interest in Buddhism, see Thomas A. Tweed and Stephen Prothero, eds., *Asian Religions in America: A Documentary History* (New York: Oxford University Press, 1999), 349–51. The Zen influences on Bill Viola's video art are evident in the exhibition *Bill Viola: A 25-Year Survey*, 16 Oct. 1999 to 9 Jan. 2000, the Art Institute of Chicago. The exhibition was organized by the Whitney Museum of American Art, New York. See David A. Ross et al., *Bill Viola* (New York: Whitney Museum of Art, 1997).

8. Emma McCloy Layman, *Buddhism in America* (Chicago: Nelson-Hall, 1976). Charles S. Prebish, *American Buddhism* (North Scituate, Mass.: Duxbury Press, 1979). Rick Fields, *How the Swans Came to the Lake: A Narrative History of Buddhism in America* (Boston: Shambhala, 1981). Layman was a psychologist, and Fields was a journalist and Buddhist convert. For an earlier attempt to review the literature and chart the emerging subfield, see Thomas A. Tweed, "Asian Religions in the United States: Reflections on an Emerging Subfield," in *Religious Diversity and American Religious History: Studies in Traditions and Cultures*, ed. Walter H. Conser Jr. and Sumner B. Twiss (Athens: University of Georgia Press, 1997), 189–217.

9. Charles S. Prebish and Kenneth K. Tanaka, eds., *The Faces of Buddhism in America* (Berkeley: University of California Press, 1998). Duncan Ryuken Williams and Christopher S. Queen, eds., *American Buddhism: Methods and Findings in Recent Scholarship* (Surrey, U.K.: Curzon Press, 1999). Williams compiled the information about dissertations. See ibid., Appendix A, 262–66.

10. Peter N. Gregory, "Describing the Elephant: Buddhism in America," *Religion in American Culture* 11 (Summer 2001), forthcoming. Martin Baumann, "American Buddhism: A Bibliography on Buddhist Traditions and Schools in the U.S.A. and Canada," www-user.uni-bremen.de/religion/baumann/bib-ambu.htm. For an earlier review, see Martin Baumann, "The Dharma Has Come West: A Survey of Recent Studies and Sources," *Journal of Buddhist Ethics* 4 (1997): 194–211: http://jbe.la.psu.edu/4/baum2.html. For a hard copy of the review, see *Critical Review of Books in Religion* 10 (1997): 1–14. Jacob Neusner, ed., *World Religions in America: An Introduction* (Louisville, Ky.: Westminster/John Knox Press, 1994). Diana Eck and the Pluralism Project, eds., *On Common Ground: World Religions in America* CD-ROM (New York: Columbia University Press, 1997). Tweed and Prothero, eds., *Asian Religions in America.* Joseph B. Tamney, *American Society in the Buddhist Mirror* (New York: Garland, 1992). Charles S. Prebish, *Luminous Passage: The Practice and Study of Buddhism in America* (Berkeley: University of California Press, 1999). Richard Hughes Seager, *Buddhism in America* (New York: Columbia University Press, 1999). Penny Van Esterik, *Taking Refuge: Lao Buddhists in North America* (Tempe: Program for Southeast Asian Studies, Arizona State University; Toronto: Centre for Refugee Studies, York University, York Lane Press, 1992). Paul David Numrich, *Old Wisdom in the New World: Americanization in Two Immigrant Theravada Buddhist Temples* (Knoxville: University of Tennessee Press, 1996). Janet McLellan, *Many Petals of the Lotus: Asian Buddhist Communities in Toronto* (Toronto: University of Toronto Press, 1999). Phillip Hammond and David Machacek, *Soka Gakkai in America: Accommodation and Conversion* (New York: Oxford University Press, 1999). Among the earlier social scientific studies were

Tetsuden Kashima, *Buddhism in America: The Social Organization of an Ethnic Religious Organization* (Westport, Conn.: Greenwood Press, 1977), and Paul Rutledge, *The Role of Religion in Ethnic Self-Identity: A Vietnamese Community* (Lanham, Md.: University Press of America, 1985). Sociologists also wrote several Ph.D. dissertations and M.A. theses on Japanese American Buddhism. For citations see Williams and Queen, eds., *American Buddhism*, 262–63. Many important articles and book chapters on American Buddhism have appeared in the past decade—too many to cite here. Several of these have addressed the central question of Buddhist identity in the United States. See Charles S. Prebish, "Two Buddhisms Reconsidered," *Buddhist Studies Review* 10 (1993): 187–206; bell hooks, "Waking Up to Racism," *Tricycle: The Buddhist Review* (Fall 1994): 42–45; Jan Nattier, "Buddhism Comes to Main Street," *Wilson Quarterly* (Spring 1997): 72–80; Jan Nattier, "Who Is a Buddhist?: Charting the Landscape of Buddhist America," in Prebish and Tanaka, eds., *Faces of Buddhism in America*, 183–95; Thomas A. Tweed, "Night-Stand Buddhists and Other Creatures: Sympathizers, Adherents, and the Study of Religion," in Williams and Queen, eds., *American Buddhism*, 71–90; and Gregory, "Describing the Elephant."

11. Martin Verhoeven, "Americanizing the Buddha: Paul Carus and the Transformation of Asian Thought," in Prebish and Tanaka, eds., *Faces of Buddhism*, 207–27. Harold Henderson, *Catalyst for Controversy: Paul Carus of Open Court* (Carbondale: Southern Illinois University Press, 1993). Tessa Bartholomeusz, *Women under the Bo Tree: Buddhist Nuns in Sri Lanka* (Cambridge: Cambridge University Press, 1994). Richard Hughes Seager, *The World's Parliament of Religions: The East-West Encounter* (Bloomington: Indiana University Press, 1995). Stephen Prothero, *The White Buddhist: The Asian Odyssey of Henry Steel Olcott* (Bloomington: Indiana University Press, 1996). See also Thomas A. Tweed, "Inclusivism and the Spiritual Journey of Marie de Souza Canavarro (1849–1933)," *Religion* 24 (Jan. 1994): 43–58.

12. [Elizabeth Palmer Peabody, translator], "The Preaching of the Buddha," *The Dial* 4 (Jan. 1844): 391–401. George Willis Cooke, "*The Dial*: An Historical and Biographical Introduction, with a List of the Contributors," *Journal of Speculative Philosophy*, 19 (July 1885): 225–65. Although no one seems to have noticed before Piez, the editors corrected Cooke's error on p. 322 of the same issue of the *Journal of Speculative Philosophy*. Cooke himself repeated the mistake in a later work, although he qualified his assertion by adding that it "probably" was Thoreau: George Willis Cooke, *An Historical and Biographical Introduction to Accompany The Dial*, 2 vols. (Cleveland: Rowfant Club, 1902), 1:134. Other scholars continued the legacy of misidentification. See Roger C. Mueller, "A Significant Buddhist Translation by Thoreau," *Thoreau Society Bulletin* (Winter 1977): 1–2. Wendell Piez, "Anonymous Was a Woman—Again," *Tricycle: The Buddhist Review*, 3 (Fall 1993): 10–11. (Note that Piez's piece appeared in the "Ancestors" column, a regular feature of the magazine, where brief profiles of many nineteenth- and twentieth-century U.S. Buddhists have appeared.) For biographies of Elizabeth Palmer Peabody, see Bruce A. Ronda, *Elizabeth Palmer Peabody: A Reformer on Her Own Terms* (Cambridge, Mass.: Harvard University Press, 1999), and Ruth M. Baylor, *Elizabeth Palmer Peabody: Kindergarten Pioneer* (Philadelphia: University of Pennsylvania Press, 1965). Among Peabody's books are *Universal History, Arranged to Illustrate Bem's Charts of Chronology* (New York: Sheldon, 1859); *Reminiscences of Rev. Wm. Ellery Channing, D.D.* (Boston: Roberts Brothers, 1880); *Last Evening with Allston* (Boston: D. Lothrop, 1886); and, co-authored with Mrs. Horace Mann, *Moral Culture of Infancy and Kindergarten Guide* (Boston: T.O.H.P. Burnham, 1863). Although Henry James denied it, many contemporaries noticed the striking similarities between Peabody and the fictional reformer in his novel, *The Bostonians*, leading some to conclude that she was the model for Miss Birdseye. On this, see Bruce A. Ronda, ed., *Letters of Elizabeth Palmer Peabody: American Renaissance Woman* (Middletown, Conn.: Wesleyan University Press, 1984), 41–42.

13. Henry David Thoreau, *The Writings of Henry David Thoreau*, 7 vols. (Boston: Houghton Mifflin, 1894–95). Edward E. Salisbury, "Memoir on the History of Buddhism," *Journal of the American Oriental Society* 1 (1843–49): 81–135. [Peabody], "Preaching of the Buddha." Hannah Adams, with an introduction by Thomas A. Tweed, *A Dictionary of All Religions and Religious Denominations* . . . , Classics in Religious Studies Series, reprint (1817; Atlanta: Scholars Press, 1992). Lydia Maria Child, *The Progress of Religious Ideas through Successive Ages*, 3 vols. (New York: Francis; London: S. Low, 1855).

14. Peabody's letter to Johnson has been reprinted: Ronda, ed., *Letters of Elizabeth Palmer Peabody*, 303–5. Samuel Johnson, *Oriental Religions and Their Relation to Universal Religion*, 3 vols. (Boston: Houghton Mifflin, 1872, 1877, 1885).

15. Martin Baumann has applied my typology of converts—esoteric, rationalist, and romantic—to analyze nineteenth- and twentieth-century Buddhism in Germany and other European nations. See "Creating a European Path to Nirvana: Historical and Contemporary Developments of Buddhism in Europe," *Journal of Contemporary Religion* 10 (1995): 55–70, and "Analytische Rationalisten und romantische Sucher: Motive der Konversion zum Buddhismus in Deutschland," *Zeitschrift für Missionswissenschaft und Religionswissenschaft* 79 (1995): 207–25. One scholar even applied the typology to U.S. converts to Baha'i: Robert Harold Stockman, "The Baha'i Faith and American Protestantism" (Th.D. diss., Harvard Divinity School, 1990), 51–88. Charles S. Prebish and Kenneth K. Tanaka have extended my argument in *The American Encounter with Buddhism* to study contemporary cradle and convert Buddhists, emphasizing "the *active* and *optimistic* approach of today's American Buddhism" (italics in the original). Prebish and Tanaka, eds., *Faces of Buddhism in America*, 10, 297–98. One of the recent developments that they have in mind is "engaged Buddhism." Among the many texts on that topic, see Christopher Queen, ed., *Engaged Buddhism in the West* (Boston: Wisdom Publications, 2000), and Thich Nhat Hanh, *Interbeing: Guidelines for Engaged Buddhism*, 3rd ed. (Berkeley: Paralax Press, 1998). I briefly discuss engaged Buddhism in the postscript of *The American Encounter with Buddhism*, 161. For more works on engaged Buddhism, see Baumann, "American Buddhism: A Bibliography on Buddhist Traditions and Schools in the U.S.A. and Canada," 12–13.

Acknowledgments

I am happy to have the opportunity to thank those who helped me as I researched and wrote this book. This is a substantially expanded and revised version of my doctoral dissertation. The project began as a research paper for Professor William Clebsch at Stanford, and he offered extremely helpful advice on this, and other matters, during the early stages of my graduate career. I owe him a great deal. Because he died before I wrote the dissertation proposal, I incurred a great many additional debts as I turned to others at Stanford and around the country for help. Van Harvey and Lee Yearley gave sage counsel all along the way. Arnold Eisen and Hester Gelber asked good questions. Both before and after I finished the dissertation, a host of American historians and Buddhist scholars offered advice. Edwin Gaustad, Henry May, George Fredrickson, Wanda Corn, Conrad Wright, and Bruce Kuklick made useful suggestions about the American religious and cultural context. Professor Daniel Howe of UCLA was especially generous during the early stages of the project. Several Buddhist specialists offered suggestions, including Masatoshi Nagatomi, David Eckel, and Peter Gregory. Robert Buswell and Luis Gomez commented on the dissertation proposal. Guy Welbon of Penn and Carl Bielefeldt of Stanford, who also served on my dissertation committee, read the entire manuscript.

I also read portions of this work to several groups. I presented a version of the last chapter to a panel titled "Asian Religions and American Culture" at the annual meeting of the American Academy of Religion in 1988. The respondents, Catherine Albanese and Stephen Reynolds, raised important issues. Members of the Harvard Colloquium on American Religious History, the Stanford Graduate Colloquium on American Studies, the Stanford-Berkeley Buddhist Studies Colloquium, and the Buddhism in America Group of the Society for Buddhist-Christian Studies also aided in a variety of ways. Robert Ellwood, Carl Jackson, Stephen Prothero, Richard Seager, and Robert Stockman were especially helpful. My colleagues in the Religious Studies Department at the University of Miami listened to a summary of the project, and they provided constant encouragement. The university also offered crucial and generous financial support: The Max Orovitz Award in the Humanities and Arts covered costs for three extended research trips and freed me to devote my attention to writing.

Most of the characters in this story were relatively or completely obscure, and many of the sources were difficult to find. Many librarians played an important role in helping me to uncover information—too many to list. Some, however, were indispensable. The interlibrary loan staff at Stanford earned their money. Barry Hinson, also of Stanford's library, passed on some of his vast knowledge about genealogical research. The staff at the

Houghton Library at Harvard was consistently helpful. William Massa, archivist at the Sterling Memorial Library at Yale, also was generous with his time. Several librarians at historical societies—especially the staffs at the Historical Society of Pennsylvania and the Massachusetts Historical Society—were kinder than they had to be. Louise Woofenden at the Swedenborg School of Religion, E. Richard McKinstry of Winterthur Museum, and Richard Terry of the California State Library helped me uncover important biographical information. So did a number of staff members at public libraries scattered around the country—Saint Paul, Philadelphia, Boston, and San Jose. Barbara Boyd of the Special Collections Department at Glendale Public Library helped me to dig up data on Marie Canavarro, one central character is this story. Descendants of several of these historical figures also helped. Benjamin LaFarge sent me photos and other material about William Sturgis Bigelow. So did Sheila LaFarge of the Cambridge Buddhist Association. She graciously received me and passed on anecdotes about both Bigelow and John LaFarge, her great grandfather. She also read the entire manuscript. I probably received the most help from Sheila Ryan at the Special Collections Department of the Morris Library at Southern Illinois University and Elson Snow at the Buddhist Churches of America in San Francisco. Mr. Snow allowed me to explore the stacks of uncataloged material in the basement of that group's headquarters. There I found crucial sources—the subscription list to a Buddhist magazine and the daily records of early Japanese Buddhist priests in San Francisco. David Gardiner of Stanford and Eiichi Tanabe of Tokyo translated portions of those daily records.

Others offered decisive aid as I wrote and revised the manuscript. The series editors, Catherine Albanese and Stephen Stein, improved the book in countless ways. Other editors associated with Indiana University Press also helped. The scholar who aided me most during the initial writing stage was William Hutchison of Harvard, who shaped the proposal and directed the dissertation. His questions and criticisms helped me to refine my argument. Professor Hutchison carefully read that original work chapter by chapter. He also made extremely useful suggestions as I planned to revise it for publication. His other students will attest to his loyalty, kindness, and thoroughness. As an "adopted" student—it was he who agreed to supervise my project after Clebsch died—I feel that I owe Professor Hutchison an even greater debt. This book, with all of its remaining flaws, is intended as partial payment.

Many others, family and friends, played an indirect but crucial role. My uncle, Joseph Tweed, offered encouragement from the start. I feel lucky to have John Mustain as my friend. His kindness and loyalty made it all easier. Steve Tublin also helped me through the loneliness of graduate school life. My children, Kevin and Bryn, helped me to keep some perspective. As I changed poopy diapers, played Ninja Turtles, and wiped glistening noses I could not take myself, or this project, too seriously. Finally, my wife, Mimi McNamee, provided boundless encouragement and unyielding support—even during some very difficult times. She listened patiently as I tried to work out new ideas. She helped me to find time to research and write. I might have finished this book without her, but I cannot imagine how. For her kindness, and all the rest, I am deeply grateful. This book is for her.

A Note on Foreign Terms

Many terms of Sanskrit, Pali, and Japanese origin are used here. Some take diacritical marks, but I do not include them. Specialists in Buddhism might welcome them, but others—American Studies scholars, for instance—might find them distracting. Diacritics will not appear, then, with terms such as nirvana or Shinto or with titles and names such as Anagarika Dharmapala and Soyen Shaku. In the same spirit, I have not italicized Buddhist terms—e.g., nirvana and karma—that are somewhat familiar to English speakers. But familiarity, of course, is relative. One way to decide the issue is to italicize all terms that are not included in an English language dictionary such as *Webster's Third New International Dictionary*. (A partial list of words that appear in that dictionary has been published, together with other guidelines on the use of Asian terms, in *The Journal of the International Association of Buddhist Studies*. See Roger Jackson, "Terms of Sanskrit and Pali Origin Acceptable as English Words," 5 [1982]: 141–42.) Appealing to a dictionary does not solve all problems, however, since many terms that appear there—e.g., prajna and sunyata—remain obscure to non-specialists. I have dealt with this issue by italicizing some Asian words that officially have entered the English language but, in my judgment, remain unfamiliar to most readers. For terms of European origin, and on other issues concerning foreign words, I generally follow the guidelines of *The Chicago Manual of Style* (13th edition).

Introduction

Ezra Stiles, the Congregationalist president of Yale, described the cultural situation accurately when he reassured those gathered to hear his election sermon of 1783 that Americans were presently "in no danger of idolatry." Yet confrontation with non-Christian religions was not so far removed as Stiles and his pious audience might have suspected. In fact, in the following year there were a number of important developments. Systematic trade with India and China began. In Bengal, William Jones and a small group of British gentlemen founded the Asiatik Society. That society's journal, in turn, would help to introduce Americans to Asian religions in general and Buddhism in particular. Also in 1784, the first edition of Hannah Adams's popular survey of Christian sects and world religions appeared. Asian religions were discussed in an eighty-three page appendix in that initial edition, and in later versions Adams gave those traditions an even more prominent place. In subsequent years other writers in America—religious liberals like Joseph Priestley and conservative Protestants like David Benedict—also offered accounts of Asian religions. Early nineteenth-century European and American missionaries, travelers, and diplomats sent back reports. Fiction writers allowed readers of American magazines to journey eastward—without the hazards of sea travel—by entering the imaginative world of the "Oriental tale." Finally, some academics in Europe took an important step toward fuller understanding by studying Asian languages and cultures: Western Indology and Sinology began. All this combined to increase literate Americans' awareness of Asian religions.[1]

In fact, the anonymous author of one retrospective review of the eighteenth century claimed that increased knowledge of India and China stood as one of the accomplishments of the past century. And awareness grew in the succeeding four decades. The extent of understanding and the depth of interest, however, should not be overemphasized. Most Americans remained apathetic or ignorant. Very few, needless to say, considered the possibility of learning from any of these religions. In fact, the intellectuals who read about Asian religions—and the traders, missionaries, and diplomats who encountered them directly—often could not distinguish among them. They tended to view the "Orient" as a single entity with only minor variations. Although they disagreed about many other matters, between the 1780s and the 1830s Americans of widely diverging perspectives agreed about how to classify the religions of the world. No significant differences appeared, for instance, in the classification schemes found in the writings of Joseph Tuckerman, the Unitarian; David Benedict, the Baptist; and Thomas Jefferson, the Deist. Almost every American interpreter drew the map of the religious world this way: There were (1)

Christians, (2) Jews, (3) "Mohametans," (4) "heathens" or "pagans." (In the late eighteenth century another category, "Deists," often was added.) These spiritual cartographers usually lumped together Confucianism, Taoism, Buddhism, Shinto, Hinduism, and all other South and East Asian traditions. Even the handful who expressed a commitment to unbiased presentation or evidenced some genuine personal interest tended to view Buddhism, and the other traditions, as part of that mass of otherness called "heathenism," "paganism," or, with only slightly greater charity and sophistication, "Oriental religion."[2]

Among interpreters who could draw distinctions, Islam, Confucianism, and Hinduism were the most widely known. A few Deists and supernatural rationalists followed the pattern set by European Enlightenment thinkers by praising the historical instantiation of "natural religion" in Confucianism, but most American authors seemed to have been intrigued more by Hinduism and Islam. Taoism and Shinto continued to be veiled in a relative obscurity that would be lifted only partially at the end of the nineteenth century. Western knowledge about Buddhism increased slightly during the second, third, and fourth decades of the nineteenth century; yet the tradition continued to be linked with—even confused with—Hinduism. As late as 1845, for example, Ralph Waldo Emerson, one of the most influential American students of Asian religions, mistakenly identified the *Bhagavad Gita* in a letter to his sister as that "much renowned book of Buddhism."[3]

It is not surprising, then, that Buddhism, or any other "heathen" religion, failed to provoke conservative Christians to defensiveness or inspire vast numbers of seekers to explore these traditions for spiritual edification. Widespread Christian defensiveness and Buddhist interest would not be expressed until the last two decades of the nineteenth century. Yet the American public discussion about the nature and value of Buddhism got under way several decades before then. The Buddha began to emerge as a historical figure in the context of a conversation that began around 1844. During the 1840s and 1850s the Buddha joined Jesus, Muhammed, Zoroaster, and Confucius as a religious founder. At the same time, the tradition he founded began to be distinguished from Hinduism and other components of "heathenism." American readers' perceptions did not change suddenly or completely, however. Although no academic scholar made this mistake, writers sometimes still confused Buddhism with other Asian traditions even after the turn of the century. In 1906, for example, the editor of one magazine that devoted significant attention to Buddhism reported that he "repeatedly received letters" urging him to remind readers not to confuse Buddhism and Hinduism.[4]

As with most cultural developments, the public discussion about Buddhism was shaped by a confluence of cultural, economic, political, and social factors. In retrospect, however, certain factors seem more influential than others. In particular, the American discussion seems to have been animated by the continuing impact of Anglo-American missionaries' and travelers' reports; and it was stimulated and refined by two developments in the 1830s and 1840s—the rise of European Buddhist studies and the emergence of New England Transcendentalism. Westerners had been commenting on the tradition for centuries, but critical and linguistically informed scholarship on Buddhism did not get underway until the nineteenth century. One specialist, J. W. deJong, has suggested that the rise of systematic European Buddhist studies can be dated from the publication of Eugène Burnouf's (1801–52) and Christian Lassen's (1800–76) *Essai sur le pali* in 1826. This was the first Pali grammar to be published in Europe. Since Pali is one of the sacred languages of Buddhism, this event was important—as was the establishment of the first European chairs in Sanskrit and Chinese more than a decade earlier. Yet, in many ways, European Buddhist studies really only began when the first systematic and scholarly book on Buddhism in a Western language appeared in 1844. That volume—Burnouf's influential *L'Introduction à l'histoire du buddhisme indien*—provided Westerners with a solid foundation for later study.[5]

The influence of European Buddhist scholarship—and Burnouf's work in particular—is clear in the "Memoir on the History of Buddhism" which Edward Elbridge Salisbury (1814–1901) read at the first annual meeting of the American Oriental Society on 28 May 1844. Salisbury, the devout Congregationalist who became America's first notable scholar of Asian languages and religions, taught Arabic and Sanskrit at Yale from 1841 to 1854. He had studied with Burnouf in France, and he passed on the latest results of that French Orientalist's research in his paper to the society. Burnouf also had influence on the Transcendentalists. In fact, only a few months before Salisbury's lecture, Elizabeth Peabody (1804–94) had translated a passage from a work by Burnouf for the *Dial*. She took it from a French translation of the *Saddharmapundarikasutra* or Lotus Sutra. Peabody's translation with commentary and Salisbury's influential lecture unofficially opened the American conversation about Buddhism.[6]

In this study I examine the writings of Christian critics, academic scholars, travel writers, and Buddhist apologists who conducted this public discussion in American books, lecture halls, and, especially, magazines. I focus on those in this community of discourse who defended Buddhism, and—as much as the sources allow—I consider those who had sympathy for Buddhism but left no written record. My aim is to enlarge our knowledge of Buddhism in the West, deepen our understanding of new and transplanted religious movements, and identify the most fundamental beliefs and values of Victorian culture in America.[7]

BUDDHISM IN THE WEST

In the spring of 1254 the great Khan arranged an interreligious debate in the Mongol capital. William of Rubruck, the Franciscan who had been dispatched by Louis IX to gather information, win converts, and form alliances, participated in this day-long conversation among Buddhists, Nestorian Christians, and Muslims in Karakorum. He left a record of this encounter: William relayed how he, and Latin Christianity, had triumphed. Other reports of early historical contacts also have survived. But it was only in the nineteenth century that Buddhism became known widely in the West and only at the end of that century that Westerners began to identify with it. There has been some study of the history of Western intellectual encounters, and some accounts of Westernized Buddhism—for example, in Britain—have appeared. Several works on Buddhism in America also have been published. Sociologists and others have investigated ethnic Buddhists—mostly Japanese-Americans. A few contemporary American Buddhists and a Buddhist scholar also have added to the narrative. An interest in twentieth-century Buddhist institutions shaped their work, and they deemphasized the wider public conversation. Of these authors, Rick Fields, a Buddhist journalist, paid the most attention to the nineteenth century. But because of his interests and training, he ignored or deemphasized much of what I study here. Scholars who have written the history of Asian immigrants or surveyed American relations with Asia have added pieces to the story as well. Yet no comprehensive analysis of the wider nineteenth-century American conversation or historical interpretation of Euro-American Victorian Buddhist sympathizers and adherents has been available.[8]

In the first chapter of this study I argue that during the years that Buddha and Buddhism began to emerge from obscurity (1844–57) Western interpreters highlighted the parallels between Buddhism and Catholicism and the similarities between Buddhism and other "heathen" religions. Influenced by new emphases in European scholars' accounts, however, after 1858 or so many American interpreters stressed Buddhism's doctrinal distinctiveness. They employed a rhetoric of negation to describe its teachings: it was "atheistic," "nihilistic," "quietistic," and "pessimistic." A handful of mid-Victorian religious radicals who were sympathetic to Buddhism—the precursors of late-Victorian apologists—struggled to present the tradition as compatible with familiar beliefs and values. The public conversation, I suggest in chapter two, intensified after 1879 and peaked between 1893 and 1907. At the same time, Buddhism became increasingly attractive to many of the spiritually disillusioned just as Christianity became increasingly problematic. In this cultural context tens of thousands of Americans of European descent read about Buddhism or attended lectures about the tradition. A few thousand even seem to have identified themselves with it. Relying on information gathered from a variety of published and unpublished sources, I offer a tentative characterization of those who had some sympathy for the religion as well as those who embraced it fully. I consider gender, region, ethnicity, and economic status.

In chapter three I offer a typology of Euro-American Buddhist advocates in late-Victorian America. Challenging the assumptions, I suggest that most Americans who expressed interest in Buddhism were not New England romantics filled with an aesthetic and mystical spirit. They were spread out in at least twenty-four states and two United States possessions—although most lived in a few major cities. The majority were rationalist inheritors of the "Skeptical Enlightenment" who advocated positivism and evolutionism or esoteric inheritors of an occult tradition who inclined toward Spiritualism and Theosophy.

NEW AND TRANSPLANTED RELIGIOUS MOVEMENTS

This study also is intended to expand our understanding of how dissenters—more specifically, members of new and transplanted religious movements—have related to the dominant religion and culture. R. Laurence Moore's work on Spiritualists, Catherine L. Albanese's analysis of Transcendentalists, Stephen Gottschalk's investigation of Christian Scientists, and Klaus J. Hansen's study of Mormonism have shown that even groups that appeared to be radically distinctive shared a great deal with those in mainline Protestantism and Victorian culture. Even the most vigorous and consistent dissenter cannot flee or reject the surrounding culture completely. In fact, if a new religious movement is to attract loyal converts and build enduring institutions—as, for example, Mormonism eventually did—the cultural tension must not be too great.[9]

The same seems to be true of transplanted traditions, in America and elsewhere. A religion's shape and texture is determined, in part, by the soil in which it sprouts. When it is transplanted, religious conflicts and cultural tensions arise. As Buddhism was carried from India to China in the first centuries of the common era, for example, Confucians expressed some of the same reservations that American Protestants would centuries later. They too, for example, found Buddhism passive or world-renouncing. Yet Buddhism adapted to that new context—by using Taoist terms and stressing Confucian parallels. In fact, it went on to exert great cultural influence there and elsewhere in East Asia. It remains to be seen, of course, how significant a force Buddhism will be in America; but it seems clear that nineteenth-century Americans who had sympathy for the religion did not thereby engage in unambiguous or unqualified dissent. They had an ambivalent relation to the prevailing religion and dominant culture.[10]

In order to sort out patterns of dissensus and consensus more precisely, I distinguish "culture" from the structure of relationships among people ("society"), the modes of regulating conflict and power ("politics"), and the relationship between society and its material resources ("economy"). Drawing on traditions in interpretive sociology, Anglo-American philosophy, and cultural anthropology, I view cultures as collectively constructed frameworks of meaning imbedded in language and symbols which orient individuals in the world. These frameworks include presuppositions, beliefs, values, attitudes, symbols, myths, and codes of conduct. They are internalized, modified, and transmitted from one generation to the next through various institutions. As Daniel Howe pointed out with reference to nineteenth-century America, society, economy, politics, and culture often change at varying rates. Therefore, some discrepancies arise between or among them. So too religions, as cultural products, can stand in various complex relationships to the given social, economic, and political structures. A particular religion can challenge certain aspects of established patterns and support others. In most cases, the relation between a religious group's beliefs and practices and other dimensions of the shared life of the larger collectivity is an extremely complex, sometimes indecipherable, mix of dissent and consent.[11]

In chapter four I consider some of the ways in which Euro-American Buddhist apologists were dissenters. I argue that they were drawn to this Asian religion to a great extent by the distinctive advantages of its alien "intellectual landscape," and they expressed significant opposition to the reigning political, economic, and social forms. Yet, as I suggest in the final two chapters, their interpretations of Buddhism also reveal deep-seated commitments to fundamental beliefs and values of the dominant culture. The nine apologists that I focus on in this study often portrayed themselves as dissenters; and, in fact, they stood apart from their contemporaries in important ways. But these public advocates, and the others I discuss, were cultural consenters as well as cultural dissenters. They had more in common with mainline Victorian Protestants than nineteenth-century Asian-American adherents or twentieth-century Beat Buddhists. In their affirmation of prevailing beliefs and values they shared a great deal with others of their era.

VICTORIAN CULTURE IN AMERICA

Finally, in this study I try to identify what they shared with their contemporaries. To put it differently, the project is intended to contribute to the discussion about the dominant culture of nineteenth-century America. Sometimes it is necessary to turn one's gaze away from an object in order to see it clearly, to examine the exotic in order to understand the familiar. And so I began this study with a premise: by considering how nineteenth-century Americans of all sorts responded to a worldview that most considered alien, fundamental beliefs and values could be uncovered. There were a number of competing cultures in the United States organized around ethnicity, region, and religion. Irish Catholics, Swedish Lutherans, Chinese Americans, African Americans, and southern Baptists all had more or less distinctive sets of beliefs and values. But the culture that dominated the print media and other communications systems of the age was a transatlantic symbol system that was associated with British heritage, English language, Protestant religion, and the new urban middle class. Victorian culture in America, the usual term for this loosely defined assortment of convictions and attitudes, had a number of regional and denominational subcultures within it—for example, the Yankee "Presbygationalists" whose capital was New Haven, the old school Calvinists centered at Princeton, and the Unitarians clustered in eastern Massachusetts. In some ways, a full-blown Victorian culture did not emerge in the South until the 1880s; and, as expected, when it did both continuities and discontinuities with its northern versions appeared. For example, the Cavalier myth—so central to that region's identity and so integral to southern Victorianism—had no obvious northern parallels. Victorian culture also changed over time. One scholar, for instance, has distinguished the emphasis on sincerity in the sentimental culture of early Victorianism (1830–50), the increasing "theatricality" of mid-Victorian culture (1850–70), and the sanctioning of aggressiveness in late Victorianism (1870–1900). Some students of women's history have suggested that there were full-blown male and female cultures in this period. The issue turns in part on how the term "culture" is defined, but it seems indisputable that women and men had some different experiences and attitudes. And the ideals for women and men varied. Although some virtues seemed appropriate to all good Victorians, the proscriptive literature warned of distinct temptations and encouraged the cultivation of different traits.[12]

Despite the variations, students of Victorian culture have identified a number of beliefs and values that seem to have been especially prevalent. This middle-class culture was characterized by an emphasis on industry, sobriety, frugality, domesticity, sentiment, nativism, competitiveness, and order. Four other components of Victorian culture—theism, individualism, activism, and optimism—played a crucial role in the discussion about Buddhism: after all, openly hostile and allegedly neutral Western interpreters presented Buddhism as a negation of these. These Victorian commitments were not unique to the United States in this period. They have roots in Hebrew and Hellenistic cultures and can be traced to the Renaissance, the Reformation, and the Enlightenment. Theism—the belief in a personal creator, sustainer, and consummator of the universe—has been a foundational belief in the modern West. Individualism has too. Since it was coined in the context of the counterrevolutionary critique of the Enlightenment, the term *individualisme* has been used to refer to a wide range of thought and action. In one of the most famous uses of the term, Alexis deTocqueville pointed to the severing of the individual from society that he believed was an observable part of American culture and an inevitable concomitant of democracy. In this study I use the term in another way. By individualism I mean the tendency to emphasize autonomy or self-reliance in all dimensions of human life and the inclination to believe in a static, substantial, and immortal self. Optimism, which also had relevance for the conversation about Buddhism, refers to that tendency to emphasize the elevated capacities of persons, the positive elements of human life, the benevolent character of the universe, and the progressive development of history. Optimism often was linked with activism. By activism I mean that inclination to emphasize the spiritual significance of vigorous moral action in the world. It is a concern to uplift individuals, reform societies, and participate energetically in the economic and political spheres. Activism and optimism might have been more intense in the United States, but they were expressed clearly in Britain and other Western nations. Activism, for example, was characteristic of the Christian Socialist movement of 1848–54 and the various efforts for economic and social reform in nineteenth-century Britain. There were parallels and precendents.[13]

If the public conversation about Buddhism is any indication, however, these beliefs and values were fundamental components of American Victorianism. I expected to find some agreement among the discussants: after all, they shared the same culture to a great extent. Yet I found much more widespread agreement among American members of this community of discourse than I had anticipated. Those with different religious affiliations and divergent assessments of Buddhism—agnostic intellectuals, academic scholars, mainline Protestants, and Buddhist advocates—affirmed these four beliefs and values. American critics of Buddhism complained that the religion negated them; its defenders countered that Buddhism harmonized with them. Dissent erupted and diversity existed, yet to the extent that groups or individuals participated in Victorian culture their religiousness was, above all, self-reliant, optimistic, and activistic. In this sense, this study offers a characterization of the dominant culture. At the same time, it delineates the limits of dissent. Some of the spiritually disillusioned in the late Victorian period were willing to give up the notion of a personal creator and a substantial self; yet very few participants in the public discourse—even the Buddhists—abandoned their deep-seated commitments to self-reliance, optimism, and activism. Despite apologists' success at stimulating interest and their attempts at harmonizing Buddhism, then, the cultural strain remained too great for many. This helps to explain why Buddhism managed to attract so much attention but, finally, failed to build enduring institutions or inspire even more seekers to embrace the religion exclusively and fully.

The American Encounter with
Buddhism
1 8 4 4 – 1 9 1 2

"THE SEEMING ANOMALY OF BUDDHIST NEGATION"

The American Conversation about Buddhism, 1844–1877, and the Contours of Mid-Victorian Culture

In 1873 James Clement Moffat (1811–80), the professor of church history from Princeton Theological Seminary, published the second volume of his *Comparative History of Religions.* In that volume he highlighted the ways in which Buddhism was a "singular belief." The Buddhist tradition, he asserted, seeks to abandon "all conception of individuality." Buddhists yearn for "salvation by death" since they hope for the annihilation of the self in nirvana. Buddhists seem to focus on negation in other ways too, he claimed: "The radical pantheism of the Brahmans [Buddha] ignored, and supplied its place with nothing." Although his followers deified him, the Buddha himself was an atheist: "his own teaching . . . took no notice of beings called gods." For several decades before Buddhism became an option for the spiritually disillusioned, Moffat and other Americans participated in a public conversation about the nature and value of the religion. After 1858 or so that discourse focused on the alleged doctrinal distinctiveness of Buddhism. To put it differently, mid-century European scholars were increasingly inclined to employ a language of otherness and a rhetoric of negation to describe many of its most basic beliefs. Buddhism was "strange" and "singular." Its doctrines were not only "atheistic" and "nihilistic" but also "quietistic" and "pessimistic." As expected, American contributors to the discussion responded in various ways to the European accounts. Some ignored them completely. Many accepted them uncritically. Yet most felt that they had to come to terms with those Buddhist teachings that seemed to challenge some of the most fundamental beliefs and values of Victorian culture in America. But this tendency to emphasize Buddhist distinctiveness—and the concomitant inclination to seek explanations for its alleged divergence—was much less pronounced in the early

Victorian period as the conversation about the Buddha and Buddhism opened.[1]

THE AMERICAN CONVERSATION, 1844–1857: DEEMPHASIZING DISTINCTIVENESS

As I have suggested, the American discussion opened in 1844 when Peabody translated a Buddhist text from the French for a Transcendentalist magazine and Salisbury gave his influential lecture on Buddhism at the American Oriental Society. Both Peabody and Salisbury had been influenced by the work of Burnouf, one of the first great European Buddhist scholars. A few American academic scholars contributed to the midcentury conversation, but they did not play nearly as great a role as they would after the emergence of the modern American university and the rise of American Buddhist studies. Until the 1880s, then, most of the voices in the discussion were those of European interpreters of various sorts and American mainline Protestants, foreign travelers, and religious liberals. Most, although not all, American members of this community of discourse were educated male New Englanders of British and Protestant heritage. Many Protestant participants were foreign missionaries who had knowledge of one or more of the languages relevant to the study of Buddhism. The liberals—Unitarians, Transcendentalists, and Free Religionists—often had some sympathy for the tradition but little or no knowledge of the original languages.[2]

These American interpreters helped to form impressions of Buddhism by speaking and writing. I focus on the discourse in books and, especially, magazines. Contributions to that conversation appeared in general interest periodicals, the American Oriental Society's journal, mainline Protestant publications, and Unitarian, Universalist, Transcendentalist, and Free Religionist magazines. Of course, characterizations of Buddhism varied according to the religious perspective of the author, but during the early-Victorian era American authors of varying views tended to minimize the singularity of its teachings. Western accounts in general tended to emphasize parallels between Buddhism and "heathenism" and Buddhism and Catholicism. Most interpreters agreed that the Buddha and his followers expressed universal religious inclinations, even if they did so in pathetically childish or dangerously demonic forms. In fact, this is one of three patterns that held among Western interpreters of Asian religions, with some variations, from the beginning of systematic contact until the middle of the nineteenth century. Buddhism also tended to receive less attention than other non-Christian traditions—Confucianism, Islam, and, by the late eighteenth century, Hinduism. Finally, although there were prominent exceptions, most accounts of Buddhism were hostile.[3]

The reports of early European missionaries, for example, followed—and helped to establish—these patterns. Jacinto Orfanel (d. 1622), the Spanish Dominican, arrived in Japan in 1607. This was just after Christian influence had reached its zenith there and just before the edicts against Christianity began to be passionately enforced again. Orfanel was arrested for preaching Christianity fourteen years later, and a crowd of approximately sixty thousand gathered in Nagasaki to watch as he burned at the stake in the "Great Martyrdom" on 10 September 1622. But during the years before Japanese hostility to missionaries and other foreigners peaked, Orfanel had an opportunity to observe living Buddhism. Like many other sixteenth- and seventeenth-century Catholic missionaries in East Asia, he sent reports back to Europe. He reported, for example, that "the Japanese are much addicted to their idolatries." Cosme deTorres (d. 1570), who labored in the mission field in Japan for twenty years, made further distinctions: "There are some people who worship an idol called Shaka [Sakyamuni Buddha] . . . other people worship an idol called Amida [Amida Buddha]." The Portuguese Jesuit Gaspar Vilela (d. 1572) even claimed that followers of Japanese Shingon Buddhism worship the devil. But the point was the same: although some aspects of practice and organization suggested Catholic parallels—the missionaries found a pope, monks, rosary beads, and penitential rites—Japanese Buddhists could be lumped with "idolaters" or "heathens" from other false traditions around the world.[4]

New England liberals were slightly more positive toward the tradition, but their writings fit these interpretive patterns established much earlier. They have a deserved reputation as leaders in the American discovery of Asian traditions. But liberals actually devoted comparatively little attention to Buddhism before the 1860s. The emerging scholarship about India appeared in magazines they read—*Asiatik Researches* (1788–1839), *Edinburgh Review* (1802–30), *Monthly Anthology* (1803–11), and *Christian Disciple* (1813–23)—and the reports of Ram Mohan Roy's (1772–1833) "conversion" to Unitarianism generated excitement about India as a mission field. These developments and others focused the attention of pre–Civil War liberals in and around Boston on Hinduism. In general, if they wrote or read about Asian religions between the 1780s and the 1860s, these New Englanders tended to focus on India and Hinduism, Persia and Islam, or, to a lesser extent, China and Confucianism. For example, although he demonstrated the tolerant tone and inclusive theory for which Unitarians became noted, even as late as 1859 James T. Dickinson hardly mentioned Buddhism in three long articles on Asian culture and religion for *The Christian Examiner*.[5]

The most comprehensive interpretation of Asian religions, and Buddhism in particular, offered by a New England liberal between 1844 and 1857 was Lydia Maria Child's (1800–1880) *The Progress of Religious Ideas through Successive Ages.* Child, the author of two popular novels and an influential antislavery book, was disappointed to find that *Progress* brought neither increased popularity nor noticeable influence. Thomas Wentworth Higginson (1823–1911), her friend, later tried to provide an explanation: "The disappointment was no doubt due partly to the fact that the book set itself in decided opposition, unequivocal though gentle, to the prevailing religious impressions of the community. It may have been, also, that it was too learned for a popular book and too popular for a learned one." Child's sources were, as her friend put it, "second rate"; but the book apparently was just learned enough to bore. Apparently, it also was just sympathetic enough to non-Christian traditions to offend.[6]

Child failed to acknowledge the precedent or mention the earlier book, but in many ways her volumes were informed by an approach that was similar to Hannah Adams's in *Alphabetical Compendium* (1784): Child announced that she aimed at "complete impartiality." Of course, Child's religious perspective still colored her interpretations. Her views were influenced by Unitarianism—her brother was a Unitarian clergyman and a Harvard Divinity School professor—but she also showed inclinations toward Transcendentalism, Swedenborgianism, Free Thought, mysticism, and, especially after her husband died, Spiritualism. As she explained in a letter to Higginson toward the end of her life, her views changed over the years. She grew less comfortable with Christianity and more drawn to, among other things, Spiritualism. But, as she suggested in this letter from 1877, Child's faith had been more traditionally Christian when she wrote her survey of religions. And at that time she had presupposed the essential unity of all religions. Both commitments informed her description of the "progress of religious ideas."[7]

In volume two, after surveying Asian religions and Judaism and before considering Christianity and Islam in volume three, she concluded that all major religions share several basic ideas: "God, the Soul, the Creation of the World, its Destruction and Renovation, a Golden Age of holiness to come in the far-off Future, were common among all the nations of antiquity." This was not surprising, she suggested: "A general resemblance in ideas on these subjects might be expected, because human nature is everywhere the same, and in all ages has had the same wants and the same aspirations, and been liable to the same infirmities." Child then offered illustrations of these essential beliefs among the religions, but she completely ignored Buddhism in doing so. This does not mean that she gave up in the effort to fit that tradition into her characterization of the nature and history of religion. In fact, in her interpretation of Buddhism she not only employed categories like God, soul, and creation—none of which has obvious parallels in "orthodox" Buddhism in South or East Asia—but also at points used Christian concepts and language. This tendency is discernible, for example, in her discussion of the Buddha. Child described him as a "Heavenly spirit" who left "Paradise." Filled with compassion for the "sins" of mankind, he "took suffering upon himself that it might expiate their crimes and mitigate the punishment they must inevitably undergo." She knew that "European writers had brought the charge of atheism" against Buddhism. Child, nonetheless, presented the Buddhist conception of ultimate reality in terms of Hindu pantheism and described the final goal as a mystical union with "God" or a mystical absorption into the "Original Source of Being; which the Buddhists name The Void." That word "Void" might have caused a few of her readers to pause, but this potentially bracing language was buried beneath the piles of Christian parallels and the stacks of contrary assertions. It goes almost unnoticed. That, presumably, was the way Child wanted it. Almost two decades after this work was published she gave Higginson a copy of the *Dhammapada*, a key Buddhist scripture. Later she also might have read the scholarly accounts that increasingly emphasized Buddhist distinctiveness. In that earlier book, however, she, like other liberals, tended to deemphasize Buddhism and harmonize it with other non-Christian, and even Christian, traditions.[8]

In one of her early letters from Burma, a New England woman with very different religious sensibilities, Ann Haseltine Judson (1789–1826), offered her first impressions of the Buddhists she encountered when she and her husband arrived to preach the Christian gospel. "If we were convinced of the importance of missions before we left our native country," she wrote, "we now *see* and *feel* their importance, as well as their practicability. We could then picture to ourselves the miserable situation of heathen nations; but we now see a whole populous empire, rational and immortal like ourselves, sunk in the grossest idolatry, given up to follow the wicked inclinations of their depraved hearts, entirely destitute of any moral principle, or the least spark of true benevolence." Her husband's letters to colleagues at home and his official reports to the corresponding secretary of the American Baptist Mission were not much more sympathetic toward the Buddhist tradition. But at least both Ann Judson, the first female to leave America for a mission field, and her husband, the first American missionary in a Buddhist nation, offered some description of the religion. In fact, American missionaries, and their European counterparts whose writings appeared in American magazines, devoted more attention to Buddhism than the liberals. There were differences in temperament and perspective among missionaries, but most of the accounts presented to American readers before 1858 also tended to present Buddhism as one more instance of heathenism and its misguided worship of false deities. Few praised the tradition, and few interpretations seemed to challenge fundamental assumptions. Yet the situation called for pity and compassion rather than defensiveness and dismay. "I beseech you to take in to compassionate consideration the perishing millions of Burmah," Adoniram Judson (1788–1850) put it in one official report, "ignorant of the eternal God, the Lord Jesus Christ, and the blessed way of salvation." Buddhists seemed to be in no more need of missionaries' attention, laypersons' compassion, theologians' criticism, or Christ's salvation than any other heathens.[9]

They were less overtly hostile than missionary reports, but travelers' accounts of Buddhism had much in common with the sketches sent by those who had gone abroad to save souls. During this period, *Harper's* and other magazines published a number of excerpts from narratives by British and American travelers that focused on Buddhist nations—including pieces on Ceylon, Tibet, Burma, Siam, and Japan. One anonymous account offered "A Peep at the 'Peraharra.'" It described a visit to an important religious festival in two towns in Ceylon: "In the month of July, 1840, I had a peep at the celebrated Peraharra of Ratnapoora. . . . Like its mountain competitor [Kandy], it has a relic of Buddha enshrined in a richly-jeweled casket, which is made an object of special veneration to the votaries of that god." A detailed description of the dress, rituals, temples, and icons followed. The piece concluded with the author confessing his tedium with the spectacle and his longing for the comforts of the familiar: "When I left Ratnapoora crowds were still flocking into the town, for on the morrow the huge temple elephants were expected to march in procession through the place, decked out in all sorts of finery, and bearing the casket and the relic; but it was a wearisome spectacle, and I was heartily glad to find myself once more on my pony, quietly winding through green paddy-fields and under shady topes." Like this anonymous author, travel writers often highlighted the mysterious, the alien, and the curious in their accounts of Buddhist cultures. Sometimes they acknowledged reports about Buddhism's singularity. But the casual reader might conclude from the mandatory descriptions of the temples, icons, relics, and priests that Buddhists were devout but misguided, that they worshipped a deity or deities of some sort, and—as the authors of these travel pieces never tired of saying—that there were surprising parallels between Buddhism and Roman Catholicism.[10]

To many mid-Victorian American readers who were filled with certainty about the superiority of the Protestant religion and the supremacy of the Anglo-Saxon race, the benign travel narratives in general magazines like *Harper's*, the hostile missionary reports in the *Missionary Herald*, and even the harmonizing interpretations of liberals like Child must have been reassuring. At least these accounts did little to challenge their presuppositions. Yet the emerging European scholarly literature did precisely that: it portrayed Buddhism as a peculiar tradition that called into question widespread assumptions.

EUROPEAN SCHOLARS AND BUDDHIST DISTINCTIVENESS

During the 1840s and 1850s several European scholars and missionaries with linguistic skill in one or more relevant languages published studies of

Buddhism. Even though Salisbury's lecture and Peabody's translation had drawn on Burnouf's scholarship, in general it was not until approximately 1858 that the force of that scholar's interpretations, and others', began to be felt in the United States. In particular, over the next two decades Eugène Burnouf's *L'Introduction à l'histoire du buddhisme indien*, Robert Spence Hardy's *Eastern Monachism* and *Manual of Buddhism*, F. Max Müller's "Buddhist Pilgrims" and "The Meaning of Nirvana," and Jules Barthélemy Saint-Hilaire's *Le Bouddha et sa religion* were reviewed, summarized, and cited in articles that appeared in a wide range of general magazines and religious periodicals.[11]

Europeans did not suddenly discover at midcentury that Buddhist beliefs seemed to vary from those in Christianity and other literate Western traditions, but they began to emphasize those differences. From the beginning of systematic contact, Western witnesses had noticed dissimilarities. In fact, those Roman Catholic missionaries in East Asia—even if they had stressed the parallels with other heathen religions—had noticed. Even more consistently and forcefully than the earlier missionaries and travelers had, however, the scholars who wrote these works stressed the distinctiveness of Buddhist teachings and used the language of negation. Burnouf's interpretation of nirvana, for example, was more subtle, qualified, and tentative than that of some of the scholars and most of the non-scholars who followed him. Yet, against Colebrooke's arguments to the contrary, Burnouf suggested that the most ancient schools of Buddhism probably had understood nirvana to mean "une annihilation." These European authors suggested that the Buddha had denied the existence of a personal creator and rejected the notion of a substantial and immortal self. Human life, the Buddha taught, is suffering; and release is found only in a systematic renunciation of the world, which leads, in turn, to a final escape into the annihilation of nirvana. In short, Buddhism became associated with atheism, nihilism, pessimism, and passivity. European academic scholars, Christian missionaries, and civil servants acknowledged that some forms of Mahayana Buddhism in East Asia seemed less negative; but, most agreed, these were the teachings of the founder.[12]

Buddha's reported challenge to theism—the belief in a personal creator—and to components of individualism—the affirmation of the substantiality and immortality of the self—seemed clear enough to most influential European interpreters between the 1840s and the 1870s. The Pali Buddhist canon presented the Buddha either as uninterested in metaphysical questions or as straightforwardly nontheistic. The doctrine of anatta (no-self) holds that the self is not a substantial and eternal entity but a confluence of physical and mental processes, and the classical texts attributed this notion to the founder. The impression that Buddhism is pessimistic arose from the canonical Buddha's proclamation that life inevitably involves suffering—the first noble truth of Buddhism—and from the understanding of nirvana as annihilation of the self. Almost all Buddhists and scholars today would reject this interpretation of the religious goal. In fairness to these early scholars, however, it is important to note that the classical Pali texts are not transparent or univocal on this point. If they do not clearly confirm nihilistic interpretations of nirvana, some passages at least leave the way open for such readings. For the few mid-Victorian readers who struggled with these matters, Schopenhauer's open embrace of Buddhism as the religion that most resembled his own gloomy world-denying philosophy only intensified the impression that this Asian tradition also was pessimistic. In fact, pessimism, Schopenhauer, and Buddhism became linked in the minds of many European and American readers.[13]

Almost all mid-century European scholars and missionaries agreed that Buddhism was atheistic, nihilistic, and pessimistic; but they often softened or qualified the usual criticism of Buddhism as passive. Noel Alexander in his *Apology of the Dominican Missionaries of China* (1700) had asserted that for Buddhists "perfection consists in perfect indifference, apathy, and an undisturbed quietude." Yet around midcentury the longstanding perception that Buddhism was unable to stimulate efforts to cultivate character, stimulate activity, and reform societies had been weakened. Almost all interpreters acknowledged the praiseworthy moral code and superior personal virtue of the Buddha; and he often was portrayed as a reformer of the Indian religious and social system. Another notion—a less widely accepted one—circulated: Buddhism had been a civilizing influence "not only on the natives of India but on the lowest barbarians of Central Asia." These views led some European interpreters to abandon or, as Albrecht Weber did, qualify the standard criticism. Weber claimed that the Buddha himself actively worked for reform of the world; but the logical or practical consequence of his philosophy was "a quietism hostile to every human activity, to an imbecilic torpor, to the most complete denial of human feelings and endeavors."[14]

MID-VICTORIAN CULTURE IN AMERICA

Whether or not they acquitted the Buddha or his tradition of the charge of passivity, a number of American readers of the European scholarly accounts seemed disquieted. These interpretations were disturbing, I suggest, because they presented Buddhism as contrary to primary beliefs and values of the dominant culture. In 1857 the author of a travel narrative that focused on Buddhism declared that "the ruling principle of man's nature is the intense desire for some object of adoration." And the Harvard Unitarian Henry Ware, Jr. also expressed the common view when he proclaimed that "no people so barbarous, none so degraded, has yet been discovered, that the idea and worship of a supreme power has not been found with them." As one historian has noted, the heritage of "personal monotheism" may be as close as we can get to religious consensus in America. The belief in a personal creator, sustainer, and consummator of the universe was so presupposed and widely shared in Victorian America that only those who attacked or defended dissenting theological views— for example, Transcendentalist pantheism, "primitive" animism, positivist atheism, or Buddhist agnosticism—even felt the need to mention it. In some ways individualism was as fundamental to Victorian culture as theism. Individualism, as I have defined it, is the tendency to emphasize autonomy in all dimensions of human life and the inclination to believe in a static, substantial, and immortal self. The latter beliefs about the nature and destiny of the self had the most significance for the mid-Victorian debate. As with the commitment to theism, the belief in an immutable, substantive, and enduring self seemed so certain to most as to be almost self-evident. Few felt the need to argue for the cogency of these beliefs or demonstrate the pervasiveness of these convictions.[15]

Some elements of the culture might seem to indicate contrary impulses. There was, for example, a cult of mourning in early- and mid-Victorian America. The preoccupation with death expressed in the vast literature available to middle-class readers after 1830—death poetry, funeral sermons, consolatory essays, and mourning manuals—might seem to reveal a yearning for a final and complete loss of self. This, of course, was not so. The death of others was accepted by the living only as an occasion to express grief, the most genteel of all sentiments, transparently and thereby to exhibit and cultivate the sincerity so important to sound character. Death also was accepted by those contemplating their own demise or others' as the consummation of the religious journey. "It is not to the tomb that God will carry those whom you love," one passage in *The Mourner's Friend* assured American readers. "The fleshly garments may be carried there," it continued, "but the living soul God places not in the tomb." The pious soul, most agreed, would be joined with God. The preoccupation with death reflected and reinforced the reigning individualism—and theism. Although some in late-Victorian America would be willing to abandon God-language and reject the notion of an immortal soul, few would do so before the 1880s. American interpreters, and most Western intellectuals of the age, presupposed or asserted that humans were naturally religious. Being religious entailed, most fundamentally, the belief in or worship of a deity and the hope of eternal enjoyment of blissful existence as a substantial self.[16]

Philip Schaff (1819–93), the influential Swiss-American church historian and astute observer of his adopted country, pointed to other Victorian convictions and attitudes that shaped the conversation about Buddhism.

He traced the character of mid-Victorian America to the influence of German and British Protestantism, especially in its Calvinist forms. In *America: A Sketch of Its Political, Social, and Religious Character* Schaff argued that these influences led to the unusually activistic and optimistic character of American society. "The Germanic and Protestant character of the United States," he claimed, "reveals itself particularly in their uncommon mobility and restless activity, contrasting with the mournful stagnation of the Romantic and Roman Catholic countries of Central and South America. The people are truly a nation of progress, both in the good sense and the bad; of the boldest, often foolhardy, enterprise; a restless people, finding no satisfaction, save in constant striving, running, chasing after a boundless future." Schaff acknowledged German and, especially, British parallels and precedents; but he found the religious life of America "uncommonly practical, energetic, and enterprising." The moral earnestness and robust optimism of nineteenth-century American Protestantism had its drawbacks, Schaff argued, but these tendencies were central components of the dominant religion and the culture it molded.[17]

The optimism that Schaff had noticed in the culture was stimulated and supported by, among other developments, the enthusiasm about Western expansion and technological advance. It also was sustained by the continuing influence of one or another versions of the longstanding view of America as a "Redeemer Nation." Whether antebellum Americans conceived of America's role as inspiring example or world's savior, or whether they were premillennialists or postmillennialists, many agreed that the new nation was destined to assume the dominant role in God's cosmic plan for the consummation of nature and history. A "cosmic optimism" characterized the thinking of many white northern Protestants on the eve of the Civil War. The horror of war burned away any residue of naive cheerfulness; but, as Abraham Lincoln's second inaugural address and Horace Bushnell's "Our Obligations to the Dead" indicate, many still found a theoretical foundation for optimism in the continuing affirmation of America's ordained destiny. Two years after the close of the war one religious radical who played a role in the conversation about Buddhism noticed "startling changes" that foreshadowed a social and religious revolution, and he still professed "boundless faith in the possibilities of the present world and the present age." In a sermon delivered a few years later, Henry Ward Beecher (1813–87), the prominent Protestant preacher, added his voice to those who saw history, and American history in particular, as "tending upward rather than downward." Americans, Beecher argued, were increasingly prosperous, refined, and educated. They also were more religious: "Religion itself, though losing many of its antique forms and services, as a spirit and as a controlling influence, was never so strong." And Beecher was grateful for all this progress: "I thank God for all the signs of the times. I thank God for the health and the prosperity of the nation."[18]

Optimism about the course of history often was coupled with increasingly positive views about the nature of humans. In "The Moral Argument against Calvinism," William Ellery Channing (1780–1842), the leading Unitarian of his day, had criticized not only the "soporific quality" of Calvinist prose but also the mistakenly pessimistic character of Calvinist theology. Channing argued that Calvinist assumptions about human nature—that we are "wholly inclined to evil"—not only contradict the letter and spirit of scripture but also offend our ideas about the goodness and justice of God. Although theological liberalism did not dominate the religious scene in the United States until after the Civil War and Reconstruction, mid-Victorian Universalists and Unitarians continued the assault on Calvinism begun by their late eighteenth-century precursors and early nineteenth-century spokespersons. They rejected the traditional five points of Calvinism as those found expression at the Synod of Dort (1618–19) and replaced the emphasis on human depravity and predestination, with a new, loftier view of the nature and destiny of humans. They replaced it with a view that seemed more commensurate with the important, even sacred, mission of the new nation—and more compatible with the interests of the urban elite. A new emphasis on the positive capacities of humans also crept into the thinking of mainline Protestants as they softened the pessimistic doctrines—some still would have said "realistic" doctrines—of "consistent Calvinism." The new tradition of Reformed theology given impetus by Timothy Dwight (1752–1817), Nathaniel William Taylor (1786–1858), and Lyman Beecher (1775–1863) was much more confident about human abilities. Charles Grandison Finney (1792–1875), the influential revivalist, edged toward perfectionism. Unconventional religious groups such as Oneida Perfectionists, Mormons, Transcendentalists, Spiritualists, Shakers, Millerites, and Adventists celebrated the mounting optimism about humans still more boisterously.[19]

This optimism was linked with activism—the inclination to emphasize the spiritual significance of vigorous moral action in the world. The escalating confidence in the capacities of persons and the continuing impact of millennialist hopes supported this concern to uplift individuals, reform societies, and participate energetically in the economic and political spheres. As one passage in *The Excellent Woman*, an advice book for women, indicated, all Victorians—women as well as men—were called to "acts of cheerful service." The Scottish Common Sense philosophy that was so popular in America during the several decades before the Civil War gave Victorian moral seriousness, even self-righteousness, a theoretical framework and a legitimating vocabulary. There was a widely shared sense that Victorian moral principles could—and must—find concrete expression in a positive transformation of individuals, society, and history. This transformation, moreover, seemed imminent.[20]

The reform impulse was expressed in a variety of forms in pulsating phases of activity throughout the century. One call to action printed in the official organ of the American Home Missionary Society captured the spirit well. The author reminded his evangelical readers that "there is always a demand upon us for 'well-doing,' for benevolent action in this world of sin and suffering." He also reprimanded the lazy and the apathetic: "There is, then, no room for inaction or repose. It will be time enough to rest in heaven." The myriad reform organizations between the 1810s and 1860s sparked and channelled this activistic impulse. There were groups dedicated to the abolition of slavery, women's rights, utopian community, educational improvement, temperance, peace, and improved conditions for the young, the blind, and the insane.[21]

The reform impulse also found expression in other aspects of the culture. The emphasis on personal transformation and social reform that already was evident in the Calvinist fiction of Anne Tuttle Bullard and others between 1825 and 1850 was taken up in a modified form in the post-Calvinist novels of Harriet Beecher Stowe and her counterparts after mid-century. The inclination to moralize and reform also shaped Protestant attitudes toward material culture. Domestic furnishings and architecture instantiated and reinforced Victorian values—and activism in particular. "For the Victorian domestic architect," Colleen McDannell has argued persuasively, "art could not exist 'for art's sake,' because it was inextricably bound to society and morality. Architecture served as both a mode of communication and a reforming enterprise." Not only personal cultivation but even social improvement began at home. Similar attitudes were expressed in Protestant painting. A longstanding ambivalence, even suspicion, toward the senses and the imagination informed Protestant, and especially Calvinist, views of painting. Some Protestants—Moravians and Episcopalians—did not feel the tension so acutely. And some felt liberated to pursue their art by their conviction that painting was acceptable if it served a didactic purpose. The Episcopalian painter Thomas Cole (1801–48) was one of the finest American artists of the nineteenth century, and a moralistic agenda was evident not only in *The Cross and the World* series begun late in life but even in the earlier series that were not explicitly religious in content—*The Course of Empire* and *The Voyage of Life*. Even fashion during the early-Victorian period served a didactic function. The sentimental view of dress that dominated *Godey's Lady's Book* during the 1830s and 1840s, for example, was based on the assumption that simple and "sincere" clothing could improve the moral condition of the wearer and those she encountered.[22]

This understanding of the nature and function of women's dress began to shift during the 1850s. Other shifts occurred too. The wild energy of the movements for individual improvement and social reform was tamed during the fifties and sixties as reform became more and more institutionalized in American Protestantism, and the activist impulse became less prominent between 1865 and 1876. Yet a concern to uplift individuals and reform society remained deeply ingrained in Victorian culture; and it was never far from the surface for those—some of whom also wrote about Buddhism—who had supported the reform movements of the prewar period.

AMERICAN INTERPRETERS AND BUDDHIST DISTINCTIVENESS, 1858–1877

If theism, individualism, activism, and optimism were as fundamental to the culture as I have suggested, then it is not difficult to understand the sources of American readers' disquiet at the European characterizations of Buddhism. They were uneasy because the religion seemed to challenge these firm commitments. In turn, their emotional reactions began to shift from pity and compassion to defensiveness and dismay, and some began to feel the need to respond to these interpretations. I have found no evidence that any midcentury American who encountered the challenge of Buddhist negation seriously considered abandoning Victorian presuppositions. To ease the disquiet, then, some American interpreters between 1858 and 1877—mainline Protestants and conservative Unitarians—accepted the negative interpretations and, at the same time, maintained the usual convictions. They found a way to explain the apparent clash between Buddhist doctrines and Victorian beliefs. Others—a handful of sympathetic religious liberals and radicals—struggled, with varying degrees of success, to harmonize the Buddha's teachings with common notions about ultimate reality, historical development, and human nature and, so, with the reigning assumptions about the character of all humans' religious needs.

Mainline Protestants and Conservative Unitarians

In 1874 the Reverend Edward Hungerford (1829–1911) of Menden, Connecticut, compared Buddhism and Christianity for *The New Englander,* a magazine connected with Congregationalism and Yale. Even more clearly than Moffat's survey that I quoted at the start of this chapter, this article provides a good example of the approach of mainline Protestants and conservative Unitarians during the 1860s and 1870s. Hungerford, who embraced the Victorian Protestant worldview, suggested that Buddhism "looks only at the dark side of existence" and contradicts not only optimism but other fundamental beliefs and values as well. Further, it fails to manifest the usual characteristics of religion: "There is no great glowing future to which faith can lift its eye, no eternal progress to inspire aspiration. No God, no soul, no Saviour from sin, no love, no heaven!" Others agreed. After concurring with Barthélemy Saint-Hilaire's negative interpretation of Buddhism and predicting that the tradition would never make any progress in America, Herman J. Warner asserted that Buddhism was not a religion. But, Warner argued in this article for the leading Unitarian magazine, neither is Buddhism a philosophy. In fact, the tradition seemed so anomalous that Warner could find no label for it. Some commentators found enough childlike groping after the true God and personal immortality in the later Buddhist traditions—especially in East Asia—to pronounce it a religion, but most mainline Protestants and conservative Unitarians who participated in the public discussion after 1858 were willing to allow Buddha's teachings to contradict established views about the nature of humans' inherent religious propensities.[23]

Yet, as a reviewer of several European books on Buddhism for the *Princeton Review* surmised, "this system must have had some power of adaptation to the wants of mankind." Most Christian contributors to the discussion agreed. Those who accepted the view that the Buddha negated fundamental human aspirations, then, still felt that they had to explain the initial spread and continued growth of Buddhism in Asia. Buddhism, after all, was not simply a gloomy, nihilistic, world-denying worldview proposed by an idiosyncratic German philosopher and embraced by a few European malcontents and misanthropes. Rather, nineteenth-century American readers were reminded again and again that Buddhism had spread rapidly in its native India and continued to advance until half or more of the world's population followed its teachings. And American Protestant and Unitarian interpreters—as if to accustom themselves to the sound of this strange and disturbing assertion—repeated this story and these statistics in their accounts. Some readers apparently felt the force of the problem that F. Max Müller confronted directly. After interpreting the tradition as atheistic and nihilistic, he described the issue this way: "How a religion which taught the annihilation of all existence, of all thought, of all individuality and personality, as the highest object of all endeavors, could have laid hold of the minds of millions of human beings . . . is a riddle which no one has been able to solve."[24]

Müller's writings were used by a wide range of American interpreters to support varying solutions to the "riddle." His writings on Buddhism can be divided into two periods, before and after 1860. In the two essays of 1857 Müller had presented the Buddha's teachings as a negation of the usual beliefs and values; however, in his 1862 essay entitled simply "Buddhism" he rejected or qualified some of his earlier interpretations. Yet even in his early essays Müller already had taken a step toward solving the puzzle by distinguishing the negative metaphysics of the founder and "a few isolated thinkers" from the positive religion and ethics of "the people at large." He suggested, then, that the Buddha's philosophy was atheistic and nihilistic, but the later tradition, acting from the deepest inherent impulses of human nature, had moved toward theism and immortality and hopefulness.[25]

In his 1862 essay Müller offered another argument from "human nature," and this time he went further. He defended even the Buddha against the usual criticisms and brought the founder's thinking into line with the dominant Western conceptions of humans' innate religious inclinations. Arguing from human nature "such as we find it in all times and countries," Müller confessed that—whatever the other great scholars had suggested—he simply could not believe that so great a moral teacher and social reformer could have "thrown away one of the most powerful weapons in the hands of every religious teacher—the belief in a future life." Because it would be contrary to human nature to be motivated by a desire for the "annihilation" of all individuality in nirvana, Buddha could not have been so deluded as to have believed that. At least, Müller asserted, he could not have been foolish enough to *teach* that![26]

Other Europeans—for example, Jules Mohl (1800–1876), one of Burnouf's friends and coworkers—offered similar arguments from human nature. But, of course, not all scholars agreed. James D'Alwiss in the mid-Victorian period and Hermann Oldenberg in the later decades both argued that although Buddha's teachings seem to contradict human nature, this alone does not provide the scholar with grounds for altering the apparent meaning of the texts. "We cannot follow the famous inquirer [Müller]," Oldenberg suggested, "when he attempts to trace the limits between the possible and the impossible. . . . Perhaps what is here beyond comprehension may there be comprehensible, and if we reach a point which to us is a limit of the comprehensible, we shall permit much to pass and stand as incomprehensible, and await the future, which may bring us nearer the solution of the enigma." During the second half of the century, especially between 1858 and 1877, few participants in the public conversation were able to "permit much to pass and stand as incomprehensible." Most felt compelled to come to firm conclusions about the meaning of these disturbing doctrines; and, although Oldenberg would have disapproved, a number of midcentury interpreters appealed to the argument from human nature when it served their purpose.[27]

American mainline Protestants and conservative Unitarians, for example, used Müller's earlier argument to explain the spread of the Buddhist tradition throughout Asia. They claimed that Buddha's later followers embraced a religion whose leading doctrines—although misguided about the proper object of devotion and the ultimate destiny of humans— "were at least partially adapted to the wants and capacities of human nature." The development of the Pure Land tradition in East Asia, for example, with its greater adaptability to God-language and its talk of a "Western Paradise" seemed to have been a move in the right direction. Humans did naturally yearn for God and immortality, and those later

Buddhists were, in this sense, human. Explaining the initial rise of Buddhism, however, seemed more difficult. These interpreters did not accept Müller's later suggestion that the Buddha probably did not—could not!—preach negation. They usually continued to present the Buddha's teaching as atheistic, nihilistic, and pessimistic. For example, that great observer of American religion and culture, Philip Schaff, portrayed the doctrines this way. Yet most felt compelled to locate some positive element of Buddha's life and teachings in order to account for Buddhism's rise in India. The desire to find such an element seems to have been crucial in Christian critics' surprising willingness to grant that the Buddha was a great moral teacher and religious and social reformer. Most Protestants and Unitarians, then, distinguished between Buddha's negative philosophical teachings and his lofty moral message and effective social reform. It was the latter, they proposed, which sparked Buddhism's rise to prominence in India. "The early spread of Buddhism," Rosewell Hobart Graves (1833–1912) argued in 1872, "is due more to its social than to its philosophical and religious elements." Graves was a missionary in China, but a similar tendency to condemn the Buddha's teachings while granting his admirable qualities and successful reforms was found in the writings of a wide range of mid-Victorian American Christians. These critics often still pointed to practical and institutional parallels between Catholicism and Buddhism, but they presented the founder and his tradition in a way that would have aroused some sympathy among those who were filled with the spirit of activism—and anti-Catholicism. Many described the Buddha as a Luther-like reformer of a corrupt religious and social system and presented Buddhism as "the Protestantism of India." As Luther had expressed a spirit of egalitarianism in religious matters in his reform of Catholicism, the Buddha regenerated the Indian religious tradition and, at the same time, challenged the oppressive caste system.[28]

I have found no reason to doubt the sincerity of Christian critics' appreciation for Buddha's moral teachings and reform activities; but this interpretation, as I have noted, did have apologetic value. It allowed Christian critics to maintain their negative critique, explain the popularity of the tradition, and grant only a limited appeal to Buddha and his teachings. But this interpretation also had other unintended consequences. It allowed a few mid-Victorian religious radicals with sympathy for the tradition—and some late-Victorians as well—to soften the longstanding criticism of Buddhism as passive. The acknowledgment by Salisbury and some other scholars that the tradition had a "civilizing" influence on the tribes of Asia also helped in this regard. Sympathetic interpreters still had to contend with claims that the ascetic thrust of the tradition and the nihilistic tone of its philosophy fostered world-denying tendencies, and some Protestants continued to claim that even though the Buddha was a reformer, the tradition he inspired was quietistic. Nonetheless, Protestant interpretations in this period, which followed those of influential European scholars, made it easier to present Buddhism as compatible with the activism of the dominant Victorian culture. Liberals and radicals who cared so much about the various "benevolent" movements of the period could appeal to authoritative interpretations of the founder as a reformer who was inspired by high moral values and filled with an egalitarian spirit. Yet they still had to confront the standard view of Buddhism as atheistic, anti-individualistic, and gloomy.

Liberal Unitarians and Religious Radicals

Some American liberals and radicals who struggled to reconcile the Buddha's teachings with the convictions of the age finally failed in this task, but they were united in their desire to harmonize and their willingness to praise. They appealed to the positive interpretations of the Buddha as a moral teacher and social reformer. They employed Müller's arguments from human nature and, more than their mainline Protestant counterparts, praised some aspect(s) of the tradition or its founder. They formed a group only in the loosest sense of the term. Most were middle- and upper-class men who hailed from the Northeast. Many had labored in the reform movements before and after the Civil War. One was a former Jew, but most attended Harvard Divinity School and had connections with Unitarianism or the dissenting movements that splintered from that tradition— Transcendentalism and the Free Religious Association. Most had direct contact and knew each other well enough to correspond. The most religiously conservative of these remained leaders or members of a Unitarian congregation. The most unconventional, on the other hand, felt uncomfortable even in the most radical of organizations—the Free Religious Association. There were real differences of temperament and perspective, then; but they shared a commitment to the most fundamental Victorian beliefs and values and a similar—although far from identical—approach to the interpretation and assessment of Buddhism. A few of these interpreters still appealed to the rhetoric of negation—even if they did so more reluctantly than mainline Protestants. Only one publicly advocated Buddhism as the superior religion, yet as a group they anticipated the sympathy for the tradition that would be expressed in the late-Victorian period.[29]

Drawn by some aspect of the tradition—usually its moral teachings— they seemed to want to minimize Buddhist differences. Finally, however, some sounded almost as negative as some European scholars and Protestant missionaries. For example, James Freeman Clarke's interpretations followed this pattern. Clarke (1810–88), the prominent Unitarian minister, was probably the first university lecturer on comparative religion in the United States and one of the most influential nineteenth-century American interpreters of Asian religions. In fact, his works on religion were probably as widely read as those of any Unitarian of his generation. And, like most Unitarians, he shared the foundational beliefs and values of Victorian culture. For Clarke, robust moral action in the world was at the heart of religion. In one letter he put his philosophy of life simply: "To do good and be good—to serve our race, even so little—to reveal Christ in our words and lives, ever so imperfectly—this is worth living for, and nothing else." And he acted on that principle. He worked on behalf of the movements for temperance and peace, but the antislavery movement was at the center of his efforts for social reform in the antebellum period. It was Clarke, for instance, who composed the public letter of protest signed by one hundred and forty-three antislavery Unitarian ministers. This letter, which was sent on to Congress in 1845, ended with a passage that reflected Clarke's religious and moral stance: "And we do hereby pledge ourselves before God and our brethren, never to be weary of laboring in the cause of human rights and freedom, till slavery be abolished and every slave made free." He also rejected Calvinist pessimism and celebrated historical progress. It is not surprising, then, that Clarke was troubled by the alleged pessimism and passivity of the Buddhist tradition. Although it was counter to his own inclinations, he apparently felt compelled to interpret Buddhism as both quietistic and gloomy. Relying on Müller's arguments from human nature, however, Clarke managed to find a belief in "God" and an affirmation of "immortality" in their doctrines. And, as expected, he praised the moral teachings and reform impulse of the founder. He seemed to try to avoid the usual criticisms and to harmonize Buddhism with the standard views of religion, but Clarke finally felt forced to concede its negativity: "Nihilism arrives sooner or later," he concluded. "God is nothing; man is nothing, life is nothing, eternity is nothing. Hence the profound sadness of Buddhism."[30]

Some of this loosely connected assortment of radicals—including Charles DeBerard Mills (1821–1900) and Felix Adler (1851–1933)—responded to Buddhism as Clarke had, although perhaps with even greater sympathy. Mills and Adler dissented from the reigning religious visions in America, and both searched for alternatives. Mills, the author of the first book-length treatment of Buddha and Buddhism written by an American (1876), sketched a portrait of the Buddha that seemed so positive to some Protestant reviewers that they wondered aloud whether he was "not actually a Buddhist." After praising the Buddha as a great reformer, however, Mills complained that Buddhist philosophers had "abolished everything, annihilated all affirmative being, and left the spirit of coldness and chill of mere negations." Adler, Reform Jew turned Free Religionist turned founder of the Ethical Culture Society, could not find a place within any existing religious structure. He constructed his own perspective and organized his own group. He also commented on Buddhism. Like Mills, he seems to have been attracted to the tradition by the moral teachings and reform impulse of its founder and by the tolerance and egalitarian spirit of the subsequent tradition, but the negative Buddhist metaphysics proved too disquieting. He lauded the Buddha as an exemplary moral teacher and social reformer, but Adler found himself unable to accept Müller's argument from human nature. He apparently felt forced to present the teachings of the founder as counter to reigning beliefs and values about the character of humans and the nature of religion. Despite the Buddha's moral character and reforming activities, the tradition itself seemed "passive and indifferent to the concerns of the present." To Adler, the founder of an organization dedicated to the development of character and the reform of society, this was a great, even insurmountable, obstacle to greater sympathy. Finally, then, both Adler and Mills interpreted the Buddha's teachings as atheistic, nihilistic, pessimistic, and, despite the qualities of its founder, leading to passivity.[31]

Yet other religious liberals and radicals took a different path. A handful of mid-Victorians who were attracted to the tradition managed to sustain and expand their sympathy for the founder and the tradition. They did so by rejecting most or all of the standard negative interpretations and implicitly or explicitly affirming Buddhism's compatibility with Victorian convictions and attitudes. Here again Müller's argument from human nature was useful. This group included William Rounseville Alger (1822–1905), the Unitarian preacher; Higginson, the social reformer and Free Religionist; and Samuel Johnson (1822–82), the fiercely individualistic and ardently reformist preacher who served an independent liberal congregation in Massachusetts. Although Alger's Unitarian Society on Bulfinch Street in Boston merged with Theodore Parker's radical Congregational Society that met in the Music Hall, Alger's theological position was traditionally Christian in many ways. Alger also was, in many ways, typically Victorian. He shared the Victorian Christian presupposition that all humans naturally long for union of the soul with God. And he embodied the reform spirit of the period: his antislavery Fourth of July address delivered in Boston in 1857 was so forceful that the board of aldermen refused the usual vote of gratitude.

The anthology of Asian poetry that Alger had published in 1856 contained Islamic, Hindu, and Confucian verse but no examples from the Buddhist tradition. He did discuss Buddhism, however, in an article for the *North American Review* two years later. In his treatment of Buddhism he relied on the argument from human nature, appealed to the logical consequences of beliefs, and considered accounts of the later tradition. Alger considered and then rejected the atheistic and nihilistic interpretations of Buddhism. The descriptions of the doctrine of no-self and nirvana could not be accurate, he argued. To deny a substantial self would be to dissolve all conceptions of individuality after death; and that, in turn, would corrode the basis for morality. Humans, he believed, are not made that way, and religions cannot function that way. Repeating Müller's claim, Alger declared that "it cannot be that a deliberate suicide of the soul is the ideal holding the deepest desire of hundred millions of people."[32]

Passages in one of Higginson's lectures delivered during the 1850s suggest that at that time he had lumped together various traditions, East and West, and dismissed them as misguided attempts to deal with the universal fear of mortality. "The great motive power in all superstitions, from the earliest Brahmanism to the latest Mormonism, is the same . . . the fear of death and the effort to remove that fear." But his commitment to optimism already was evident. In that speech delivered near the peak of American interest in Spiritualism he praised that movement as "a gospel of gladness." He contrasted Spiritualism's optimistic teachings with the "gloomy" preaching of the traditional churches. Most Christian preachers, he suggested, do not demonstrate the gleefulness that would come if they really believed in immortality. His own optimism was almost boundless. Higginson spoke confidently of "the progress of the world" and asserted boldly that "the tendency of humanity is onward." And Higginson did his part to nudge the social world toward its perfected state. This Harvard Divinity School graduate served at the First Religious Society of Newburyport and then at a "Free Church" in Worcester, but he found time to be active in the temperance movement, educational reform, women's suffrage, and the antislavery cause. During the Civil War he led the first African American regiment in the Union Army, the First South Carolina Volunteers. In many ways he was a paradigmatic Victorian reformer, and in one journal entry Higginson explained the importance of activity: "We all need action. This is shown by the way it transforms us, just as the water of a brook that glides turbid and dull along its common bed, becomes radiant and of a sunny purity when compelled to find its way over a cascade of rocks." Many contemporaries believed that Higginson had developed just such a "sunny purity" from his activist struggles. In 1903 one French biographer lavishly praised his activist spirit and, even further, portrayed him as A Typical American. Of course, there was no typical Victorian American. Yet Higginson did express a number of the dominant convictions and attitudes—including theism, individualism, optimism, and activism. He continued to hold to these commitments late in life.[33]

His attitude toward Buddhism and other religions, however, seemed to change by the 1870s. This Asian religion apparently had not been enough on his mind in the 1850s to bother dismissing. Later he showed the openness to this and other traditions that irked some mainline Protestants. In his influential lecture "The Sympathy of Religions," which was first delivered and published in 1871, Higginson advocated tolerance and set out an inclusivistic theology of religions. And in two articles on Buddhism for the Radical and the Index he presented this Asian tradition with great sympathy. "The Buddhist Path of Virtue," for example, contained brief comments on the tradition and selections from the recently published translation of the Dhammapada by Müller. Higginson praised the beauty and insight of this important Buddhist text and concluded this way: "I do not envy the man who does not find the depth of his soul stirred by a book like this." Clearly Higginson's soul was stirred—and, to a great extent, so was Samuel Johnson's.[34]

Higginson praised the first volume of Johnson's three-volume *Oriental Religions and Their Relation to Universal Religion*. It was, he asserted, far superior to Child's *Progress of Religious Ideas*, since Johnson appealed to the latest European authorities. It also was superior to Clarke's *Ten Great Religions*, since he had avoided Clarke's "polemical" spirit. In fact, Johnson was so concerned to be inclusivistic, nonsectarian, and tolerant that he felt unable to officially join even the Free Religious Association—that organization dedicated to, among other things, inclusivity, nonsectarianism, and tolerance. Ralph Waldo Emerson, one of the speakers at the first meeting of that radical group, reportedly called his fellow Harvard Divinity School graduate "a man of the desert" because of his refusal to join any religious organization. Johnson confirmed Emerson's impression. When asked which religion he adhered to, Johnson once replied, "You shall count me nowhere; but you shall exclude me nowhere. I will have the freedom of all times and all hearts; but I will, of my own motion, take on no special bonds, and wear the special labels, of none." This attitude informed his interpretations of Asian religions. Because Johnson's volumes on India (1872) and China (1877) did not evidence the sectarian spirit of Clarke's *Ten Great Religions*, however, does not mean that they were not informed by a particular religious vision. Johnson set out his approach in the introduction to volume one: "I have written not as an advocate of Christianity or any other distinctive religion, but as attracted on the one hand by the identity of the religious sentiment under all the great historic forms, and on the other by the movement indicated toward a higher plane of unity, on which their exclusive claims should disappear."[35]

Committed to a belief in the essential unity of all religions, then, Johnson struggled to come to terms with "the seeming anomaly of Buddhist negation." Was Buddhism, as many interpreters had claimed, an exception to "the principles of universal religion"? Was it incompatible with much that Victorian Americans held dear? Johnson showed a relatively good understanding of the diversity within Buddhism and pointed to some of the ways in which Buddhist answers to Western questions about the nature of ultimate reality and the destiny of the self might vary from sect to sect. Yet he did not allow this awareness of diversity to dissolve the questions about "Buddhism's" distinctiveness, as it might have done. Instead, in the volumes on India and China he tried to address the questions as most

Westerners of his day had formulated them. Relying on the argument from human nature, Johnson affirmed the compatibility between Buddha's teachings, human nature, and universal religion. He rejected atheistic and nihilistic interpretations by asserting that "the prodigious power exercised by this faith over the destinies of mankind" would be inexplicable if its adherents, in fact, "worship nonentity." This would contradict the widely accepted understanding of humans as seeking affirmation and not negation. In his volume on India he put it this way: "It would indeed be fatal to our hopes for human nature, if we could be forced to believe that four hundred millions of at least partially civilized people have made a religion out of love of nonentity, or indeed, out of mere negation."[36]

In an 1870 essay entitled "The Search for God" Johnson proclaimed, "I do not hesitate to affirm . . . that there is no one who does not intrinsically desire to find God." As one anonymous reviewer of the posthumously published collection of his writings noticed, "To convict men of atheism was never his delight. He much preferred finding the essential theism implicated in their negations." Johnson treated the few Westerners who professed atheism in this way, and he applied the same principle to Buddhists. He found no affirmation of a personal creator in Buddhism, but he could locate a belief in "Eternal Being." In a similar way, Johnson found no desire for annihilation in the Buddhist nirvana, but only the quest for a state of bliss.[37]

Johnson's commitments to activism and optimism also shaped his account. Johnson, who blended mystical and free thought sentiments, rejected much of the Unitarian theology he had learned at Harvard Divinity School in favor of Transcendentalism and Free Religion—and especially Parker's brand of religious radicalism. Johnson also had supported various reform movements. Between 1848 and 1858, for instance, he had lectured for the Massachusetts Anti-Slavery Society. His religious radicalism and political activism were connected: both were grounded in his affirmation of liberty in all areas of human life and in his conviction that all persons were formed in the divine image. That was why he was so disturbed when some of his reformer friends seemed to misunderstand his unconventional religious views. He defended himself to Wendell Phillips, the eminent reformer, in a letter in 1869: "I confess I am a touch sensitive about being understood by my anti-slavery friends on this matter: because my religious radicalism springs from the same root with my political." Johnson also was "a touch sensitive" about religious views that seemed to inhibit the activist impulse, and he was aware that some had brought the charge of passivity against Buddhism. In an essay entitled "Fate" he overlooked the traditional Buddhist emphasis on personal moral responsibility—in the doctrine of karma—as, at the same time, he presented a qualified defense of the tradition. "The Buddhists carried their fatalism down to the minutest actions and events," Johnson claimed, "yet they were the most energetic and devoted proselytizers and the most enterprising and active colonizers of the East. Out of the dogma that everything was fixed by fate they drew the duty to seek the present good and final release of all mankind." In his volumes on Oriental religions Johnson suggested that Buddhism inherited a potential element of "fatalism" in the Indian notions of rebirth and karma; but, like most other mid-Victorian participants in the discussion, he celebrated the moral teachings, tolerant tone, and reform spirit of the Buddha and his tradition.[38]

One Christian reviewer of Johnson's work on China complained that "he boldly compared Confucius, Buddha, and Jesus Christ, and calmly pronounced Confucius, to his thinking, the greatest of the three." Like many disillusioned Enlightenment intellectuals and subsequent religious rationalists, Johnson admired the humanistic and ethical thrust of Confucian teachings. Nonetheless, he also clearly expressed appreciation for the life and teachings of the Buddha. In fact, Adler, Mills, Higginson, and Johnson all expressed some sympathy for Buddhism; and, in some passages, they praised it lavishly. Yet no one was more sympathetic than Dyer Daniel Lum (1839–93), the religious radical and political anarchist. In fact, Lum probably was the first American of European descent to publicly proclaim allegiance to Buddhism. Although Lum's article on Buddhism was published in the *Index* during this early period, in most ways he belonged to the next. His response to Buddhism followed the pattern that would be set in the late-Victorian period. He found a celebration of the "infinite perfectibility of man's nature" at the bottom of Buddhism; and this optimistic foundation, he asserted, supported Buddhism's lofty moral code. Like many other American participants in the discourse, Lum praised Buddha's ethics and reform impulse, and he lauded the tradition's tolerant spirit. He even suggested that Buddhism could pass the "test of history": it had beneficial cultural influences in Asia. Yet rather than struggle to reconcile Buddhism's reported rejection of a personal God and an immortal soul with Victorian values—as Johnson and other mid-Victorian radicals with sympathy for Buddhism had done—he celebrated its negation of these. This, Lum announced, rendered Buddhism more compatible with "Western science." Like many late-Victorian American advocates, Lum was attracted to Buddhism by its reported compatibility with science and tolerance. And, although he was willing to abandon the belief in a personal creator and substantial self, he still felt compelled to emphasize Buddhism's harmony with Victorian self-reliance, optimism, and activism.[39]

Few mid-Victorians were as sympathetic to Buddhism as Lum or Higginson. However, more attractive portraits began to appear in American periodicals and books during the 1870s, and more mainline Protestants offered their defensive rebuttals. In the same year that Lum publicly had advocated Buddhism, John Ogden Gordon (1850–1923) reported that it was a time "when we hear so much of the beauty of this system." This young Presbyterian pastor felt obliged to reprimand those who had been "praising Buddhism as a mild system of faith and practice." Those who were disillusioned by the harshness of the traditional "orthodox" Protestant—he meant Calvinist—views of election and hell were being unwittingly drawn to a tradition that has an infinitely more repugnant view of hell. Buddhism, Gordon admitted, does "inculcate a very high morality," but its hyperbolic depictions of the number of hells, the length of stay required, and the intensity of suffering endured makes Buddhism anything but mild. With dry humor Gordon warned those who were intrigued by Buddhism "that in turning to this highly lauded religion, they almost literally jump from the frying pan into the fire." The most revealing element of this article published in 1875 is that its Protestant author already felt compelled to defend Christianity in the face of increasingly sympathetic accounts of this alien tradition.[40]

Another example of a sympathetic portrait and a defensive response can be seen in a public exchange between Higginson and Hungerford. In a lecture in Horticultural Hall in Boston on Sunday, 3 March 1872 Higginson praised "The Character of the Buddha." He ended his very appreciative account by alluding to King Asoka's discovery of the tomb of the Buddha. Those who opened the tomb, so the story goes, found the lamps that had been lighted two hundred years earlier still burning and the flowers that had been offered in homage still fresh and fragrant. Higginson saw a parallel to his own age: "More than two thousand years have now passed, and we are opening this tomb again; the lights still burn, the flowers are still fresh, the perfume of that noble life, yet remains immortal." As I have suggested, Americans had begun to pry open "the tomb of the Buddha" almost three decades earlier; and not everyone was as blinded by the sudden illumination or as overcome by the sweet fragrance as Higginson.[41]

The Reverend Hungerford, for example, found little in Buddhism that stirred his senses. In fact, this mainline Protestant was annoyed by Higginson's positive assessment of the religion—and those offered by other radicals. In a public response that seems to have been aimed directly at Higginson he complained:

And notwithstanding the almost universal testimony of scholars to the unquestionable superiority of the Christian faith, it has been very much the fashion for a certain class of writers and speakers, such as those who have made Horticultural Hall in Boston their temple, to hold up in one hand Christianity to a rap and in the other hand Buddhism to praise. If they have not been in the habit of asserting the superiority of the latter over the former, they have been in the habit of dismissing their readers or their popular audiences with the impression that one was just about as good as the other.[42]

It was not long before the spiritually disillusioned got into the habit of asserting the superiority of Buddhism over Christianity. As I argue in the next chapter, only a few years after the exchange between Higginson and Hungerford the public conversation about Buddhism grew even more lively and widespread. And thousands of Americans who were disenchanted with Christianity found themselves drawn to that Asian religion.

TWO

"SHALL WE ALL BECOME BUDDHISTS?"

The Conversation and the Converts, 1879–1912

> Possibly the impression gained in India from the reception of its representatives in Chicago may be correct, viz., that there is great religious unrest among us, and a growing dissatisfaction with Christianity, that people are longing for another more satisfying faith, and that the present is a most favorable time for the dissemination of Buddhistic views. Possibly Professor Davids' visit to this country was most providential in point of time, and that the aim which one of his hearers ascribed to him, viz., to convert us all to Buddhism, has some hope of being realized. Possibly to some of the most excellent people among us, even Buddhism might be an improvement upon their present unsettled, agnostic mental condition. At any rate, it may be well to take a fresh and, if we can, impartial review of Buddhism . . . and to inquire seriously—Shall we all become Buddhists?
>
> Henry M. King (1895)

Henry Melville King (1838–1919), the prominent pastor of the First Baptist Church of Providence, was worried. And, if the discussion in the magazines, books, and lecture halls of the period is any indication, so were other mainline Protestants. Intellectual forces such as Darwinism, biblical criticism, and comparative religion, and social forces such as industrialization, urbanization, and immigration were combining to produce a "spiritual crisis." These developments made Protestantism problematic for significant numbers of literate Americans. At the same time, many observers noted—especially between 1893 and 1907—that Buddhism was increasingly popular. In 1883 one Shaker follower noticed the rise of interest:

"Buddhism is at present attracting great attention from scholars and liberal thinkers." William Davies (1848–1922), the Methodist minister and university professor, reported in an article for *Atlantic* in 1894 that "of the religions of the East, Buddhism is the best known and most popularly appreciated." Four years later an anonymous reviewer for the *American Ecclesiastical Review* told his Catholic readers what most of them probably wanted to hear: there is "much absurdity" in Buddhism and especially in the "curious superstitions" concerning, for example, the Buddha's tooth in Ceylon. This reviewer, of course, was preaching to the converted; but even he, and presumably many of his readers, felt compelled to acknowledge that Buddhism had "numerous enthusiastic admirers" in America.[1]

Newspapers in a number of cities also cited evidence of the increased interest in Buddhism. *The Chicago Record* reported on 8 August 1899 that Harry Holst, a twenty-seven-year-old Danish immigrant, spoke regularly about Buddhism on the street corners of the city; and it announced that Holst's topic on the coming Sunday would be karma and rebirth. The city had a small branch of the Maha Bodhi Society, the international Buddhist organization founded in India in 1891, to nurture those with serious interest. But in Chicago even unwitting pedestrians could hear about Buddhist doctrines. Some Buddhist supporters saw in this the seeds of a growing Western Buddhism; and they let the improved transportation and communications systems of the turn of the century scatter these newspaper reports of Buddhist visibility and interest far and wide. Perhaps, they thought, with some cultivation a transplanted Buddhism could root and sprout on American soil. So, for example, Paul Carus (1852–1919), the German-American philosopher and editor, passed on news of this street-corner preacher. He communicated the story and other evidence of American interest to Anagarika Dharamapala (Don David Hewavitarne, 1864–1933), the influential founder of the Maha Bodhi Society. This Buddhist from Ceylon, in turn, spread the news of the advance of the Dharma by reprinting the clipping from the Chicago newspaper in his magazine, *Maha Bodhi*. American magazines kept the news circulating by reprinting *Maha Bodhi*'s story about Holst's Buddhist evangelizing.[2]

But accounts of Buddhist visibility and proclamations of Buddhist popularity were not found only in Chicago. Observers reported interest in other major urban centers such as Boston, New York, and San Francisco. In a letter to his sister-in-law dated 1883, Phillips Brooks (1835–93), the influential Episcopal priest and bishop, wryly explained his visit to a crucial Buddhist shrine in India by suggesting that "in these days when a large part of Boston prefers to consider itself Buddhist rather than Christian, I consider it to be a duty of a minister who preaches to Bostonians." And one follower of the emerging New Thought movement suggested in a newspaper series about Boston that "the term 'American Buddhist' is not an uncommon one at date." *The New York Journal* reported the same swelling interest: "it is no uncommon thing to hear a New Yorker say he is a Buddhist nowadays."[3]

Asian-American and Euro-American Buddhists usually celebrated the reports. For example, writing at the height of the tradition's popularity, Thomas B. Wilson was dizzy with optimism. "The philosophy of Buddhism," he announced, "is making a deep and no doubt lasting impression upon thinking people in America." On the other hand, mainline Protestants like King found the heightened sympathy for the religion troubling. As I will indicate, contemporary observers sometimes exaggerated Buddhism's popularity; but there was much more personal interest in the tradition between 1879 and 1912 than most scholars have recognized. One historian who noticed its popularity suggested that Buddhism was in "vogue" during this period. The term "vogue" might be too strong, but many found themselves attracted to it. At the same time, Christian critics who were alarmed by the reports joined Americans of various perspectives—academic scholars, travel writers, and Buddhist advocates—in a heated and sustained public discussion about the nature and value of this tradition that was attracting so much interest.[4]

THE CONVERSATION ABOUT BUDDHISM, 1879–1912

In July 1853 Commodore Matthew Calbraith Perry reached Japanese shores with eleven armed ships and a letter to the Emperor from President Pierce. Within several years the Japanese, who felt they had few options, signed treaties that allowed for the opening of ports and commerce. There were a variety of reasons for the official American interest in Japan—Nagasaki would be a convenient fueling stop for ships bound from San Francisco to Shanghai—but a raging curiosity about the insights of Buddhist doctrine or the efficacy of Buddhist meditation were not among them. The "opening" of Japan, nonetheless, helped to determine the course of the American discussion about that Asian religion. The treaties ended the Tokugawa government's sustained policy of seclusion, and the resulting political instability helped to prepare the way for a change in leadership. Under the new Meiji leadership (1868–1912) Japan was increasingly open to Westerners. Starting in the 1870s, a number of American intellectuals, for a variety of reasons, decided to see the exotic East for themselves—including Edward Morse, Ernest Fenollosa, William Sturgis Bigelow, Percival Lowell, Henry Adams, John LaFarge, and Lafcadio Hearn. These travelers wrote accounts of the "traits and customs" of the Japanese, and they compared them with those of "the West." They all had direct contact with Buddhism in Japan, and they all later wrote about the tradition in one form or another. A few of them even returned as Buddhist advocates. Their writings helped to initiate the American public discussion about Buddhism; but a number of other persons, texts, institutions, and events played an important role as well.[5]

In 1879 Edwin Arnold (1832–1904), the British writer, published a life of the Buddha rendered in free verse. His sympathetic account emphasized the parallels between the lives of Sakyamuni and Jesus—without explicitly arguing that the life and thought of the two founders was similar or identical. The impact of Arnold's *The Light of Asia* on literate Americans was strong and immediate. The book was, one historian has suggested, "an instant success and one of the literary events of the late nineteenth century." Arnold's biographer has estimated that the work sold between five hundred thousand and one million copies in the United States. To put this in perspective, if this estimate is correct then the poem sold as many copies as bestsellers like Frances Hodgson Burnett's *Little Lord Fauntleroy* and Helen Hunt Jackson's *Ramona* and perhaps as many as Mark Twain's *Huckleberry Finn*. Reviews in religious periodicals ranging from *The Theosophist* to *Catholic World* assessed the poem, and contributors to a large number of secular magazines did the same. In fact, interest in the book and in Buddhism was stimulated by enthusiastic reviews penned by a number of New England intellectuals—for example, William Henry Channing, George Ripley, Franklin Benjamin Sanborn, Francis Ellingwood Abbot, and Oliver Wendell Holmes.[6]

The popularity of Arnold's poem, the extent of Buddhist interest, and the book's influence in drawing Americans to the tradition is witnessed in the opening passage of a book-length rebuttal by Samuel Henry Kellogg (1839–99), the Presbyterian clergyman and professor of systematic theology at the Western Theological Seminary in Allegheny, Pennsylvania:

> The interest that has been of late in Buddhism by a large number of intelligent people . . . is one of the most peculiar and suggestive religious phenomena of our day. In the United States this interest has prevailed for a considerable time among a somewhat restricted number of persons who have known or thought that they knew something of Buddhism; but since 1879, through the publication of Mr. Edwin Arnold's *Light of Asia,* the popularity of the subject has in a very marked degree increased.

In later years Arnold extended his influence, and American interest in Buddhism, as he lectured widely in the United States.[7]

At the same time, European Buddhist studies grew more sophisticated after 1877 or so, and the field continued to have influence in the United States. American scholars, having been dependent on Europe for a generation, also began to make their own international contributions during the 1890s. The first edition of Noah Webster's *Dictionary of the English Language* (1828) had included a one-sentence description of Buddhism: "The doctrines of Buddhists in Asia." Academic scholars associated with the American Oriental Society helped to expand the "official" understanding of Buddhism by writing later entries for that dictionary. Edward Salisbury wrote the definition for the third edition in 1848, and it increased from one line to eighteen. William Dwight Whitney (1827–94), his successor at Yale, was involved with the fourth edition in 1859, and he added further to the sophistication of the treatment. In this small way, American academic scholars slowly added to American awareness of the tradition: they wrote accounts for this dictionary and other standard sources of information. Of even greater long-term impact, early scholars such as Salisbury and Whitney also expanded awareness, and even interest, by stimulating the development of academic Buddhist studies in America through their writing and, especially, their teaching. Salisbury had studied with the great scholars in Europe, and he passed on what he had learned to Whitney at Yale. Whitney taught Charles Rockwell Lanman (1850–1941) of Harvard; and Lanman, in turn, tutored Henry Clarke Warren (1854–99). It was Warren who, with the publication of his *Buddhism in Translations* (1896), made important contributions to the international conversation about Pali Buddhism.[8]

A number of the most influential nineteenth-century scholars of Asian religions were Protestant missionaries, and the foreign missionary efforts that had helped to stimulate discussion about Buddhism in the earlier period continued and intensified between 1880 and 1920. As in the earlier era, the reports of American and European missionaries in Asia helped to shape the reading public's image of Buddhism. The accounts of Buddhism in the *Missionary Herald*, the *Missionary Review of the World*, and similar American periodicals were generally negative. In fact, almost all of the missionaries' interpretations were hostile. Missionaries added to the liveliness of the American conversation, however, both through their own accounts and their often passionate responses to popular sympathetic interpretations of the religion.[9]

One group that consistently offered sympathetic interpretations of Buddhism was the Theosophical Society. In fact, it played a very important role in popularizing Buddhism. The attention of Theosophists and those who followed their activities was directed toward Buddhism when Henry Steel Olcott (1832–1907) and Helena Petrovna Blavatsky (1831–91) formally professed their allegiance to the faith at a temple in Ceylon on 25 May 1880. Kneeling before a huge statue of the Buddha and a large crowd of spectators, the founders of this group took *pansil* as many other Theravada Buddhists had done before. They promised to observe the five basic moral rules and declared that they would take refuge in the Buddha, his teachings, and the Buddhist community. Olcott later diminished the significance of this event. He suggested that he and Blavatsky "had previously declared [themselves] Buddhists long before, in America, both privately and publicly, so that this was but a formal confirmation of [their] previous professions." Olcott's *Buddhist Catechism* was published a year after his public profession, and *The Theosophist*, the organ of the society, regularly included sympathetic pieces about the tradition. Whether or not the ceremony in Ceylon was Olcott's initial profession of allegiance, then, that event—and his and Blavatsky's other efforts to promote Buddhism— stimulated American interest.[10]

All these developments increased the attention given to Buddhism between 1879 and 1912; but, with the possible exception of the publication of Arnold's *Light of Asia*, no single event had more impact than the World's Parliament of Religions of 1893. The Parliament, which opened on 11 September and closed on 27 September, was held in Chicago's "White City" in conjunction with the Columbian Exposition of 1893. At this event Buddhists from Asia had the opportunity to present their tradition to overflow audiences. A number of Asian Buddhists read papers. Two of the most influential were Dharmapala and Soyen Shaku (1856–1919), the Rinzai Zen master from Japan. After the Parliament, both men returned to America to lecture—Soyen in 1905–6 and Dharmapala in 1897 and 1902–4. And both were influential in arousing and sustaining interest in Buddhism. Soyen's sermons, for example, were published in 1906 as *Sermons of a Buddhist Abbot*, and he was instrumental in sending Daisetz Teitaro Suzuki (1870–1966) to America. Suzuki, the Japanese Zen layman, went on to become one of the most important promoters of Buddhism in the West. As I already have hinted, Dharmapala also was very influential. During his second visit to America, in 1897, he founded the American branch of the Maha Bodhi Society. Within a few years there were branches of this international organization in Chicago, New York, and San Francisco. This charismatic Buddhist leader made a strong personal impact on a number of Euro-American Buddhist supporters.[11]

The public discourse that was initiated by these various developments was carried on in all sorts of forums and publications. A look at any of these would reveal something of how widespread and lively the debate about Buddhism was. However, since the nineteenth century was the age of magazines, I concentrate on the discussion that appeared in the pages of important weekly, monthly, and quarterly publications. In later chapters I discuss in detail the content of this conversation and the characteristics of the discussants. Here I only want to give some indication of the intensity of the discussion and the number of participants.

A very wide range of American periodicals included contributions to this discussion between 1879 and 1912. There were two English-language Buddhist magazines published on the West coast: *The Buddhist Ray* (1888– 94) in Santa Cruz and *The Light of Dharma* (1901–7) in San Francisco. *The Buddhist Ray*, which blended occult tendencies with more traditional

Buddhist themes, seems to have been the first English-language Buddhist magazine published in the United States. *The Light of Dharma*, published by the Japanese Pure Land Buddhist Mission, was of much higher quality and exerted greater influence. A number of the most influential participants in the international conversation about Buddhism wrote for the magazine or found their articles reprinted in it. Among those who had pieces appear in the magazine were influential Asian Buddhists like Suzuki, Soyen, and Dharmapala; prominent Western Buddhist scholars such as Thomas William Rhys Davids (1843–1922) in Great Britain and Lanman in the United States; and several of the most influential American Buddhist apologists— including Carus, Olcott, and Marie deSouza Canavarro (1849–1933). A number of more obscure but still influential Asian and Asian-American Buddhist leaders also wrote for the magazine, most of them Japanese. The magazine was sent to many of the major universities and a number of the most eminent scholars of religion.[12]

As one would expect, the magazines connected with the Theosophical Society and the American Oriental Society included articles on Buddhism. Madame Blavatsky, for instance, contributed an article entitled "New York Buddhists" to the *Theosophist*, published in India; and similar pieces appeared in *The Path* and other Theosophical magazines printed in America. Although the *Journal of the American Oriental Society* did not by any means focus on Buddhism, several scholars and philosophers offered relatively sophisticated treatments in its pages. Literary and general-interest magazines from *Atlantic Monthly* in Boston to *Overland Monthly* in San Francisco also added to the discussion. *Atlantic*, for example, offered its readers an overview of "The Religion of Gotama Buddha." David Brainard Spooner (1879–1925), the American tutor at the Siamese Legation in Tokyo, described for readers of the West Coast equivalent of *Atlantic* the "very beautiful and very interesting" ceremonies that accompanied the Japanese reception of alleged relics of the Buddha.[13]

One interesting contribution appeared in *Open Court* (1887–1936), the magazine founded as the successor to *The Index*. The latter had been the organ of the Free Religious Association, that group formed by New England religious liberals and radicals who found even Unitarianism too narrow, unscientific, and dogmatic. Carus, the editor of *Open Court*, arranged and published a revealing debate among Soyen, John Henry Barrows (1847–1902), the Protestant minister who was the leading force behind the Parliament of Religions, and Frank Field Ellinwood (1826–1908), the Presbyterian lecturer in comparative religion at the University of the City of New York. It had happened this way: The year after the Parliament, Barrows was appointed to the Haskell lectureship on comparative religion at the University of Chicago. And in January 1896 Barrows, who often was praised for his inclusivity and tolerance, delivered a public lecture on Buddhism at that university. In the same month Carus wrote to Soyen in

Japan to complain that Barrows's lecture had revealed a "strange" Christian bias. Carus's disappointment and irritation was evident. Instead of offering his own corrective, however, he asked Soyen to "set him right." He would respond himself, Carus explained, but Barrows might counter by citing the findings of an authoritative Western scholar who shared Barrows's Christian bias—Sir Monier Monier-Williams. So Carus decided to "leave the defense of Buddhism to a prominent foreign Buddhist." But he cared too much to allow the apologetic advantage to fall to the Christian critics because of poor word choice or unwittingly hostile tone. So Carus offered precise instructions to Soyen—"be as polite as possible in your letter"—and even sent a first draft of a response: "In order to make the work as easy as possible for you I enclose a reply such as I suppose might impress Dr. Barrows." Carus did not want to insult Soyen or limit his freedom of expression: "Of course, you must write it as you deem fit." But, Carus believed, a great deal was at stake in such public exchanges. In any case, Soyen did send off a response. Carus then published Soyen's response alongside letters by Barrows and Ellinwood as "A Controversy on Buddhism" in the January 1897 issue of *Open Court*. A month later Dharmapala also entered the debate by offering a reply to Ellinwood's negative remarks about Buddhism. Between 1893 and 1907 many other pieces about Buddhism appeared in this magazine, which was devoted to the reconciliation of science and religion and the promotion of inclusivism and tolerance. The discussion also was conducted in other liberal and radical religious periodicals such as the new *Dial, Christian Examiner, Arena, International Journal of Ethics*, and *Unitarian Review*.[14]

Articles and reviews about Buddhist topics appeared in a wide range of mainline Protestant magazines as well, including *The Andover Review, The Baptist Quarterly, Biblical World, Christian Literature, The Methodist Review*, and *The Princeton Review*. The historical relation and relative merits of Christianity and Buddhism were discussed by Congregationalists and Methodists as well as Ethical Culturists and Unitarians. For example, in 1898 John Wesley Johnston, pastor of the First Methodist Episcopal Church in Meriden, Connecticut, discussed the "resemblances and contrasts" between Christ and Buddha in the *Methodist Review*. The *Andover Review* published several articles about Buddhism during the 1880s. In fact, the two by Marquis Lafayette Gordon (1843–1900), who entered Japan as a missionary of the American Board of Commissioners for Foreign Missions in 1872, were among the most sophisticated pieces by a non-scholar published during the nineteenth century.[15]

Roman Catholics were preoccupied with other pressing concerns such as building and staffing churches and schools and fighting Protestant hostility and urban poverty. Yet even Catholic periodicals devoted attention to Buddhism. John Gmeiner (1847–1913), best known as a German-American defender of Roman Catholic adaptation to the American context, reviewed

Sir Edwin Arnold's *Light of Asia* for *Catholic World* in 1885. R. M. Ryan shed "More Light on 'The Light of Asia' " in 1895 and added another article in the same year called "The Lustre of 'The Light of Asia.' " A well-informed and carefully argued analysis of the reports about parallels between the two traditions and their founders appeared in an 1897 issue of *American Catholic Quarterly Review*. And Merwin-Marie Snell, an uncompromisingly exclusivistic Roman Catholic, wrote a number of articles on Buddhism for Protestant as well as Catholic periodicals.[16]

Foreign authors and periodicals also played an important role in the American discussion. American Buddhist advocates read foreign magazines, especially those published in Great Britain, India, and Ceylon; and a few Americans also published pieces in these periodicals. Of these magazines, *Maha Bodhi,* organ of the Maha Bodhi Society, was one of the most important at the peak of American interest in Buddhism. European scholars and Asian Buddhists also contributed to the American conversation by contributing to American periodicals. For example, both F. Max Müller, whose writings had been so influential in the earlier period, and Rhys Davids, the eminent British scholar of Buddhism, published pieces about the religion in the *North American Review*.[17]

AMERICAN BUDDHIST SYMPATHIZERS AND ADHERENTS

Not only was Buddhism widely discussed between 1879 and 1912, but there were a number of Americans—of European as well as Asian descent—who either identified themselves as Buddhists or expressed sympathy for the tradition.

Asian-American Buddhists

Ah Nam (d. 1817), a cook for the Spanish Governor at Monterey, California, is the first Chinese immigrant on record. Chinese immigration was only a trickle for the next forty years or so. But the Chinese, the first Asians to arrive in significant numbers, became a visible presence along the West Coast between the 1850s and the 1880s. Koreans, Filipinos, and, in much greater numbers, Japanese also arrived in Hawaii and on the Pacific Coast during the nineteenth and early twentieth centuries. There were Buddhists among the Koreans who immigrated to Hawaii between 1902 and 1905 as "scab" replacements for striking Japanese plantation workers. There were some Buddhists from other Asian nations as well: K. Y. Kira of Ceylon resided in New York and played an active role in the Maha Bodhi Society. But these latter immigrants were a minor portion of the Asian Buddhists in America; the majority were Chinese and Japanese living on the West Coast and in Hawaii. Hawaii became a United States possession in 1898 and welcomed Buddhist missionaries as early as 1889.[18]

It is unlikely that we will ever be able to reconstruct the religious beliefs and practices of Ah Nam, that earliest recorded Chinese immigrant; and it is only slightly easier to do so for the thousands of Chinese who followed him during the century. We can look to published accounts by contemporaries for aid in reconstructing the religious life of nineteenth-century Chinese Americans. In 1892, for instance, Frederick J. Masters offered a depiction of the fifteen "pagan temples" in San Francisco for *The Californian*. Masters was relatively well-informed about Chinese religions— although his Christian allegiance was never far from the surface—and his account was as rich and ornate as the temples and icons he described. For all the detail, however, he failed to distinguish among Buddhist, Taoist, and Confucian figures and themes. And this is not surprising in some ways. Following long-established patterns, Chinese-Americans were syncretistic. They were much less inclined than their American Christian contemporaries to define their religiousness in terms of exclusive allegiance to a single tradition; and so it is difficult to sort Buddhist from Taoist, Confucian, and native folk elements in the immigrants' religious life.[19]

It is safe to say that Buddhism was a significant part of the religious life of many Chinese-Americans. But it is difficult to estimate the number of Buddhists for another reason: Chinese-American Buddhism remained unorganized. No membership statistics are available; and so speculations must be based on population figures and the number of "temples" reported to the Bureau of the Census. In any case, there seem to have been tens of thousands of Chinese who were predominantly Buddhist by heritage and conviction at any point between the 1850s and 1910s. However, Chinese Buddhists did not send missionaries to nurture their American immigrant communities as the Japanese would, and this led to a loosening of Buddhist ties among second- and third-generation Chinese Americans. The influence of Buddhism was not extinguished completely or suddenly among the Chinese, but because of the lack of institutional support the vitality of Buddhist life probably was greatest among the first generation. By the time the Japanese began arriving in significant numbers during the 1890s, the pervasiveness and liveliness of Chinese-American Buddhism already was beginning to decline.[20]

It is slightly less difficult to determine the number of Buddhists among Japanese immigrants. It depends, of course, on how one defines a Buddhist "adherent." If the term refers to individuals who were registered as Buddhists in Japan or those whose parents were Buddhist, the percentage in the immigrant population was quite high. If it refers only to those who were formal members of a particular Buddhist church in the United States, then the numbers would be less. The only census figures we have for the period come from 1906, and they record 3,165 Japanese Buddhists. Yet the number of Japanese-Americans who remained loosely affiliated with the tradition might have been much higher.[21]

As I have noted, the Japanese provided greater support for their immigrant Buddhist communities than the Chinese. They apparently did so, in part, in response to Christian missionary efforts. The Japanese Gospel Society of San Francisco was founded in 1877, and during the next decade the Presbyterian and Methodist Boards of Missions formally committed themselves to preaching the Gospel among the Japanese. The governing body of the *Hompa Hongwanji*, one of the forms of *Jodo-Shin-shu* (True Pure Land Sect) in Japan, decided to send two representatives to the United States to study the spiritual condition of immigrants. The leaders of this group felt that they had a real stake in the American developments since approximately two-thirds of the immigrants came from prefectures in Japan that were dominated by the Pure Land Buddhist faith. The group's ordained representatives, Eryu Honda and Ejun Miyamoto, arrived in San Francisco on 6 July 1898. Soon after, the Young Men's Buddhist Association of San Francisco was formed, and on 17 September the first Buddhist temple in the United States was established on Mason Street in that city. All this was unofficial, however: Honda and Miyamoto had been commissioned only to study the problem. It was only on 2 September 1899 that the Japanese headquarters in Kyoto gave official recognition to the Buddhist mission in America by sending two missionaries—Shuye Sonoda and Kakuryo Nishijima. By 1906, twelve Pure Land Buddhist groups had been established—nine in California, two in Washington, and one in Oregon. Eight more temples would be added by 1912.[22]

These Japanese Buddhists were viewed as alien and treated with hostility because of both their race and religion. As some scholars have suggested, in many ways Asian-Americans were the "ultimate aliens." Like the Chinese, Japanese immigrants were "aliens ineligible to citizenship." Since the first naturalization act of 1790, the right to naturalization was restricted to "free white persons." Their distinctiveness was intensified by their religious affiliation. To many, the Japanese who had been converted to Christianity by the Protestant missionaries in Japan or on the West Coast seemed less alien, less repulsive, less dangerous. In short, Christian converts seemed more American. American Protestant ministers, many of whom had been missionaries in Asia, were prominent among the defenders of the Chinese and the Japanese. Yet these same ministers—for instance, Otis Gibson (1826–89), under whom Japanese immigrants founded the San Francisco Gospel Society, and Sydney Lewis Gulick (1860–1945) of the Federal Council of Churches' Commission on Relations with Japan—also often identified assimilation with conversion. Gulick, a former Congregationalist missionary to Japan, found a significant difference in attitude among Japanese-American converts to Christianity. He argued that "a Christian Japanese is ready to go more than halfway in establishing right relations with American neighbors." For these Protestants, America was a Christian nation; and becoming American meant adopting beliefs and values that were linked not only with democratic government but also Protestant religion.[23]

By the time the Japanese started to arrive in significant numbers, hostility to the Chinese—formalized in the Chinese Exclusion Act of 1882—had been raging for some time. And Japanese immigrants, often repeating American criticisms of the Chinese, tried to distinguish themselves from the "lower class" Chinese who seemed unable to assimilate. Most of the *issei*, first-generation Japanese immigrants, intended to return to Japan, but there is some evidence of assimilation even during the initial period of Japanese-American history (1885–1907). As early as 1892, Tadashichi Tanaka, the illiterate but shrewd Japanese-American contractor who supplied laborers for railroad construction, insisted that his Japanese workers wear American clothes and eat American food.[24]

A limited amount of Americanization and Protestantization also occurred in Japanese Pure Land Buddhist communities before World War I. The official name of the group was not changed to "Buddhist Churches of America" until 1944, but as early as 1905 its fourth director renamed the "Hongwanji Branch Office" the "Buddhist Church of San Francisco." It is probably no coincidence that in that same year the *San Francisco Chronicle* had launched an anti-Japanese campaign in a series of sensational articles. But there were precedents in Japan. In 1891 one Protestant minister in Tokyo complained about the "parasitic" qualities of Buddhism: "Besides adopting other Christian methods of propagation, it is plagiarizing Christian names. For instance, instead of using the word *temple* as the designation for their religious houses, they say *church* now." There is other evidence of relatively superficial Protestantization. The Young Men's Buddhist Association self-consciously modeled itself after its Protestant counterpart, the Y.M.C.A. Buddhist priests sometimes were addressed as "Reverend." The Sunday School, so prominent in nineteenth-century American Protestantism, appeared in Japanese Buddhist groups by 1913. Finally, most of the religious buildings constructed in the early years followed Western patterns. This was mostly for economic reasons: immigrants of limited means who intend to return to their native land usually do not invest in grand religious architecture. But other considerations probably played a role: an Oriental roof only invites notice and recalls difference. By the 1920s, some Japanese-American Buddhists were singing "Onward Buddhist Soldiers" at English-language services.[25]

A few Euro-Americans with sympathy for Buddhism had personal influence on the leaders of the Japanese Pure Land community in America. Sonoda, one of the two original Buddhist missionaries, wrote to Paul Carus in 1899 to thank him for his writings on Buddhism. Carus's works, it turns out, were rather influential among some Buddhists in Japan around the turn of the century. Sonoda reported that he had assigned Carus's collection of passages from the Buddhist scriptures as the main text for a course in English at a Japanese college. And the influence continued and expanded on American shores: another correspondent who was associated with the Buddhist Mission in San Francisco told Carus in 1903 that that group used his Buddhist anthology and Buddhist hymns for their services.[26]

But more significant for the present study, the influence also went in the other direction. This study analyzes the public conversation about Buddhism (in English) and focuses on Euro-American Buddhists. The history of Asian-American Buddhism has relevance insofar as its spokesmen—and they were men—shaped the American discussion and insofar as its leaders, institutions, and publications influenced Euro-Americans. There is, in fact, clear evidence of influence; and apparently this was not accidental. Sonoda confided to Carus that his concerns extended beyond the Japanese-American Buddhist community. He hoped to "gradually propagate our doctrine among Americans." On 4 January 1900 the Buddhist Mission in San Francisco formally reached out to Euro-Americans by instituting weekly lectures for Occidental inquirers. In April of that year the Japanese priests helped to establish the Dharma Sangha of Buddha, a group for Caucasian Buddhists in the area. In the same year the San Francisco Mission published an overview of Buddhist doctrine and practice in English. A magazine aimed at Japanese Buddhist immigrants, Beikoku Bukkyo (Buddhism in America), also was founded in the same year; but the influential English-language Buddhist magazine, The Light of Dharma, followed in 1901. Further, the daily records (nisshi) left by the Japanese priests in San Francisco suggest that there was frequent, informal contact between Caucasians interested in Buddhism and the Japanese priests at the mission. They mention not only business meetings of the Dharma Sangha of Buddha but also visits to the homes of Caucasians. There is even some evidence of intimacy: One entry records a Japanese priest's exchange of Christmas gifts with a Caucasian supporter. In one letter Sonoda described Jenny Ward Hayes, a member of the Dharma Sangha of Buddha and an "earnest Buddhist" who composed Buddhist hymns, as "my friend."[27]

Nishijima, the other original Japanese missionary in San Francisco, wrote to Dharmapala in Asia of the great success of their efforts among Euro-Americans: "It is a fact now that there is a great number of English speaking people in America, who are deeply interested in Buddhism." But, such assessments aside, these efforts did not lead to unrestricted sympathy for the Japanese or universal appreciation for Buddhism. One event, for example, offers some indication of the complex nature and varying extent of Japanese influence on American attitudes toward this immigrant community and its alien faith. On 8 April 1900 the San Francisco Pure Land group sponsored an elaborate festival celebrating the Buddha's birthday. At two o'clock there was a service—in English—that was attended by approximately 150 Caucasians. Included in the audience were dignitaries and officials from the San Francisco area. Some of these same dignitaries later participated in the "drive out the Japs" campaign; others in that audience subsequently established friendships with the Japanese-Americans and found themselves drawn to Buddhism. Most Americans of European descent treated Asian immigrants, and the Buddhist religion, with apathy or hostility. But some—like Jenny Hayes—apparently had their interest in Buddhism sparked and sustained by Japanese Pure Land priests and their institutions.[28]

Euro-American Buddhist Adherents and Sympathizers

When the Reverend King wondered aloud whether he and his contemporaries should convert to Buddhism he was not revealing his own submerged attraction to the Asian tradition: he was a committed Christian with little sympathy for Buddhism. Yet his disingenuous query was not as preposterous as it first might appear. Certainly Buddhism was not about to displace Christianity as the dominant religion in the United States. But even King implicitly acknowledged that Buddhism had become, to use Williams James's phrase, a "live option" for the spiritually disillusioned. Whether or not they were first drawn to the tradition through the influence of the Japanese Buddhist Mission—and most were not—significant numbers of Americans of European heritage found Buddhism attractive between 1879 and 1912.

In rural camp meetings, urban church revivals, and, today, football stadium rallies, Americans have been stirred by the revivalists' rhetoric of sin, repentance, and salvation ritually to pronounce or reconfirm their Protestant faith. After a public lecture by Dharmapala on Buddhism and Theosophy in 1893, C. T. Strauss, a Swiss-American businessman of Jewish descent, strode purposefully to the front of a Chicago auditorium like a repentant Protestant at a revival meeting and ritually professed his commitment to a very different sort of faith. Those in the overflow crowd in that Chicago hall were informed that Mr. Strauss was about to formally accept Buddhism. As they apparently had planned before the lecture, Strauss repeated the formulas after Dharmapala and proclaimed that he, too, took refuge in the Buddha, his teaching, and his community. After the public ceremony, Strauss had regular correspondence and intermittent visits with Dharmapala and other Asian and Western Buddhists; he remained a devoted Buddhist for the rest of his life.[29]

Several accounts describe Strauss as the first American formally to convert to Buddhism on American soil. That seems correct. But, as I noted in the previous chapter, Dyer Daniel Lum seems to have been the first American to advocate Buddhism publicly—although there was no ceremony to formalize and legitimate his personal commitment. He had defended Buddhism as "the true method of salvation" in a lecture to the

Channing Club of Northampton, Massachusetts, on 8 April 1875, and he continued to see himself as a Buddhist until his death. There were others before 1893 who publicly advocated Buddhism but did not formalize that commitment in a traditional Buddhist ceremony. E. D. Root described himself as an "American Buddhist" in *Sakya Buddha,* his poetic life of the Buddha that was published in 1880. Philangi Dasa (Herman C. Vetterling, 1849–1931) came to see himself as a follower of the Buddha around 1884, and he publicly promoted the tradition as editor of that first American Buddhist magazine, founded in 1888, *The Buddhist Ray.* Other Americans, like Olcott, formally embraced the religion in traditional Buddhist ceremonies held outside the United States. Ernest Francisco Fenollosa (1851–1903) and William Sturgis Bigelow (1850–1926), two aesthetically inclined Boston intellectuals who lived in Japan for years, received the precepts of Tendai Buddhism on 21 September 1885.[30]

Fixing the religious identity of those—like Bigelow and Fenollosa—who declared their allegiance in traditional ceremonies officiated by authoritative Asian Buddhists is not too difficult. Questions remain—for example, about how deeply they understood the tradition and how consistently they practiced it—but few would argue that they were not Buddhists in any sense. Determining religious identity is trickier in many other cases. As I will indicate more fully in later chapters, many Caucasian Buddhist followers combined traditional Buddhist doctrines with beliefs derived from Western sources. Many of those who were syncretistic blended forms of esoteric spirituality with Buddhist themes; but some also fashioned their Buddhism by setting traditional doctrines in a framework constructed from the writings of, for example, Herbert Spencer, the British philosopher, or Auguste Comte, the French positivist. In both instances, especially with those inclined toward the occult, the question arose: But were they *real* Buddhists? Western Buddhist scholars, Protestant critics of the tradition, and even a handful of Euro-American Buddhists questioned the authenticity of some self-proclaimed adherents. The American scholar Edward Washburn Hopkins (1857–1932) complained vigorously that the beliefs and practices of so-called American Buddhists diverged from the picture of the tradition that was emerging in Western scholarship. He felt the need to remind "the many that profess themselves Buddhists" that they had adopted "a very unreal Buddhism." M. L. Gordon, the Congregationalist missionary, also worried about inauthentic Buddhists. He witnessed with concern the excitement stirred by *The Light of Asia,* and he warned that the Buddhism of Arnold's seductive poem was not the real stuff of everyday Mahayana Buddhist belief and practice in Japan. The real thing was much less attractive than that.[31]

Gordon's attack on the authenticity of Euro-American Buddhist followers was driven by a concern to support and extend a shaken Christianity, not to preserve and propagate a purer Buddhism. But even a few who advocated Buddhism challenged the genuineness of the American syncretists. Herman Vetterling's authenticity as a "real" Buddhist might have been challenged by many because he blended a number of perspectives in his understanding of the tradition—including Swedenborgianism, homeopathy, Theosophy, and Spiritualism. Yet he printed a notice from the *Boston Record* in his magazine that challenged the widespread perception that there were swarms of Buddhists buzzing around urban centers like Boston during the 1890s. The unidentified author of this reprinted piece asserted that "of actual buddhists there are two or three" in Boston. The article concluded by suggesting that Fenollosa probably was "the only out and out buddhist in the city." Another piece, written by Vetterling himself for the same magazine, aimed some of the same criticisms at other self-proclaimed Buddhists that might have been directed against its spiritually eclectic author. He warned his Asian Buddhist brethren not to conclude that "one needs but go into the street to elbow buddhists at every step" since many of the so-called Buddhists were merely esoteric dilettantes or, what he called in another article on the topic, "the hysteric women, weak-minded men, and plagiarists that have formed the 'aryan'-'buddhist'-astrologic cliques of Boston."[32]

There is little evidence that those who were being attacked as inauthentic worried much about the charge, and such concerns need not produce much anxiety for the historian. It might be useful to know where American interpretations of the tradition diverged widely from the nineteenth-century scholarly literature or from the consensus of Buddhism scholars today. It might be useful to know that an individual or group combined beliefs or practices in a manner that seems novel in the history of Asian Buddhism. Yet innovation and syncretism in the transplanting of Buddhism and other religions as well is hardly new: over the centuries, as I suggested, the Chinese transformed Indian Buddhism rather significantly. Innovation by itself should raise few serious questions. Those nineteenth-century writers who did question the authenticity of some Buddhists were expressing, implicitly or explicitly, either competing personal religious convictions or naively self-assured notions about the true "essence" of Buddhism.

For a variety of reasons, twentieth-century authors also have questioned the authenticity of some professed followers. The author of the most comprehensive treatment of Buddhism in Victorian Britain, for example, completely ignored occult Buddhists. In a footnote, Philip C. Almond explained: "I have not dealt with the Esoteric Buddhism of Madame Blavatsky and her English disciple, Alfred Sinnett. Esoteric, it may have been. Buddhism, it certainly was not, at least in the eyes of most late-nineteenth-century interpreters of Buddhism." However, I suggest, it is not useful to exclude a great number of individuals and groups on these grounds. If the concern is to understand sympathetic responses to Buddhism and uncover as much as possible about Victorian religion and culture, as it is in the present study, whether or not Olcott or Vetterling met some standard of orthodoxy or orthopraxy is not crucial. There are a number of more important questions: Why were they attracted to Buddhism? How did they, and their opponents, interpret it? What presuppositions, beliefs, and values informed those interpretations? What do their accounts reveal about the contours of the wider culture? It is unnecessarily restrictive to apply the term "adherent" only to those who, for example, affirmed a particular interpretation of nirvana, studied with an Asian Buddhist teacher, formally professed Buddhism in a public ceremony, or diligently followed the practices of a particular sect. To apply such criteria is to become tangled in thorny issues about the true essence of the tradition. It also seems to lead only to unilluminating conclusions—that most nineteenth-century followers got it wrong, that only a handful were "real" Buddhists, or that we know more about Buddhism than they. Many persons whose experience seems to have been shaped by Buddhist categories would be ignored, and the extent of American interest in the tradition during the nineteenth century would be obscured. Concomitantly, we would uncover less than we might about American religion and culture in this period. The most useful way to determine the religious identities of these nineteenth-century Americans, I suggest, is to rely on self-definition as much as possible. For the purposes of this study, then, Euro-American Buddhist adherents were those Americans of European heritage who identified themselves as Buddhists or those for whom other reliable evidence exists that suggests they thought of themselves in this way.[33]

Of course, relying on self-definition is not always possible, and it is never without its dangers. Often not enough evidence survives to reconstruct religious self-understanding with certainty or precision. Further, some individuals who thought of themselves as Buddhists might not have confessed their beliefs, because they wanted to avoid the censure that such a public proclamation often brought. On the other hand, some who proudly and publicly proclaimed their allegiance might have had very little genuine commitment to the tradition. They might have been driven more by the love of the exotic or the quest for attention. Nonetheless, self-definition still seems the most parsimonious and useful method for identifying adherents.

But adherents were not the whole story. Others who did not see themselves as Buddhists but had sympathy for the religion were an important part of the American encounter with Buddhism as well. I call those who were attracted to Buddhism but did not embrace it fully or exclusively "sympathizers." To ignore them is to fail to gauge the full level of interest in the tradition during this period and to miss another opportunity to understand Victorian religious culture. It is crucial, of course, to consider why adherents were led to Buddhism. But it can be as illuminating, even more so, to investigate why sympathizers were attracted and why they failed to embrace the tradition fully and exclusively.

"Sympathizer" is a rather vague term that could include a fairly wide range of perspectives and practices. In its loosest sense, the term might refer to individuals who simply said a few positive things about Buddha and Buddhism. In this sense, Andrew Jackson Davis (1826–1910), the Spiritualist leader, Warren Felt Evans (1817–89), the cofounder of the New Thought movement, and many others could be labeled sympathizers. I generally use the term, however, in a slightly more restricted way. Sympathizers were those individuals who confessed—in an article, book, lecture, diary, or letter—that they were attracted to Buddhism. Or, if self-description is lacking, sympathizers are those for whom I have relatively reliable evidence that they found Buddhist doctrines attractive. For example, they might have offered a vigorous public defense of Buddhism, regularly attended lectures about the tradition, or read Buddhist literature for a sustained period of time. They need not have spent their religious lives teetering on the fulcrum between belief and doubt, but there must be some reason to think that they were drawn to Buddhism—even if they remained unaffiliated or affiliated with some other religious group. Of course, some who read about Buddhism, defended it publicly, or attended lectures on the subject might have had little or no personal sympathy for the tradition. Perhaps some were Christian opponents of the tradition involved in some sort of spiritual espionage. In general, however, I think it is fair to assume that many or most of those who expressed interest in these ways were sympathetic.[34]

Some sympathizers—for instance Paul Carus—were drawn to Buddhism but refused to join any particular religion or sect. Others expressed significant interest in Buddhism but saved their primary allegiance for another tradition. In August 1836 the Reverend Adoniram Judson, that first American missionary to Burma whom I discussed in chapter one, wrote to his son in the United States about his new daughter, Abby Ann Judson (1835–1902). "Your little sister, Abigail, is a sweet, fat baby," Adoniram reported. "You would love her very much if you were here. Pray for her, that she may live, and may become a child of God." Abby, a Buddhist sympathizer, did not turn out exactly as her pious Protestant father had hoped. She came to believe that "the religion of the Buddha is far superior to what is known as Christianity." Her first allegiance, however, was to Spiritualism, and she rejected those elements of Buddhism that "did not enter into [her] conception of Spiritualism."[35]

Abby Judson hailed from an old New England family. Yet many sympathizers and adherents were first- or second-generation Americans, and they were found in at least twenty-four states and two United States possessions—from Maine and Vermont to Oregon and California (see table 1). Some were scattered in the South and Midwest, but most were concentrated in the Northeast and along the Pacific Coast. Some persons in small rural communities expressed interest in the tradition—in places like Mount Vernon, Maine; Brownsville, Texas; and Vermillion, South Dakota. The self-proclaimed Buddhist in Vermillion, for instance, was Frank Graeme Davis, a student at the University of South Dakota. He corresponded with Japanese Buddhists in San Francisco and subscribed to the magazine they published. In one letter he proclaimed his allegiance to Buddhism and encouraged missionary efforts in America: "You say you do not attempt to make converts among Christians, but surely there are persons innumerable in this land, that would joyfully receive the teachings of the Lord Buddha, if they could but be reached. My sympathies are altogether with you and your work; it is my hope that I may sometime be able and worthy to aid in working for the same cause, for I believe Buddhism to be the religion of humanity." But being a Buddhist in South Dakota had its difficulties. "You cannot know how utterly alone I have felt during the past years," he wrote to a Buddhist priest, "knowing of no other person in America attempting to follow the teachings of the Lord Buddha, and how I desire to be of service to His cause." Davis sought the Buddhist community he longed for by organizing a small and informal group of his own: four students at the University of South Dakota met every Friday evening in the room of one of Davis's friends "for the purpose of studying Buddhism." Few Buddhist followers, however, were as isolated as Davis and his friends. Most lived in or around a few urban areas—Boston, New York, San Francisco, Honolulu, Philadelphia, and Chicago.[36]

As I have noted, those in Chicago enjoyed the support of an official organization. In May 1898, for instance, the branch of the Maha Bodhi Society in that city planned a celebration of the Buddha's birthday. The vice president of that group, Arba N. Waterman (1836–1917), agreed to have the ceremonies in his spacious home. At the time, Waterman served as a judge in Circuit Court of Cook County. While not all sympathizers were professionals, most seem to have come from the middle and upper classes. Given the paucity of sources, it is often difficult to identify the occupations of many of those who did not contribute to the public discussion or enjoy relatively high social or economic status. Even if further research uncovers more laborers, however, it seems safe to suggest that attorneys, professors, and physicians were represented in disproportionate numbers.[37]

The business community also seems to have been well represented. Andrew Carnegie (1835–1919), for example, though not a Buddhist, was sympathetic to the tradition. This extremely influential manufacturer and philanthropist even suggested that Arnold's *The Light of Asia* gave him "greater delight than any similar poetical work I had recently read." He also called his original manuscript of that poetic life of the Buddha "one of my most precious treasures." From someone with Carnegie's affection for books and his stockpile of treasures that was high praise. Other relatively prominent local business and civic leaders could be counted among the sympathizers. Alexander Russell (1855–1919) of San Francisco, who worked as sales manager of the Bowers Rubber Works and later made money in real estate and mining investments, subscribed to the *Light of Dharma*. He and his wife, Ida, were instructed in meditation by Soyen while they visited Japan, and in 1905 the whole family participated in regular Zen meditation and devotion while Soyen stayed for months in their mansion. Not all those who worked in the business and financial communities were as wealthy and prominent as Carnegie or even Russell. Charles W. G. Withee (1848–1911) of St. Paul, Minnesota, subscribed to the *Light of Dharma* and donated money to the Maha Bodhi Society's projects. He seems to have worked as a bookkeeper before he began to practice law. Clarence Clowe, who described himself as "an American Buddhist" in an angry letter to Carus, worked at a store that sold "dry goods, groceries, and ladies and gentlemen's furnishings"—The Miner's Supply Company in Bossburg, Washington.[38]

There also were journalists, publishers, bookbinders, mediums, students, public officials, librarians, artists, printers, poets, teachers, and governesses among the American Buddhists. Yet many of those I have identified seem to have been homemakers—including I. W. Gardner of Los Angeles, Louise I. Hall of Chicago, Rosa Young of New Orleans, Gila Mireles of Brownsville, and Ines G. Capron of Portland, Maine. This, of course, raises the question of gender. Some women—Marie Canavarro, for example—were prominent apologists for the tradition. Yet roughly equivalent numbers of men and women seem to have expressed interest in the tradition. About forty percent of the American subscribers to the *Light of Dharma* were women, and in general they probably did not constitute more than half of the sympathizers and adherents. To put this in perspective, in 1906 women seem to have been a clear majority among Christian Science, Spiritualist, and Theosophical groups. Even some mainline Protestant groups like the Methodists had over sixty percent female membership. The proportion of women, then, does not seem to have been unusually high.[39]

I have offered a tentative characterization of Buddhist advocates in terms of gender, class, ethnicity, and region, and I will return to these issues again in the next chapter. But an obvious question remains unanswered: How many were there? I have uncovered at least some information about several hundred persons who, by the criteria I have established, were Euro-American Buddhist sympathizers or adherents. Yet many more were either attracted to the tradition or identified themselves with it. The circulation figures for a few important periodicals and books and the membership estimates for religious groups that included Buddhist followers offer some clues. Between five hundred and one thousand copies of the *Light of Dharma* circulated each year. Yet others who were not listed in the subscription book might have received the periodical, and many more might have read the magazine at the many university libraries, publishing institutions, and Buddhist organizations that received it. Although it is difficult to reach conclusions about the number of sympathizers on such grounds, the circulation of *Open Court*, which published many contributions to the public conversation about Buddhism, was almost five thousand copies; and many Americans also had access to articles and reviews about Buddhism that regularly appeared in secular and religious magazines with larger circulations.[40]

If we considered only the popularity of three books we might have to conclude that a significant number of Americans had some personal interest—Arnold's *The Light of Asia* (1879), Olcott's *Buddhist Catechism* (1881), and Carus's *The Gospel of Buddha* (1894). All three had sizable circulations and were cited frequently. Carus's *Gospel of Buddha* went through thirteen editions by 1910, and Olcott's *Buddhist Catechism* went through more than forty editions before the author died in 1907. As I reported above, Arnold's poetic life of the Buddha sold between five hundred thousand and one million copies. It went through eighty American editions. Even if some of the readers of these books had no serious interest or personal sympathy and even if some were Protestant critics studying their religious adversary, many also must have been sympathetic to the tradition.[41]

The hall of the Golden Gate Lodge, the Theosophical group in San Francisco, was "overflowing" when Dharmapala spoke there one Sunday in 1902. Its library and reading room were open to the public every afternoon, and Buddhist periodicals and books found a place beside the Theosophical and New Thought literature. As one notice reported, "The *Light of Dharma* [found] many an appreciative reader among visitors." And, as I argue in the next chapter, there were other signs of interest in Buddhism in this and other Theosophical societies. Altogether there were probably a few thousand Euro-American sympathizers and adherents associated with one religious group or another—the Theosophical Society, the Spiritualists, the Free Religious Association, the Ethical Culture Society, the Pure Land Buddhist temples, or the Maha Bodhi Society.[42]

I estimate, then, that in each year at the peak of American interest (1893 to 1907) there were probably two or three thousand Euro-Americans who thought of themselves primarily or secondarily as Buddhists and tens of thousands more who had some sympathy for the tradition. But estimating the number of followers of alternative groups is notoriously difficult when, as in this case, there are no authoritative membership lists to count adherents, and, by definition almost, there can be no certain way to count sympathizers. Part of the difficulty arises because of the usual slipperiness and potential ambiguity of quantitative analysis. For example, it is possible to claim that there were as many Buddhists at Harvard in 1908, just after the interest had peaked, as there were members of Lutheran, Dutch Reformed, or Quaker bodies. This is accurate, in a sense, since a survey of Harvard college seniors in that year found that two persons had identified themselves as Buddhist and two each as Lutheran, Dutch Reformed, and Quaker. Yet this easily could lead to overestimation: not only do we not know whether these Buddhists were Euro-Americans, but the figures, of course, do not offer a fair picture of the influence and distribution of these groups.[43]

There are other potential difficulties with such estimates. Olcott, the Theosophical Buddhist, claimed that there were "at least 50,000" Buddhist adherents in the United States in 1889. This seems highly exaggerated if he meant Caucasian Buddhists. It is not surprising that an advocate would overestimate; nor is it surprising that many other neutral or even hostile observers spoke as if American Buddhists flooded the streets. Contemporaries, sympathetic and hostile, often overestimate the membership of new religious movements and traditions transplanted from alien shores. As with Deists in the 1790s or "Moonies" in the 1970s, the amount of public attention, anxiety, and influence can be disproportionate to actual numbers. Olcott's estimates clearly were wrong; but even if there only had been two hundred Buddhist followers their visibility might have been almost as great. I have tried to suggest there were many more than that. As with most new or transplanted movements, the visibility of Buddhism in Victorian America can be traced to the work of a small number of influential public advocates; but thousands of more obscure Americans were drawn to the religion.[44]

Who were those Americans who were drawn to this alien faith? Even with the paucity of information already introduced, a dizzying diversity of characteristics and perspectives has emerged. Vetterling, the homeopathic physician in California, combined Asian Buddhist and Western occult themes. Bigelow, the aesthetically inclined Bostonian, practiced Tendai and Shingon Buddhism in Japan. Carus, the German-American philosopher in Illinois, presented a sympathetic portrait of the founder and a rationalistic interpretation of the religion that drew praise from Asian Buddhists eager to introduce Buddhism to the West. Yet he never joined this or any other religion. In order to discern patterns—and highlight idiosyncrasies—in the next chapter I offer a typology of Euro-American Buddhist sympathizers and adherents.

THREE

ESOTERICS, RATIONALISTS, AND ROMANTICS

A Typology of Euro-American Buddhist Sympathizers and Adherents, 1875–1912

A short story published in 1891 recounts Maxwell Lawrence's visit to a meeting of the "Buddhist Inquirers," a society dedicated to the exploration of Buddhism and occult phenomena. "Under the Bodhi Tree" is set in the town of Stoneville, a small city with a large portion of people of "culture and ideality" who "send their sons to Yale or Harvard and their daughters to Vassar" and have "a frequent ephemeral interest in newly imported cults of one kind or other." A friend asks Lawrence, of keen intelligence, dry wit, and more than a little skepticism, to explore this "wisdom-religion." Lawrence replies: "I have looked into that as into other things in the course of my business and took no stock in it; because, perhaps, the wisdom-religion I was born and reared in would suffice to make a saint of me if constantly practised."[1]

Despite his reservations, Lawrence reluctantly agrees to give Madame Regnier, the foreign-born woman who presides over the group, a chance to persuade him of the truth of her occult form of Buddhism. A "mysterious hush" fell over the group as she sat in the armchair to begin the meeting: "Now, spoke madame musically, dear friends, we will resume our studies in psychic lore. In what better mode can we pass the weary moments until we are reabsorbed into cosmic space than in learning to conquer the earthly part of us and perfect the development of our psychic senses?" Then she informed the group of an unfortunate development: the Indian adept, Coomara Theris, could come not come tonight. They would have to wait for the "occult manifestations" they all had hoped for. They had to fall back on their faith.

We must content ourselves, for the present, with humble faith and simple truthfulness. We sit, she said with graceful enthusiasm, like Gautama himself, under the shade of the sacred tree, waiting for the light of truth to come to us!

And, in the meantime, we have our Buddhist catechism. At this anti-climax Lawrence bit his lip, and might have smiled but that he felt her eye upon him. She actually produced a small book here labelled "Catechism," and began propounding the questions as to a class of little boys.

The group recites from this catechism, an obvious reference to Olcott's popular summary of the Buddhist faith:

> Madame: "What benefit does a Buddhist derive by the observance of the five Precepts, the Panca Sila?"
> Steinfeld: "More or less merit, according to the manner and time of observing the Precepts and the number observed."

Then they read aloud from Arnold's *Light of Asia*. Mr. Lawrence, the skeptical observer in this fictional account, had to fight back a smile. Without the eye of Madame Regnier to inhibit them, more than a few of the American readers of "Under the Bodhi Tree" presumably grinned, as Lawrence could not, at this scene.[2]

Jeanie Drake, the author of this short story, portrayed the members of Madame Regnier's society as comically credulous; but, most important for this study, she also pointed to one discernible kind of American Buddhist. Drake was not sympathetic to Buddhism, but even many of those who were felt the need to distinguish this kind of Buddhist. Most adherents who did so, however, were not interested primarily in sharing a good laugh. It was more serious than that. These occult Buddhists, some American followers believed, had distorted the Asian faith and made it more difficult for the tradition to get a fair hearing in the West. For example, C. T. Strauss, who worried about their influence, encouraged Carus to advise Dharmapala on his visit to the United States of "the necessity of leaving aside all mysticism, theosophy, etc." Whatever their assessment of them, most late-Victorian observers seemed to agree that those Buddhists who affirmed "mysticism, theosophy, etc." represented a discernible type. I call them esoterics. And, I suggest, there were other types as well—rationalists and romantics (see table 2).[3]

Max Weber was the first to use "ideal types" self-consciously in the interpretation of religion, and my application of ideal-type theory here is based on his theory and recent reconstructions of it. Ideal types, as I use the term, are theoretical constructs that function as more or less useful interpretive tools. They are designed by accentuating and exaggerating some feature(s) of empirical reality and then formulating a logically consistent construct. No historical individual, position, or group will correspond perfectly to any of the types; and the types always are linked with the particular interests and guiding questions of the investigator. Some scholars, especially historians, squirm at the mention of ideal types. These sorts of interpretive constructs seem ahistorical. They seem to lead inevitably to a lack of concern for the peculiarities of each period and culture. This concern is understandable but, finally, unwarranted. Some of the several basic kinds of ideal-typical constructs that Weber used in his work were conceived after comparative investigation of a variety of cultures and periods and intended to illuminate a broad range of belief or action. Yet he also used historical or contextual types, and these present fewer potential difficulties for historical analysis. They are derived from and employed in the study of a particular culture and era.[4]

In this chapter I hope to demonstrate that the historical types that I have constructed can help make sense of the diversity of characteristics and perspectives of sympathizers and adherents in late-Victorian America and, at the same time, highlight the uniqueness of any particular individual's traits and position. They do not represent all possible sympathetic responses an individual or group could make to Buddhism; nor do they reconstruct all the responses that individuals or groups have made. Rather, they only point to some of the most important patterns that can be discerned among Buddhist apologists in one time and place. So this typology might or might not be useful in interpreting the encounter with Buddhism in twentieth-century America or in other cultural or historical contexts. And it might or might not be helpful in analyzing the perspectives of nineteenth-century converts to other alternative traditions. I claim only that it helps to illuminate the range and complexity of sympathetic responses to Buddhism in the United States between 1875 and 1912.[5]

For each type I identify cultural sources, institutional expressions, and individual exemplars. I also tentatively explore the "elective affinities"—to use Weber's term—between these three ideal-typical compilations of religious beliefs and values and a range of nonintellectual factors—gender, socioeconomic status, region, and ethnicity. By using Weber's language I want to note the convergence of intellectual and nonintellectual factors without interpreting beliefs as merely the expression of social or economic interests. Although Weber was most interested in the correlations with social and economic status, I also point to affinities between these three ideal-typical belief patterns and other intellectual factors.[6]

THE ESOTERIC TYPE

The fictional "Buddhist inquirers" in Jeanie Drake's short story were, in my terms, esoteric or occult Buddhists. This first type points to those whose perspective—even if the influence was at second hand—tended to be shaped by Neoplatonism, Theosophy, Mesmerism, Spiritualism, and Swedenborgianism. In particular, Emanuel Swedenborg's (1688–1772) thought was a very important intellectual source for a great number of the forms of alternative spirituality in nineteenth-century America and for esoteric Buddhism in particular. A number of the sympathetic participants in the American discussion about Buddhism demonstrated interest in the teachings of Swedenborg, including Herman Vetterling, Albert J. Edmunds (1857–1941), and even D. T. Suzuki.

The esoteric or occult type was characterized, in part, by an emphasis on hidden sources of religious truth and meaning and by belief in a spiritual or nonmaterial realm that is populated by a plurality of nonhuman or suprahuman realities that can be contacted through one or another practices or extraordinary states of consciousness. According to the *Oxford English Dictionary*, the primary meaning of "occult" is "hidden" or "concealed," and in general the term "esoteric" can be considered a synonym—with the exception that the latter term includes the added meaning of "abstruse" or "recondite" that often applies to writings of this type. In order to excavate some of the buried meanings of "occult" we can rely on Robert Galbreath's definition:

Modern occultism pertains to matters that are "hidden" or "secret" in one or more of the following senses: (1) extraordinary matters that by virtue of their intrusion into the mundane world are thought to possess special significance (e.g., omens, portents, apparitions, prophetic dreams); (2) matters such as the teachings of the so-called mystery schools that are kept hidden from the uninitiated and the unworthy; and (3) matters that are intrinsically hidden from ordinary cognition and understanding but are nonetheless knowable through the awakening of hidden, latent faculties of appropriate sensitivity.[7]

Esoteric Buddhists sometimes had connections with one or another esoteric religious movement. In chapter two I noted that Abby Judson combined interest in Buddhism and Spiritualism. Others did too. In the 1890s Anna Eva Fay, a "Spiritualist lecturer," confessed that she was "deeply interested in Buddhism." One of the original officers of the Dharma Sangha of Buddha in San Francisco, Eliza R. H. Stoddard, was a medium. Many esoteric Buddhists also were affiliated with the Theosophical Society. Some contemporaries treated esoteric Buddhism, even Western Buddhism, as if it were synonymous with Theosophy. In fact, this conviction was widespread enough that Madame Blavatsky felt the need to demonstrate that "Theosophy is not Buddhism." She blamed the misunderstanding on the influence of Sinnett's *Esoteric Buddhism*, but Blavatsky's and Olcott's formal profession of Buddhism in Ceylon and Olcott's subsequent attempts to link the two explicitly did little to counter the common impression. Blavatsky acknowledged that "some of us are Buddhist by religion," and she granted that the "secret" religious teachings and the lofty ethical principles preached by the Buddha were identical to those of Theosophy. Yet, she noted, the "exoteric" doctrines of Hinayana Buddhism deny two basic beliefs of Theosophists—"(a) the existence of any Deity, and (b) any conscious post-mortem life, or even any self-conscious surviving individuality in man."

Blavatsky correctly noted some of the doctrinal incompatibilities. The rejection of God and self seemed to strain against the most basic Theosophical teachings. Other Asian traditions—especially Vedanta Hinduism—seemed much more compatible. In fact, in the twentieth century the society returned more emphatically to the Hindu tradition. But individuals do not always act logically, and history does not take the course that retrospection might indicate. Many Victorian esoterics—including Blavatsky and Olcott—generally overlooked or minimized doctrinal discontinuities as they expressed sympathy for Buddhism. A portion of the several thousand members of the Theosophical Society in America—it is impossible to say how many—saw themselves most fundamentally as Buddhists or viewed Theosophy and Buddhism as indistinguishable. In the end, many late-Victorian Theosophists seem to take the position announced by Blavatsky: Buddhism and Theosophy are not identical, but even the exoteric Buddhism of South Asia is superior to all other traditions. "But how much grander and more noble, more philosophical and scientific, even in its dead letter, is this teaching than that of any other Church or religion." Several years later, William H. Galvani of Portland, Oregon, who had pieces published in several Buddhist magazines, took a similar stand: "Buddhism is not Theosophy, but in its course of development it has departed from the fundamental principles of Theosophy much less than any other system of religious thought."[8]

However the relation between the two was conceived, Buddhism remained prominent in the group's teachings between approximately 1881 and 1907—i.e., from the publication of Olcott's *Buddhist Catechism* to the year of his death. The link was strengthened by, among other things, the connections between Theosophical Society founders and the Sinhalese founder of the Maha Bodhi Society. Dharmapala, who went on to become one of the most influential Asian Buddhists of the age, had been stimulated to pursue both occult studies and Buddhist studies by Olcott and Blavatsky. He had been present at the public ceremony in which they took the three refuges and the five precepts. Even before they arrived, the adolescent Dharmapala had been inspired by them: a letter they wrote offering their help to the Buddhists of Ceylon was translated and circulated in his native country. "My heart warmed towards these two strangers," Dharmapala recalled, "so far away and yet so sympathetic, and I made up my mind that, when they came to Ceylon, I would join them." He met them a few years later in Colombo, when he was sixteen; and he joined the Theosophical Society. In fact, in 1884, at the age of nineteen, he had decided to spend his life "in the study of occult science." It was Blavatsky who convinced him to study Pali and "serve humanity" instead. After dedicating his life to these new goals, Dharmapala traveled and lectured with Olcott in Japan in 1889. Even after Dharmapala established the Maha Bodhi Society in 1891, the association between Asian Buddhism and Theosophy continued. It continued in an official way as Olcott served as both president of the Theosophical Society and "Director and Chief Advisor" of the Maha Bodhi Society. It also continued unofficially: the periodicals associated with the two groups, the *Theosophist* and the *Maha Bodhi*, published a great deal of news and advertisements relating to each other. This bond would be loosened gradually, but during the 1890s it was strong.[9]

There also were contacts between Theosophists and Buddhists who were not connected with the Maha Bodhi Society. For example, Olcott lectured at the Japanese Pure Land Buddhist mission in San Francisco in 1901, and D. T. Suzuki spoke at the Theosophical Society in the same city in 1903. Despite the protests of Blavatsky and others, then, there was an undeniable link between Theosophy and Buddhism in late-Victorian America. A significant number of esoteric Buddhists do not seem to have been affiliated with occult groups. Some members of the Maha Bodhi Society and the Dharma Sangha of Buddha could be classified as esoteric. But the Theosophical Society institutionalized this sort of Buddhist perspective as much as any of the three types under discussion found expression in a single organization.[10]

Whether or not they were members of the Theosophical Society, esoteric groups and individuals had certain common features. Women, first of all, were more visible and numerous among them. Several female esoterics contributed to the promotion of the tradition. Marie Canavarro is the most obvious example, but others did their part, including A. Christina Albers (1866–1948), Mary Elizabeth Foster (1844–1930), Sarah Jane Farmer (1847–1916), and Catherine Shearer (d. 1909). The proportion of women was not overwhelmingly high: it probably approximated that found among unconventional groups such as the Spiritualists, Theosophists, and Baha'is—between 55 and 65 percent. But it was higher than that found among rationalist and romantic Buddhists. This disproportionate representation fits what we know about nineteenth-century American religion. Many Victorian women found occult groups and alternative forms of spirituality—including, for example, Shakerism and Christian Science—more congenial to their egalitarian impulses and religious needs.[11]

Occult sympathizers also were more likely than the other types to be found in rural areas, and there seem to have been regional patterns as well. Canavarro, who by my standards was an esoteric, nonetheless criticized the "craving for the mysterious" that she found among Caucasian sympathizers in San Francisco in 1900. On the other hand, when she moved to Chicago several months later the contrasts surprised her. She reported that their Sunday services—presumably she meant the meetings of the local Maha Bodhi Society—were "having success." She also observed that "there seems to be a different class of people coming here, mostly doctors and professors, and the majority men." If Canavarro's impressionistic account was correct, the social and economic status of sympathizers varied somewhat from region to region. This, and other evidence, suggests that more women and more esoterics—and fewer professionals—followed Buddhism in San Francisco. Some of those doctors and professors in Chicago might have been esoterics, and clearly there were wealthy and educated occult sympathizers who hailed from prominent American families. As Martin E. Marty noticed about occultists of a different sort in the 1970s, Victorian esoteric sympathizers often belonged to "middle America." For example, Thomas Moore Johnson (1851–1919), who had interest in Platonism, Neoplatonism, and Buddhism, was a prominent citizen of the rural community where he was born and died—Osceola, Missouri. Johnson earned a master's degree, worked as a prosecuting attorney, belonged to the local school board, and served for thirteen years as mayor. Yet, on the whole, esoterics were more economically marginal—although not lower class. They also were more socially marginal—with less formal education and more ethnic diversity. Esoterics were more likely to be immigrants or the children of immigrants.[12]

Esoterics also tended to be more spiritually eclectic. Many were attracted by several groups simultaneously—Western and Eastern—and switched their allegiance from one tradition to another. When they turned their attention to Buddhism they tended to focus on the forms of Buddhism in South Asia, especially Ceylon. In a sense, this seems odd. As Olcott noted when he met with the chief priest of the Shingon sect in Japan in 1889, Theosophy and some forms of Buddhism "held many ideas in common." More specifically, it is easy to imagine esoterics like Olcott being more drawn to the Tantric traditions of Buddhism in Tibet or Japan with their emphasis on "hidden" truths and practices. But for a variety of reasons the Theravada Buddhism of Ceylon preoccupied Olcott and Blavatsky. This focus then was reinforced by the strong inclination among prominent American and British Buddhist scholars of the late nineteenth century to champion the Pali scriptures and Theravada Buddhism as the earliest and most pristine form of the tradition. Some, of course, expressed interest in "esoteric" forms of Japanese Mahayana; and those forms might seem more intrinsically compatible. Yet most took Sinhalese Theravada as most authoritative. So, for instance, when Anna M. Brown, a Theosophist and Buddhist sympathizer who ran a boarding house in Philadelphia, wanted to travel to Asia to study the tradition, it was to Ceylon that she went for spiritual sustenance.[13]

Many—and probably the majority—of the Americans of European descent who were attracted to Buddhism shared some or most of the characteristics of this esoteric type. Albert J. Edmunds, who once stayed in Anna Brown's boarding house for several months, was a nonacademic interpreter of Pali Buddhism and a perpetual religious seeker. His friend, D. T. Suzuki, described him as "a devout Christian, that is, a Quaker, Swedenborgian, and a great sympathizer with Buddhism." That term "devout" seems misleading, however. He was hardly an orthodox Christian, by almost any standard; and he never could give exclusive or final allegiance to any tradition. In fact, he was drawn by elements in a number of religious perspectives. Yet there was some unity throughout his life-long religious search: he never completely severed his relation with the Quaker tradition in which he was reared; and, most important here, he sustained an interest in occult or esoteric groups for most of his adult life. In the late nineteenth century, he regularly attended a Swedenborgian church. He had continuing interested in Spiritualism, Theosophy, and "psychic phenomena." His diaries overflow with evidence that he believed that he received messages from the dead and heard voices "telepathically" from the living. This idiosyncratic Buddhist sympathizer blended selected Buddhist teachings with those of a variety of Western teachers of occult spirituality—especially the Swedish mystic Swedenborg.[14]

Other esoterics included Joseph M. Wade (1833–1905) and a woman I mentioned above, A. Christina Albers. Wade was a friend of the Japanese and a student of the occult. He presided over an esoteric magazine, *Occultism,* and even published the messages of Madame Blavatsky from beyond the grave! He also had personal interest in Buddhism. He subscribed to the *Light of Dharma,* and the editors of that Buddhist magazine published pieces by and about him. He housed in the "occult room" of his home in Dorcester, Massachusetts, an ancient Japanese statue of Amida Buddha that he had received as a gift from Buddhists in Japan. Wade's Buddhist interests seem to have been set in the larger context of his commitment to occultism. To a lesser extent, so were Albers's. This German-American member of the Maha Bodhi Society lived in India for years and visited several Buddhist nations. She had contacts with many influential Eastern and Western Buddhists, wrote books on Buddhism for children, and contributed poems to a number of Buddhist magazines. Her esoteric interests were noticeable to those who knew her well. Paul Carus, who corresponded with Albers, put it this way: She was "quite gifted but not without some strange aberrations in her beliefs which may upon the whole be characterized as theosophic."[15]

Of the many individuals who resemble this type, Henry Steel Olcott, Sister Sanghamitta (Marie deSouza Canavarro), and Philangi Dasa (Herman C. Vetterling) can be taken as an exemplars. They might not have accepted the label—remember that both Vetterling and Canavarro doubted the authenticity of occult Buddhists—but they clearly showed the characteristics that I have associated with this type. Olcott, who has been mentioned several times already, is, by far, the best known of these three. Unlike most esoterics, Olcott was born into an old American family: he was a descendant of Thomas Olcott, one of the founders of Hartford, Connecticut. Henry Olcott began his career as a farmer in Ohio, New Jersey, and New York (1849–59) and later became associate agricultural editor for the *New York Tribune* (1859–61). Olcott briefly attended the University of the City of New York before serving as an officer in the Union Army (1861–65). After the war, he returned to New York. This time he went to learn the law in a New York firm, and he worked as an attorney there for a number of years after he passed the bar in 1868.[16]

The turning point of Olcott's personal and professional life came in the summer of 1874. While he was still doing legal work, he decided to renew his interest in Spiritualism. After reading an account of "certain incredible phenomena" in a Spiritualist magazine, he set off for the Eddy farm in Vermont, the cite of the occurrences, to investigate. Olcott then wrote sympathetic accounts of the mysterious phenomena that were occurring at the "Eddy Homestead" for the *New York Sun* and the *New York Daily Graphic*. It was his accounts of the "Eddy ghosts" that brought Madame Blavatsky to the Vermont farm. The two became intimate friends; and in the next year they formed the group that blended, among other things, Spiritualism, Mesmerism, Hinduism, and Buddhism—the Theosophical Society. Olcott, who had been raised in a pious Presbyterian home, became a leading figure in one of the most unconventional and influential forms of alternative spirituality in the nineteenth century.[17]

Some remained skeptical about his intentions, but many Buddhists in Burma, Japan, America, and Ceylon welcomed his work on behalf of the Asian tradition. And his contributions were significant. He edited a Theosophical magazine that devoted a substantial portion of its pages to Buddhism. He also lectured about Buddhism on several continents; authored the popular *Buddhist Catechism* (1881); designed a Buddhist flag (1886); organized an ecumenical meeting of Japanese Buddhists (1889); drafted a "Buddhist Platform" signed by Buddhists from Ceylon, Burma, and Japan (1891); and stimulated educational reform and Buddhist revival in Ceylon. Many Asian Buddhists found him orthodox, and he continued to see himself as a Buddhist until the day he died. Yet Olcott had an enduring interest in spiritualism and psychic phenomena, and he mixed traditional Buddhist themes with a variety of occult beliefs and practices. His *Buddhist Catechism*, for example, contained references to "auras" and "astrology" as well as to *arhat* and *Abhidhamma* and to "psychic phenomena" as well as to *prajna*. In many ways, then, Olcott was a paradigmatic esoteric Buddhist.[18]

Another esoteric adherent who promoted Buddhism in Ceylon and America was Marie deSouza Canavarro. Canavarro, who took the Buddhist name of Sister Sanghamitta, is virtually unremembered even though she lectured widely, authored several articles and books, and played an important role in the promotion of Buddhism around the turn of the century. The facts of her life and work must be pieced together from a variety of sometimes conflicting sources, and gaps and uncertainties in her biography remain. Even her place of birth is uncertain. Contemporary accounts suggested, alternately, that she hailed from Europe, Mexico, the United States, and South America. Apparently she claimed to be of noble Spanish descent. Most likely, she was born in San Antonio, Texas, to a father from Mexico and a mother from Virginia. She might have spent most of her preschool years in Mexico; and it is possible, as some accounts suggest, that she was born in Mexico City. In any case, it seems almost certain that her family moved to Mariposa County, California when she was a girl. It was apparently there that she married "an American gentle-man," Samuel C. Bates, at the age of sixteen. After she was widowed or divorced "at an early age"—again the records disagree—Marie married His Excellency Señor A. deSouza Canavarro, the Portuguese representative to the Sandwich Islands. She then lived with him in Honolulu for several years. Although she had wealth and status, it was in Honolulu that she began to feel "an unsatisfied craving for something." It was there that her religious quest began in earnest.[19]

Like many other esoterics, Canavarro was a life-long religious seeker who, along the way, turned to several traditions. The first step on her pilgrimage was to reject the Roman Catholicism that she had inherited in favor of the teachings of the Theosophical Society. Through that society and personal contact with Dharmapala, the Countess—as she was fre-quently referred to in the press—felt herself drawn toward Buddhism. With Dharmapala officiating, she formally converted to Buddhism in 1897 in a public ceremony held in the New Century Hall on Fifth Avenue in New York. She was the second American—Strauss had been the first—and the first woman formally to profess allegiance to Buddhism on American soil. It is no surprise that this event attracted the attention of the local and foreign press. After that ceremony she set off for Ceylon in order to help revive Asian Buddhism and nurture Sinhalese girls.[20]

During the three years she lived in Ceylon (1897–1900) Canavarro ran an orphanage, a school for girls, and a Buddhist convent; and she lectured on Buddhism in Ceylon, India, and Burma. Although it is difficult to de-termine exactly what happened, around 1900 Canavarro seems to have been forced to leave the Sanghamitta School and Orphanage. In her letters to Carus, she suggested that Catherine Shearer, who had come to help her in her work, had conspired against her. Carus apparently believed this account since he repeated the story. In any case, Canavarro was back in the United States in the fall of 1900. There she enjoyed the status of a minor celebrity as she lectured in cities such as San Francisco, Chicago, and New York. During 1900 and 1901 she was very active in promoting Buddhism in America, especially in Chicago and New York. In fact, she was one of the leaders of the American branch of the Maha Bodhi Society during this time.[21]

She later returned to Ceylon for a brief time, but around 1901—just at the peak of her influence as a Western interpreter of Buddhism—Canavarro seems to have begun to lose interest in the religion. Or, to put it more precisely, she was more and more attracted to another tradition. Even though she still asked Paul Carus for news of Buddhist activities and still received the journal of the Maha Bodhi Society at least as late as 1909, around 1901 she felt herself pulled toward the Baha'i faith. Canavarro had encountered American converts to this tolerant and syncretistic Persian tradition in Chicago and at Sarah Farmer's Greenacre Conferences in Maine. She was so impressed by their demeanor and teachings that she traveled to the Middle East to meet with 'Abdu'l-Bahá, son of Bahá'u'lláh (1817–92), who founded that Persian religious tradition. Canavarro was known in the American Baha'i community just after the turn of the century, and she even lectured on the tradition. In fact, Canavarro is still remembered among historians of Baha'i as the anonymous coauthor of an important book on the tradition attributed to her companion of those years, Myron Phelps.[22]

Canavarro's spiritual journey did not end with Baha'i. When Canavarro emerged again into the public view in the 1920s she was living in California and extremely sympathetic to Vedanta Hinduism. Swami Paramananda, the Vedantic teacher who presided at the Ananda Ashrama in La Crescenta, California, wrote the preface to her spiritual autobiography that was published in 1925. She visited his community in the hills above her home in Glendale and was drawn to his teachings. Yet she never repudiated her previous affiliation with Buddhism. And while she had worked as a public advocate of Buddhism, she had been among the half-dozen most influential American promoters of the religion.

Her occult interests seemed to have been somewhat suppressed during the years that she interpreted and promoted Buddhism, but there is evidence of long-term interest in occult teachings and practices. She continued to be a member of the Theosophical Society during her years in Ceylon and at the height of her notoriety as a Buddhist representative. Later she apparently even claimed supranormal powers as well: in 1908 a Spiritualist wrote to the editor of the *Open Court* to defend Sister Sanghamitta's claim that "voices conveyed to her, definite and precise supernormal information in three instances." Carus, the editor and Canavarro's friend, apparently had publicly dismissed the occurrences as "noises in the ear." She continued to have close relations with others with "theosophic" interests—like her friend Christina Albers—throughout her life; and her sentimental novels of spiritual quest that were published during the last decade of her life portrayed "occult things" sympathetically. So although she studied Pali and could discuss the doctrines of Theravada Buddhism in terms that were recognized as orthodox, Canavarro certainly shared many of the characteristics of the esoteric type.[23]

So did Philangi Dasa (Herman Carl Vetterling). Although he edited the first English-language Buddhist magazine in America, *The Buddhist Ray*, Vetterling is almost as obscure as Canavarro. Yet most of the twists and turns in his life can be reconstructed. Soon after Vetterling emigrated from Sweden he became a follower of the (Swedenborgian) Church of the New Jerusalem. He then studied for the ministry, and was ordained by that institution on 10 June 1877. He served as a minister, off and on, to New Church communities in Greenford, Ohio; Pittsburgh, Pennsylvania; and Detroit, Michigan, until 1881. Controversy and scandal, however, marred his ministerial career. During the mid-1880s Vetterling dissociated himself from the New Church. He joined the Theosophical Society and wrote a series of articles entitled "Studies in Swedenborg" for *The Theosophist*. It was around this time that he identified himself with Buddhism.[24]

This esoteric adherent had a number of occupations before and after he turned to Buddhism—including working as typesetter, minister, homeopathic physician, and farmer. Yet it is his work as author and editor that is most relevant here. In 1887 *Swedenborg the Buddhist; or, The Higher Swedenborgianism: Its Secrets and Thibetan Origins* was published in Los Angeles. In this work Vetterling, writing under the pseudonym of Philangi Dasa, set out a religious view that combined Buddhist teachings with those of the Theosophical Society and Emanuel Swedenborg. The book recounts a dream by "Philangi Dasa" in which a number of characters—a Chinese, a Parsee, an American woman, a Brahman, a Buddhist monk, an Aztec Indian, an Icelander, Philangi Dasa, and Emanuel Swedenborg—engage in spirited dialogue about religious matters. In the foreword to that book the narrator, Philangi Dasa, defiantly announces that both he and Swedenborg are "Pagans." He suggests that "the sign of a Pagan soul" is the ability "to stop the breathing at will," and claims that Swedenborg had "a piece of Asia in him" since he had possessed this supranormal capacity from birth. Philangi Dasa argues, indirectly and directly, that a form of esoteric Buddhism is the highest spiritual teaching and Swedenborg was actually a Buddhist. He acknowledges that there were Christian themes in the Swedish mystic's writings but suggests that "hidden under Judaic-Christian names, phrases, and symbols, and scattered throughout dreary, dogmatic, and soporific octavos, are pure, precious, blessed truths of Buddhism." How did Swedenborg come to see the truths of this Asian religion if he never read Buddhist literature? Philangi Dasa claims that Swedenborg had direct contact with "Great Buddhist Ascetics" on a suprasensual plane.[25]

Needless to say, although the work was praised in periodicals connected with the Theosophical Society and other esoteric groups, Vetterling's idiosyncratic and iconoclastic interpretation was not warmly received in Swedenborgian circles. Reviews of the work in New Church periodicals harshly criticized the author's rejection of a personal conception of God, the divinity of Christ, and the authority of the Judeo-Christian scriptures. They were most outraged, however, by Vetterling's linking of their spiritual patriarch with Buddhism. If the reviewers did not "murder him in the name of the Lord," as the Christians did to Philangi Dasa in the dream recounted in Vetterling's book, it was not because the book had failed to stir sufficient anger in them.[26]

At the end of *Swedenborg the Buddhist*, Philangi Dasa awakens from his dream and repeats the familiar profession of Buddhist faith: "I follow Buddha as my guide. I follow the Law as my guide. I follow the order as my guide." Philangi Dasa surfaced next in Santa Cruz County, California, as a self-proclaimed Buddhist. There he promoted his brand of esoteric Buddhism as publisher and editor of *The Buddhist Ray*. Vetterling continued to blend Theosophical and Swedenborgian influences in his own contributions and in the material he chose to include in the magazine. In fact, the synthesis of these diverse elements already was evident in the prospectus:

> *The Buddhist Ray* will be devoted to the divulgation of the philosophy and life of Buddhism: of Karma, of Transmigration, and of Mystic Communion with the Divine in Humanity. . . . It will set forth the teachings imparted by the Mongolian Buddhists to Emanuel Swedenborg, and published by him in his mystic writings. . . . As a work of love, we ask the moral and pecuniary cooperation of all lovers of the Ancient Wisdom; and we invoke upon it the blessings of the SOULS REGENERATE throughout the world![27]

THE RATIONALIST TYPE

"If I aid Buddhism," Paul Carus once divulged in a letter, "I do it solely in the interest of antagonizing occultism. Genuine Buddhism is no occultism." Those Buddhist advocates who "antagonized" esoterics most vigorously were rationalists. By rationalists I refer to those who were influenced most emphatically by Enlightenment rationalism, Auguste Comte's positivism, and Herbert Spencer's evolutionism. This ideal-typical constellation of intellectual tendencies can be traced through Deism and, to a lesser extent, through the "supernatural-rationalist" stream in British and American Unitarianism. The more iconoclastic Enlightenment ideas about religion, expressed in the writings of French and British authors like Voltaire and Hume, had a rather small following in the United States, and attempts to promote institutionalized Deism in America were not very successful. Nonetheless, forms of Enlightenment thought—especially the Scottish Common Sense philosophy—had significant influence among American intellectuals almost until the Civil War. Moderate as well as more radical versions of this rationalistic religiousness were kept alive not only by the rationalist stream in Unitarianism but also by Transcendentalists like Theodore Parker and, later, the members of the Free Religious Association and Ethical Culture Society. So at the time when Buddhist ideas first became widely accessible to literate Americans (1879–1912) this form of religious radicalism was still available. Comte's positivism and Spencer's evolutionism then transformed and invigorated it.[28]

Rationalists, as I am using the term, focused on rational-discursive means of attaining religious truth and meaning as opposed to revelational or experiential means and emphasized the authority of the individual in religious matters rather than that of creeds, texts, officials, or institutions. They also can be characterized by a sometimes uncritical affirmation of "science"—whether Lyell's or Darwin's—and an always fierce advocacy of religious and political tolerance. The overall effect was a focus on anthropological and ethical issues rather than theological and metaphysical ones.

Some spiritually disillusioned late-Victorians who could be called rationalists drifted away from all forms of religion and identified themselves as atheists or agnostics. Others still wanted to be religious in some way, and so they searched for a form of religiousness that was compatible with their unconventional beliefs and values. Of this group some were attracted to Buddhism. Perhaps he was just being polite, but even the notorious freethinker and "great agnostic" Robert Green Ingersoll (1833–99) expressed appreciation for Buddhism. Ingersoll thanked Carus for sending him a copy of his *Gospel of Buddha*: "I have read it with the greatest pleasure." Buddhism's originality, he suggested, would "surprise and educate many." Ingersoll was not—by my standards—a Buddhist sympathizer. Like Ingersoll, however, those rationalists who did have sympathy often were, by principle and personality, suspicious of religious institutions. Yet a number were linked with liberal and radical religious groups such as the Free Religious Association and the Ethical Culture Society.[29]

Felix Adler, who served as president of the Free Religious Association and founded the Ethical Culture Society, was one of several radicals to participate in the mid-Victorian debate who lived long enough to witness the swell of interest after 1879. Adler had expressed dismay at the apparent "passivity" of institutionalized Buddhism in an early article, but it is clear that he had been moved by elements of the Buddha's message. He did not see himself as a sympathizer; but there is, I think, some residue of Buddhist influence evident in Adler's later thought. His few references to Buddhism in a collection of addresses published in 1905 all were positive. And even though similar issues and themes could have emerged from Western religious and philosophical traditions, some of the issues he continued to struggle with and the themes he continued to emphasize echoed those in the Buddhist tradition. Adler emphasized compassion, a dominant theme in Mahayana Buddhism, and he even used a parable from Buddhist literature to illustrate his point. He also advocated a "tragic" view of life that accepted the universality and inevitability of suffering without falling into "pessimism." Reminiscent of Buddha's championing of the

"Middle Path," Adler also argued that the moral path ran between the extremes of asceticism and self-indulgence. Even in his constant focus on activism as opposed to passivity—where Adler seems to reject the "quietistic" Buddhism he was offered—some continuing influence as a negative model seems possible.[30]

Even if Adler—despite this evidence of influence—was not a Buddhist advocate, periodicals associated with the group he founded contributed to the conversation, and other Ethical Culturists seemed to have had significant sympathy for Buddhism. When Albert J. Edmunds heard Adler deliver an "extraordinary" lecture on the distinction between "tragic" and "pessimistic" views of life at the Philadelphia branch of the Ethical Society in the spring of 1904, Edmunds had just completed a series of lectures on Buddhism before that same body. The Philadelphia Society had some interest in this and other Asian religions. Other branches evidenced even more interest in the tradition. Dharmapala lectured to the Brooklyn Ethical Association on 22 November 1896. The next year there were reports in newspapers and magazines about that group's interest: " 'The Brooklyn Ethical Society' is seriously considering the subject of Buddhism as a substitute for Christianity. They have grown weary of the supernatural, and crave something with a purely scientific basis. The New Testament taxes their credulity to the point of snapping, and, with an intense longing for what is at the same time intellectual and reasonable, they prostrate themselves in the presence of the Buddha." For most, presumably, this devotional impulse passed. Some members of that Brooklyn group, however, had enduring links with Asian and alternative spirituality. Four years later (1901) the corresponding secretary of the branch, Henry Hoyt Moore, served on the Advisory Board of Farmer's School for Comparative Religion in Eliot, Maine; and Dr. Lewis G. Janes, former president of both the Free Religious Association and the Brooklyn Ethical Association, was its director. Janes was recognized as a Buddhist sympathizer—or at least a Westerner open to the religion—by members of Buddhist institutions in America and elsewhere. The notice of his death that appeared in the *Light of Dharma* announced that "Buddhism had a staunch friend in Dr. Janes." Janes was deemed important enough by the editor of the *Maha Bodhi* that that Asian periodical reprinted his obituary from the *Boston Evening Transcript* on the front page of their November 1901 issue. There were, then, rationalist sympathizers associated with groups like the Free Religious Association and Ethical Culture Society. Some rationalists were members of the Maha Bodhi Society. But many were not affiliated officially with any religious group.[31]

Whether they were affiliated with a group or not, fewer female advocates fit this ideal-typical pattern. The predominance of males among rationalists mirrors membership patterns in the Ethical Culture Society. In 1906, for instance, only about 36% of the members of the Ethical Culture

Society recorded in the census were women. This almost reverses the statistics for the female-dominated Theosophical Societies. Rationalists, to note other affinities, were more likely than esoterics to be professionals. Although there were a few exceptions, they also seemed most open to radical political and economic views. Of course, their religious views were "radical" in many ways too. Rationalists emphasized Buddhist parallels with the teachings of radical thinkers like Comte and the literature of radical groups like the Free Religious Association. Buddhism for them meant, above all, the Pali canon and the Theravada tradition. This hardly seems surprising or incongruous. Some Asian representatives of Japanese Mahayana sounded similar themes in their efforts to attract Caucasian converts, but Theravada Buddhism had been presented by Western scholars and Asian adherents as a rational tradition that emphasizes self-reliance, tolerance, psychology, and ethics. The tradition, the story went, rejects the unscientific and superstitious doctrines of Christianity such as the notion of a substantial self and a personal deity.

A number of contributors to the public discussion fit the rationalist type to some extent. Moncure Daniel Conway (1832–1907) was one of the mid-Victorian radicals who continued to express sympathy for Buddhism during the last years of the century, and his interpretations most closely resembled those of the rationalists. Conway never saw himself as a Buddhist, but he found a number of things in the tradition that attracted him. This freethinker who despised the "superstition" and sectarianism of the Protestantism in which he had been raised, wryly announced in an article published in the earlier period that he preferred the atheism of Asian Buddhists to the theism of Christian missionaries. Later, Conway had the opportunity to encounter Asian Buddhists directly. In fact, at the request of a delegation of young Buddhists, he lectured in Ceylon on Christmas Day in 1883. His topic was the birth legends of Jesus and Gautama; and, in the course of his speech, he contrasted Buddhism's emphasis on happiness in this world with Christianity's stress on the rewards of the next. It was insufficient to inspire him to convert, but Conway had found enough freethought and rationalism in the Pali scriptures and Sinhalese Buddhism to elicit his praise. For example, he was stirred by a scriptural passage that he heard read at a ceremony in Ceylon: "To me, indeed, it was thrilling that from a past of seventy generations should come this voice [i.e., the Buddha's] summoning man to rest his faith on his own reason, and trust his life for eternity to virtues rooted in his own consciousness."

Almost all of the elements of this rationalist type also can be found in the writings of Eleanor Hiestand Moore (1859–1923), the Philadelphia physician, medical school instructor, journalist, and lecturer. One contemporary biographical dictionary listed her faith as Episcopalian, but the Japanese Buddhists at the San Francisco mission knew her as a "friend, contributor, a lady, a Buddhist believer." In one of her articles for the Buddhist magazine in San Francisco she offered a firm defense of Buddhism as a rational and scientific tradition. Rationalist impulses were even clearer in the work of C. T. Strauss who, around the time of his conversion, was a "dealer in lace curtains" in New York City. Before his turn to Buddhism Strauss had been involved in the Ethical Culture Society. Years later, as a member of the Maha Bodhi Society, he authored a sustained explication and defense of Buddhist beliefs entitled *The Buddha and His Doctrine*. In that book he forcefully criticized the "Esoteric Buddhists" of the West as inauthentic. He portrayed Buddhism as an ethical, tolerant, and empirical tradition that emphasized self-reliance and liberty and harmonized with science and reason. Yet of the rationalist Buddhist sympathizers and adherents in the United States, Dyer Daniel Lum, Paul Carus, and Thomas B. Wilson are particularly representative.[32]

The radical Lum, who wrote an important article in the 1870s, continued his interest in the succeeding decades. This rationalist adherent was born in Geneva, New York, and raised in New York State's "burned-over district." Like most other young people in that section of the state, Lum had been an active abolitionist. He volunteered to fight for the emancipation of slaves and served four years in the Union Army as an infantryman and cavalry soldier. After the war, he apprenticed himself to a bookbinder and worked for a short time in that trade. By the late 1870s he had become increasingly interested in economics and involved in politics. In his last years he struggled with financial insecurities and battled an addiction to alcohol, but Lum was a relatively prolific author and an active participant in many of the public disputes of his day.[33]

Historians of the American political left know Lum as a leading spokesman for anarchism and trade unionism, but there has been very little attention to his religious position. During the 1870s and 1880s he wrote a critique of Spiritualism and a defense of Mormonism. Lum was certainly not a Spiritualist, nor was he a Mormon. He was an iconoclast who confessed to having a "critical and analytical nature." His thinking was shaped by the radical traditions of the Enlightenment and some recent philosophical developments. The works of Comte and Spencer were especially influential, and he returned to them periodically. Three years before his death, Lum reported, "I have again plunged anew into Comte's 'Positive Philosophy,' an old favorite of mine." Lum's writings were published in magazines as diverse as the *Catholic World* and the *Monist*, but most of his articles appeared in periodicals that were dedicated to religious and/or political radicalism, periodicals such as *Alarm, Liberty, The Radical Review, The Index, Open Court,* and *The Twentieth Century*.[34]

Lum's writings on Buddhism offer an especially revealing example of the rationalist type. In his important essay, "Buddhism Notwithstanding," he had attempted to "interpret Buddha from a Buddhist standpoint." In that piece, which was published in the magazine associated with the "scientific theist" branch of the Free Religious Association, Lum presented Buddhism as "the religion of reason." His interpretation of Buddhism was colored by commitments characteristic of the rationalist type: he championed the authority of the individual, focused on ethics, promoted tolerance, and embraced "modern science." For Lum, biological and moral evolution were intertwined, and the path to the moral perfection of humanity, and so ethics, was found in the laws of the natural world. All ethical systems, and all religions too, must be judged by, and be compatible with, the laws uncovered by modern geology and biology. By this criterion, Lum argued, Buddhism is superior to Christianity and other traditions. Buddhists are not asked to "sacrifice reason" by believing in notions that are contradicted by modern science—such as the belief in a supernatural being and an immortal soul. The doctrine of the moral law of cause and effect (karma), for instance, provides the basis for a religious view which is in perfect harmony with biological evolution, natural selection, and heredity. In its doctrine of karma Buddhism is able to account for the "moral government of the world, without a personal governor."[35]

The only published pieces that focus exclusively on Buddhism— "Buddhism Notwithstanding" (1875) and "Nirvana" (1877)—appeared mid-career; but Lum continued to refer positively to the tradition in later philosophical articles. And he seems to have continued his allegiance to the tradition until his death. In a posthumous tribute, his niece, who knew him better than anyone, suggested that Lum had "directed all his conscious efforts to read the riddle of life into the channel of Buddhism." Whether a Westernized Theravada Buddhism or an idiosyncratic evolutionist-positivist philosophy formed the "channel" through which his beliefs and values flowed, it seems clear that Buddhism was an important part of his worldview.[36]

Although Lum deserves recognition as the first Euro-American to advocate Buddhism publicly, the philosopher Paul Carus was a much more influential interpreter and popularizer. With the possible exception of Olcott, Carus probably was more influential in stimulating and sustaining American interest in Buddhism than any other person living in the United States. Through his books and articles about Buddhism, his contacts with Asian and Western Buddhists, and his work as editor of *Open Court*, Carus made crucial contributions to the public discussion about the nature and value of Buddhism. Carus was born and educated in Germany. After he received his doctorate from Tübingen in 1876, he served in the army and then taught school. He had been raised in a pious and orthodox Protestant home, but he gradually moved away from his inherited tradition. In 1884 Carus came to the United States, where he believed he could proclaim and promote his liberal religious views more freely. By December 1887 his career would be set for life: he became the editor of *Open Court* and managing editor of the publishing company as well. He held those posts until his death in February 1919.[37]

There is evidence that Carus knew about Buddhism before he came to America; but his interest in Asian religions and in Buddhism in particular seems to have intensified at the World's Parliament of Religions of 1893. For years after that event Carus defended Buddhist ideas, composed Buddhist hymns, and encouraged Buddhist missionaries. Yet, like many other rationalists, he stopped short of offering exclusive devotion to this, or any other, religion. Carus's refusal to commit to Buddhism or any particular religious tradition was known, if not wholly accepted, by his Buddhist friends. For example, in one letter Canavarro expressed her gratitude for his interpretations and his work on behalf of Buddhism. She even suggested that he already had done more for its promotion in the West than anyone except Dharmapala. And she implied that it would be even more helpful if he openly professed allegiance to Buddhism. Yet she seemed resigned to Carus's stance: "It is true you cannot be sectarian, therefore you cannot champion one religion to the exclusion of all others." Carus, then, was a strong sympathizer.[38]

In calling Carus a rationalist sympathizer I am merely repeating his own description of his position. For example, in accepting his honorary membership in the Rationalist Press Association of London, Carus announced, "I am in perfect agreement with the idea of rationalism, that is to say, of applying reasoning and scientific thought to the problem of religion, and all my work is evidence of the sense in which I would carry this principle into effect." In works before and after the Parliament, Carus outlined his own notion of rational religion, or what he called the "religion of science," and he argued that Buddhism was compatible with it. Buddhism harmonizes with the findings of science, the conclusions of reason, the demands of morality, and the requirements of interreligious cooperation.[39]

The perspective of this rationalist sympathizer was shaped by, among other things, the heritage of the Enlightenment, the evolutionary framework of Darwin, the spirit of laissez-faire capitalism, and the principles of "Monism." Like Ernest Haeckel (1834–1919), the German biologist who offered the most influential articulation of monistic philosophy, Carus emphasized the reliability of knowledge derived from the senses—i.e., from science and experience. Carus also accepted Haeckel's claim—and here is the derivation of the label "monist"—that the whole universe, including both organic and inorganic matter, and spirit as well as matter, is "unified" because it is regulated by the same natural laws. Of course, there was much more to Carus's "monism," but no more than these broad outlines of that philosophy are relevant here.[40]

In fact, in many ways, his rationalist interpretation of Buddhism can be illustrated best by highlighting the heritage of the Enlightenment and the parallels with freethought. Like Voltaire and other Enlightenment figures, Carus was concerned to define the true essence of religion. That essence would be the kernel of religious truth that remained after the dogmatic and superstitious elements were removed. Like Theodore Parker, another inheritor of the spirit of the "Skeptical Enlightenment," Dr. Carus hoped to "distinguish . . . the essential from the accidental, the eternal from the transient." This concern was expressed clearly in the way Carus selected passages for his anthology of Buddhist scriptures. Like the presentation of Christianity in Thomas Jefferson's Bible, Carus's *Gospel of Buddha* (1894) offered a Buddhism freed from superstitious and dogmatic accretions. Carus tried to arrange the diverse passages into "harmonious and systematic form" in order to construct "an ideal position upon which all true Buddhists may stand as upon common ground." In this process he had to "cut off most of [the] apocryphal adornments" of the Mahayana tradition that he believed had been added when Buddhist leaders tried to reach out to the masses. This critical and selective approach to the Buddhist scriptures also characterized his approach to the tradition as a whole and, in fact, to all religions. Carus believed—and here the influence of Darwin, Spencer, and laissez-faire capitalism seems clear—that religions evolve over time. After a battle for survival, a "cosmic religion of universal truth" will emerge. He encouraged comparison, competition, and conversation—especially between "the two greatest traditions in the world"—because he believed that this would hasten the identification of the essence of each tradition and accelerate the emergence of a universal, nonsectarian, and rational religion.[41]

Carus, as I have suggested, was very influential. One of the American participants in the public discussion who read and internalized his interpretations was Thomas B. Wilson. Although characterizing Wilson's understanding of Buddhism is relatively simple, since he wrote a number of articles on the subject and his interpretation fits the rationalist type very closely, reconstructing his biography is much more difficult. In 1905 Wilson apparently edited the *Overland Monthly*, the most prestigious magazine on the West Coast, and he went on to write for this periodical after that time as well. Although the San Francisco City Directory for 1905 listed his occupation as "journalist" and his copy of the *Light of Dharma* was sent to a San Francisco address, he seems to have worked at other occupations and lived in other localities. The byline of the later articles indicate that Wilson had been awarded an honorary doctor of laws degree. The extremely sympathetic attitude toward the business community and the advocacy of the accumulation of wealth that found its way into his articles for the *Light of Dharma* and *Overland Monthly* suggest that either he had wealth or aspired to it. Wilson's accounts of Asia and Asians, especially the Chinese, imply a firsthand acquaintance with non-Western cultures.[42]

The daily records of the priests connected with the Japanese Pure Land mission in San Francisco indicate that Wilson had regular and informal contact with Asian-American and Euro-American Buddhists. He probably was a member of the Dharma Sangha of Buddha, that Caucasian Buddhist group associated with the San Francisco mission. He lectured at the mission one summer Sunday in 1901. Although Wilson forcefully defended and sympathetically interpreted Buddhism in lectures and articles, it is impossible to determine whether he saw himself as a Buddhist adherent. In any case, he was at least a strong sympathizer.[43]

And he was a rationalist. Although there was no branch of the Free Religious Association or the Ethical Culture Society in the Bay Area, Wilson probably would have felt comfortable with these groups. Like these religious liberals and radicals and rationalist Buddhist advocates, Wilson emphasized the centrality of ethics, the importance of tolerance, the authority of the individual, and the primacy of reason. According to Wilson, Buddhism asks no one to believe assertions about the nature of the universe, the self, or ultimate reality on the authority of others: "Every Buddhist is free to investigate the facts from which the Buddhist doctrines have been derived." Wilson argued that the revealed "dogmas" which Christians are compelled to believe—such as the notion of a personal God—are illogical and unscientific. On the other hand, Buddhism is more rational and scientific than Christianity since, for example, it substitutes the moral law of cause and effect (karma) for the arbitrary rules of a capricious God. In fact, borrowing from Carus, Wilson asserted that "a conflict between religion and science is impossible in Buddhism." Some notion of God is saved in Wilson's interpretation since "Causation," the law of cause and effect that is sewn into the fabric of the universe, plays the role in his scheme which God plays in the Judeo-Christian one; but, needless to say, few of the orthodox Christian readers who happened to glance at his articles would have found Wilson's "God" intellectually or emotionally satisfying.[44]

Not only was Buddhism more rational and less dogmatic, it also provided a superior ethical framework. For Wilson, as for most rationalists, the heart of religion was ethics. Religions do provide conceptions of the self and the world; and since Buddhist views are empirically verifiable and compatible with science, they are superior. Yet Wilson assumed—and sometimes argued—that religion was most fundamentally a this-worldly path in which the individual strives to acquire more and more "nobility of character." Religions offer guidelines for the development of moral character, and as "a religion of ethics" Buddhism provides a compelling picture of how the universe supports moral evolution (karma). It also offers effective guidelines for achieving moral perfection (the noble eightfold path).[45]

THE ROMANTIC TYPE

Wilson not only emphasized all of the themes I have associated with the rationalist type, he firmly and explicitly rejected esoteric interpretations of Buddhism. Buddhism proclaims no "secret doctrine" and has nothing to do with "occultism," "mysticism," "psychic power," or "esotericism." "Buddha," he asserted, "taught an open and positive system of ethics and philosophy, and left no room anywhere for the injection of mystery or inner meaning." Ernest Fenollosa, an American Buddhist with a rather different perspective, agreed. He shared Wilson's concern about occultists, and he condemned forms of Buddhism that seemed to be little more than "theosophy mixed with a little diluted Hegel." Despite the commonalities on this point, the Buddhist perspective of Fenollosa diverged from the rationalism of Wilson as well as the esotericism of, say, Olcott in significant ways. Although some esoterics and rationalists expressed interest in the nonreligious spheres of Buddhist cultures and some even visited nations in which the tradition survived, their concern centered on religious beliefs and practices. For the third type of Buddhist advocate, the romantic or exotic-culture type, the attraction to Buddhism was part of an immersion in, and attachment to, a Buddhist culture as a whole—its art, architecture, music, drama, customs, language, and literature as well as its religion. In ways more characteristic of post-World War II American Buddhism, these nineteenth-century sympathizers tended to study the culture of a particular Buddhist nation and even adopt some of its customs. Due to historical circumstances, they tended to focus on Tibet and, especially, Japan. Most important, they focused on aesthetic rather than esoteric or rational approaches to religious meaning. Although apologists of this type often were committed to science and influenced by Spencer, they focused on the imagination more than reason. Further, supranormal access to hidden sources of religious truth interested them less than the ordinary workings of the human aesthetic faculties.[46]

Individuals of this type were indebted, in part, to Romanticism. Many of those who have been linked with the Romantic movement in Europe and the United States were attracted by the exotic and the distant. They read and wrote about the cultures of "the East" as well as those of nonliterate peoples and classical Greece and Rome. American exotic-culture Buddhists were the intellectual descendants of German Romantics like Goethe and American Romantics like Emerson. They continued the emphasis on feeling, exploration of imagination, and concern for aesthetics. And they perpetuated and intensified the Romantic interest in Asian cultures.

The emergence of this exotic-culture type also was stimulated by increased contact with Asian nations. American mariners, merchants, and missionaries had confronted Asian cultures earlier. However, improvements in communication, advances in transportation, changes in immigration patterns, and especially Japan's new openness to the West made it easier to travel to Asia—or to spend leisure hours reading the accounts of those who had. Most Americans, of course, still were hostile or apathetic; but some were attracted by what they were learning of Asian cultures. For example, there was a vogue of things Japanese in Western literary and artistic communities. *Japonisme* raged in France, Britain, Germany, and the United States from approximately 1865 until 1895. More specifically, it can be seen in the influence of Japanese woodblock prints on a large number of American artists—including Frederick Edwin Church, James Abbot McNeill Whistler, Mary Cassatt, Winslow Homer, William Merritt Chase, and John LaFarge.[47]

Many romantics liked the Western art forms inspired by the East but were even more fascinated by Asian art itself. They also had the time, education, and means to pursue those interests. They usually were members of the elite of major urban centers—especially Boston and New York. A disproportionate number, for example, were born into prominent American families. They also inclined toward more conservative political and economic views: they were least likely to be found distributing communist literature, inciting labor riots, or advocating anarchist views on street corners. Their Buddhist interests centered on the aesthetically rich forms of Mahayana Buddhism found in East Asia. The special focus on Japanese Buddhism was both a logical consequence of their aesthetic concerns and an arbitrary result of the confluence of forces that led to greater opportunities for contact with Japanese culture during this period. If there is an image of Victorian Buddhists among historians it is that of a self-indulgent Bostonian of wealth and influence dabbling in an exotic religion out of ennui, curiosity, psychic turmoil, or just plain silliness. Of the three types, romantic apologists fit this picture best. Yet this image is misleading. It fails to describe the romantics accurately, and it misrepresents the proportion of romantics among American followers. Some of these romantics, for instance, did much more than dabble: they had serious and sustained interest. Consider the sophistication of Fenollosa's notes on Tendai and Shingon Buddhism or Bigelow's published interpretations. Also, these romantics formed only a portion—and probably the smallest portion—of those who were drawn to the religion.[48]

John LaFarge (1835–1910), who took advantage of the opening of Japan, was one American who evidenced some of the traits of the romantic type. He was fascinated by the beauty of the art that he and Henry Adams (1838–1918) encountered in Japan in 1886. In *An Artist's Letters from Japan* he reported that of all the art he saw there he was most moved by the images of the bodhisattva Kannon "when shown absorbed in the meditations of Nirvana." The two even took a second trip to Asia in 1891, traveling to the Buddhist temples in Ceylon in order "to see the art." Although the attraction was not sufficiently strong for him to leave the Roman Catholic tradition, LaFarge also had sympathy for and interest in Buddhism. So did Adams. When he first went to Japan in 1886, just after his wife's suicide, Adams seemed hungry for some exotic spiritual nourishment. He even suggested that he had been very sympathetic to Buddhism before he arrived. Adams did not like Fenollosa, with whom he had frequent contact in Japan; and he playfully confessed that Fenollosa had unconverted him: "[Fenollosa] has joined a Buddhist sect; I myself was a Buddhist when I left America, but he has converted me to Calvinism with leanings toward the Methodists." Adams mocked his own earlier interest in Buddhism when he sent his poem "Buddha and Brahma" to his friend John Hay; but he also asked Augustus Saint-Gaudens, the sculptor of the famous memorial to his wife, to use a Japanese Bodhisattva figure as the model. Toward the end of his life, Adams confessed that he had "admiration" for his friend Bigelow's new book on Buddhism. He thanked Bigelow for sending a copy: "I will, as usual, take refuge in the Lotus. There we will meet. We shall not be alone." One scholar has suggested that the Lotus here symbolizes the silence of nirvana and that the "philosophy of silence" that unites Adams's corpus is grounded in a mystical understanding of Buddhism and its goal. Whether or not Buddhism influenced his view this radically, it seems that, despite his ironic confessions and cynical asides, his renunciations and mis-directions, Adams seriously considered the tradition.[49]

Mary McNeil Fenollosa (d. 1954), Ernest Fenollosa's second wife, was a romantic adherent who also had the chance to visit Japan. In the spring of 1896 she and her husband went back to the temple where he had formally professed allegiance to Tendai Buddhism, and there both of them studied with Keiyen Ajari. She too then converted. Half of the poems that appeared three years later in *Out of the Nest* were inspired by her encounters with "Eastern," especially Japanese, religion and culture. She offered, for instance, a poetic reconstruction of one of her visits to a Japanese shrine to Kannon, the Buddhist bodhisattva of compassion who answers the petitions of the devout. Struck by the beauty, mystery, and simplicity of the scene, she had scribbled her own petition on paper and tied it to the shrine where those of other pilgrims fluttered in wind: "Ah, simple faith! The sun was in the west;/And darkness smote with flails his quivery light./Beside the path I knelt; and, with the rest,/My alien prayer was planted in the night." William Woodville Rockhill (1854–1914), who studied Tibetan culture and sympathized with Buddhism, and George Cabot Lodge (1873–1909), who wrote a poetic tribute to nirvana and meditated with Bigelow in Boston, left no evidence that they had "planted" "alien prayers" at Buddhist shrines. But they too might be labeled romantics. Yet Ernest Francisco Fenollosa, who introduced his wife to the tradition, William Sturgis Bigelow, and Lafcadio Hearn displayed the characteristics of this type as clearly and fully as any.[50]

Ernest Fenollosa was a poet and student of Oriental art who played an important role in the introduction of Asian cultures to late-nineteenth-century America through articles in literary magazines, a collection of poems, a classic work on East Asian Art, and service as curator of the Department of Oriental Art at the Boston Museum of Fine Arts. He had significant contact with Japanese culture in the course of two extended visits to East Asia (1878–89 and 1896–1900). During his stays in Japan, Fenollosa taught political economy and philosophy and, later, English literature. For two of those years abroad (1878–80) he was manager of a museum and fine arts academy in Tokyo. Fenollosa, who longed for the union of the "feminine" East and the "masculine" West, was drawn to the delicate contours of Japanese culture, especially its art, architecture, poetry, and classical drama.[51] Fenollosa, of course, also was attracted to Japanese Buddhism. As I have noted, he received the precepts of the Tendai sect, along with William Sturgis Bigelow, in 1885. He studied the philosophies of Hegel and Spencer as an undergraduate at Harvard. He even promoted Spencer's system in his lectures at the University of Tokyo. Yet Fenollosa seems to have been more interested in the aesthetic than the metaphysical. He was more animated by the search for beauty than for truth. In fact, his wife suggested that he first came to Buddhism through his appreciation for Japanese art and architecture: "It was during these temple sojourns that his interest in Buddhism, both as a religion and a constructive philosophy, was aroused." And as Fenollosa's biographer has suggested, an aesthetic concern was crucial in stimulating and sustaining his attraction to Tendai and Shingon Buddhism: "The beauties of Buddhist worship," Chisolm claimed, "lent added and perhaps decisive persuasion." Fenollosa found in the symbols and rituals of these Buddhist groups a richness and sensuality that was reminiscent of Roman Catholic cathedrals and absent in the bone-white Protestant churches of New England.[52]

Another romantic adherent who was drawn to Japanese culture and the aesthetic elements in Japanese Buddhism was Fenollosa's friend, William Sturgis Bigelow. Bigelow was born into an old, prominent New England family. He attended Harvard College and Harvard Medical School and enjoyed the advantages that wealth and status can offer. After graduating from medical school in 1874, Bigelow went to Europe to continue his training in science and medicine. He lived in several European cities and studied for more than a year with Louis Pasteur in Paris. When he returned to the United States to begin his career, Bigelow consented to the wishes of his father and followed in his footsteps by becoming a surgeon at Massachusetts General Hospital and an assistant in surgery at Harvard Medical School. But he only practiced medicine for two years (1879–81). Complaining of ill health, he gave up the profession that he did not seem to enjoy. As others who knew him suggested, he might have been happy and productive as a researcher; but he apparently did not possess the courage to challenge the wishes of his father.[53]

It never led to a full-time paid position, but Bigelow discovered a new center around which to orient the rest of his life when—after being inspired by Edward Morse's Lowell Lectures on Japan—he set off for that country in 1882. He went for a brief visit but stayed seven years. During that time he was an appreciative student of Japanese culture, and he was drawn to Tendai and Shingon Buddhism. He studied with a Tendai Buddhist teacher, Sakurai Keitoku, and formally professed his allegiance with his friend Fenollosa. Three years later, in 1888, Bigelow participated in another formal ceremony that might be described as a "lay ordination" or perhaps, as Bigelow himself once described it, a Buddhist "sacrament." Bigelow often told friends that he would have become a Buddhist priest if his health and constitution had allowed it. In any case, apparently Bigelow faithfully engaged in meditation and the Tantric practices of Shingon and Tendai after he left Japan in 1889 following the death of his Buddhist teacher. These practices included repetition of a mantra or sacred formula, use of mudras or ritual gestures, and contemplation of mandalas or symbolic representations of the Buddhist cosmos.[54]

Bigelow can be viewed as a romantic Buddhist adherent in several ways. First, he seems to have been indebted to literary and philosophical Romanticism and, like Fenollosa, especially to the writings of Emerson. Emerson's idealism and pantheism provided Bigelow with an intellectual framework that could incorporate the insights of Tendai and Shingon Buddhism. For Bigelow, these forms of Buddhism stressed the primacy and power of consciousness and the ultimate unity of all reality. In an attempt to describe Buddhism for the Reverend Phillips Brooks of Boston, Bigelow emphasized the parallels: "As far as I have got it, Buddhist philosophy is a sort of Spiritual Pantheism—Emerson almost exactly." Bigelow also was a romantic adherent insofar as he was immersed in and attracted to several aspects of Japanese culture—above all, Japanese prints, lacquer, swords, sculpture, and gardens. Bigelow had begun exploring and collecting Japanese art while he was studying in Paris in the 1870s, and during his first stay in Japan he spent a great deal of his time and money in this pursuit. While in Japan he encouraged the Japanese to sustain their native traditions in the arts, and to this day he is remembered for his $10,000 contribution to the founding funds for the Japan Art Institute. In recognition of his contributions to Japanese art, in 1909 he was awarded the decoration of the Third Order of the Rising Sun, the highest honor given to a private foreigner by the Japanese government. Although Fenollosa was more widely known, Bigelow's contributions to the understanding of Japanese art also were recognized in America. He had, after all, served as a Trustee of the Boston Museum of Fine Arts and had donated tens of thousands of items of Far Eastern art to the museum, which, together with the Morse and Fenollosa-Weld collections, made that institution the finest early repository of Japanese art in America.[55]

As with Fenollosa, Bigelow's fascination with Japanese art sparked his Buddhist interest. One of his friends suggested that it was his investigation of Japanese gardens that "led him to the religion." Whatever the path, it seems clear that the aesthetic appeal of Tendai and Shingon Buddhism were crucial in sustaining his interest. This is another sense in which his Buddhist commitment was romantic. Although one scholar has suggested that, unlike Fenollosa, Bigelow had a "muted response to the aesthetic aspects of Buddhism," Bigelow's correspondence and other unpublished sources indicate that he shared Fenollosa's appreciation for the richness of Buddhist iconography and ritual. For example, in a conversation about Buddhism that was recorded by his secretary, Bigelow praised the aesthetic character of the forms of Japanese Buddhism he had studied and practiced: "In Tendai and Shingon they use the old forms of Northern Buddhism. Have kept the ritual very closely. Very beautiful ritual."[56]

The romantic sympathizer Lafcadio Hearn (1850–1904) did not attend Harvard, or any other college; and, unlike Bigelow, he did not have to wrestle with the ghosts of New England Puritans. Yet this immigrant son of an Anglo-Irish father and a Greek mother also was drawn to the beauty and richness of Japanese culture. He immersed himself in that culture perhaps as fully as any other Westerner of his day—living in Japan for fourteen years (1890–1904), marrying a Japanese woman, adopting a Japanese name (Yakumo Koizumi), dying a Japanese citizen, and being buried at a Buddhist monastery in Tokyo. In his twelve books—from *Glimpses of Unfamiliar Japan* (1894) to *Japan: An Attempt at Interpretation* (1904)—he interpreted the whole gamut of Japanese culture for Western audiences.[57]

Scattered throughout these works were interpretations of Buddhism. Despite great interest in the tradition, Hearn never identified himself as an adherent. When his readers mistook him for one—as one Yale undergraduate did—he corrected them: "I am not a Buddhist but still a follower of Herbert Spencer." Committed to nonsectarianism in religion and, to a large extent, sympathetic to the agnosticism of Spencer's philosophy, Hearn apparently was unable or unwilling to accept any particular religion or sect. Of the Western and Eastern traditions available to him, however, Buddhism was the most attractive. He once suggested that "if it were possible for me to adopt a faith, I should adopt it [Buddhism]." It was Tendai's and Shingon's apparent compatibility with "the German monism of Professor Haeckel's school"—which Carus also had noticed—and with the evolutionary monism of Spencer's philosophy that were important sources of Buddhism's attractiveness for Hearn. Spencer's thought was especially influential in Hearn's interpretation of the "Higher Buddhism." This "philosophical Buddhism" intended for the intellectual elite was, to put it crudely, a gnostic version of Spencer's agnostic evolutionist system. An experience of ultimate reality in the nirvanic transcendence of subject and object took the place of Spencer's sense of dual consciousness's inability to encounter the "Unknown Reality," and karma—not heredity—functioned as the mechanism of evolutionary change. In Hearn's interpretation of the "Higher Buddhism," even the development of inorganic substances falls under the causal power of the moral law. Hearn viewed this higher Buddhism, then, as a form of spiritual evolutionism compatible with Spencer's thought and, therefore, with reason and science.[58]

Although I have described his position as romantic, Hearn's interpretation of Buddhism also contained elements more characteristic of another type. It is important to recognize the ways in which Hearn and almost all Buddhist advocates fail to fit perfectly any single ideal-typical constellation of traits. Almost every individual expressed tendencies of more than one type. Hearn certainly was no occultist: his antagonism toward Western "esoteric" Buddhists was clear and strong. But his writings evidenced some parallels with the rationalists. Hearn immersed himself in a number of aspects of Japanese culture and was interested in its art and literature; but he also, like the rationalists, emphasized the authority of the individual and the centrality of ethics. He also hoped for the emergence of a universal religion and assessed religions by appealing to the principles of reason and the findings of science. So, in a sense, his view could be characterized either as an example of the romantic type with rationalist tendencies, as I suggest, or even as a variation of the rationalist type.[59]

Other Buddhist advocates exhibited elements of both the romantic and esoteric types. The esoteric sympathizer Joseph Wade shared the romantics' affection for a Buddhist culture: he collected Japanese art, maintained a Japanese garden, supported Japanese students, and, like Bigelow, even was honored by the Japanese government for his contributions. On the other hand, there is some hint of "esoteric" sympathies in the unpublished writings of the romantic adherent, Bigelow. For instance, he told one of his Japanese mentors that he believed that Buddhism had ideas that paralleled those of Laurence Oliphant and Western Spiritualists. Kanryo Naobayashi responded by correcting Bigelow's mistaken impression. "I am inclined to think," Bigelow wrote in another letter, "Thibet is the great centre of knowledge, from which it has spread both ways, and there if anywhere, are preserved the facts which the West has lost with the burning of the Alexandrian library and the extinction of the Rosicrucians." One scholar has taken this last remark to indicate that Bigelow had an "almost Faustian curiosity toward [Buddhism] as a source of great and esoteric and occult knowledge." It does suggest some affinities with the esoteric type, but the bulk of the evidence indicates that those parallels should not be over-emphasized.[60]

The trouble here, in part, turns on the multiple uses of the term "esoteric." After their first meeting in 1887, Theodore Roosevelt, who later would become a close friend, described Bigelow as an "esoteric": "but, Cabot, why did you not tell me he was an esoteric Buddhist? I would have then have been spared some frantic floundering when the subject of religion happened to be broached." It is most likely, however, that Roosevelt meant that Bigelow belonged to a Japanese sect that is often referred to as "esoteric." Forms of Buddhism associated with the Tantric tradition often have been described in this way, and the Shingon and Tendai sects with which Bigelow was associated included elements from this Tantric tradition. Yet it is important to distinguish between Tantric beliefs and practices and Western occult elements. Bigelow himself came to see the importance of this distinction. Because he wanted to distance himself from the "esoteric" Buddhists of Boston who were connected with Theosophical and Spiritualist groups, he consistently avoided the terms "exoteric" and "esoteric" in his published accounts. In his Ingersoll Lecture of 1908, for example, he distinguished between two fundamental perspectives in Mahayana Buddhism. There was *Kengyo* or the "non-apparent" and *Mikkyo* or the "apparent." In defending the "non-apparent" wisdom and practice of Shingon and Tendai Buddhism Bigelow avoided translating *Mikkyo* as "esoteric," as is usual, because this had "led to some popular misconceptions." Both Bigelow's version of Tantric Buddhism and, for example, Olcott's understanding of Theosophical Buddhism include references to "hidden" or "secret" beliefs and practices. In this sense, there was some overlap. It would be misleading, however, to describe Bigelow as a paradigmatic example of an esoteric adherent.[61]

Esotericism and rationalism also overlapped. For example, Dr. Eleanor M. Hiestand Moore presented Buddhism as a reasonable tradition that was in "harmony" with the latest results of modern scientific inquiry. Yet, in a surprising aside, she also praised "the wise disciples of esoteric truth" who might have anticipated some of the conclusions of modern science. On the other hand, a number of esoterics evidenced some traits of the rationalist type. Edmunds, for instance, found some aspects of the Western rationalist tradition very attractive. He had belonged to a Free Church in England, considered ordination to the Unitarian ministry, and "resolved" to join the Ethical Culture Society. In fact, he might have joined the latter if the minister of the Swedenborgian church in Philadelphia had agreed to allow him multiple religious identities. The esoteric Canavarro, to offer a final example, praised the "rational" and "scientific" teachings of Theravada Buddhism in articles for *The Light of Dharma* while revealing only a hint of esoteric influence. I point to these instances of ambiguity and overlap to remind the reader that these types are only more or less useful theoretical constructs. At the same time, I want to demonstrate how this typology not only can identify patterns among the perspectives but also highlight the uniqueness of particular positions. By interpreting an apologist's stance in terms of this typology, both its continuities and discontinuities with other sympathetic responses to Buddhism become clearer.[62]

In the preceding chapter I argued that there was a vibrant public conversation about Buddhism and that the tradition became a serious option for the spiritually disenchanted. Here I have suggested that although individual variations were significant, three main types of sympathizers and adherents stood out. Contrary to the prevailing assumptions, I have contended that the majority were not romantics but esoterics. Further, romantics' interest often was as serious and enduring as the absence of Asian Buddhist teachers and institutions would allow. Yet I have said little about why they grasped onto Buddhism and not another of the various forms of traditional and alternative spirituality available in turn-of-the-century America. I next analyze the sources of Buddhism's appeal and, at the same time, consider Buddhist advocates' relation to the dominant culture.

FOUR

"WALKING IN FAIRYLAND"

Buddhism's Appeal and Cultural Dissent

There is much truth in the claim that during the 1890s "the leading doctrine of Boston was not to offend," and William Sturgis Bigelow struggled to be an orthodox Bostonian. It was not easy, however, since he also yearned to be a faithful Buddhist. Needless to say, he was not completely successful. In a letter to a prominent Boston minister, Bigelow described his father's reaction to his formal conversion to Buddhism: "He does not take any stock in Buddhism, & thinks that I am hovering on the verge of lunacy, because I do not come home & get up some grandchildren for him, like a well-regulated Bostonian." Clearly his father's reaction bothered him. Some Buddhist followers, like the sensitive Bigelow, were hurt or annoyed by the condescending grins, disdainful glances, and bewildered expressions. Others seemed less troubled. The cost to Bigelow was disintegration and loneliness. He was in a unique position to act as a leader of American, even Western, Buddhism: he had time, money, a Harvard education, influential contacts, and formal Buddhist training. Yet he did less than, for example, Carus or Olcott to popularize the tradition. Bigelow was aware that others in Boston besides his influential father were embarrassed, amused, or disturbed by his commitment to Tendai and Shingon Buddhism, and to avoid further rejection he cloistered himself in his house on Beacon Street and his summer home on Tuckernuck Island. Or, more accurately, he presented a public self that fit reasonably well with the mores of "well-regulated Bostonians" and cultivated a private self that was, in many ways, contrary. Working at the Boston Museum of Fine Arts, attending afternoon concerts with his friend Margaret Chanler, performing his duties as trustee of Massachusetts General Hospital, and staying with Theodore Roosevelt at the White House, Dr. Bigelow wore "beautiful haberdashery and hand-some English clothes" and gave off the subtle aroma of toilet water.[1]

According to his wishes, half of his ashes were buried in Boston; the other half were shipped to Japan. It was his public self that was eulogized at Trinity Episcopal Church in Boston by a Harvard classmate and buried at prestigious Mount Auburn Cemetery—the cemetery that his grandfather had founded. In the seclusion of his Boston home, Japanese house, or island retreat, Gesshin Koji (Bigelow's Buddhist title) struggled to reconcile the Victorian self that eventually would be buried in Mount Auburn with his Buddhist self. That self would be laid out in his Buddhist robes in his dining room on Beacon street and buried at the Homyoin Temple in Japan, a subtemple of the Tendai monastery where he and Fenollosa had studied. For the most part he lived his Buddhist life away from the eyes of the elite of Boston. On Tuckernuck Island, he engaged in the "esoteric" practices of the Tendai and Shingon traditions and tutored George Cabot Lodge in Buddhist meditation. While in his various Japanese lodgings, Bigelow wore traditional Japanese dress. In his home on Beacon Street, he slept beneath a picture of Keitoku Sakurai, his beloved Japanese Buddhist teacher.[2]

He acknowledged his Buddhist commitment to his closest friends—e.g., Henry Cabot Lodge and Theodore Roosevelt—but could discuss his deepest religious concerns with only a handful of persons. Most important to Bigelow, of course, was his teacher Sakurai. He also shared his devotion to Buddhism with Fenollosa, George Cabot Lodge, Wajo Chiman, and Kakuzo Okakura, Curator of the Department of Chinese and Japanese Art at the Boston museum. But, one by one, they all died before Bigelow—starting with his teacher who passed away in December of 1889 after Bigelow had nursed him "as a filial child would his benevolent father." He wrote to Sakurai's successor at Homyoin temple, Kanryo Naobayashi, for spiritual advice from 1890 to 1921. Yet from the time that Sakurai died (1889), and even more intensely by the time his friend Okakura died (1913), Bigelow often was left alone in his struggle to be faithful to the vows he took in 1885. Five years before his death, physically debilitated and spiritually "dead," a guilt-ridden Bigelow confessed his failings as a Buddhist to Sakurai's successor in Japan. He also expressed his loneliness: "Since Mr. Okakura's death there is no one in this country to whom I can talk of Buddhism."[3]

American Buddhists, then, did not have to live in Vermillion, South Dakota—like F. Graeme Davis—to feel isolated. Nor did they have to be as sensitive as Bigelow to notice that many dismissed their unconventional beliefs and practices. Of course, not all sympathizers and adherents reacted as Bigelow did to the signs of rejection. Some even seemed to welcome the dismissals as validation of the correctness of their views and the nobility of their character. However they reacted, one thing seems clear: in their natural idiosyncrasy, their cultivated marginality, or their genuine cultural nonconformity, most Euro-American Buddhist sympathizers and adherents stood apart from their contemporaries. Most Americans who cared enough to have an opinion on the subject seemed to have shared Frank Field Ellinwood's perception that Buddhism appealed to "all types of religious apostates and social malcontents."[4]

In fact, many of those who were attracted to Buddhism—including Bigelow—had personal eccentricities of various sorts that only contributed to the view that they were different. Adding further support for this interpretation, in public debate Buddhist apologists often used the fiery rhetoric of dissent. In their accounts of the sources of Buddhism's appeal they often emphasized the tradition's distinctiveness. Christian critics, of course, also emphasized its divergence; and some, like the Reverend Clarence Edgar Rice, even reluctantly acknowledged the lure of Buddhism's exotic and alien world:

> When I first arrived in Japan I took up my residence in a city some distance from European and American residents. Hardly a hundred yards away, across a narrow ravine, stood a Buddhist temple surrounded by pine trees. At evening, when the wind was whispering in the pines, the mellow tones of the temple bell and the droning chants and litanies of the priests floated in at my study window. The *strange surroundings*, the quiet evening, the cadences of the bell and song lent a *peculiar fascination* to the scene; and one could almost imagine himself transported to *another world*, or a witness of *strange events* in medieval ages. My first glimpse of Buddhism under these conditions presents an aspect of this religion that explains in part the *peculiar charm* it has for some minds.

A handful of Buddhist apologists, like their Christian opponents, also used this exotic language of enchantment, and even the bracing idiom of negation, to describe the religion. To live the Buddhist life was to abide in a remote land—a "fairyland"—where inhabitants celebrated the absence of all that was familiar and dear. In short, those interested in Buddhism seemed to be dissenters. In this chapter I begin the task of sorting out the complicated patterns of dissensus and consensus that were expressed in Euro-Americans' responses to Buddhism. I analyze some of the ways in which sympathizers and adherents between 1879 and 1912 consciously rejected the dominant social, political, economic, and cultural patterns.[5]

POLITICAL, ECONOMIC, AND SOCIAL DISSENT

The period of significant interest in Buddhism (1879–1912) was also a time of social, political, and economic turmoil. As one scholar has suggested, the three decades following the Civil War were "a period of trauma, of change so swift and thorough that many Americans seemed unable to fathom the extent of the upheaval." Industrialization, incorporation, urbanization, immigration, and rapid technological innovation changed the character of daily life for Americans as many of the characteristics of twentieth-century American economy and society began to emerge. Many pondered "the labor question" in the 1870s and 1880s as tensions between management and labor periodically erupted into violence. Cynicism and frustration about corruption in civil service and politics was widespread.[6]

Many American historians have borrowed Mark Twain and Charles Dudley Warner's cynical phrase "The Gilded Age" to describe the period between 1870 and 1900, and textbooks usually label the period that followed (1901–17) the "Progressive Era" or the "Age of Reform." These labels can be deceptive, however. Efforts at reform of all sorts were initiated during the Gilded Age; and political corruption, economic unrest, and social dislocation continued during the Progressive Era. I return to this point in the final chapter. Here it is important to note only that dissent emerged from a variety of sources between 1879 and 1912. There were, for example, protests by groups of farmers and workers with more conventional religious affiliations as well as by associations of atheistic anarchists. Some of the most popular and effective protests were linked directly or indirectly with the Protestant mainstream. Buddhists, then, were neither the loudest nor the most effective dissenters in this period; but there were undeniable expressions of social, economic, and political opposition among some who were drawn to the religion. Some challenged, for example, prevailing dietary habits, medical practices, research procedures, ethnic relations, and gender roles. A handful even rejected elements of the accepted order as fundamental as capitalism and democracy.[7]

A small but significant number of late-Victorians challenged the reigning attitudes toward the nonhuman world. In Philadelphia, for instance, the American Anti-Vivisection Society was established in 1883. That society was dedicated to "the total abolition of all vivi-sectional experiments on animals and other experiments of a painful character." By the turn of the century, that city had at least sixteen organizations dedicated in one way or another to promoting more humane treatment of animals. Because they wanted to improve their health or avoid maltreatment of animals, a small group of Philadelphians even decided to eat differently. The Vegetarian Society of America, which published a magazine called *Food, Home, and Garden*, was founded in that city in 1886. But unconventional attitudes toward diet had been institutionalized there much earlier. The Philadelphia Bible-Christian Church, or so-called Vegetarian Church, was established as early as 1817 when forty-one former members of the Bible-Christian Church of Salford in England arrived. They had split from the parent church, which apparently had been influenced by Swedenborgianism, because they and their minister came to believe that the Bible required not only abstinence from war, capital punishment, and slavery, but also from meat and liquor.[8]

Some Buddhist followers openly rejected vegetarianism and favored vivisection. The rationalist sympathizer Carus came to the conclusion that "the antivivisection movement is wrong." He did publish a small number of the many pieces he received on vegetarianism and vivisection, but apparently not enough to satisfy those involved in the movement. With characteristic politeness and gentleness, for example, Carus thanked William H. Galvani, the Buddhist sympathizer and ardent vegetarian and antivivisectionist, for his thoughts on "man's moral attitude toward animals." But he felt compelled to reject the submission because the magazine did not have enough space "for a controversy on the subject."[9]

Galvani, who was so committed to the cause that he announced plans for a vegetarian colony at his farm in Oregon, was unwavering. And his persistence found him periodicals that welcomed his notices and articles. In one brief note that appeared in *Food, Home, and Garden* he cited statistics about the annual American consumption of pork and then drew a connection between diet and character: "Can a mass of humanity whose bodies are made up of so much of the flesh of swine be refined, generous, loving and kind? I fail to see it." It is difficult to say whether, as Galvani's logic implied, swineless Buddhists were more refined and kind than their swine-eating counterparts. But it is certain that a number of Buddhist advocates—especially those with esoteric tendencies such as Galvani, Vetterling, and Wade—were among the late-Victorians who challenged the socially accepted ways of dealing with the nonhuman world. They advocated vegetarianism, as is usual for Buddhists, and they rejected vivisection. Pieces on these topics were published in Buddhist magazines such as *Light of Dharma, Maha Bodhi,* and *Buddhist Ray.* In the opening issue of *The Buddhist Ray* its eccentric editor, Vetterling, suggested that one of Buddhism's appealing traits is that "it does not deny justice to any living creature by slaying it." Later in his life Vetterling continued to support humane treatment for animals by donating $50,000—a significant sum at the time—to erect an animal shelter in San Jose, California.[10]

On the East Coast, the rationalist C. T. Strauss of New York City and the esoteric Albert Edmunds of Philadelphia were associated with the Philadelphia-based Vegetarian Society of America. Edmunds, for instance, had personal interest in Christianity and Buddhism; and he believed that both called for more benevolent relations with the nonhuman world. Buddhism's views on this matter seemed clear and exemplary, he thought; but Christianity also held promise. The traditional Christian anthropocentrism was based on a distortion of scripture and must be corrected. He did his part to correct the distortions through his writing and lecturing. (He even took the pulpit of the "Vegetarian Church" in Philadelphia one Sunday in 1893 in the pastor's absence.) And Edmunds struggled to follow the diet that his religious beliefs demanded. The unmarried Edmunds apparently did not cook for himself. And, so, he could manage to eat "fruit and nuts" for breakfast before his ten mile walk one spring morning in 1891, but he often felt forced to go against his deepest beliefs and endure the "agonies" that accompanied the many nonvegetarian meals he dutifully consumed in dining halls and boarding houses.[11]

Perhaps Edmunds's struggle might have been eased if he had provided those boarding house cooks with a copy of Laura Carter Holloway

Langford's *Buddhist Diet Book*. This work contained the vegetarian recipes Langford compiled while spending several months with Western Buddhists in England and Prussia. Langford, a prominent journalist, editor, feminist, author, and lecturer, was raised amidst Southern plantation affluence. Her father was a governor of Tennessee, and she lived for a period at the White House with fellow Tennesseeans President Andrew Johnson and his wife. While at the White House Langford wrote her most popular book, *The Ladies of the White House*. She also authored biographies, household manuals, and volumes of poetry. In many ways she appeared to be the consummate "insider"; yet her views on religion, women, and diet were unconventional. A member of the Theosophical Society, this esoteric Buddhist sympathizer corresponded with others who belonged to groups outside the religious mainstream—including Shaker elder Frederick W. Evans and eldress Anna White. Although Langford never accepted the invitation to join that group, vegetarianism was one topic on which she concurred with her Shaker correspondents. Evans and White, like Langford, advocated vegetarianism. Others in the Shaker community in Mt. Lebanon did too. In fact, the organ of the Vegetarian Society of America published portions of a letter from Evans in 1889 in which he claimed that almost all of the sixty believers in the "North Family" avoided meat. But as White told her "dear friend" Laura in one letter, when Evans first introduced vegetarianism into that community in 1849 "it was a great innovation and made a great talk." Although her friend Anna White had congratulated her for giving up "foods detrimental to health," there was, no doubt, also "great talk" in some quarters when Langford publicly recommended vegetarianism. To make matters worse, she linked it with an alien faith—Buddhism.[12]

In her *Buddhist Diet Book* Langford offered recipes to Western Buddhists and other interested readers for their physical and spiritual improvement. Most reviewers of Langford's work seemed troubled by her advocacy of Buddhist beliefs and practices and her explanations of the religious grounds for vegetarianism in particular. Yet most still recommended the book: "The author appears to be a devout Buddhist, but the recipes can be appreciated by those who hold a different faith, and who use vegetables as auxiliaries to meat, instead of as the staff of life." One reviewer found the book benign enough to commend it to "all good housewives," and another reassured readers that "the directions for preparing food bear a strong resemblance to the methods already in vogue in any American kitchen." Yet for most reviewers, and presumably most readers of this collection of vegetarian recipes, Buddhism clearly was associated with a challenge to culinary custom.[13]

Caucasian Buddhists, again mostly esoterics, sometimes challenged medical practices as well. During the mid- and late-nineteenth century, the loosening of licensing laws opened the medical field to a variety of alternative forms of healing. In fact, one historian of the period has argued that "doctors of the people—allopaths, homeopaths, eclectics, and later osteopaths—roamed the land at will." Vetterling provides an excellent example. With a degree in medicine from Hahnemann in Philadelphia in hand, he went on to practice and advocate homeopathy—a form of medical practice in which disease is treated by the administration of minute doses of a remedy that would in healthy persons produce symptoms of the disease.[14]

A handful of sympathizers and adherents—esoterics such as Albert J. Edmunds and rationalists like Dyer Daniel Lum—even challenged elements as fundamental to the reigning political and economic order as democracy and laissez-faire capitalism. Just off the ship from England in 1885, Edmunds spoke to a Baptist Church in New York state on the topic, "Christianity Applied to Business." Three days earlier, Edmunds reported in his diary, he had "dined on snow." He was having a hard time in his adopted land, and the evening of his speech, anxiety about his own financial situation might have combined with lingering memories of his impoverished childhood—as the eldest of thirteen children of a tailor—to make his economic and political views even more radical than usual. In any case, Edmunds complained that he had collected less from his substantial audience than he had hoped because he "offended the plutocrat by my socialism." Edmunds's unconventional views came to the surface again when the National Guard was sent to the site of the coal miners' strike in Pennsylvania in 1902: "Trade unions are beginning to talk revolution, and I already foresee, not far off, the social war which I have believed in since 1884."[15]

Lum also hoped for a "social war," and he provides perhaps the clearest example of political and economic dissent. He played a role in organizing the bookbinders into a union during the 1870s—the period in which he embraced Buddhism; and as the years passed Lum turned his attention more and more toward political, social, and economic questions. He argued publicly against the anti-Oriental sentiment that raged among workers during the 1870s and 1880s. In 1876 he ran for lieutenant governor of Massachusetts on the Greenback-Labor ticket with Wendell Phillips, the labor reformer and abolitionist. The following year he served as secretary of a congressional committee to investigate the "depression of labor." Then the Railroad Strike of 1877 and the Pittsburgh riots which accompanied it propelled him on a career in radical politics. He lost faith in the reigning economic and political system and in the possibility of incremental change of that system from within. Lum moved toward socialism and, finally, anarchism. In 1883 he joined the newly formed Anarchist International Working People's Association, which condemned church, state, and schools for their perpetuation of poor conditions for workers, and he wrote for anarchist magazines that called for violence (*Alarm*) as well as those that were pacifist (*Liberty*). Lum even served briefly as editor of the anarchist publication *Alarm* when its editor and several other leaders of the rally of anarchists in Chicago's Haymarket Square were arrested and convicted for conspiracy after a bombing in May 1886. Lum defended the "Haymarket victims," advocated terrorism to free them, and allegedly smuggled a stick of dynamite to one of the condemned men who then used it to commit suicide. When the other condemned anarchists were executed Lum called for violent revenge in the pages of *Alarm*. He subsequently published a "history" of that famous trial.[16]

Besides this work, he authored several other books on the political, social, and economic issues of the day. Never one for popular causes, at the height of anti-Mormon sentiment Lum wrote a defense of Mormonism from an anarchist perspective. Toward the end of his life he came to reject violence, but he continued to advocate anarchism. As late as 1890—the year he wrote *The Economics of Anarchy* and two years before the influential *Philosophy of Trade Unions* appeared—he described himself as a "Social Revolutionist."[17]

Buddhist advocates stood apart from their contemporaries in other ways. A Victorian "Cult of True Womanhood" emerged between 1820 and 1850. This cult prescribed, as one influential scholar put it, a female role "bounded by kitchen and nursery, overlaid with piety and purity, and crowned with subservience." Some Victorian women and men appealed to Christianity to challenge the beliefs of this "cult," and they gave Christianity credit for progress already made. Other influential participants in the public conversation about women—for example, Elizabeth Cady Stanton—gave religions no credit for elevating women and placed little hope in any tradition: "She is not indebted to any religion for one step of progress, or one new liberty. . . . All religions thus far have taught the headship and superiority of man, the inferiority and subordination of woman. . . . It is not to any form of religion we are to look for woman's advancement, but to material civilization." Some Buddhist sympathizers, like Edmunds, did indeed seem rather uninterested in "woman's advancement." After attending a meeting at the Germantown Hicksite Friends one Sunday, for example, Edmunds praised the "conciseness" of one woman who felt moved to speak regularly. But, he confessed to a friend after meeting, "I don't believe in feminine ministrations as an every day thing." And he gave this as one reason he would not join the Quaker group. Yet a number of the women and men who were sympathetic to Buddhism disagreed with the positions of Stanton on the one hand and Edmunds on the other. Unlike Edmunds, they challenged reigning conceptions of the status and role of women; and, unlike Stanton, they retained hope in the transforming power of religion. They seemed to have been drawn to Buddhism, in part, by its supposed compatibility with an elevation of the status of women.[18]

Some Christian missionaries and Buddhist scholars pointed to Buddha's reluctance in admitting women into the order, and implied that the founder and his tradition were less egalitarian than Christianity. On the other hand, there also was some support in the Buddhist scholarship of the day for an egalitarian interpretation of Buddhism. For example, the eminent British scholar Rhys Davids pointed to passages in the Pali Buddhist canon that seemed to acknowledge the early contributions and spiritual capacities of women. Those Buddhist advocates who cared about what the scholars said—and there were some—could find a cloak of authority to wrap around their views about gender.[19]

Such social dissent was associated more frequently with esoterics like Vetterling and rationalists like Lum than with romantics like Bigelow. In separate defenses of Buddhism, for example, rationalists Myra Withee and C. T. Strauss suggested that Buddhism does not, as some Westerners had claimed, degrade women. In fact, Withee suggested, the tradition is superior to Christianity on this point since its scriptures do not contain admonitions, like St. Paul's, to be silent and submissive. Eleanor Hiestand Moore was another rationalist who found those Pauline admonitions annoying. Moore attended elite women's colleges—Bryn Mawr and Vassar—and earned a medical degree at a time when female physicians still were rare. She also was an active member of the Equal Franchise Society of Pennsylvania. Perhaps her feminist views emerged during her college days, or perhaps her experiences as a female physician, chemistry instructor, lecturer, and journalist radicalized her. Either way, her challenge to traditional attitudes and roles was clear and firm.[20]

Marie Canavarro's views on the subject were ambivalent; but this esoteric Buddhist challenged prevailing conceptions of marriage and the family and even of women's role in the larger society in important ways. She believed that Buddhism was particularly suited to the elevation of women. It was the first religion, she suggested, to put woman "on a level equal to man," and she did her best to translate Buddhist egalitarian principles into action. After she converted she left her grown children and her second husband and set off for Asia to run a school, orphanage, and convent. Canavarro explained several years later that she went, in part, because she felt that the women of India and Ceylon "needed liberation." Perhaps surprised by her own actions, Canavarro wrote to Carus in 1897: "Do you know what I have done, my friend! Loving husband, children, home, affluence, position, friends, *all* have I given for Truth." Her decision to leave family and friends, as expected, brought her some disapproval and difficulties. And those who supported her activities in Ceylon, like Carus, felt that they had to defend her against the charge that she was advocating full-scale rebellion against Victorian social practices. Carus, that religious radical with somewhat mainstream social, economic, and political views, reassured readers of *Open Court*: "She is far from encouraging wives to leave their husbands or mothers to neglect their children. On the contrary she says that she has repeatedly upon certain occasions when women have showed an inclination to leave their homes, insisted that it was their duty to stay with their husbands."[21]

Canavarro transgressed the boundaries of Victorian social norms even more clearly and forcefully, however, when she began her secret "spiritual marriage" to Myron Henry Phelps (1856–1916), the Buddhist sympathizer, New York attorney, and director of the Monsalvat School of Comparative Religion in Maine. Friends and mentors warned against it because both were still married to others during the initial stages of the relationship, but Canavarro decided to ignore the advice and live with Phelps. Although Canavarro eventually agreed to Señor Canavarro's repeated requests for a divorce, she and Phelps apparently never married. They considered taking that step—but not because they believed in the convention. "Personally," she wrote to the happily married Carus, "marriage is a thing quite out of my desires." She also justified her unconventional relationship with Phelps: "But marriage in my opinion is not simply a formula gone over before a Magistrate or Priest—it means to me more. To be bound by mistaken vows—as nine tenths of our civil and religious marriages are—to me is but a licensed adultery." To Canavarro, then, adultery was defined as continuing in an intimate relationship with a man with whom one did not share a "spiritual" bond. Her extramarital relationship with Phelps, on the other hand, was one that embodied all that the intimate relation between women and men should. In her letter of May 1902, Canavarro acknowledged that she had "overstepped the laws of social bondage"; and she seemed resigned to "not defy public opinion." A month later, however, she expressed the defiance that characterized her stand for years: "why need I take upon myself other ties just to please the world!" But, for Canavarro, this defiance of social norms had a price—just as her choice of Buddhism had. She swore Carus to secrecy and even asked him to burn some letters that contained details of her illicit relationship. To avoid public scrutiny and embarrassment, Phelps and Canavarro posed as brother and sister while on a trip to Ceylon, and she felt forced to live in seclusion with Phelps on a farm in Middlesex County, New Jersey. When Phelps left her in 1907, Canavarro continued her self-imposed rural exile at "Bloomfield Farm" and later on a farm in Virginia.[22]

Canavarro and others like her could draw on traditions of social dissent from a number of marginal spiritual groups in nineteenth-century America. Various antebellum utopian religious communities, sometimes for contradictory reasons and with opposing goals, had challenged the Victorian mores about sexuality, marriage, and family. It was probably Spiritualism and Theosophy, however, that provided the theories and examples that sustained esoterics like Canavarro in their oppositional values and practices. Spiritualists frequently had to defend themselves against the charge of promoting free love. Although they denied the charge, there was some substance to it. Many did reject some of the conventional legal and moral codes regulating sexuality, marriage, and the family. They believed, like Canavarro, that those with "spiritual affinities" should be allowed to unite whether or not arbitrary and misguided social conventions prohibited it. Theosophists' concern to balance the masculine and feminine cosmic principles, their devotion to the Mother Goddess, and the models of egalitarian relations among Theosophical leaders also provided resources for those who were discontented with standard conceptions of the status and role of women. A number of the esoteric Buddhists drew on these native traditions, as well as those in Buddhism, to question conventional social practice. But although Euro-American Buddhists challenged the dominant social, political, and economic patterns in various ways, their dissent was most fundamentally cultural.[23]

BUDDHISM'S APPEAL AND CULTURAL DISSENT

This chapter opened with an account of the consequences of Bigelow's conversion to Buddhism. He paid a price, I suggested, for embracing this Asian tradition. But why was he attracted to Buddhism in the first place? Why were others attracted? Bigelow had begun by investigating Japanese gardens and art and had come to the tradition through those aesthetic interests. He apparently was struck by the beauty of the Tendai and Shingon's symbols, art, and rituals. Bigelow entered the tradition under the tutelage of Sakurai—for whom he had intense and enduring affection—and was led deeper, in part, by the powerful influence of his teacher's personality. Other romantics who traveled to Asia, such as Fenollosa, had similar experiences.

Yet Americans came to Buddhism in a variety of ways. Canavarro had the support of an esoteric group with Buddhist influences—the Theosophical Society of Honolulu. Through that group she encountered Dharmapala. Years later she described the immediate circumstances of her turn to Buddhism in this way: "Through connection with this fraternity I came to know a Buddhist from Ceylon. I told him of my long search for truth, and explained that I had not yet found what I had been seeking. He then told me of the Buddha and his long search for truth. He spoke no ill of anyone, and had sympathy for everything that lived. I became interested, and commenced the study of Buddhist scriptures." Although there were Buddhists of Asian descent in Honolulu at the time, Canavarro apparently had no direct experience with them or their rituals. She could not have been drawn, then, by the beauty of the rituals; but, like Bigelow, the charisma of an Asian teacher seems to have played an important role.[24]

Bigelow formally professed his allegiance to Buddhism in a ceremony in Japan after seeing it practiced and practicing it himself among Asian Buddhists; and Canavarro had contact with Dharmapala and, later, other

Buddhists in Ceylon. Yet many Americans who viewed themselves as Buddhists had little or no contact with either Buddhist leaders or institutions. For example, Lum's bold proclamation of the superiority of Buddhism in the 1870s was the result of a purely intellectual encounter with the tradition through Western translations and accounts. Twenty-five years later some converts—like Davis of Vermillion, South Dakota and Clarence Clowe of Bossburg, Washington—still seemed as isolated as Lum had been before Buddhist interest had swelled. Add to these portraits those of sympathizers such as Carus or Edmunds who never fully or formally embraced Buddhism and the difficulties in making generalizations about how and why Americans were drawn to the religion intensify.

It is clear that there were varying levels of commitment, different types of conversion, and assorted sources of attraction. The analysis of the differences between sympathizers and adherents found in chapter two was an attempt to acknowledge the varying levels of commitment. This chapter and earlier ones have described different types of conversion. The typology of Buddhist advocates provides some hints about the sources of attraction among esoterics, rationalists, and romantics. But, in fact, a variety of factors were at work—often in the same individual. Bigelow identified some of the sources of Buddhism's appeal in a letter to a Japanese Buddhist who had inquired about American receptivity to the tradition: "You ask if there are any other persons who would like to study *Buppo* [Buddhism]. I think there would be a considerable number, but not all from the best motives. Some from curiosity. Some from vanity. Some in the hope of learning how to do miracles. And some from the real spirit of kindness and help to others." (Did Bigelow believe that the latter was decisive in his own turn to the tradition?) Other motives—conscious and unconscious, intellectual and nonintellectual, noble and base—could be added to Bigelow's list. For example, a wide range of unconscious psychological factors seem to have played a role. Many proponents—such as Bigelow, Canavarro, and the esoteric Mary Foster—seem to have been drawn, in part, by the charismatic appeal of Asian teachers such as Dharmapala or Sakurai. And Jackson Lears's psychological analysis of Bigelow is persuasive: "In embracing Buddhism, Bigelow preserved his dependent role by leaving a stern father for a benign Ajari." It is also possible to argue—less persuasively I believe—that psychological instability and emotional need were dominant factors in Canavarro's turn to Buddhism. Not only was she drawn by an attachment to Dharmapala, but there is evidence of personality problems before and after her conversion. After her conversion, fellow Buddhists in Asia complained about her "eccentric and sensational disposition," and even she admitted that her behavior might have seemed "erratic." A little more than a decade later a friend reported that Canavarro had been "ill with a complete nervous breakdown."[25]

But most psychological and sociological theories of conversion to alternative traditions—deprivation, brainwashing, developmental, and role theories, for example—have limited interpretive value in this case. They obscure many of the most significant aspects of the sympathetic responses of Victorian Buddhists. Deprivation theories that emphasize the psychological, sociological, or economic deficiencies of the converts tend to overemphasize the pathological motives, presuppose the passivity of the convert, ignore the role of intellectual factors, and overlook the importance of the cultural context. Brainwashing theories are unilluminating for similar reasons. Role theories that focus on the adoption of successive roles in a religious organization are rather unhelpful in understanding Buddhist interest in Victorian America since there were few structured institutions. They are almost completely useless in the analysis of the responses of the thousands of Buddhist sympathizers who stood outside the few Buddhist institutions and even held multiple religious identities.[26]

Theories that emphasize the importance of the developmental tasks involved in the transition from adolescence to young adulthood—such as that of J. Gordon Melton and Robert L. Moore—might help to interpret the conversion of college students such as Davis and his small circle of friends at the University of South Dakota. But they can offer little insight concerning the Buddhist interest found among the majority of nineteenth-century Americans. In contemporary America, as Melton and Moore point out, most persons join new and transplanted religious movements in their early twenties. Nineteenth-century Buddhist adherents and sympathizers, however, did not seem to fit that pattern. If anything, a developmental theory of Victorian Buddhist conversion would have to emphasize the dynamics of the transition from mature adulthood to old age.[27]

Of the available theories of conversion a modified "interactionist" approach that draws on traditions in sociology and anthropology provides the greatest interpretive power. Religions provide frameworks of meaning that orient adherents in the world, and Victorians' turn to Buddhism can be understood as gradual and more or less complete shifts of frameworks of meaning or universes of discourse. Adopting a Buddhist framework of meaning might have involved, for example, interpreting moral action by using categories such as karma, rebirth, and nirvana rather than God, sin, and grace. This adoption of a Buddhist symbolic universe can be understood as more or less complete, because distinct and even contradictory frameworks of meaning can, and often did, function in an individual. Sympathizers internalized a Buddhist framework less completely than adherents. They used it less systematically and comprehensively to interpret ordinary events and cosmic processes. So, for example, a sympathizer might have appealed to the notion of karma to understand moral action and, at the same time, have clung to a conception of the self—as "soul"—that is incompatible with almost all forms of Asian Buddhism.

In this process of appropriating a new framework of meaning, I suggest, psychological dynamics, personal choices, and cultural forces interacted. Such an understanding of the process acknowledges the role of psychological predispositions without transforming the actors into merely passive victims of uncontrollable forces. This is important because all three types of Buddhists tended to be active seekers who were disillusioned with inherited traditions and vigorously pursued other religious options. This approach also restores some of the original complexity by situating individual religious quests in the context of the larger culture. Finally, it permits an appeal to intellectual factors; and, as I will argue, these factors were crucial. If the self-reports and published and unpublished accounts of the tradition are to be considered seriously, the appeal of a Buddhist framework of meaning seems to have been decisive for most.[28]

Exactly how, then, did most late-Victorian sympathizers and adherents come to adopt, more or less completely, a Buddhist framework of meaning? In their frequently cited analysis of a "West coast millenarian cult" (the Unification Church of the Reverend Sun Myung Moon), John Lofland and Rodney Stark offered a list of necessary but not sufficient conditions for conversion to an alternative religious group. As Lofland recognized later, this original model had some limitations. The authors, for example, overemphasized the passivity of the convert. For the purposes of analyzing nineteenth-century American interest in Buddhism, their analysis obscures somewhat the significance of the appeal of a religion's beliefs and values. By modifying their model, however, and conceiving of conversion as a change of frameworks of meaning informed by the interaction of conscious choices, psychological forces, and cultural dynamics, it is possible to point to several necessary but not sufficient conditions for late-Victorian Americans' attraction to Buddhism. Along the way, I will highlight adherents' and sympathizers' role as intellectual nonconformists or cultural dissenters.[29]

First, the potential convert usually experienced some sort of personal crisis that allowed for consideration of a variety of resolutions, secular and religious. The nature and intensity of the crises varied, but almost all the Buddhist followers I have identified seem to have experienced the effects of the broader religious crisis of their age. Carus's struggle was representative in many ways. He was reared in an intensely religious household in Germany. His father, a prominent Protestant clergyman, even became superintendent of the Church of Eastern and Western Prussia. The son planned to become a Christian missionary. That plan, of course, had to be abandoned when Carus discovered that he no longer believed the message he was expected to proclaim. There is some evidence that Carus actually had become "heterodox" when he was quite young: it was at the age of twelve, he told Edmunds one evening in Philadelphia in 1906. In any case, as Soyen noted, Carus "deviated considerably from the traditional Christianity represented by his father." This loss of faith put distance between him and his father. It cost him his teaching position at the military academy of the Royal Saxon Cadet Corps, and it propelled him to seek a more hospitable religious climate first in England and finally, in 1884, in the United States.[30]

The loss of faith tormented him. Like many other disillusioned late-Victorians who privately or publicly mourned the loss of the God and world of their childhood, Carus remained ambivalent and nostalgic. Years after his religious crisis had passed, Carus confessed to a conservative Protestant minister his continuing attachment to the views he felt compelled to abandon: "I grew up in the position which you take and have given it up only reluctantly, in fact, against my own inclinations and intentions. I cannot help cherishing a great regard for these views, and at the same time they possess an allurement that is almost enviable." Many others also felt both the enduring lure of inherited faiths and the shattering force of decisive challenges.[31]

In order for a Protestant worldview—or any other collectively constructed framework of meaning—to function it must be internalized and, implicitly or explicitly, affirmed. It must appear "uniquely realistic" to provide meaning and orientation. Tension in the cultural order is continuous; but there are times when a network of assumptions, beliefs, and values may become especially problematic. Although we must be careful not to make too much of this, since historians have shown an inexhaustible capacity to discern crises in almost every age and culture, a number of scholars have pointed to a significant cultural crisis in Europe and America that peaked around the turn of the century.[32]

The "spiritual crisis" that was part of this larger pattern of unrest and disquietude made Americans more open to alternatives in general and to Buddhism in particular. Just as the numbers of mainline church members in the United States continued to increase steadily, many literate Americans, simultaneously, felt a jolt to the foundations of Christian belief. O. B. Frothingham, the Transcendentalist and Free Religionist, was correct when he suggested in 1872 that "ours is an age of restatements and reconstructions, of conversions and 'new departures' in many directions. There is an uneasy feeling in regard to the foundation of belief. The old foundations have been sorely shaken." Some American observers, especially religious liberals and radicals who followed European intellectual trends closely, could feel the first rumblings earlier in the century; yet a spiritual crisis was easily detectable only after 1870. Within a decade or two, however, even those huddled in the shelter of an ethnic or regional subculture were at least dimly aware that there was something going on out there.[33]

What was going on? A confluence of social and intellectual forces was shaking the foundations of "orthodox" Christian faith. To change the metaphor, the foundations were being dissolved by the acids of biblical criticism, the new geology, the new biology, anthropology, and comparative religion. The accuracy of the biblical accounts of the age, origin, and nature of the human and nonhuman world was challenged by Lyell's geology, Darwin's biology, and the Higher Criticism. Continuing a process that had begun at least as early as the seventeenth century, the explanatory power of the doctrine of God also seemed less and less clear. Although uncertainties and gaps remained, there seemed to be a naturalistic explanation for events and processes that traditionally had been the province of a personal creator, sustainer, and consummator of the universe. The three-story universe seemed to collapse, and with it, belief in a personal God and individual immortality. A poem published in an 1892 issue of the *Twentieth Century*, a magazine dedicated to political and religious radicalism, put it succinctly:

> Science has made to disappear
> The three-floored house we used to fear!
> Heaven above and hell below,
> With earth between to suffer woe.[34]

The Christian churches of the last quarter of the century also had to respond to the social and economic problems produced by industrialization, urbanization, incorporation, and immigration. The waves of immigrants, for example, eroded the numerical dominance of Anglo-American Protestants and increased ethnic and religious pluralism. Yet it was not just this limited sense of pluralism but also an increasing awareness of the diversity of cultures and religions outside the West that presented a decisive intellectual challenge to Protestant faith. Building on work that had begun earlier, American, British, and continental students of anthropology, comparative linguistics, comparative mythology, and comparative religion challenged the uniqueness, finality, and supernatural origin of Christianity. Of course, few scholars in these fields saw their primary task as debunking Christian claims; nonetheless, this was one of the effects of their study. At least since 1784, when Hannah Adams acknowledged the "great and sad truth" that Christians were a minority in the religious world, a handful of Americans had struggled with the problems presented by an awareness of nonliterate and Asian religions. In the late nineteenth century the issue of how to defend traditional claims about the distinctiveness and superiority of Christianity moved toward the center of the American theological discussion.[35]

The late-Victorian conversation about the historical relation and relative merits of Buddhism and Christianity grew out of the wider spiritual crisis and, at the same time, contributed to it. As I will indicate in greater detail in the next chapter, sympathetic accounts often emphasized the parallels between the founders of both religions and their teachings. The discovery of these apparent continuities was part of the confluence of forces that made Christianity problematic for many. Yet, in turn, the attention to other traditions and the search for parallels also had been driven by the spiritual restlessness set loose in Anglo-American culture by the religious crisis. The force with which some Christian apologists denied doctrinal parallels and historical influence is, to a degree, a measure of how threatened some leaders felt. Christian responses to these threats varied, of course. Some Christian apologists accommodated the faith to the new intellectual developments. Some did this by demonstrating the "scientific" character of the tradition. Others used Freidrich Schleiermacher's approach: they championed a noncognitive view that located religion in "feeling" or "sentiment" and not in an assent to propositions about the nature of things. Some fiercely and consciously resisted all modifications. Many others, in the pews and in the pulpits, went on as if the new science, comparative religion, and biblical criticism were as insubstantial and undiverting as a warm wind whispering through a revivalist's tent in Kentucky. Yet, as I have suggested, a number of persons abandoned inherited faiths. There was an openness to visions—secular and religious—that repudiated some or most of the beliefs and values of Protestantism and Victorianism.

There was a second necessary but not sufficient condition for turning to Buddhism. The individual must have been inclined to seek and find a solution to the crisis in a religious community of one sort or another. As I have hinted, a number of the spiritually disillusioned turned to secular visions and remained in more or less comfortable forms of agnosticism or atheism. Promoters of Buddhism recognized that not all of the disillusioned were open to religious resolutions. In 1899, for example, C. H. Currier addressed his public appeal for Buddhist converts in a Boston newspaper to others who were "dissatisfied with current theology, and therefore, [could] find no place in the church life of to-day, yet still believe in personal endeavor and *association* in the pursuit of righteousness." Currier received at least one reply—from Carus. Carus promised to send some Buddhist literature, and he closed the letter by "wishing [Currier] the best success and satisfaction in [his] work." Carus could not become a Buddhist; but he encouraged those, like Currier, who wanted to spread Buddhism in the West and revitalize it in the East. And, whatever his views about joining institutions, he certainly sought to resolve his spiritual crisis by appealing to religions—Eastern and Western.[36]

Some Buddhist apologists thought that the spiritual crisis led directly and inevitably to Buddhism. Thomas Wilson found the elevated status and increased popularity of Buddhism understandable, even inevitable: "it is not at all surprising that Buddhism should get the attention of thinking people in America. The thinkers of all classes of American people are and have been for many years drifting away from the currents of Christian theology and church dogmatics, and very naturally into a sea of unrest and uncertainty." Buddhism, he believed, provided the only safe refuge for those bobbing in that sea of doubt. Yet, it is important to remember, Victorians sought resolution of their crises in a variety of forms. The turn to Buddhism was not nearly as inevitable as Wilson would have it.[37]

For those who still wanted to be religious in some way there were a number of alternatives. Some romantics, such as Lodge and Bigelow, were drawn by the aesthetic appeal of Roman Catholic practice. Lodge read *The Imitation of Christ* and felt the pull of Catholicism. He called the tradition "the most religious sect in all Christendom." Although Bigelow had an unpleasant encounter with a priest late in life that seemed to reinforce some negative perceptions, he too apparently found Catholicism appealing. He found it attractive enough, in fact, to ask a Japanese Buddhist advisor about the possibility of dual religious identity: "If all religions have the same goal, why is it better to study one rather than another? If a man takes the *kai* of more than one religion, what happens! Suppose I received the sacraments of the *Romakyo* [Catholicism], would it interfere with my *Buppo* [Buddhism]?" Those with esoteric tendencies and interest in mental healing or psychic phenomena might have chosen exclusive devotion to Spiritualism, Swedenborgianism, New Thought, or Christian Science. For others, philosophical idealism "provided the means to make individual religious commitment compatible with science and with rigorous philosophical reasoning." Some of the disillusioned with rationalist inclinations found in the idealist philosophy of Hegel or others support for their religiousness—even if they remained outside the boundaries of all religious organizations. As I have suggested, other rationalists drifted toward radical groups like the Free Religious Association, the Ethical Culture Society, and the "free churches" of various sorts. Among the communities on the liberal fringes of American Christianity, the Unitarians and Quakers were among the most attractive; but they still had too many doctrinal commonalities with Protestantism to draw those unable to accept, for example, belief in a personal God or immortal soul. Among the available non-Christian religions, Islam, Judaism, and Baha'i had limited appeal since these traditions also affirmed personal theism and other beliefs these seekers rejected. Vedanta Hinduism and Buddhism, especially after the Parliament of Religions of 1893, seem to have been the most serious alternatives among the world religions.[38]

Although this may seem obvious it deserves notice: potential Buddhists also needed the requisite money, leisure, and skills to pursue a religious option that met their needs. Disillusionment, in a sense, was a privilege. They need not have had the wealth, time, and education of Bigelow, but they needed some minimum resources. If discontent and the search for alternatives were not limited only to the elite, they did require at least enough literacy and leisure to read books and magazines and to attend lectures and meetings.

Finally, the potential sympathizer or adherent obviously had to have some encounter, direct or indirect, with Buddhist beliefs and practices; and those who came to identify with the tradition more or less completely found some resolution of their spiritual crisis in that Asian religion. What I have asserted to this point can now be argued: many found their crisis fully or partially resolved by Buddhism's alien intellectual scheme. Henry Clarke Warren, the American scholar of Pali Buddhism, was not a follower, but he could feel the attraction. "Now a large part of the pleasure that I have experienced in the study of Buddhism has arisen from the strangeness of what I may call the intellectual landscape. All the ideas, the modes of argument, even the postulates assumed and not argued about, have always seemed so strange, so different from anything to which I have been accustomed, that I feel all the time as though walking in fairyland." Those who accepted Buddhism did not always use this language of enchantment, but they too noted its doctrinal distinctiveness. Most important, they reported that it was this that drew them. They were attracted by elements in Buddhism's worldview that challenged fundamental convictions of Protestant Christianity and the dominant Victorian culture with which it was so intimately linked. The perception that a Buddhist framework allowed for egalitarian relations between the sexes and fostered benevolent relations with the nonhuman world drew some. The intellectual sources of Buddhism's appeal also varied, to some extent, according to the three types. Esoterics—like Anna Eva Fay, the Spiritualist—often were lured by the impression that Buddhism was compatible with occult beliefs and practices. For Fay this meant that Buddhism's doctrine of reincarnation provided the "logical cause" for the spiritual manifestations from the other world. Rationalists were drawn especially by Buddhism's personal moral code. Strauss, for example, suggested that "the part of Buddhism which exercises the greatest attraction on those who begin to study is its sublime ethics." However, for most public apologists—and presumably many of those who left no written record—two particular cultural-intellectual factors were crucial: they believed that they had found in Buddhism not simply an inspiring ethical tradition but, most important, a "scientific" and tolerant one as well.[39]

Unaware of, or unimpressed by, the attempts of liberal Protestants and others to reconcile Christianity with tolerance and science, Buddhist apologists portrayed themselves as cultural dissenters compelled to reject an inherently unscientific and intolerant religion and culture and moved to embrace Buddhism by the distinct advantages of its alien "intellectual landscape." Insofar as they misrepresented the beliefs and values of a significant number of their contemporaries by failing to acknowledge that they shared their commitment to "science" and tolerance, these apologists seemed to be following a pattern that R. Laurence Moore has noticed. An "outsider" group often "invents" a dominant culture to set itself against in order to help create and maintain its sense of cohesiveness and identity. As I argue in the next chapter, Buddhist apologists often rejected the dominant framework of meaning in the name of commitments—to science and tolerance—that were shared by a number of their contemporaries. Yet their cultural dissent also was genuine and significant in many ways. To be more precise, then, they did not so much "invent" the religion and culture that they rejected as they exaggerated discontinuities and obscured continuities.[40]

With regard to a few of the most basic beliefs and values of the most influential religion and culture, the discontinuities were real enough. After all, Buddhist advocates were not suggesting only minor revisions in the Judeo-Christian worldview. They did not merely add or subtract books to the canon but completely challenged the authority of the Bible and the revelation that it embodied or proclaimed. They did not only question the chronology of the biblical accounts of creation but rejected the very notion of creation in favor of a Buddhist picture of eternal cycles of existence regulated by impersonal forces. They did not argue about whether Augustinian or Pelagian, Calvinist or Arminian views of human nature were more adequate, but challenged the predominant Western notion that the self is substantial and static. They did not worry about whether the Judeo-Christian God was unitary or triune, immanent or transcendent, but challenged the very notion of a personal creator and sustainer of the universe. In fact, the tradition seemed to contradict so much that was familiar that late-Victorian Christian critics—such as secretary of the American Board of Commissioners for Foreign Missions, Nathaniel George Clark (1825–96) continued the hoary Western tradition of wondering aloud whether Buddhism qualified as a religion at all.[41]

So, too, Buddhist apologists' claims about the intolerance of the Christian tradition and Victorian culture had some basis in historical reality; and their self-understanding as dissenters against the reigning attitudes and policies toward religious, ethnic, and cultural "outsiders" seems generally accurate. Protestant apologists might argue that the Inquisition, the European religious wars, the maltreatment of African Americans, Native Americans, Chinese Americans, Mormons, Catholics, and Jews violated the norms of the Christian tradition and Victorian culture. Few, however, could deny that that tradition and culture had been associated with intolerance, exclusion, and violence. There was an important sense, then, in which Buddhist advocates had not "invented" the intolerance of the tradition and culture. They challenged hard realities—the exclusivism of conservative Christians, the condescension of liberals, and the consistent pattern of maltreatment of those who fell outside the boundaries of Anglo-Protestant Victorian culture.[42]

Buddhism and Tolerance

The prevailing perception that Buddhism provided a better theoretical foundation for inclusivistic theology and enjoyed a better historical record of peaceful relations with foreign traditions and cultures, then, was a major source of its appeal for the spiritually disillusioned of the age. Europeans had systematic contacts with non-Western religions at least as early as the Renaissance voyages of discovery and subsequent Catholic missions to Asia. This increasing awareness of religious diversity, together with a pervasive sense of weariness at the sectarian strife that had burned across Europe during the Age of Religious Wars (1559–1689), combined to help stimulate the Enlightenment search for a common "essence" of religion. Moderate and radical Enlightenment thinkers alike hoped that a reduction of religion to the barest essentials could bring liberty and tolerance just as the overemphasis on dogma had provoked coercion and discord.

The official American conception of the relation of church and state, of course, had been conceived in this theoretical context: the framers of the Constitution wanted to institutionalize toleration. The region that ultimately became the United States had been the site of greater religious diversity and liberty than most European nations of the time; yet the New World settlers, before and after the drafting of the Constitution, were hardly without sectarian strife. In fact, it is only a slight exaggeration to suggest that American religious history in the seventeenth and eighteenth centuries was a series of disputes and persecutions, separations and exiles. Recent studies have shown that the colonies pulsed with greater pluralism than most students of American religion had realized; but it is still true that, in many ways, significant religious diversity did not begin to appear until the mid- and late nineteenth century as waves of immigration brought, for example, Irish, Italian, and Polish Roman Catholics, Eastern European Jews, and even Chinese and Japanese Buddhists. The diversity of Christian sects—and in the late eighteenth century the handful of Deists—hardly approached the extent of religious and ethnic pluralism that emerged a century later.[43]

American Buddhists' commitment to inclusive theory and tolerant practice was, in part, a protest against nineteenth-century Anglo-Protestant harassment, persecution, and exclusion of "outsiders" in the United States. Yet the intellectual and moral difficulties went deeper than that: many questioned reigning attitudes toward those outside the West and began to wonder if there were any secure grounds for preferring one tradition over another. Many Buddhist sympathizers felt that the intellectual difficulties that accompanied exclusivistic positions were insurmountable. And the loss of solid theoretical grounds for absolutizing any particular religion made Christianity's reputed history of persecution and coercion seem even more reprehensible. It made the discovery of tolerant religious forms seem even more morally urgent.

The perception was based to some extent on a romanticized Buddhism, but almost everyone seemed to agree that the religion was inclusivistic and tolerant. This image of Buddhism recurred throughout the nineteenth century. Mid-Victorian religious liberals and radicals such as Child, Clarke, and Johnson had presented it that way. Late-Victorian scholars agreed. Even late-Victorian Christian critics reluctantly concurred. The nineteenth-century rediscovery, translation, and publication of the edicts of King Asoka (ca. 272–232 B.C.E.) played an important role in sharpening the Western perception of Buddhism as especially inclusive and tolerant. Several of the stone inscriptions of this influential Buddhist emperor of India emphasized the need for acceptance, even celebration, of religious diversity and called for peaceful relations among nations. Rock Edict XII, for example, includes this passage: "The faiths of others all deserve to be honored for one reason or another. By honoring them, one exalts one's own faith and at the same time performs a service to the faith of others. By acting otherwise, one injures one's own faith, and also does disservice to that of others." It is easy to see how this passage, and others, might increase Buddhism's reputation as a gentle tradition.[44]

Whether or not they had heard about Asoka's policy of benevolence toward non-Buddhist traditions and states, many found the theoretical foundation for and historical record of tolerance they sought in Buddhism. Just as many Enlightenment intellectuals were drawn to the Confucianism of the Jesuit interpreters of the seventeenth and eighteenth century by its apparent instantiation of the tolerant "natural religion" they championed, many late-Victorian advocates—esoterics, rationalists, and romantics—were attracted by Buddhism's apparent openness to other traditions.

In his long poem "East and West," for instance, the romantic adherent Fenollosa not only called for toleration but envisioned "the future union" of Eastern and Western religions and cultures. Hearn, too, valued tolerance highly. In his letters he condemned "missionary jackasses." It was not that he rejected Christianity completely: he was angered by the destructiveness, arrogance, and intolerance of Christian missionaries. Hearn often commented on the gentleness of Buddhism and the Japanese, and he seemed to believe that Buddhism's record in this regard was superior to Christianity's. Yet he did not think that that Asian tradition provided the only theoretical foundation for mutual respect. For example, in a letter to a Japanese young man wrestling with religious questions, Hearn drew a distinction between religions and sects: "A religion is a moral belief which causes men to live honestly and to be kind and good to each other. A sect is made by a *difference* of belief as to what is true religious teaching." Christianity had assumed myriad sectarian forms; but pristine Christianity, like Buddhism, is tolerant and respectful to those of other faiths. Missionaries and others, he implied, have not been preaching or practicing authentic Christianity. Hearn closed by reminding the young man who was leaning toward Christianity that "a true gentleman respects *all* religions." Bigelow, to offer another example, also valued tolerance; and he found it most clearly in Buddhism. Overlooking Nichiren's approval of coercion, he suggested that it was "characteristic of Buddhists not to press or force people's interest; never to interfere with a man who doesn't come to them first and ask for help." And he relayed to a Japanese Buddhist that he believed that tolerance—even inclusivity bordering on syncretism—was crucial for the continued vitality of religions: "The form of belief that must live longest is the one which can *include*, not *exclude*, the others."[45]

Buddhism's reputed tolerant spirit seems to have been an even more important source of its appeal for rationalists and esoterics. Continuing patterns inherited from the Enlightenment, rationalists demanded a religiousness that would grant diverse traditions their due and support amiable relations among religions and nations. Carus, for instance, deplored "sectarianism" so much that he was unable to join any tradition— even the tolerant Buddhism that attracted him so strongly. Many who have embraced tolerance have failed to embrace the intolerant, but Carus was different. In his work as editor of *Open Court* he would not allow any disrespect or inequity—even toward conservative, exclusivistic forms of Christianity. Carus told one prospective author, for example, that his article would be published only if he would "omit some words in the beginning, which seem . . . too hard on orthodox believers."[46]

Carus even reprimanded Asian and American Buddhists when he thought that they failed to show the charity and benevolence their tradition and its founder demanded. In response to one American Buddhist's harsh criticism of his *Gospel of Buddha* Carus exhorted his correspondent to change his tone: "if you confess the doctrine of Buddhism, you will in the surroundings in which you live not show the irritable mood of a dogmatic fanatic, for nothing is more foreign to the doctrines of the Tathagata [i.e., the Buddha]." Even Dharmapala, who let his seething hostility to Christianity and its missionaries boil over at times, received a similar rebuke. Dharmapala's printed announcement for his new Buddhist organization seemed too openly hostile: "I am very sorry at the tone in which the note has been written, and I can only wish that the expressions which are attributed to you may soon be forgotten. The charges which are made in these remarks against Christianity are not true, and even if they were true they ought to be expressed in a different way. Buddha certainly would not have used this language."[47]

Like other sympathizers and adherents, Carus extended the principle of tolerance beyond mutual respect. He tended toward eclecticism, even syncretism, and yearned for a "cosmic religion of universal truth." In response to Dharmapala's urgings to be more forceful and unambiguous in his public pronouncements about his commitment to Buddhism, Carus sent a reply that revealed his eclecticism and appealed to the tolerant principles of Buddha, Asoka, and the World's Parliament of Religions all at the same time:

> I have said repeatedly that I am a Buddhist, but you must not forget that I am at the same time a Christian in so far as I accept certain teachings of Christ. I am even a Taoist. . . . I am a Israelite [*sic*]. . . . In one word, I am, as it were, a religious parliament incarnate. To say that I am a Buddhist and nothing else but a Buddhist would be a misstatement, and, indeed, it would be un-Buddhistic, it would be against the teachings of Buddha himself. In this sense we read in Ashoka's twelfth edict: "The beloved of the gods honors all forms of religious faith."

Buddhist tolerance, in Carus's interpretation, was so complete that it condemned exclusive devotion—even to Buddhism itself.[48]

Dyer Lum, another rationalist, was no "Parliament incarnate." But he approvingly quoted a passage from Clarke's extremely popular *Ten Great Religions* in which that Unitarian who argued for the superiority of Christianity in most regards had praised the Asian tradition: "Buddhism has made all its conquests honorably, by a process of rational appeal to the human mind. It was never propagated by force, even when it had the power of imperial rajahs to support it. . . . In this respect it can teach Christians a lesson. . . . The Buddhists have founded no Inquisition; they have combined the zeal which converted kingdoms with a toleration almost inexplicable to our Western experience." C. T. Strauss, who even proposed an artificial international language to promote cooperation, also recommended Buddhism because of its gentle spirit. Mentioning the edicts of India's King Asoka specifically, Strauss reminded the readers of his survey that although the tradition had spread throughout Central and Eastern Asia, followers had not spilt "a single drop of blood for the propagation of the doctrine."[49]

Esoteric Buddhists also drew on some of the same traditions of anti-sectarianism, rejected Christianity's theory and practice, and found Buddhism's reputed inclusivism and tolerance attractive. Like many Enlightenment thinkers and rationalist Buddhists, esoterics believed that there was an identifiable "essence" of religion, and they believed that this essence could form the theoretical basis for interreligious unity and international peace. Esoteric apologists, however, sometimes presented a different account of that common core. Like Madame Blavatsky in *Isis Unveiled*, Buddhists associated with the Theosophical Society, for example, tended to conceive of this essence as an aggregate of ancient esoteric doctrines. The theoretical foundation for their religious eclecticism and tolerance was the view that this ancient core of esoteric wisdom had formed the ground of all the historical religions and would form the foundation of the nonsectarian religion of the future.[50]

Whether or not this position was the basis of their antisectarianism, many esoterics were drawn by Buddhism's tolerant spirit. Vetterling, for example, advocated Buddhism "because it does not propagate itself by cheat, torture, sword, and fire." Christianity, by comparison, had used all these methods. Olcott, too, used harsh language to condemn the abuses of Christian missionaries and reminded his Asian and Western readers about the edicts of Asoka and Buddhism's record of benevolence: "So far as we know, it has not caused the spilling of a drop of blood." This Theosophical leader praised Buddhism as "a religion of noble tolerance, of universal brotherhood, of righteousness, and justice" that had no taint of "selfishness, sectarianism, or intolerance."[51]

Like Olcott, Edmunds also condemned the abuses of "narrow orthodoxy" and associated Buddhism with gentleness and tolerance. In his diary, he praised the Quaker tradition that he inherited and never completely abandoned by pointing to its "Buddhist elements"—such as "meekness." In fact, wherever he found these qualities Edmunds tended to link them with Buddhism and its founder. In an earlier entry, for example, he confided to his diary that Charles R. Lanman, with whom he corresponded, was "a splendid fellow:" "He is full of Buddha, non-resistance and charity." Edmunds also hoped for a synthesis of East and West and foresaw the emergence of a world culture and universal religion. He never granted Buddhism—or any other religion or sect—his exclusive allegiance; but the tradition appealed to him, in part, because it seemed to be capable of broadening Christianity and fusing cultures. For example, this sympathizer explained his acceptance of the position as American representative of the International Buddhist Society in these terms: "I have taken this Rangoon representativeship so as to be useful and justify my existence. I am not a Buddhist, but a philosopher who believes that a knowledge of Buddhism will liberalize Christianity and bring the ends of the world together."[52]

Canavarro did not expect Buddhism to "liberalize" Christianity or blend cultures, but she did value interreligious tolerance. In her explanation of her conversion to Buddhism, Canavarro confessed that she had rejected Christianity, in part, because Christians had been "too unyielding and ununited." In fact, the search for an inclusive and tolerant framework seems to have been a crucial factor in the spiritual journey that led her from Roman Catholicism to Theosophy, Theravada Buddhism, Baha'i, and finally Vedanta Hinduism. In a sense, Canavarro, like some others of her day, converted to inclusivism and tolerance. Although different strands within these religious groups offer various interpretations of the relation among the religions—essentialist inclusivism, fulfillment inclusivism, and even approximations of a pluralist position in some Vedanta Hindu traditions—all in some way affirm the partial truth of other faiths. There is evidence that her perception that these groups were inclusive was crucial for her exploration of each. I already have cited Canavarro's mention of tolerance in connection with her Buddhist conversion. In her address to Baha'is in Chicago in 1904 she described the motives for her turn from Catholicism to Theosophy and from Theosophy to Buddhism in a similar way: "So I came into contact with Buddhism through studying on Theosophical lines, and it touched very keenly into my soul. Why? Because it was so universal that it took in every thing and every one and all religions." A related concern seems to have been operative in her later exploration of Baha'i: "But in this religion, you see, there is the unity of all religions. The greatness of it is that the truths of all religions are combined and brought together and put into this religion." Finally, in the concluding chapter of her 1923 spiritual autobiography, Canavarro described her attraction to Vedanta Hinduism by quoting this passage from a pamphlet by Swami Paramananda, whom she met in California: "Vedanta does not interfere with any man's natural way of thinking, but furthers his growth by lending him a sympathetic and helping hand wherever he stands. It accepts all the Sacred Scriptures of the world and bows in reverence before all saviours and prophets. It believes that the same Gospel of Truth is preached by all, the only difference is that of language and not of the essential meaning. There is, therefore, no room for proselytizing in Vedanta." Her formal affirmation of Buddhism in 1897, then, was united with her previous conversion to Theosophy and her subsequent explorations of Baha'i and Vedanta by a common rejection of the exclusivity and intolerance of Christianity and an affirmation of the inclusivity and tolerance of these spiritual paths.[53]

Buddhism and Science

In 1899 Carus described the slant of the journal he edited to the great French historian of religion Albert Réville: "We advocate in the Open Court what we term 'The Religion of Science,' which means that scientific truth itself will be the last guide of a religious conception of mankind." And, as I indicated in chapter three, Carus identified this "religion of science" explicitly with Buddhism. In one letter to Dharmapala he put it simply and boldly: "In my opinion Buddha's intention was nothing else than to establish what we call a Religion of Science. 'Enlightenment' and 'Science' are interchangeable words." Probably the most crucial source of Buddhism's appeal in nineteenth-century America was the perception that the tradition was more "scientific" than other available religious options. Although the force of this attraction was strongest for rationalists like Carus, all three types of sympathizers and adherents were drawn to Buddhism in part because it seemed more adaptable to, for example, the findings of the new geology, the new biology, and the new psychology.[54]

Many rationalists and esoterics took from Theravada Buddhism, or a Westernized version of it, a new foundation for religiousness that was based on either an indifference to metaphysical issues or, more characteristically, an understanding of "God" as the impersonal animating force of the cycles of existence. Romantics who were drawn to Japanese Mahayana traditions with more elaborate cosmologies also found in Buddhism an understanding of ultimate reality that appeared to be compatible with evolutionary theory. The metaphysical monism of Tendai, Shingon, and Zen suggests that reality is ultimately one; but the conventional realm in which we all live is governed by karma, the moral law of cause and effect. This karmic "law" was interpreted by many as one of the natural forces that regulate the evolutionary process. Late-Victorian Buddhist advocates of all perspectives, then, found it easy to blend the reigning Darwinian or Spencerian evolutionism with Theravada or Mahayana frameworks—and in particular with the common Buddhist doctrines of karma and samsara— and emerge with a picture of a universe driven ever upward by individual choice and impersonal law. Buddhism also seemed compatible with the latest findings in the emerging "science" of psychology. Recent developments in that field seemed to point to a processive, dynamic, nonsubstantialist notion of the self, and so a number of advocates came to view Buddhist psychology as more scientific than its substantialist Christian counterpart.[55]

The apologetic advantage and potential appeal of Buddhism's apparent compatibility with the natural and behavioral sciences was recognized and exploited by those who popularized and promoted the tradition in Europe and the United States. For example, Edwin Arnold was friends with a number of the most famous British scientists of his day, and this Buddhist popularizer proclaimed that "between Buddhism and modern science there exists a close intellectual bond." Several of the Asian Buddhist speakers at the Parliament of Religions, for instance Soyen and Dharmapala, noted their traditions' compatibility with science. When Dharmapala spoke to an overflow crowd that included "the best known and most intellectual residents" of Oakland in the same year, he even managed to suggest that the scientific attitude would lead to tolerance: "Intolerance has been rampant and bigotry supreme. Now, thanks to the researches of Huxley, Darwin, and Tyndall and the great scientists of the century, man is in a position to think; is freed from dogma and theology and is prepared to shake the hand of the brethren of Asia." The Reverend Shuye Sonoda of the San Francisco Buddhist Mission, in his first lecture on Buddhism to a Caucasian audience, already emphasized Buddhism's scientific character. C. H. Currier's public appeal for converts drew on the same theme, and so did one published invitation to join the Dharma Sangha of Buddha, the Caucasian Buddhist group in San Francisco: "Its doors are open to all . . . who are earnestly seeking the truth based on the scientific laws of life; as set forth in the Dharma of the Lord Buddha."[56]

The appeal of the "scientific" character of Buddhism was strong among rationalists. In 1875, just as the force of evolutionary theory was beginning to have its strong and belated impact in the United States, Lum looked into the future and envisioned a day "when modern science shall have cut the connections by which Christian life is fed" and so it will "wither and die." Yet Buddhism, animated by its scientific doctrines, will be left with life pulsing through its veins. Wilson, using a different metaphor, implied that those Americans who were "drifting in a sea of uncertainty" because of the Victorian spiritual crisis clutched at Buddhism, in part, because of its empirical and scientific character. Moore, the physician and chemistry instructor, expressed the views of many Buddhist followers in an article published in 1903. She recounted the personal and cultural crisis—the "mortal wound" that Western theism had received "when Darwin and Spencer launched the unassailable doctrine of physical evolution"—and she described its resolution in Buddhism's "scientific" doctrines. In fact, filled with a sense of the vast interpretive power of its worldview, Moore even suggested that the "obvious harmony between the new dogma of science and the teachings of Buddhism marked an epoch in the history of human thought."[57]

As I have indicated, the emphasis on science also was dominant and clear in the work of rationalist sympathizer Paul Carus. Before the Parliament of Religions he had suggested that Confucius, Zarathustra, Moses, Buddha, and Christ were all "prophets" of the "religion of science." After Soyen and Dharmapala emphasized Buddhism's compatibility with science in their addresses, Carus elevated the Buddha to the position of "the first prophet of the religion of science" and proclaimed that his tradition was more "scientific" than Western alternatives. In fact, Carus argued that "a conflict between religion and science is impossible in Buddhism." Buddhism's rejection of a personal deity and a substantial soul in favor of an impersonal cosmic principle and a dynamic, nonsubstantial self made the tradition more consistent with the latest findings in biology and psychology. Its empirical and pragmatic bent also made the tradition attractive to Carus and other rationalists since, as Carus wrote, a Buddhist must accept only propositions derived from personal experience or those that have been "proved to be true by careful scientific investigation."[58]

But Carus recognized that not all Buddhists or all Buddhisms were equally scientific. Over the years, he believed, even Buddhism had become tainted by some "superstitious" beliefs and practices—such as the Sinhalese reverence for relics of the Buddha. Carus found himself repelled by the impurities of popular Buddhism and, at the same time, attracted by the scientific doctrines of "pure Buddhism." He could not identify with the tradition if it meant accepting its superstitious beliefs and practices, and he could not affiliate with any other since none was more scientific than Buddhism. At the same time, he could not form a new sect or church. It inevitably would repeat the mistakes of the past. Instead, Carus envisioned a "purification" of all existing religions in the flame of science.

Even some forms of Buddhism needed this. Carus hoped, then, that by burning off the residue of elements that were incompatible with science—and tolerance—a single "cosmical religion" would emerge from the fire. That religion would require no intellectual sacrifice or moral compromise. Its contours, no doubt, would resemble "scientific" Buddhism in many ways.[59]

The aesthetic appeal of Mahayana sects was more important for romantics, but they also seem to have been drawn by Buddhism's compatibility with "modern science." Fenollosa eagerly studied Spencer's philosophy—with its attempt to apply evolutionary theory to all areas of human life—as an undergraduate at Harvard, and he later promoted that system in his lectures at the University of Tokyo. But as I noted in the previous chapter, it was Lafcadio Hearn who was an especially devoted student of Spencer's thought, and he was attracted by Buddhism's parallels with Spencer and "science." Unlike Fenollosa, Hearn was so devoted to Spencer's views that he only could accept Buddhism insofar as it was aligned with the philosopher's system. Spencer's views, for Hearn, were more comprehensive and even more authoritative than Darwin's. Spencer's evolutionary scheme, he wrote in a letter in 1895, provided the framework for understanding natural and spiritual evolution while Darwin, Huxley, and Tyndall added only "small detail." Darwin's theory of natural selection helped to explain "one factor of evolution." It was Spencer who discovered the "cosmic law" of evolution "governing the growth of a solar system as well as the growth of a gnat."[60]

But even Spencer's illuminating system and the "details" added by natural science had limitations. Science tells us, Hearn believed, that the solar system will undergo recurring cycles of evolution and dissolution. Yet if we rely only on science, and Spencer's system, we are left perplexed and disquieted. What is the ultimate meaning of the cycles of existence? In the search for meaning and consolation, Hearn turned to Asian religions and especially Buddhism. "But again," Hearn sighed in another letter, "in the eternal order of things, what is the use? What is even the use of the life of the solar system—evolution and dissolution—re-evolution, re-dissolution, forever more? Really Buddhism alone gives us any consolatory ideas on the subject." It is not clear from this exactly how Buddhism consoles, but a letter on the same subject five years later offers some hints. Buddhism, and Hinduism too, provide meaning and comfort by suggesting that humans have some control over natural and moral evolution and that the ultimate conquest of the good is possible:

Why a cosmos must be dissipated into a nebula, and the nebula again resolved into a sun-swarm, [Science] confesses that she does not know. There is no comfort in her except the comfort of doubt,—and that is wholesome. But she says one encouraging thing. No thought can utterly perish. As all life is force, the record of everything must pass into the infinite. Now what is this force that shapes and unshapes the universes? Might it be old thoughts and words and passions of men? The ancient East so declares.

Hearn was drawn, then, by the notion that through the positive force of human thoughts and desires the "rest eternal" that all humans seek can be secured.[61]

But, for Hearn, Buddhism not only adds meaning and provides consolation. Buddhist cosmology also has the advantage that it harmonizes with a "scientific" worldview grounded in Spencer's scheme. In one letter Hearn noted the continuities between Spencerian views of the evolution and dissolution of the solar system and Indian Buddhists' "ancient theory of cycles." "Buddhism and Spencer, before the Ultimate," he asserted, "stand upon the same ground." And, Hearn continued, if he were to take his faith "ready made," as his correspondent had suggested, instead of blending Spencer with established religions in an idiosyncratic mix, then he would prefer Buddhism. Similar references to Buddhism's unique correspondence with science and the appeal its "scientific" character held for him are scattered throughout Hearn's letters and books. Before he left for Japan, for example, Hearn confessed to one of his correspondents that he believed that "science gives an harmonious commentary" on the Buddhist notions of karma, discipline, no-self, and enlightenment that "it refuses to the more barbarous faith of the Occident." Later, in a more systematic and mature interpretation of Buddhism, he continued this insistence that the tradition was uniquely compatible with science. He argued that "some Buddhist ideas do offer the most startling analogy with the evolutional ideas of our own time." Hearn even confessed that it was because Buddhism was "a theory of evolution" and so was compatible with Spencer's philosophy and modern science that he came to have "a more than romantic interest" in the tradition.[62]

The romantic Bigelow, who trained as a physician, apprenticed as a researcher, and even authored scientific articles, also affirmed the compatibility of Buddhism and science. In fact, the appeals to "modern scientific research" are frequent in his major published work on Buddhism, and an evolutionary framework was central to his interpretation of the tradition. In *Buddhism and Immortality*, Bigelow offered a sustained conceptual analysis of human consciousness leading to a brief sketch of the Tendai and Shingon sects. He distinguished between the spiritual and material realms and between spiritual and material evolution. He leaned on the authority of Darwin's theory of natural selection and continually used language taken from the biological sciences to describe spiritual as well as material development. He described the process of spiritual evolution as one in which the individual emerges from "unconditioned consciousness" and "move[s] up the scale of evolution guided by natural selection." Next the individual progresses to an intermediate step of celestial existence, which all other religions mistake for the zenith of development. Finally, the enlightened Mahayana Buddhist is able to return to the unconditioned consciousness from which all things emerged.[63]

Although it might seem that esoterics would have been uninterested in the claims that Buddhism was especially compatible with science, this was not the case. As scholars have noted, through the Renaissance occultism often was coupled with science; and the connection was still strong in the writings of eighteenth-century authors like Swedenborg. The scientific revolution of the seventeenth century, however, began the long process of severing science and esotericism. By the time Lyell's geology and Darwin's biology stirred controversy the process was almost complete. Nonetheless, whether or not their beliefs would be judged compatible with the findings of contemporary science, many non-mainstream groups in this period, including those influenced by esotericism of one sort or another, appealed to "science" to legitimate their perspectives. Those devoted to, for example, Spiritualism, Theosophy, or psychic research wanted to call their doctrines "scientific." For them, interest in contact with deceased relatives or occult masters and investigation of supranormal psychic phenomena was consistent with the positivist's quest for facts and the scientist's search for proof. Participants in these groups often confessed to worshipping at the altar of science and told of being filled with the spirit of "scientific" inquiry. They required "empirical" verification for beliefs regarding the supranatural world and humanity's place in it. This tendency is evident, for example, in Marie A. Walsh's preface to *The Human Aura* by A. Marques and in that pamphlet as a whole. Marques, the head of the Theosophical Society in Honolulu, had delivered a lecture in San Francisco in 1896 on this occult topic. Walsh recommended the published version of Marques's lecture in this way: "Today we like theories, but we demand facts,—and facts this author gives. Dr. Marques claims no authority save that of experience,—experience confirmed by repeated experiments, the results of which have been subjected to critical analysis. It has been my privilege to see a little of that method followed in this study by Dr. Marques, and I can truly say the personal equation has been carefully eliminated, and a severe *scientific* judgment passed upon every observation." Esoterics of various sorts claimed they did not reject science but only those narrow interpreters who, in their view, distorted it into a perspective that obscured all truths that transcend the material realm.[64]

It is not surprising, then, that esoteric Buddhists pointed to parallels between Buddhism and science—although sometimes they directed their readers' or listeners' attention to "occult science" and not the mainstream science of Darwin. For example, the British Theosophist A. P. Sinnett used the language and authority of "science," "the Darwinian law," and "evolution" in his occult interpretation of the tradition. Canavarro, who told

Carus that she had collaborated with Marques on *The Human Aura*, confessed that she first had sought a solution to her spiritual crisis in science. Canavarro claimed she had systematically studied chemistry and astronomy for three years in order to reconcile religion with the cruelty of the law of the survival of the fittest. After she had found some resolution of her own crisis in the teachings of the Buddha, she announced to an audience in San Francisco that Buddhism was "more in accord with modern scientific thought of the law of cause and effect." She also revealed her esoteric tendencies in that lecture, however, by suggesting that the "scientific" investigation of this law by means of physics, biology, and psychology might lead into "occult science."[65]

One esoteric Buddhist sympathizer who found himself led into occult science was Edmunds. Despite overwhelming evidence, he observed, "orthodox science" had unfairly ridiculed investigators of the occult. Edmunds himself wholeheartedly accepted reports of spirit communications and psychic phenomena. He also offered accounts of his own occult experiences. For example, one of his diaries contains an uncharacteristically long entry about a séance he attended in Philadelphia on a winter morning in 1906. It had been a bit more than two decades since his last encounter with the spirit world, he explained, but he was "so low and depraved [that] week that [he] felt like Saul at Endor, when the Lord spake no more." The medium, Samuel C. Fenner, received two dollars to provide answers to three questions Edmunds asked his deceased father and two dead friends. He received answers from the other world and even unsolicited support for the authenticity of the maligned Madame Blavatsky. Overall, Edmunds judged the séance a success: "For a séance with a stranger of moderate intellect, this is quite good." Following the teachings of the British spiritualist F.W.H. Meyers, Edmunds also believed that sleep was "more profound" than waking; and he repeatedly recorded his interpretations of the communications received in his dreams.[66]

Edmunds offered an esoteric interpretation of Buddhism that emphasized the compatibility of the tradition with the "laws" of occult science as well as orthodox science. In a brief dialogue called "A Sunday Noon in the Thirtieth Century" Edmunds expressed his own views through the voice of one character. Like that character, Edmunds "leaned to the idea that Buddhism had the doctrine of Evolution in embryo." He stressed Buddhism's correspondence with the "occult branch" of science in an article published in the *Proceedings of the American Society for Psychical Research*. In that piece he interpreted the Buddha as a seer who provided "another case of lifelong trance-phenomena." In fact, Edmunds believed that the Buddha's record compared favorably with that of the Swedish mystic Swedenborg, whom he admired so much. Gautama experienced forty-five years of "open communication with the unseen world" while Swedenborg enjoyed only twenty-seven. Buddha—he argued by citing passages in Pali scriptures—even transported himself to the spiritual world to confer with angels.[67]

Like Edmunds, Olcott believed that occult science had substantiated the claims of spiritualists, telepaths, and others who had experienced esoteric phenomena; and he too was disappointed by "the prejudiced disbelief of Western scientists." "Forty-six years of modern mediumistic phenomena have not yet taught Western scientists the principles of the law of spirit intercourse," Olcott complained, "nor those of psycho-physiological abnormalism." More directly relevant, Olcott's section on "Buddhism and Science" in his *Buddhist Catechism* reveals the interesting mingling of "respectable" science with occult views and practices that was characteristic of esoteric Buddhists. He began the section by alluding to the compatibility between Buddhist doctrine and "the law of evolution" and implying that Christianity was inferior in this regard. Yet he then moved on to discuss auras, hypnosis, supranormal powers such as retrospection and foresight, and he presented Buddhist parallels to these occult phenomena. The implication throughout the section was that Buddhism is more "scientific" than competing religious views. Euro-American sympathizers and adherents of all types agreed.[68]

I have argued that, despite many other differences among them, esoterics, rationalists, and romantics all were drawn to Buddhism by the reports of its greater compatibility with science and tolerance. In the name of commitments to science and tolerance, they denounced fundamental beliefs and values of the Protestant-Christian framework and the Anglo-American Victorian culture. Apologists often portrayed themselves as cultural dissenters who were attracted to Buddhism by the unique advantages of its alternative framework of meaning. In fact, their dissent was genuine and significant in many ways. Yet if we listened only to their impassioned protests, we might overlook—as they and their contemporary critics did—the important ways in which these Buddhist advocates, even in their most forceful denunciations, also were consenters. They shared a great deal with the scholars, travelers, and critics who participated in the late-Victorian conversation. In the next chapter, then, I begin to explore the nature and extent of their cultural consent.

FIVE

STROLLING DOWN MAIN STREET

Cultural Consent and the Accessibility of Buddhism

In a letter written in September 1897 Paul Carus reported his desire to see an American artist create a visual image of the Buddha to express and supplement that verbal picture which was being sketched in books, articles, and lectures. He believed that this might contribute to the conversation and promote the religion. Carus also had some ideas about how such a portrait might be executed: "I thought that especially painters could make quite a hit if they succeeded in giving a fixed type to the conception of Buddha, not according to Japanese and Chinese style, but according to more modern *American* notions." He did not elaborate further. Perhaps Carus envisioned a starched-collared, businessman Buddha painted in the tradition of sober Victorian portraiture. Perhaps he had in mind something like John Quincy Adams Ward's sculpture of the Protestant preacher, Henry Ward Beecher. Ward had portrayed Beecher as a respectable and serious, if slightly portly, public figure. For readers with an iconoclastic temperament, other images might come to mind: a Frederic Remington Buddha astride a horse on the western plains or an "American Gothic" Buddha clutching a pitchfork on a Midwestern farm. Carus's suggestion might seem odd—and might inspire playfully exaggerated images. Yet he was serious. And his call for a tangible representation of an American Buddha revealed an inclination shared by many other apologists—to harmonize Buddhism with some fundamental features of the leading religion and dominant culture.[1]

This inclination is common among leaders and followers of successful new and transplanted religious traditions. One sociologist, Rodney Stark, has argued that there are several conditions that determine the success of new religious movements. The first two are relevant here. In order to achieve some popularity and stability they must, first, "retain *cultural continuity* with the conventional faiths of the societies in which they appear or originate." Groups, of course, must offer some features that appear distinctive if they are to attract followers. If nothing new is offered, why would the potential convert abandon the old framework of meaning? At the same time, if the contrast is too great, conversions will be few and institutions will be weak. Successful movements, Stark also proposed, "maintain a *medium* level of *tension* with their surrounding environment; are deviant, but not too deviant." You do not have to be a sociologist to notice this pattern. In an insightful series of articles on one new religious movement of the nineteenth century, Christian Science, Mark Twain predicted that Mary Baker Eddy's group had "a better chance to grow and prosper and achieve permanency" than any other "ism" of his day. Among Christian Science's many advantages was its continuity with the dominant religion and wider culture. "The past teaches us," Twain suggested, "that in order to succeed a movement . . . must not claim entire originality, but content itself with passing for an improvement on an *existing* religion, and show its hand later, when strong and prosperous."[2]

Twain had included "Buddhism" and "Blavatsky-Buddhism" in his long list of groups, or "isms." Euro-American Buddhism, finally, did not succeed as Mormonism, or even Christian Science, did. Unless we count the Theosophical Society, Buddhism failed, for example, to leave stable and lasting institutions. Yet Buddhist advocates often explicitly or implicitly highlighted parallels, as Twain's and Stark's observations suggest any skillful apologist might. Buddhist apologists, and probably many of the sympathetic thousands with no public voice, seemed to yearn for a tradition that was different, but not too different. They wanted to dissent—but not too much. Defenders of the tradition, then, rejected some elements of the dominant religion and culture, but they did so within the context of a broader consent. The harmonizing impulse was not always conscious or predominant, but, I argue in this chapter, it was discernible in the published and unpublished writings of most American apologists. Most seem to have been drawn to the tradition by its discontinuities with Christianity and Victorianism. More specifically, the intellectual advantages of its allegedly scientific and tolerant worldview attracted many of them. Yet unrecognized elements of consent surfaced even in their most vigorous denunciations and most vocal proclamations. It was the pervasiveness of the commitment to science and tolerance in the culture that gave their opposition its persuasive power. Once attracted to the tradition, they seem to have been sustained in their dissent by the discovery of other real or imagined points of religious and cultural continuity. Buddhism's attractive founder, personal ethics, "Protestant" spirit, "God-idea," modified "immortality," and self-reliant tone made the Asian tradition seem more familiar and accessible. Christian opponents and academic scholars often still focused on Buddhist distinctiveness. For potential converts, however, the perceived continuities made partial or complete identification with the tradition seem less eccentric.[3]

CONSENT IN DISSENT: SCIENCE AND TOLERANCE

Even when apologists' cultural opposition was most clear and strong it often was in the name of commitments—to science and tolerance—that were shared by a much wider range of their contemporaries than they realized or acknowledged. As I noted in the last chapter, the exclusivist theory and intolerant practice of Victorian culture and Protestant religion were undeniably real. Apologists, however, usually failed to acknowledge that others in the culture had called for more inclusive theologies and more tolerant policies toward those who fell outside Anglo-Protestant culture. In many ways, liberals and radicals outside the mainline denominations (e.g., Unitarians) led the way in the search for greater openness; but some mainline Protestant leaders granted some truth and value to non-Protestant traditions and advocated tolerance toward "outsiders" of all sorts. Having won the battle against a Calvinist anthropology, for example, the proponents of the liberal "New Theology" of the 1870s and 1880s faced the problem of how to deal with the "heathens." These New England liberals in the mainline denominations appropriated the notion of an ethical, caring deity to help construct a theology that would allow them to acknowledge that those outside the tradition had some hope of salvation. During the 1890s, just as interest in Buddhism was peaking, Protestant liberals not only debated the status of non-Christians but focused on the more fundamental issue raised by the new theological developments and the increased awareness of non-Christian religions: What is the justification for the traditional claim that Christianity is unique and "final"? A number of liberal Protestant ministers—like the Baptist William Newton Clarke (1840–1912)—tried to formulate a persuasive understanding of Christianity's uniqueness and superiority and, at the same time, acknowledge truth and value in other traditions. A rhetoric of inclusion often coexisted with expressions of Protestant triumphalism, ethnocentrism, and racism. This can be seen in late-Victorian attitudes toward Asian and European immigrants; and it is clear, for instance, in the exhibits and proceedings of the Columbian Exposition of 1893. Yet Buddhist apologists' call for greater openness and benevolence toward religious and cultural outsiders was not as unique and unprecedented as they often argued or implied.[4]

If there were some grounds for questioning the authenticity and force of Protestants' expressed commitment to tolerance, Protestant leaders' affirmation of science was more clear and consistent. In turn, Buddhist sympathizers' and adherents' rejection of Christianity as inherently and inevitably "unscientific" seems less fair. Their self-perception as cultural dissenters in this regard seems more exaggerated. There is some truth to the claim that a Westernized Theravada Buddhist framework harmonized more easily with the theory of evolution, but there were a number of others in the culture—for example, Unitarians, Spiritualists, Christian Scientists, Swedenborgians, Ethical Culturists, and mainline Protestants—who also said they wanted a tradition that was compatible with the latest scientific developments.

Many evangelical and liberal modernists in the mainline Protestant denominations—men such as Henry Ward Beecher, James McCosh (1811–94), Lyman Abbott (1835–1922), and Newman Smyth (1843–1925)—accepted, even celebrated, the new developments in biology and geology. For example, in an 1882 article, Beecher acknowledged the anxieties of his more conservative Christian contemporaries; but he urged them to embrace the new science. "The dread of Darwinian views is sincere," he observed, "yet a secret fear prevails that they may be true. . . . Instead of dreading the prevalence of the scientific doctrine, Christian men should rush toward it with open arms and exultation." Some, aware of the many assertions to the contrary, not only explicitly argued that Christianity was adaptable to the new science, but that it was inherently more scientific than Buddhism. In one article for the *Andover Review*, William M. Bryant dismissed the supposed conflict between modern science and Christian doctrines by suggesting that the only conflict was "between narrow dogmatic theologians on the one side and equally narrow skeptical scientists on the other." Further, he claimed, if the disillusioned are anxious to find a scientific tradition, they need look no farther than their own backyards. Buddhism is, in truth, based on "superstition." On the other hand, Christianity is "the religion of Reason, and as therefore involving within itself the very soul of true scientific method, is not merely aided by but is also itself in reality a mighty aid to the advance of science."[5]

Many conservative evangelicals also believed that their doctrines were "scientific." Carus once reported in a letter that he found less opposition to science among those "in the most orthodox circles" than he had encountered among some allegedly liberal Unitarian clergymen. This assessment seems distorted, but conservative Protestants did share the tendency of the age to legitimate their beliefs by describing them as "empirical" and "scientific"—even when their doctrines did not seem to reflect the conclusions of the latest theories in biology and geology. As George M. Marsden has noted, conservative evangelicals of the late nineteenth and early twentieth century "stood in an intellectual tradition that had the highest regard for one understanding of true scientific method and proper rationality." Their conception of science was grounded in the principle of careful observation and classification of the facts that was championed by the seventeenth-century philosopher Francis Bacon, and their philosophy was articulated in terms of the Scottish Common Sense Realism that had been so influential in antebellum America and continued to have influence among Evangelicals during the Gilded Age. In one sense, then, their claim was that Darwin's theory was not "scientific" and "empirical" enough. It was, by their principles, bad science. Even the Evangelicals who battled so fiercely against the perceived threat of Lyell's geology and Darwin's biology seemed to participate in the common celebration of the "scientific." Insofar as Buddhist advocates challenged the notions of a personal God and a substantial self in the name of science, then, they were appealing to widespread commitments. They were cultural consenters.[6]

RELIGIOUS PARALLELS AND CULTURAL CONTINUITIES

Apologists were consenters in other ways as well. Even more consistently and effectively than their mid-Victorian precursors, they often focused on elements in Buddhism that seemed to be continuous with contemporary developments in Protestantism and essential themes in Victorianism. They did so either because they were unaware of the evidence of divergencies; or, more likely, they intentionally or unintentionally ignored or de-emphasized that evidence.

Influences, Parallels, and "Protestant Spirit"

Between approximately 1879 and 1907 American readers encountered impassioned discussions about parallels and possible historical influence between Buddhism and Christianity in the pages of a variety of periodicals. The emphasis on continuities was not unprecedented, of course. That had been the general tendency of Western interpreters, with a few exceptions, until the middle of the nineteenth century. But that interpretive pattern usually had reinforced—not challenged—Western religious and cultural assumptions. Buddhists, interpreters had suggested, were like other heathens—or, only a bit better, like Roman Catholics. In either case, the reports hardly questioned traditional notions about the uniqueness or finality of Christianity. And, until the 1870s or so, few had used the alleged parallels to support claims about the equality or superiority of Buddhism. Many did this in the late-Victorian era. Participants in the later discussion also felt somewhat less compelled to explain Buddhism's distinctiveness. A firm sense of doctrinal difference carried over from the mid-Victorian period; yet it was the parallels with Christianity that now seemed to require more scrutiny. In these ways, the late-Victorian discussion had changed.[7]

This slightly altered conversation about similarities was stimulated, in part, by popular sympathetic accounts of Buddha and Buddhism. Arnold's poem *The Light of Asia* and a few other seminal works emphasized the correspondences between the two founders and their traditions. Some Christians and scholars minimized the continuities—and so the need to explain them. Other participants in the discussion reluctantly acknowledged or triumphantly proclaimed essential similarities. Some even entertained arguments about the possibility of historical influence. Sometimes interpreters attributed similarities to coincidence, but both Buddhist and Christian apologists explained the supposed parallels by implying or asserting that one tradition had influenced the other. They disagreed, of course, about the direction of the influence. Some, like Carus, suggested that it had gone in both directions. Critics like the American Protestant Samuel Henry Kellogg refuted or discounted the evidence about possible Buddhist impact. Sometimes he and others even countered with speculations about the possibility of Christian influence on Buddhism. On the other hand, Ernest von Bunsen's *The Angel-Messiah of Buddhists, Essenes, and Christians* (1880), Rudolf Seydel's *Das Evangelium von Jesu in seinen Verhältnissen zu Buddha-sage und Buddha-lehre* (1882), and Arthur Lillie's *Buddhism in Christendom; or Jesus, the Essene* (1887) argued for Buddhist influence on early Christianity through the Essenes or by some other means. One American commentator, Felix Oswald, even suggested that the resemblances were understandable since Jesus had been a Buddhist! Oswald was certain that comparative study of Gnostic-Christian and Buddhist scriptures soon would show conclusively that "the Prophet of Nazareth was a Buddhistic emissary, and preached his gospel in the name of Buddha Sakyamuni." His claim helped to intensify the dispute, and other claims—more and less eccentric than his—were seriously debated.

In fact, a number of prominent European and American scholars had entered the discussion—including Emile Burnouf, Müller, Rhys Davids, Renan, Monier-Williams, and Hopkins. And, as Christian critics reminded their opponents, the weight of scholarly opinion seemed to be against those who claimed significant parallels and direct influence. A few apologists continued to pursue parallels and influence, and a noted American scholar of Asian religions still felt the need to address the issue as late as 1918. Yet by 1906 or so interest in the question of parallels and contact had waned. Many had come to agree with Albert Schweitzer's conclusion that although some indirect influence through the wider culture was "not inherently impossible," the hypothesis that Jesus' novel ideas were borrowed directly from Buddhism was "unproved, unprovable, and unthinkable."[8]

Before it had waned, the debate about religious parallels and historical contact seems to have exerted influence on the religious position of some American readers. A number of Christian critics complained that the reports had "furnished the opponents of Christianity with a weapon of attack." As I indicated in the previous chapter, for some literate Americans the discovery of apparent parallels, if not direct influence, was part of the confluence of intellectual and social forces that precipitated their own spiritual crisis. The claims about historical influence were more difficult to support, but even if direct contact could not be proven, the parallels still seemed to call into question traditional assertions about the uniqueness and superiority of Christianity. In this way the alleged correspondences between the two founders and traditions helped lead some away from Christianity. They also drew some of the spiritually disillusioned closer to Buddhism.[9]

Not all reports of continuities, however, made the religion more accessible to the disillusioned: the longstanding tradition of noting parallels between Buddhism—often Tibetan Buddhism or "Lamaism"—and Roman Catholicism continued to some extent. For example, Fernand Grénard's account of his travels in Central Asia reminded a new generation of American readers about the reported continuities. Some of the earlier sources that had reinforced and spread the notion—e.g., Father Evariste Regis Huc's *Travels in Tartary, Thibet, and China*—were still in print after the turn of the century. Lydia Maria Child, who had consulted Huc's book soon after it appeared in the United States in 1852, later tried to use the reports for positive purposes. She pleaded for more benevolent treatment of Chinese immigrants by pointing to parallels between Buddhism and Catholicism. She suggested that the Chinese Buddhists were no more "foreign" than Irish Catholics and that both "John Chinaman and Patrick O'Dublin have an equal right to the free exercise of their religion under our impartial laws." Child's appeal, needless to say, did not have much influence. Her questionable strategy of defending the Chinese and their religion in Anglo-Protestant America by comparing them to the Irish and theirs probably had something to do with that.[10]

Few other sympathetic interpreters tried to use Catholic parallels for positive ends. Protestant critics and travel writers who continued to underscore ceremonial or institutional similarities did so to degrade and dismiss Buddhism—and Catholicism. Catholic leaders themselves—or at least those who could turn themselves away from the more pressing needs of the immigrant American church—did not like the talk of parallels and influence at all. Their strategies differed, but most Catholic participants in the late-Victorian discussion denied Buddhist influence, challenged reported parallels, and reasserted Christian—i.e., Catholic—superiority. Merwin-Marie Snell tried to shift the discussion by ignoring Catholic correspondences and stressing Protestant ones with Pure Land Buddhism. Even the few Catholics who granted some Catholic parallels used them to advance their cause among their Christian contemporaries. Here too the correspondences were used as a weapon in intrareligious combat. In an article for the *American Catholic Quarterly Review* Darley Dale asserted that the similarities indicated that only Catholic, and not Protestant, missionaries could achieve any success in converting the Tibetans.[11]

American Buddhist apologists usually ignored, deemphasized, or denied these continuities with Catholicism. Their motives are unclear. Perhaps they were revealing their own biases or modifying their message to the Protestant cultural context. It is clear, however, that they continued a contrary tendency that had been firmly established by both sympathetic and hostile interpreters earlier in the century: they highlighted the continuities with Protestantism. Europeans such as Müller and Americans such as James Freeman Clarke had stressed the "Protestant" elements in Buddhism. For example, Clarke acknowledged the "external" resemblances to Roman Catholicism, but he argued that "the internal resemblance is to "Protestantism." "Buddhism in Asia, like Protestantism in Europe," Clarke claimed, "is a revolt of nature against spirit, of humanity against caste, of individual freedom against the despotism of an order, of salvation by faith against salvation by sacraments." Clarke's and Müller's works continued to be read and cited in the late-Victorian period, and some of the scholars who rose to prominence in the later period—such as Rhys Davids—continued this hermeneutical tradition. They pointed to the correspondences between the historical Buddha and the Protestant reformers and between Buddhism—especially Indian and Sinhalese forms—and Protestantism.[12]

The impression that Buddhism embodied a "Protestant spirit" seems both correct and incorrect. On the one hand, it would be easy to show the errors Clarke and others made and the complexities in Buddhism they missed. At the same time, the Buddhism that Americans received—from Dharmapala and the Maha Bodhi Society, for example—already had been "Protestantized" to some extent. Several scholars of Buddhism in Sri Lanka actually have used the term "Protestant Buddhism" to describe the activistic and individualistic tradition that emerged under Western influence during this period. Yet it is not crucial to determine whether—or to what extent—Americans actually encountered a "Protestant" Buddhism. The intended and unintended consequences of the prevailing interpretation are more relevant to the central concerns of this chapter: To what extent were apologists consenters? How did the suggestions of continuities affect their religious positions? Clarke himself did not suffer from the more virulent strain of anti-Catholicism that infected large numbers of nineteenth-century Americans, but by playing on the widespread anti-Catholic sentiment his interpretation functioned to make Buddhism seem less alien and less worrisome for many. Directing attention away from Catholicism could only help the case for Buddhism. It only could help among alienated Protestants, unaffiliated Americans who had been stained with some trace of anti-Catholicism, and raging rationalists who had rejected all forms of "superstition" and challenged all constraints on autonomy. A few intellectuals with romantic inclinations might have been drawn by the aesthetic power of medieval Catholic culture, but most who considered Buddhism seriously welcomed these suggestions of continuity with Protestantism and the wider Victorian culture with which it was linked.[13]

Appealing Founders and Noble Ethics

It was not only the assertions and hints about broad continuities between Buddhism and Protestantism that helped make the tradition more approachable. Among the other more specific religious and cultural parallels that were reported, the supposed similarities between the biographies and ethical teachings of the two founders were crucial. These reports might have provoked interested reactions of all sorts—hostile, curious, excited— in almost any period. They had special force and significance in the late nineteenth century. As James Stalker, the Scottish author of a life of Jesus, noticed in a retrospective essay published in 1900, "No characteristic of the theology of the second half of the nineteenth century has been more outstanding than its preoccupation with the life of Christ." Liberal Protestant leaders—such as Albrecht Ritschl (1822–89) in Germany and William Adams Brown (1865–1943) in America—had directed the attention of the pious in the pews to the historical Jesus. They also had defined Christianity's uniqueness and defended its finality by pointing to the moral example and ethical principles of its founder.[14]

Many acknowledged, in Edmunds's phrase, "the hard biographical facts." There seemed to be a number of parallels. Edmunds and his contemporaries, for example, pointed to "their fasting and desert meditation; their missionary charge; their appointment of a successor; their preaching to the poor; their sympathy with the oppressed," It is not surprising that sympathetic accounts—like Edmunds's comparative scriptural study or Arnold's poetic life of the Buddha—stressed the biographical correspondences. Yet even Christian critics and academic scholars sometimes acknowledged both the familiarity and attractiveness of the canonical Buddha. For example, Hopkins explained the surprising spread of Buddha's negative religion by pointing to the character and charisma of its founder. "It was the individual Buddha that captivated men," he claimed; "from every page [of the Buddhist scriptures] stands out the strong, attractive personality of this teacher and winner of hearts. No man ever lived so godless yet so godlike. . . . His voice was singularly vibrant and eloquent; his very tones convinced the hearer, his looks inspired awe." Despite his claims to scholarly objectivity, Hopkins's Christian biases surfaced occasionally. Perhaps he genuinely was moved by the scriptural portrait of the Buddha. Or perhaps, like mid-Victorian Christian critics, he reluctantly offered his positive interpretation of the Buddha because he felt compelled to provide some explanation of the expansion of the tradition in Asia. In either case, this interpretation, too, was reassuring. The offer of an appealing founder, with striking similarities to Jesus, was comforting even to iconoclasts who had rejected the Christian God and heaven and had willfully ignored the latest twists and turns in Protestant theology. What one scholar has noted with regard to the disillusioned in Britain applies also to the American context: "The universal testimony of Victorian agnostics is that they preserved great affection and reverence—accompanied by a wistful nostalgia—for the figure of Jesus long after they had given up belief in Christian metaphysics."[15]

The nobility of the Buddha's ethical teachings also was acknowledged by a variety of participants in the discourse—Buddhist apologists, Western scholars, and Christian critics. This too had seductive power because it corresponded with patterns in Protestant thinking. Late-Victorian Protestant leaders often supported the usual claims to Christian finality by pointing to Jesus' superior ethical teachings and their benevolent effects. I will consider the significance of the nineteenth-century tendency to evaluate religions in terms of their ability to create and sustain just and effective social, political, and economic forms in the next chapter. Here it is important only to note some of the ways in which Buddhist personal ethics made it more approachable.

As I suggested in the last chapter, rationalists, and most advocates, found Buddhism's lofty moral code appealing. Apologists' concern for ethics, of course, did not set them apart from their contemporaries. A number of late nineteenth-century religious groups—including Unitarians, Ethical Culturists, Reform Jews, as well as mainline Protestants—placed ethics at or near the center of their framework of meaning. But the special advantage of Buddhism, discussants boasted or complained, was that it was able to reject Christian doctrines that some had found incompatible with logical reasoning and scientific investigation—a personal God and an eternal soul—yet still provide a sound basis for morality. Even before Kant, Western thinkers had argued for the *moral* necessity of God and immortality. For centuries Westerners had believed that these doctrines were indispensable supports for the moral life. For this reason even the most radical Enlightenment thinkers had been reluctant to give them up. Yet Buddhism seemed to offer new possibilities. One Christian critic who worried about the "peculiar purpose" that Buddhism had come to play in the late-Victorian theological and ethical discussion accurately described the implications of the "discovery" of its lofty personal ethic:

> There was one obstacle which the non-believer could not overcome, namely, the impracticability of destroying, together with religion, morality itself. . . . Without religion, that is, without the belief in a God and a future state, how would it be possible to maintain morality? . . . Behold in the East, a practical demonstration of such a condition of things! Here was a religion Atheistic or Agnostic, and even Nihilistic, and behold, its moral code is excellent, its tenets have been promulgated over more than half the world.

Even some Christian critics acknowledged, then, that Buddhism's acclaimed personal code allowed the spiritually disillusioned to reject fundamental components of Christian doctrine and remain both religious and moral. In fact, like the liberals in the mainline Protestant denominations, Buddhists could stress personal morality.[16]

I have asserted that Buddhist defenders of the tradition were able to reject God and self, but it was more complex than that. In this regard too their dissent actually was more partial and tentative. The peculiarities of their consent and the ambiguities of their dissent were discernible not only in their affirmation of science and tolerance and their embrace of a "Protestant" tradition with an appealing founder and attractive ethics. They were discernible in the residue of theism and individualism found in the Buddhist perspectives of some of the most vocal and influential apologists. The affirmations, conscious and unconscious, of these key elements of late-Victorian culture indicates that they were more a part of their cultural milieu than their emphasis on the unique advantages of Buddhism's distinctive system might suggest. This also meant that sympathetic American readers could encounter a Buddhism that seemed more like an intellectually satisfying modification of a familiar tradition than a bracing contradiction of all that Victorians held most dear.

THEISM AND INDIVIDUALISM: THE AMBIGUITIES OF DISSENT

Most Christian antagonists and some Western scholars continued to use a rhetoric of negation to describe Buddhist doctrine. One writer for the *Methodist Review*, J. Wesley Johnston, managed to squeeze more than twenty-five negations, with a few repetitions, into one paragraph of an article. Consider just these portions: "In Buddhism there is neither God nor heaven, neither prayer nor pardon, neither faith nor providence, neither resurrection nor future. It is without one ray of light or gleam of hope from beginning to end." "For in Buddhism," he continued—now beginning to repeat himself, "there is no personal God, no gracious divine Spirit, no atoning Saviour, no overruling providence, no place of prayer, no absolution from sin, nothing of blessing, nothing of help, or comfort, or guidance, or strength." Just warming up, Johnston complained that "the purest and holiest affections wither at its touch, for with Nirvana personal consciousness ends, and when consciousness ends all love passes away." Of all the negations noted by unapologetically hostile and allegedly neutral interpreters, four stand out. As in the earlier period, Buddhism, above all, seemed to challenge theism, individualism, activism, and optimism. I consider the latter two in the next chapter. In the remainder of this chapter I focus on the discourse about God and self.[17]

The view that Buddhism contradicted traditional notions of God and soul was repeated by Christian apologists—like Johnston—and academic scholars with overt Christian allegiance—for instance, Monier-Williams. They sometimes disagreed about whether Buddhism was agnostic, atheistic, or pantheistic. Almost all critics agreed, however, that Buddhism denied the notion of a personal creator. They also concurred that the doctrines of no-self and nirvana—the latter still interpreted by many critics as "annihilation"—meant that the tradition was unable to speak about a soul that could enjoy eternal rewards or punishments. So Buddhists seemed unable to affirm two crucial components of Victorian individualism—belief in the substantiality and immortality of the self.[18]

This picture of Buddhism prompted several questions. First, Christian discussants continued to ask whether Buddhism was a religion. R. M. Ryan in an 1885 article expressed a common view when he declared that Buddhism, because of its rejection of theism and individualism, was not a religion but a "system of philosophy" and "a sorry one at that." Second, like their mid-Victorian predecessors, they also continued to be perplexed by the success of Buddhism in Asia. A new generation of Americans asked the question that Müller and others had posed: how could a religion that seemed to challenge much that Westerners believed about the desires of humans, the character of ultimate reality, and the nature of religion have attracted so many adherents? The Baptist minister Henry M. King formulated it this way: "It seems unaccountable that a religion (if, as I have said, it can be called a religion) which ignores the being of a personal God, and denies the continued existence of the individual soul, . . . and whose highest destiny for man is Nirvana, the extinction of conscious being, the infinite emptiness of the non-self, should have been accepted by so many millions of people." Some still pointed to the founder's religious and social reform, but explanations varied widely. Whatever the sources of its appeal in Asia, American Christian interpreters claimed to be unaffected by its charms. They continued to criticize the religion—if it could be called that at all!—for its rejection of basic verities.[19]

Some Western scholars offered accounts that Christians took as supporting their own negative interpretations. The prominent British scholar Rhys Davids and the American Orientalist Hopkins agreed that Buddha himself was atheistic or agnostic. Hopkins continued to present Buddha's teachings about the self and its ultimate destiny as "nihilistic" since the founder allegedly envisioned no state of bliss after death. Some Christian critics also welcomed Oldenberg's hints that the doctrine of nirvana logically should lead to a nihilistic view as confirmation of their views.[20]

Yet Oldenberg's interpretation—as well Rhys Davids's, Hopkins's, and most of these later Western scholars—actually was much more complex than Christian antagonists granted. They showed a greater appreciation for the complexity of the issues and the multivocality of the sacred texts. After 1881 more scholars clearly and consistently began to distinguish among the beliefs of the Buddha, his early followers, and the later traditions. More acknowledged the diversity of the Buddhist tradition and the variety of answers provided to Westerners' questions. This new approach is evident in the work of leading scholars of the Anglo-German school that dominated Buddhist Studies during this later period (Rhys Davids and Oldenberg) and in the work of Americans who followed their lead (Hopkins and Warren). This more subtle approach to the old debates about Buddhism's atheism and nihilism is evident, for example, in Oldenberg's analysis of the meaning of nirvana. He found three attitudes toward nirvana in the Pali canon. First, there was Buddha's dismissal of all such metaphysical concerns. Second, there were the implicit suggestions by the writers of the sacred texts that some early followers believed that nirvana ultimately meant annihilation. Finally, there were hints that others rejected the nihilistic interpretation. Scholars directly or indirectly associated with this Anglo-German school tended to assume or affirm the primacy and purity of the Pali scriptures and the Theravada tradition. Yet they also acknowledged that finding a single Buddhist answer to questions about the character of ultimate reality or the destiny of the self was made difficult, if not impossible, by the plurality of perspectives in the later Hinayana and Mahayana texts and traditions.[21]

Occasionally a Protestant leader granted this diversity of answers in Buddhism. For example, Marquis Lafayette Gordon, the missionary to Japan, quoted a passage from Rhys Davids's Hibbert Lectures on Buddhism that pointed to plurality within the tradition. He then went on to argue that it is necessary to speak of "Buddhisms" and not "Buddhism" when inquiring about the teachings of the tradition. In fact, Gordon suggested, great "heterogeneity" exists among the teachings of the various groups that have claimed allegiance to the Buddha. Some, for example, seem to have been theistic and others atheistic. The confusion about the meaning of Buddhism has resulted, Gordon argued, from a failure to qualify characterizations of its teachings about God, self, and other matters. In another article that appeared earlier in the same year (1886), Gordon discussed Japanese Pure Land Buddhism, and he acknowledged that this popular form of Mahayana Buddhism—with its affirmation of "grace," "faith," a supernatural being (Amida), and a paradise (Amida's Pure Land)—"promises most to needy men." He even hinted that it coincided with Western notions of religion. Yet Gordon retrieved with one hand what he offered with the other: although this more "Protestant" Pure Land tradition is "Buddhism's best gospel," it is inauthentic since it does not represent the views of its founder.[22]

Christian critics, then, either failed to acknowledge the diversity within the Buddhist tradition or, like Gordon, used the lack of unanimity among its sects and schools for their own apologetic ends. On the other hand, these new developments in scholarship provided American Buddhist apologists with the resources to offer a more sophisticated response to their Christian critics and, more important, less jarring interpretations of Buddhism. These interpretations allowed them some measure of consent. Of course, many apologists—especially rationalists—forcefully and fully disavowed all uses of the terms "God" and "soul" and "immortality." But some felt comfortable adapting this language to a Buddhist context. Many discovered—or constructed—a religion that seemed compatible with elements of the reigning theism and individualism. They constructed this Buddhism by attributing negative or disturbing features to a form of the Asian tradition that they were willing to sacrifice for a final apologetic victory: Another form of Buddhism does have those features, but not the sect I follow! Or, leaning on the increased sophistication of late-Victorian scholarship, some found partial parallels and located comforting continuities.[23]

The "God-Idea" in Buddhism

The confusions that have accompanied Western discussions of whether Buddhism is "really" atheist or not have derived from a lack of appreciation for Buddhist diversity and a lack of clarity in the formulation of the question. Which form of the tradition and which "god" are we speaking about? The Buddhist scholar Edward Conze's approach to this issue seems as judicious as any. He suggested that Buddhism had been indifferent on the question of a personal creator, but that it left open the possibility of belief in a Godhead, conceived as impersonal or suprapersonal. It also tended to encourage, or sometimes tolerate, devotion to a myriad of suprapersonal beings.[24]

Some late-Victorian scholars, as susceptible as anyone else to intellectual fashion, reflected the interests of antimetaphysical, positivist thinkers of the age. These interests entered the conversation as scholars stressed Buddhism's antimetaphysical, even atheistic, impulses. Rhys Davids's work is the clearest example. As Edmunds complained in his later years, Rhys Davids "wrote when Victorian agnosticism was at the crest of its wave, and could not resist the temptation of making poor old Buddha the great agnostic of antiquity." Edmunds, who felt comfortable with metaphysics and spoke of "the Buddhist Godhead," departed from this great scholar on this point. Those who did the same also could appeal to other authorities. Dharmapala, for instance, tried to counter "the erroneous conclusion that Buddhism is Agnosticism." The Buddha, he acknowledged, had set aside some metaphysical questions as unprofitable— the relation of body and mind, the future destiny of the self, the origin of the world. But he did so to help save those of limited wisdom from errors, not to deny all metaphysical truths. In this way, Dharmapala and some other authoritative voices left open the possibility of finding impersonal parallels to Western conceptions of ultimate reality.[25]

No Euro-American Buddhist who participated in the public discussion searched for parallels to the notion of a personal creator. They all self-consciously and unambiguously rejected that idea. So did some others in the culture: atheism and agnosticism had become live options for Westerners during the last decades of the nineteenth century. Yet theism—the belief in a personal creator—remained an important component of late-Victorian culture in America. In this sense, then, Buddhist advocates were dissenters. A number of American apologists, however, also used God-language in their interpretations of Buddhism—or did not seem to object strongly to such language. For instance, the sympathizer George Cabot Lodge used the term "God" in his poem, "Nirvana." Or advocates employed terms for ultimate reality, the All or the Absolute, that—although inclining more to pantheism than theism—conjured images of an ultimate reality similar to that which some Christian mystics and philosophers had sketched. Sympathizers and adherents of all three types were united in their rejection of the "unscientific" idea of a personal originator of the universe, but many acknowledged a "God-idea" in Buddhism.[26]

Child and others in the early-Victorian period had done the same. Sympathetic late-Victorians, however, often were more sophisticated. Romantics—and esoterics and rationalists with mystical tendencies or an acquaintance with non-Theravadin traditions—pointed to the Mahayana concept of the cosmic Buddha or universal Buddha-body. But most apologists located this impersonal "God" in the doctrine of the "moral law of cause and effect" (karma). Both notions of the locus and function of the divine in the Buddhist scheme can be found, for example, in the writings of Carus. In *Buddhism and its Christian Critics* he argued that the "God-idea" can be discovered in "the law of cause and effect" since it provides Buddhists with "an ultimate authority of conduct" and since—this claim seems overstated—Buddhists "gain a personal attitude toward it" that is similar to that of Christians when they speak of God. Further, Carus suggested, there are striking parallels between the Christian doctrine of the Trinity and the Buddhist notion of the Three Bodies of the Buddha. In Carus's view, the cosmic body of the Buddha, or the notion of Buddha as reality itself, functions very similarly to Christian ideas of God the Father. Buddha as the cosmic body, he informed his readers, is eternal, omnipresent, omnipotent. In fact, "He is the life of all that lives and the reality of all that exists. Thus he is the All in All, in whom we live and move and have our being." Carus simultaneously reassured and taunted his Christian readers by concluding that "Buddhistic atheism, apparently, is not wholly unlike Christian theism." Especially when they were in an apologetic mood, other defenders of the faith concurred. In a similar way, advocates' responses to Victorian individualism involved a complex blend of dissent and consent. They rejected some component beliefs and values. They affirmed others.[27]

Anatman, Nirvana, and "Immortality"

Individualism involves belief in the substantiality, immortality, and autonomy of the self. As with theism, there were a few isolated and limited challenges to this cluster of convictions in late-Victorian culture. Of these three, the commitments to the substantiality and immortality of the self seemed somewhat less firm. Some late-Victorian psychologists and philosophers explicitly rejected or significantly modified common notions of selfhood. They found a self that was insubstantial and fluid, always in the process of becoming. Taken in the loosest sense, some ambivalence toward the temporary suspension or transcendence of personal identity surfaced in the continuing popularity of religious revivals and theater productions as well as the new interest in athletic competitions. In a different way, Protestant moral crusaders and social reformers called for altruism, a loss of self in moral action. In fact, some sympathetic interpreters claimed that the two religions were united in this way: "both proclaim the necessity of a second death, a death of self: 'whoso seeketh his soul shall lose it, but he that loseth it shall find it.' "[28]

Traditional notions of an immortal soul enjoying eternal reward in heaven were jettisoned by some along with orthodox conceptions of God as personal creator. And in the wider culture some even seemed to feel ambivalently toward the "suicide of the soul" that critics had condemned in Buddhism. There was some preoccupation, even fascination, with suicide. In Bridgeton, New Jersey, an odd expression of this fascination erupted: a "suicide club" was founded in 1893. Every year on Washington's birthday, its rules stated, the fifty members would hold a banquet at which each would draw a ball from an opaque container. The man—as one newspaper account suggested, no woman would be stupid enough to join!—who drew the black ball would be forced to kill himself within the year. All his wealth would be contributed to the club "for the social amusement of the surviving members."[29]

Despite a few indications to the contrary, belief in the substantiality and immortality of the self was firm and abiding. Belief in an afterlife was rejected by very few, and impulses toward self-destruction were, finally, condemned. Most Americans who discussed suicide in books and articles complained about the increase in reported cases and searched for explanations and remedies. As in Victorian Britain, there were conflicting ideas and feelings about taking one's life, the ultimate act of self-negation. Often, horror combined with fascination. But, naturally enough, most seemed more repelled than attracted. The commitment to the notion of a unified and enduring personal center was intense. Discomfort, even terror, at the thought of selflessness, even temporary, was widespread. The protagonist in Edward Bellamy's popular utopian novel *Looking Backward* (1888) expressed this well. Julian West awakens in the Boston of the year 2000 to witness enormous social, economic, and political transformations. On the morning after he had been told of his suspended animation, West had forgotten who and where he was. His account of that experience captures the widely shared sense of anxiety about the loss of personal identity: "There are no words for the mental torture I endured during this helpless, eyeless groping for myself in a boundless void. No other experience of the mind gives probably anything like the sense of absolute intellectual arrest from the loss of a mental fulcrum, a starting point of thought, which comes during such a momentary obscuration of the sense of one's identity."[30]

Some Buddhist defenders offered sweeping and impassioned condemnations of individualism. Consider, for instance, Hearn's hostile response to Percival Lowell's championing of Western individualism in *The Soul of the Far East* (1888): "Much of what is called personality and individuality is intensely repellent, and makes the principal misery of Occidental life." But Buddhist apologists' relation to Victorian individualism was more complex than clear and complete opposition. Most often they focused their dissent on the idea of a static and substantial self. Embracing the traditional doctrine of anatman or no-self, they described the individual as a constantly changing aggregate of mental and physical forces. Some seemed to adopt this traditional element of Buddhist teachings without explanation or justification—or they offered less sophisticated versions of the usual Buddhist arguments. Others, speaking more directly to the wider culture, challenged the notion of self in the name of science and the "modern." Carus, for example, suggested that Buddhism—he meant the Theravada tradition and the Pali Canon—contained a "scientific soul conception"; that is, it seemed compatible with some recent developments in the new "science" of psychology. Like Carus, a few of the most theoretically inclined and highly educated apologists noted that Buddhism seemed more congruent with the processive, nonsubstantialist notions of individuality that were emerging in some fields. Whatever their motive or reasoning in their rejection of a substantial self, Buddhism's defenders clearly stood apart from most of their contemporaries.[31]

Yet even here there were occasional and partial compromises. Either because of their inability to break old habits or their concern to persuade Western audiences, a few advocates even used the term "soul." Dharmapala, in fact, criticized Carus's *Gospel of Buddha* precisely for this reason. "But I used the word 'soul' purposely," Carus explained in a private response, "because a denial of the soul is more confusing than to use the word in such a sense as it makes it agree with Buddhist psychology. To avoid the word altogether is just as objectionable, or at least difficult, because it is the most important term in religion." Not many would have agreed that "soul" is so crucial: "God" seems more important in Christianity. Yet Carus's aim was clear. He wanted to maintain the traditional Buddhist emphasis on no-self while harmonizing the doctrine with some recent intellectual developments and guarding against the accusation that Buddhists deny the conventional reality of mind and personality.[32]

Not all participants in the public discourse were as concerned about conceptions of the self as the philosophically inclined Carus. Many critics worried, however, about the implications of this doctrine and, even more, the doctrine of nirvana for the traditional understandings of another component of individualism—the conviction that the self is eternal. Johnston, who was so consumed with Buddhism's negations, had claimed that the tradition had no heaven, no resurrection, no future state. Critics who required a reward in the afterlife not only as the foundation of the moral life but also as the culmination of the religious struggle wondered about the implications of its teachings. If there is no self and nirvana involves annihilation, some antagonists reasoned, there can be no individual to enjoy the bliss of the afterlife. They found this disquieting.

Public advocates of Buddhism argued or implied that their opponents had misunderstood them. The doctrines of anatman and nirvana, they claimed, are compatible with some modified notions of an afterlife. Appealing to the authority of one of the founders of anthropology, Edmunds suggested that "the doctrine that there is no enduring soul is a piece of metaphysics, as Tylor long ago pointed out in his *Primitive Culture*: it in no way conflicts with a very well-defined belief in a future life." Esoterics like Edmunds, Vetterling, and Olcott were strongly disinclined to abandon one of the centers of their spirituality—the belief in an "other world" populated by spirits. Edmunds, who knew the Pali scriptures well, even quoted the sutras' condemnation of the "heresy that there is no other world" to support his position. Rationalists and romantics joined esoterics in asserting that no-self did not imply the denial of an existence after death. In one book, Carus sorted out its negations and affirmations this way: "Further, it is undeniable that Buddhists do not believe in the atman or Self which is the Brahman philosopher's definition of soul, but they do not deny the existence of mind and the continuance of man's spiritual existence after death."[33]

They also suggested that the doctrine of nirvana too—when properly understood and combined with the idea of rebirth—was compatible with some notion of immortality. Apologists who spoke to this issue admitted that no substantial soul could enjoy the rewards of heaven, but some conception of an afterlife was possible if the emphasis shifted to rebirth and the misinterpretation of nirvana was corrected. Several advocates used the term "immortality" to describe rebirth. Some even suggested that Buddhism's conception of immortality was superior to competing notions. Fenollosa, in his "Ode on Reincarnation," asserted that the notion of rebirth provided a sense of "immortality" that was far superior to modern scientific notions of the "continuity of the race" and Christian notions of heaven. But Fenollosa obscured some traditional Buddhist teachings in that versified tribute to the spiritual advantages of belief in rebirth. Despite the emphasis in the Mahayana traditions of East Asia on the identity of samsara and nirvana—i.e., the identity of ordinary existence and the ultimate state—rebirth itself rarely has been seen as the religious goal.

Theravadins sometimes might speak more frankly about the concern to be released from the cycle of birth, death, and rebirth. But even the Mahayana sects that Fenollosa had studied point to some perfected state that is now not recognized or attained by most humans.[34]

Of course, it was precisely on this point—the conception of nirvana—that antagonists had criticized Buddhism. Nirvana, which the sacred texts suggest is ultimately beyond comprehension or description, often has been described as a blissful liberation from suffering and rebirth. Sometimes, especially in East Asia, Buddhists have used the language of oceanic mysticism to convey this bliss of the perfected state. Some American defenders with mystical inclinations alluded to a final state in which the aggregate of fleeting forces that constitutes the individual merges with the one reality—often conceived of as the cosmic or universal Buddha. In this sense, then, apologists were dissenters: they diminished the force of commitments not only to the substantiality but also the immortality of the self. As Jackson Lears has noted, many late-Victorians equated "oceanic and suicidal impulses" and feared "the self-extinction in an oceanic unconsciousness." Some Euro-American Buddhists, however, let mysticism wash over them. Fenollosa, for example, apparently believed not only that there would be "no more West and no more East" in "the silence of Nirwana's Glory," but also that there would be no self or other. The nature of their mysticism, together with their commitment to no-self, meant that these Buddhists could not speak meaningfully about a soul in heaven or even, like St. Theresa of Avila or St. John of the Cross, an intimate ultimate union with the beloved.[35]

Romantics tended to soften their commitment to these aspects of individualism more than the other types. But a mystical impulse, or sometimes a philosophical monism, led to similar tendencies among esoterics and rationalists as well. For instance, the rationalist Lum considered the self as "the veriest of soap-bubbles, a thing to be dispelled by the merest whiff of wind." His dissent in this regard seems to have been related to a number of personal factors—in his despair he finally committed suicide—and religious inclinations: he displayed mystical tendencies. Lum seemed to welcome the possibility of being absorbed at death into an undifferentiated Whole. Sometimes, especially in his Buddhist pieces of the 1870s, he wrote of the Whole in abstract terms. It was the "All," and final union with it was the blissful release from suffering that Buddhists spoke of as "nirvana." At other times, he seemed to conceive of this Whole toward which all things move in social terms: we derive meaning from life by recognizing that our nobler efforts have added to the moral evolution of the species. We have our immortality in the future development of "Humanity." These two conceptions of the ultimate aim sometimes merged in his thinking. In his poetic treatment of nirvana for the *Radical Review*, for example, he contrasted "nirvana" with the "modern nirvana."

He envisioned the former as an oceanic immersion into "Infinity." The latter, Lum's formulation of "nirvana" for the modern context, he saw as a "mystic impulse toward a common goal—Humanity."[36]

In a related way, the esoteric Canavarro revealed a mystical sensibility in her affirmation of the no-self doctrine; and, in a suggestion that would have unsettled many Victorians, she granted that the final loss of self in nirvana might be, in one sense, the "annihilation" so many had feared. "Only in perfect union is there harmony," she claimed. "Selfhood separates us and we suffer,—so my friends, Nirvana is complete harmony and union with all. It is going out of the individual will to live, the extinction of matter in any form, however tenuous, however holy or sublime. From this point of view, perhaps it may be considered by many annihilation."[37]

If I am right about the intensity of the Victorian commitment to the notion of a substantial and enduring self, then it is not difficult to explain the stir caused by apologists' occasional and qualified use of a rhetoric of dissent or critics' frequent and exaggerated claims of negation. Canavarro's concession and Lum's suicide aside, American Buddhists generally did not long for a complete "suicide of the soul." It is true, of course, that they could not speak of immortality in traditional Christian terms. But, like a number of Westerners with tendencies toward pantheism and mysticism, apologists could talk about a positive final goal in the bliss of oceanic union. Here too American Buddhist apologists' dissent was not as complete as the rhetoric of their critics, or sometimes their own rhetoric, might imply. In this sense, advocates were consenters. Or, more precisely, they seem no more heterodox or countercultural than, for example, Emerson. Despite contrary elements in Emerson's poetry and prose, there was in his work an expressed desire to lose the self in the natural or cosmic totality: "I yielded myself to the perfect whole."[38]

Self-Reliance and Buddhism

The third and final component of Victorian individualism was the emphasis on self-reliance. By self-reliance I mean that call for mature self-regulation that echoed in the writings of Protestant reformers like Martin Luther, Enlightenment thinkers like Immanuel Kant, and Romantic writers like Emerson. It found expression in various areas of American life. It has been associated with life on the frontier. It was evident in the economic sphere. The Gilded Age, in fact, seemed to be the age of economic individualism: business was viewed as personal competition, survival of the fittest, heroic endeavor. Such individualism also was expressed in the religious sphere. A number of nineteenth-century Americans—e.g., Protestants, Transcendentalists, and freethinkers—saw autonomy as a central aspect of their spiritual stance.[39]

This religious individualism—as Emerson put it, to "love God without mediation or veil"—often was linked with anti-Catholicism. But its significance in this context is that it became associated with Buddhism and affirmed by a number of American promoters of the religion. Even Christian critics sometimes acknowledged that Indian and Sinhalese Buddhism had emphasized self-reliance. Instead of praising the tradition for its "Protestant spirit," however, they often tried to turn this against Buddhism. Frank F. Ellinwood, for example, suggested that Buddhists distorted or perverted self-reliance into a lack of concern for others and a disregard for community. In fact, Ellinwood proposed, this helped to explain its attractiveness for some misguided Americans. They were drawn by its principle of "every man for himself." But the championing of self-reliance in some early Buddhist scriptures was portrayed in a much more positive way by most of the leading scholars. And, appealing to those authorities for support, most American advocates continued in their commitment to this component of the dominant individualism even when they softened or abandoned traditional Western notions of the nature and destiny of the self.[40]

The emphasis on self-reliance was more muted and less clear among some romantics. Jackson Lears has shown that Bigelow, Lodge, and Percival Lowell expressed ambivalence toward self-reliance. He has argued persuasively that ambivalence toward this and other components of individualism worked itself out in their Buddhist investigations. He claimed that part of Buddhism's appeal for these men was—as I too have suggested—the promise of a loss of self in oceanic mysticism. These three struggled with contrary impulses toward both autonomy and dependence in their personal lives. Lears correctly noted, for example, Bigelow's intense dependence on his Japanese Buddhist teacher and the attraction this relationship held for him. In some unpublished remarks Bigelow overtly rejected most forms of religious individualism by stressing the decisive role of the teacher in religious development. Actually, however, the three men whom Lears discussed were, in my terms, all romantics, and the challenge to notions of self-reliance was much more common among this type than the others. This is not to say that there were no romantics who embraced self-reliance in the religious realm or in other areas of human endeavor. Hearn did. Romantics, if I am right, simply were less likely than esoterics or rationalists to do so.[41]

Ignoring contrary themes in Mahayana traditions like Pure Land, the esoteric Olcott, for example, asserted that Buddhism's emphasis on "redemption by oneself as the Redeemer" was one of the "striking contrasts" between Buddhism and Christianity and, by implication, one of its distinct advantages. Vetterling proclaimed that Buddhism's religious individualism made the tradition more attractive and accessible for him and his contemporaries: "it does not insult the Human Soul by placing mediators between it and the Divine Spirit." The championing of self-reliance in religion and all spheres of life was perhaps strongest among rationalists. Wilson, for instance, declared that the many who had been drawn to Buddhism had found "a system of religion wholly without a personal god, without dogmas, and with faith only in man's own ability to be a manly man, and thus by working out his own salvation become a god when 'mortality puts on immortality.' " In a similar way, Strauss highlighted the advantages of Buddhism by quoting from a contemporary Asian Buddhist catechism that he had translated into English. Buddhism, this catechism declared, offered the possibility of redemption without a vicarious "redeemer, a salvation in which every one is his own saviour and which can be attained . . . by the exercise of our own faculties without prayers, sacrifices, penances, and ceremonies, without ordained priests, without the mediation of saints, and without divine grace." A commitment to self-reliance, then, was shared by esoterics and rationalists and many others of their age. And Buddhism, it seemed, was as American as Emersonianism and Protestantism, robber barons and inventors, pioneers and cowboys.[42]

American Buddhist apologists were not as sweeping or unambiguous in their dissent as it seemed. And the discovery—or construction—of religious parallels and cultural continuities made Buddhism, for them and their sympathetic readers, a more approachable and less alien tradition. Of course, its distinctive intellectual advantages needed to be preserved and emphasized, but it was important to those considering the tradition that Buddhism could be presented as compatible with a range of convictions and attitudes associated with Protestantism and Victorianism. Yet two other widely shared values—activism and optimism—were important, even decisive, in determining both the nature and intensity of religious commitment among the spiritually disillusioned and the character and force of responses to the tradition by scholars, travelers, and critics. I turn to this in the final chapter.

OPTIMISM AND ACTIVISM

Responses to Buddhism, Victorian Religious Culture,
and the Limits of Dissent

Responding to sympathetic accounts of Buddhism, the Reverend J. T. Gracey of Rochester, New York, reminded the Christian readers of *The Homiletic Review* about Buddhism's most serious defects. "It is," he claimed, "one lone, helpless, hopeless bondage, driving men to despondency or paralyzing all moral purpose, save as they rise above it or are indifferent to it." Whether or not other late-Victorian Christian critics used this language, the point was the same. They agreed that Buddhism was passive and pessimistic. Even if Buddhist apologists had tried to stress its compatibility with Protestantism and Victorianism in other ways, critics argued, no one could ignore these disturbing negations. In response, Buddhism's defenders did not explain or justify its passive and pessimistic impulses. They rejected the critics' interpretations altogether. Buddhism, they claimed, had been misunderstood. In this way too apologists were consenters: they expressed their own allegiance to optimism and activism, and they argued, asserted, or implied that Buddhism was compatible with that cluster of beliefs and values. The impassioned rhetoric on both sides of the debate sometimes obscured how widespread these commitments were. Both the critics' vigorous repudiations and the apologists' forceful rebuttals indicate their intensity and pervasiveness in the culture. If this discussion is any indication, activism and optimism were fundamental to Victorian religious culture and as difficult to denounce as theism and individualism. In fact, many of the spiritually disillusioned who turned to Buddhism were more willing to give up a personal God and a substantial self. In this way, this discourse delineates the limits of dissent in Victorian America. At the same time, the debate about its alleged passivity and pessimism offers some clues about why Victorian Buddhism was not even more successful.[1]

OPTIMISM AND ACTIVISM IN LATE-VICTORIAN CULTURE

I have noted some of the ways in which mid-Victorian American interpreters of all perspectives affirmed optimism and activism and struggled with Western accounts that challenged those affirmations. These convictions and attitudes continued to be an important part of Victorian culture in the United States as Buddhist interest intensified (1879–1912). Although the cultural context had changed in some important ways, most participants in the dominant culture continued to embrace, first, optimism. They emphasized the elevated capacities of persons, the positive elements of human life, the benevolent character of the universe, and the progressive development of history. In other words, most believed that humans were fundamentally good or capable of becoming good. The world seemed suited for the promotion of the good, and nature and history were getting better and better. Several developments supported the reigning optimism. The tragic era of Civil War and Reconstruction closed. "Progress" in science and technology escalated: the number of patents issued, for example, increased dramatically during the last decades of the century. American territory continued to expand and develop, and a belief in America's unique role as a "Redeemer Nation" survived in modified form.

Many American authors expressed their belief in the perfectibility of individuals and society and the linear advance of nature and history in the philosophical language of Spencer's comprehensive evolutionism, Hegel's philosophy of history, or Comte's positivistic worldview. Similar themes were expressed differently in other aspects of the culture. Horatio Alger's (1834–99) "rags to riches" stories reassured young male readers that the benefits of the American economy were open to all. Like history itself, the virtuous, lucky, and diligent could move ever upward. William Holmes McGuffey's (1800–73) *Eclectic Reader* performed some of the same functions for rural America that Alger's fiction performed in the cities. These popular textbooks continued to exert influence after McGuffey's death, and their message was reassuringly hopeful in several ways. As one scholar put it, their viewpoint paralleled that of Dr. Pangloss: "no matter how distressing things might seem, all was for the best—the workings of Providence, the arrangements of society, the vicissitudes of the economy." The authors of popular religious fiction of the period—for example, Lewis Wallace (1827–1905), Elizabeth Stuart Phelps (1844–1911), and Edward Payson Roe (1838–88)—also bubbled with confidence. Even when the heroine fell in love with a benevolently irreligious man, the traditional plot formula of these novels allowed love, and Christian faith, to triumph. Even when doubts arose, they were overcome—as in Wallace's *Ben Hur*. Even when these religious novelists protested social and economic injustices, an incorruptible faith in the possibility—the inevitability—of change prevailed.[2]

The rhetoric of optimism also appeared often in the sermons, articles, and books of a wide variety of religious leaders. Mainline Protestants such as Henry Ward Beecher of Brooklyn and George Angier Gordon (1853–1929) of Boston both expressed this attitude. In an 1882 essay Beecher, for instance, rejected Calvinism's reputed pessimism about humans and history. He welcomed, among other things, the evolution of a more optimistic attitude toward worship so that one no longer would feel the need "to abase oneself, to fall prostrate before the unknown, to dwell upon one's inferiority." Optimism was especially strong and clear in the writings of John Fiske (1842–1901). This modernistic liberal who helped popularize Darwinian and Spencerian ideas believed that God's immanence in the cosmic process assured its ultimate goodness. In *The Destiny of Man Viewed in the Light of His Origin,* he celebrated both Darwinism and optimism: "it is Darwinism which has placed Humanity upon a higher pinnacle than ever. The future is lighted for us with the radiant colors of hope. Strife and sorrow shall disappear. Peace and love shall reign supreme."[3]

This confidence in the nature of humans and the course of history also was evident in groups that fell outside the Protestant mainstream. As scholars have recognized, proponents of Unitarianism, Free Religion, Ethical Culture, Mormonism, Spiritualism, New Thought, and Christian Science all expressed the reigning optimism in various ways. Despite their obvious differences, they were united in their common rejection of Calvinism's "pessimistic" evaluation of humans and history. Even more forcefully and directly than liberals in the mainline Protestant denominations, for example, late-Victorian Unitarians and Universalists continued the assault on Calvinism's allegedly gloomy anthropology. Or they simply assumed its demise. In an attack on "the five points of Calvinism," James Freeman Clarke emphasized the "essential goodness which God has put into the soul" and rejoiced in the "new theology's" focus on "progress." He announced in this 1886 essay that an optimistic attitude harmonizes with all the evidence—"with the long processes of geologic development by which the earth became fitted to be the home of man; with the slow ascent of organized beings from humbler to fuller life; with the progress of society from age to age; with the gradual diffusion of knowledge, advancement of civilization, growth of free institutions, and ever higher conceptions of God and religious truth."[4]

Although the tendency toward optimism was strong in the culture, there were a few pessimistic voices during the 1880s and 1890s. Perhaps William James was right when he observed that individuals can be optimistic or pessimistic by "temperament" and "healthy-minded" on one day and "sick-souled" the next. Yet some late-Victorian American intellectuals who leaned toward gloominess believed that they had found justification for their attitude outside the self in the larger culture. They seriously began to question the freedom and value of the individual and the meaningfulness and direction of history. They did so by building on the potential pessimism and fatalism in evolutionism and other forms of naturalistic determinism and by pointing to counterevidence to the theory of inevitable progress in the political corruption, labor unrest, class conflict, and urban squalor of their day. This challenge to the reigning optimism was clear, for example, in Mark Twain's *A Connecticut Yankee* (1889) and Brooks Adams's *Law of Civilization and Its Decay* (1893). Others—such as George Santayana and Edgar Saltus—retreated into various forms of subjectivism and aestheticism under the influence of European writers like Schopenhauer. Yet, as John Higham has recognized, the "pessimistic mood" that scholars have found in *fin-de-siècle* Europe did not seem to be as intense or pervasive on the other side of the Atlantic: "When all this is said, the fact remains that pessimism became in America neither general nor profound. . . . Most intellectuals resisted pessimism. Philosophers (with the possible exception of Santayana) rallied against it; literary critics denounced it; social scientists were challenged rather than overcome by it."[5]

Even those who could not embrace the strongest versions of the reigning optimism because of naturalistic fatalism, Calvinist residue, or some other factor usually accepted the "doctrine of meliorism" as formulated by William James: although individuals and the world are mixtures of good and evil they can be improved by appropriate action. James, who struggled to come to terms with personal impulses toward both pessimism and passivity, promoted meliorism. He saw it as a stance midway between the view which holds that "the salvation of the world is impossible" and that which holds that "the world's salvation is inevitable." Meliorism, on the other hand, considers a positive conclusion "neither necessary nor impossible." The decisive variable, James said, was the nature and character of human action. Some late-Victorian reformers denounced the quietistic implications of the optimistic mood. Richard T. Ely (1854–1943), the Episcopalian economist, exhorted Protestants to fight "a manly contest against the deadly optimism of the day which aims to retard improvement and to blind men to actual dangers." "I believe," Ely continued, "the social consequences of optimism [are] even more disastrous than those of pessimism, though both are bad enough." Yet for James and many of his contemporaries, attitudes about the goodness of persons and the benevolence of the universe—or at least the malleability and perfectibility of both—were linked with the activistic spirit that permeated late-Victorian culture.[6]

Activism, as I have defined it, is the inclination to emphasize the spiritual significance of vigorous moral action in the world. It is the concern to uplift individuals, reform societies, and participate energetically in the political and economic spheres. It took a variety of forms in the last two decades of the nineteenth century and the first of the twentieth. At the personal level and in the character of daily life, some European observers noted a "nervousness" and "jerkiness" among Americans. Some Americans concurred. One Boston Episcopalian preacher attributed this to the enduring effects of Calvinism; and—showing the influence of New Thought—he found the cure in the "mental healing" of a liberalized Protestantism. James also felt that this "absence of repose, this bottled-lightning quality in us Americans" was harmful, and prescribed "The Gospel of Relaxation" preached by Annie Payson Call. He was not condoning passivity. James and many other privileged Americans of his day, in fact, battled the paralyzing effects of the epidemic of depression and listlessness his contemporaries called "neurasthenia." Few consciously surrendered to this psychic malady of the age. Rather, James recommended repose in order to stimulate activity. Since unfocused energy and nervousness renders activity less efficient, Americans needed to relax more to increase the efficaciousness of individual and collective action. After all, as James asserted in another essay entitled "The Energies of Men," nations are judged by how many individuals they can stimulate to function at the "highest pitch" of energy.[7]

Some activist energy crackled during the 1870s and 1880s. There were efforts to attack political corruption and solve the economic and social problems of the Gilded Age. Farmers protested and workers struck. Often, violence broke out. "Reforming Darwinists" also led efforts to alter the status quo. With diverse intentions and varied results, they interpreted economic, social, religious, and political issues in terms of the evolutionary framework that was so popular. In evolutionism's most malevolent form, Spencer's notion of "the survival of the fittest" was used to justify the inequitable distribution of economic benefits and social rights as well as the supremacy of the Anglo-Saxon race and the Protestant Christian religion. Yet, as with Henry George (1839–97) and Edward Bellamy, it also provided a theoretical framework for reform. George's *Progress and Poverty* (1879)—with its condemnation of monopolies and call for the imposition of a "single tax"—went through over one hundred editions within twenty-five years, and it stimulated the creation of "Single Tax Clubs." Bellamy's utopian novel *Looking Backward* (1888) became a bestseller in a few years, and over one hundred and sixty Nationalist Clubs sprang up to propagate his revisionary ideas.

Although some cultural historians have overemphasized the point, activism was more evident in American popular culture after the 1880s. The "activist mood" of the Progressive Era (1890–1917) took various shapes. It was evident in the "Cult of the Strenuous" presided over by Theodore Roosevelt and others. It found expression in the intense interest in competitive athletics (e.g., football), the rage for outdoor activities of all sorts (e.g., bicycling), and the quickened pace of popular music (e.g., ragtime). A commitment to activism also was revealed in the "reformer-individualist" Anglo-Saxon political culture of the Progressive Era and the numerous movements for reform in this period. For instance, leaders of the Progressive Movement campaigned for women's suffrage, regulation of liquor traffic and interstate commerce, revised banking and currency laws, effective antitrust legislation and equitable income tax statutes, an eight-hour work day, and prohibition of child labor.[8]

Many efforts at reform were associated directly or indirectly with religion. In fact, European observers sometimes equated the optimistic, world-affirming activism of Protestantism between the 1880s and the 1920s with "Americanism" in religion. The distinctiveness of American religion can be overemphasized; yet a this-worldly spirit and world-transforming impulse were important components of late-Victorian American Protestantism. Some who stood outside the Anglo-Protestant mainstream because of religious affiliation or ethnic background still affirmed activism. In an article for the *North American Review*, Booker T. Washington exhorted his fellow African American Protestants to adopt middle-class Victorian values such as industry, earnestness, and steadiness; and, most important, he urged them to channel the emotional vitality of black worship into efforts to uplift and reform. African American churches needed, he argued, "more of the spirit of service." Protestants outside and inside the mainline denominations seemed to agree about the need for "service." Henry Ward Beecher, to turn to that paradigmatic Victorian Protestant again, proclaimed that the Christian churches of America were "fountains of benevolence." "They are in every village the organized centers of influence for morality, for education, for public spirit." Although this force for patriotism, education, and morality was not confined to the Christian churches, Beecher acknowledged, it found its most effective and profound expression there.[9]

This makes sense, Beecher and others suggested, since these functions are at the heart of Protestant Christianity. In an 1890 essay, for instance, Beecher's successor, Lyman Abbott, claimed that the essential aim of Christianity is "human welfare." In the same year, Professor Charles W. Shields and Bishop Henry C. Potter argued in a piece for *The Century Magazine* that "to instruct and preserve society is at least one design, if not the chief design, of the Christian religion as organized in the Church." In fact, activistic Christianity could provide "the only perfect remedy" for the present "social ills." Other leaders of the movement that came to be called the Social Gospel—such as Washington Gladden (1836–1918), George D. Herron (1862–1925), and Walter Rauschenbusch (1861–1918)—concurred. Some with similar views, like the Congregationalist pastor Charles M. Sheldon (1857–1946), turned to fiction to communicate their message of social change. Sheldon asked the millions who read his *In His Steps* to confront unemployment, alcoholism, crime, and poverty as Jesus might have. To be a Christian, the fictional minister in Sheldon's popular novel proclaimed, is to imitate Jesus. More precisely, he meant that it is to follow in the steps of the Jesus who passionately condemned the money changers and unapologetically embraced the dispossessed.[10]

An activist spirit also infused efforts at commercial, cultural, political, and religious expansion. Since the Second Great Awakening, reform had meant converting the "heathen" at home and abroad. In an 1884 description of the "theological purpose" of the new Andover Review, Egbert C. Smyth articulated what many already were feeling—that it was "a missionary age." Almost two decades later, the corresponding secretary of the American Board of Commissioners for Foreign Missions offered a retrospective review. He proudly proclaimed that "the nineteenth century has gone into history with an imperishable name and glory." As evidence of its enormous "progress" in all dimensions of life he pointed to gains in technology, education, literature, arts, and, especially, foreign missions. He suggested that the "aggressive spirit" of Christianity created 449 Protestant missionary organizations, sustained 13,607 missionaries, and saved 1,289,289 "souls." All this clearly demonstrated, he asserted, the inevitable "advance" of Christianity and the unavoidable decline of other faiths. While his claims about the spread of Christianity proved to be overblown, it was true that more American missionaries were going abroad. And Protestants at home in the pulpits and the pews provided more support than ever before—or since.[11]

There were the expected disagreements about the nature and function of missions. Some wanted to civilize as well as evangelize. And, more broadly, there were the expected disagreements about how America should interact with other nations. Some wanted isolation; others expansion. Some, both inside and outside the Protestant churches, protested the "emancipation" of Cuba in the Spanish-American War, the annexation of the Philippines and Guam, and the acquisition of the Hawaiian islands. Some who could not support the new nationalism and imperialism of the 1890s—or could not do so without reservations—found a more benign substitute in "the fine spiritual imperialism" of foreign missions. Yet many mainline Protestants remained undisturbed by the new developments. They linked the extension of Christianity with attempts to expand American commerce, territory, and political influence. Abbott, for instance, explicitly coupled religion with nationalism and expansionism, and he defended the war with Spain. During the 1890s other Americans also felt the older "ideological constraints" of antiexpansionism begin to lift. Under the influence of Theodore Roosevelt, Henry Cabot Lodge, and John Hay, a new foreign policy began to emerge. Advocates of this modified stance toward other nations sometimes justified their attitudes and actions by appealing to lofty motives—such as saving Cubans from Spanish cruelties and preserving the "independence and integrity" of China. In general, however, the policy seemed to be grounded in enduring beliefs about

America's sacred destiny and Anglo-Saxon supremacy, and it seemed to be aimed at the protection and expansion of American commercial and political interests.[12]

BUDDHISM AS PESSIMISTIC AND PASSIVE: SCHOLARS, TRAVELERS, AND CRITICS

Activism, then, in more and less benevolent forms, was an element in the dominant culture of the period. So was optimism. This was significant for the public discussion about Buddhism because most scholars, travelers, and critics accepted these Victorian beliefs and values, and, at the same time, most claimed that Buddhism contradicted them. Perpetuating a long tradition in the West, interpreters implied or argued that Buddhism was pessimistic because of its emphasis on pervasive suffering and celebration of nirvanic negation. It also seemed passive or quietistic. As in the mid-Victorian period, commentators often reluctantly praised Buddha's moral teachings. But later in the century, hostile interpreters were even less likely to grant that the religion he founded was world-transforming. In fact, many argued, history has proven that Buddhism is unable to spark technological innovation, support democratic government, encourage religious expansion, foster economic growth, or stimulate organized reform. The Harvard philosopher Josiah Royce (1855–1916) succinctly expressed the sentiment of many when he contrasted Buddhism's "quietism" with Christianity's "activity," Buddhism's "pessimism" with Christianity's "hope."[13]

American attitudes toward Buddhism continued to be shaped in part by European scholarship. Rhys Davids tended to deemphasize or openly challenge the interpretations of Buddhism as pessimistic and passive; yet other leading European scholars reinforced negative views. Scholars of the Anglo-German school showed a much greater awareness of the complexity of the issues and the diversity of the tradition than most of their predecessors; yet some continued either explicitly to interpret Buddhism as pessimistic and passive, or they presented the "facts" in such a way that the reader could easily reach that conclusion. Oldenberg opened his influential book by asserting that the Buddha's earliest disciples were bound together by "the deeply felt and clearly and sternly expressed consciousness, that all existence is full of sorrow, and that the only deliverance from sorrow is in renunciation of the world and eternal rest." However, he argued, Buddhism's "pessimism" and concomitant lack of concern for worldly matters were not, as many had supposed, rooted in a celebration of "the Nothing." Oldenberg pointed to the silence of the historical Buddha in the Pali scriptures concerning questions about the origin of the universe and the destiny of the individual after death, and he argued for the plurality of "answers" offered by other authorities inside and outside the Pali tradition. This eminent German scholar located Buddhism's gloominess and otherworldliness instead in its founder's claim that life is suffering and in the continuing emphasis on that theme in the later tradition. The roots of pessimism, world-rejection, and passivity were watered by larger currents in the Indian cultural context, and similar themes emerged in other religions. Yet, Oldenberg suggested, Buddhism's focus on the inevitability of suffering distinguishes it from other traditions.[14]

Other European scholars' writings were less nuanced and more negative. Monier Monier-Williams, Boden Professor of Sanskrit at Oxford, not only disqualified Buddhism as a religion because of its rejection of a personal God and immortal soul, but also portrayed this Asian version of "the gospel of Humanity preached by the Positivists" as gloomy and quietistic. In fact, Monier-Williams openly confessed in the preface to his 1889 work that he "depicted Buddhism from the standpoint of a believer in Christianity." It is not surprising, then, to find that later in the book he compared "the utter apathy and indifference to which [Buddha's] doctrines logically led" with Christianity's ability to "stir the soul of the recipient [of Christ's gifts] with a living energy."[15]

Few American academics had knowledge of the relevant Asian languages, but, for the most part, a similar pattern emerged in their writings. Charles Rockwell Lanman, Harvard professor and Buddhist sympathizer, was an exception. He is remembered for his *Sanskrit Reader*, textual translations, technical articles, and, most of all, his role as editor of the Harvard Oriental Series. But he played a limited role in the public conversation since he tended to avoid controversial characterizations and usually offered no more than philological analysis or close reconstruction. Lanman's writings, in short, focused more on noun inflection than on the meaning of nirvana. Henry Clarke Warren, one of Lanman's students, was more speculative in temperament and more willing to offer characterizations of Buddhist doctrine. As his teacher noted in an obituary notice, Warren had been "an intelligent student of Plato, Kant, and Schopenhauer; and . . . the natural trend of his mind toward speculative questions showed clearly in his scientific investigations of Buddhism." It was not that Warren was an inferior student of Pali. In fact, he was the first American scholar to attain distinction in the study of Pali and "one of the leading Pali scholars of the Occident." For a variety of reasons, Warren simply seemed more willing to enter the discussion about the character of Buddhist thought. In the interpretations interspersed throughout his *Buddhism in Translations*, for example, Warren challenged the claim that Buddhism was nihilistic; but he agreed that Buddhism's analysis of the universe was "pessimistic."[16]

I noted in the previous chapter that E. Washburn Hopkins, another prominent American scholar, clearly had sided with those who viewed Buddhism as nihilistic, pessimistic, and passive. Actually, he was more precise than that. In *The Religions of India* (1895) Professor Hopkins distinguished between Hinayana and Mahayana traditions and between elite and popular Buddhism. (He wanted to say "exoteric" and "esoteric," but these terms had been lost to scholars because of the unwanted associations of the term "esoteric.") He linked pessimism, nihilism, and passivity with the historical Buddha, his elite disciples, and the Hinayana tradition. The Buddha allowed "the mass of his disciples" to adopt a more limited and positive interpretation, Hopkins claimed, but he shared the full truth about his negative teachings with "the strong and wise." Hopkins acknowledged some pessimistic elements in Judaism, Christianity, Hinduism, and Jainism; but he found in Buddhism a "formal and complete pessimism." It reigned in Buddhism because of the influence of the founder's characterization of human existence (the four noble truths and the chain of causality) and the implications of his denial of a state of bliss beyond the grave (nirvana as annihilation).[17]

Buddhism, Hopkins suggested, also was world-denying and passive. The belief in karma "lessens man's compassionate interest in his fellows." The inclination toward passivity found in all Indian religions that affirm this doctrine was intensified by Buddhism's emphasis on the universality of suffering. Apparently annoyed or threatened by the continuing appeal of the image of Buddha as a reformer, Hopkins argued that although Buddha had initiated reforms of all sorts that "made the lowest equal with the highest," that was not his original intention. Buddha, he suggested, "was no democrat." In an apparent attempt to defend against Buddhism's incursion into the activistic domain reserved for Christianity, he declared that the historical Buddha had originally sought salvation only for himself. The founder's mounting compassion for the multitude held in bondage to a superstitious religion (Hinduism) and an oppressive social structure (the caste system) set loose a reforming impulse in a social system that already was unstable. Hopkins wanted to link Christianity, and not Buddhism, with the democratic principles and the activist spirit of his culture and era. He left the impression that any reforming impulse or egalitarian spirit discernible in Buddhism was an unintended consequence of the founder's personal spiritual quest, not a defining trait of the tradition.[18]

American travelers in Asia portrayed Buddhism only slightly more positively. During the last decades of the nineteenth century and the first of the twentieth a number of American diplomats, businessmen, and intellectuals wrote about Asian nations—especially Japan, China, and Tibet. Some of those travel narratives presented Buddhism sympathetically. Occasionally, a passage in these sympathetic portraits even reversed interpretive trends. In a series of articles on Japan for *The Century*, for instance, John LaFarge reinforced stereotypes by speaking of the "feminine" (i.e., passive) qualities of the culture and its religious goal (nirvana) and emphasized the contemplative and mystical aspects of the religion. But he also pointed to one of the theoretical grounds for activism in the

Mahayana tradition: "For, in the Buddhist doctrine, compassion is the first of all virtues, and leads and is the essence of the five cardinal virtues, which are—note the sequence—pity, justice, urbanity, sincerity, and wise behavior. . . . For the happiness, which is the aim of Buddhism, is not limited to the individual but is to be useful, to be of profit, to all mankind." Yet this passage was uncharacteristic. Usually the travel narratives that appeared in popular books or influential secular magazines like *Century*, *Atlantic*, and the *Overland Monthly* gave the impression that Asian nations, and Buddhist ones in particular, were lifeless. These attitudes sometimes were expressed in frankly hostile assertions, other times buried in a heap of detail. Either way, the effect was the same.[19]

Yet even when narrators expressed sympathy or claimed objectivity, the standard views were often explicitly or implicitly reinforced. William Woodville Rockhill's well-received book on Buddha and early Buddhism aimed at impartial description; and, in fact, he avoided assessments of his subject. Yet the accounts of his travels in Mongolia and Tibet that appeared in the pages of *The Century* in 1890 did not challenge many of American readers' negative impressions. Rockhill penetrated an Asian culture almost as fully and presented Buddhism almost as fairly as any American of his generation. But his travel narratives—which had the texture and spirit of contemporary ethnography—included explicit references to the "ignorance" of the Tibetans, the undemocratic tendencies of its religious leaders, and the "primitive political organization" that Buddhism had supported there. Even when Rockhill managed to avoid highly charged words like "primitive"—which was usually the case—his descriptions of Chinese, Mongolian, and Tibetan cultures, nonetheless, would have allowed his readers to feel confirmed in their convictions about the passivity of Buddhism and the activity of Christianity.[20]

A handful of late-Victorian scholars and travelers clearly challenged the negative interpretations. Some veiled their hostile attitudes in detailed descriptions of everyday life. Others expressed ambivalence toward the Buddhist traditions and Asian cultures they encountered. American Christian critics, however, usually showed little charity or ambiguity as they gleefully pointed to the tradition's gloominess and vigorously denounced its quietism. They condemned its overemphasis on suffering, its devaluation of the individual, its preoccupation with rest and release, and the passive attitude that resulted from these intellectual tendencies. American Christians brought to their criticism of Buddhism a number of different religious perspectives. They belonged to a wide range of denominations. For example, Unitarians and Catholics as well as mainline Protestants were members of this community of discourse. Catholic participants in the discussion pointed to Buddhism's pessimism and passivity in passing, but they seemed more concerned to refute the troubling claims about Catholic parallels and Buddhist influence. Unitarians qualified their condemnations of Buddhism more than their more conservative Protestant contemporaries and their mid-Victorian predecessors, but the assertions about Buddhism's gloomy assessment of human nature and inadequate theoretical foundation for reform still disturbed them. The criticisms of mid-Victorian Unitarians like James Freeman Clarke echoed in the later period. In fact, Clarke continued to contribute to the conversation. Yet other members of the denomination spoke out as well. Charles Henry Appleton Dall (1836–85), the Unitarian missionary in India, lived long enough to see the increased interest in the tradition; and in an 1882 article he contrasted Buddhism's and Christianity's ultimate aims and practical results. Dall acknowledged that God might "reprove the reckless haste of our American life." But God certainly would not approve of Buddhism's world-negation. "He bids us know that this is a glorious world," Dall countered, "not all a cheat; and that there is much to do in it." Like many other late-Victorians, Dall appealed to pragmatic criteria to assess religions: "What Buddhism has accomplished in the world, that it is." Finally, he pronounced Christianity superior. Buddhism's emphasis on renunciation and its quest for "rest" has had ill effects. The tradition has been unable to generate the requisite "energy": because of the somniferous teachings of Buddhism, he claimed, "the properly Buddhist nations of the world are all asleep." James Thompson Bixby (1843–1921) also condemned its drowsiness. Readied for the task by three degrees from Harvard and a Ph.D. from Leipzig, he turned his attention to comparative religions and Buddhism in particular in articles for the *Unitarian Review, The Arena,* and the *New World.* In one piece, for example, this professor of religious philosophy and ethnic religions at the Meadville Theological School contrasted Christianity's world-affirming "cheerful view of life" with Buddhism's world-rejecting "pessimism."[21]

Offering arguments that often paralleled those found in the works of British and German Protestant critics such as R. Spence Hardy, Adolph Thomas, and Monier-Williams, liberal and conservative mainline Protestants were united in their rejection of Buddhism. In his account of his years as a missionary in Japan, for instance, M. L. Gordon applied the same pragmatic criterion that Dall had—by their fruits you shall know them. "This is the divine test for all things," he claimed,"—a test ordained not only by the words of our Lord, but also by the reason divinely implanted in every soul of man." Buddhism had failed this test. Just one example: although the Japanese treated women better than some other non-Christian nations—India, Turkey, and China—they still failed to accord them the respect they deserve. "According to Buddhism," Gordon argued, "women are greater sinners than men, hardly knowing the difference between truth and falsehood." Citing a traditional Buddhist teaching, he continued: "Only men can enter Nirvana, or become Buddhas." On this issue, and others, Buddhism had shown its quietistic tendencies and

Christianity had shown its transformative impulses. In fact, Gordon suggested, Christian missions already had produced positive results in Japan and other nations. "What has been true of Christianity everywhere, and in all ages, is markedly true of its history in Japan; the divine characteristics of the fruit prove the divine nature of the tree."[22]

Others connected with American Protestant foreign missions agreed about both Christianity's activism and Buddhism's passivity—Samuel Henry Kellogg, who worked as a Presbyterian missionary to India; Frank Field Ellinwood, who acted as corresponding secretary of the Board of Foreign Missions of the Presbyterian Church; and Henry Melville King, who served on the executive committee of the American Baptist Missionary Union. King, for instance, complained that Buddhism devalues the individual by failing to recognize humanity's "exalted origin and immortal destiny." Instead, the tradition presents a "pessimistic philosophy of life" which aims at nothingness and promotes a way of life in which the individual is "wholly idle, and to all besides himself absolutely useless." In fact, one woman with sympathies for missions, Constance F. Gordon Cumming, could explain her encounter with hints of "civilization" among the "heathen" in a Chinese town only by pointing to the "humanizing influence of the American mission, which has had a station here for some years." No native influences, she felt certain, could have been at work.[23]

Other mainline Protestants expressed similar views in articles for religious and secular periodicals. In a piece for *Atlantic* in 1894, for instance, William Davies denounced Buddhism's quietism. "If we make a comparison of Buddhism and Christianity," he suggested, "however great a similarity may appear in some of the elements of its teaching, its distinct inferiority in scope, purpose, and adaptability will become apparent. The religion of the Buddha could never be brought to combine with the advancement and progressive amelioration of society. It works by abandonment, leaving the world every way as it finds it. It lacks the helpful and actively loving spirit of Christianity." Another Protestant discussant, William M. Bryant, alluded to its pessimism as well as its passivity in a two-part article for the *Andover Review*. Troubled by the increased interest in Buddhism, he set out to compare the two traditions and demonstrate the superiority of Christianity. Buddhism as "the religion of Pessimism" promotes a negative view of life by its emphasis on endless transmigration and universal pain. It seeks only "the attainment of final and complete passivity" and "a negative release from pain through the ultimate suppression of activity." On the other hand, as "the religion of Optimism," Christianity stands as "the predestined final Religion of the World." It "teaches man to value himself as a being possessed of infinite capabilities," stimulates persons to work to transform evil into good, and affirms the "unlimited power of development."[24]

BUDDHIST APOLOGISTS' AFFIRMATIONS OF OPTIMISM AND ACTIVISM

Euro-American Buddhist apologists, needless to say, found these criticisms disturbing. Carus defended American expansionist policy in Cuba and the Philippines. Edmunds participated in the cycling craze of the 1890s. Lum reported that he had inherited activist impulses—he proudly called them "cranky notions"—from abolitionist ancestors on his mother's side. In short, Buddhist apologists were late-Victorian Americans. And Buddhism, of course, was presented as contrary to the most incontrovertible of Victorian convictions. In response, almost all sympathizers and adherents who participated in the public conversation portrayed the tradition as optimistic and activistic. This tendency was strongest among esoterics and rationalists, but even romantics—those with inclinations toward mysticism, aestheticism, or "Schopenhauerismus" included— could not reject these dominant values completely or unambiguously.[25]

Yet, given the tone and content of the prevailing interpretations, defending Buddhism as activistic and optimistic presented a challenge. To counter the charge of pessimism, apologists could—and did—point out Buddhism's ultimate hopefulness. After all, the canonical Buddha did not end his famous speech on the four noble truths with an analysis of the universality of suffering. He went on to offer a way out. Carus noted this in one article on "the prophet of pessimism," Schopenhauer. Trying to disentangle Schopenhauer's teachings from Buddha's, Carus suggested that the German philosopher's appreciation of Buddhism was rooted in its recognition of universal misery. "But," Carus reminded American readers, "he blinds himself to the third and fourth [noble truth], which proclaims there is salvation from misery and that the eightfold noble path of righteousness unfailingly leads to the attainment of salvation." Yet no matter how often apologists emphasized the final hopefulness of his teachings, many American participants in the conversation seemed unable or unwilling to divert attention from Buddha's "pessimistic" diagnosis of the human condition. Many Americans had rejected or softened one pessimistic anthropology—Calvinism. They were not about to embrace, or even tolerate, another.[26]

Dislodging reigning views of Buddhist passivity proved just as difficult—or even more so. Several factors made it especially challenging. Even at the turn of the century, few translations of Buddhist texts were available; and so interested American readers could not see all the counterevidence, especially in those Mahayana Buddhist scriptures that emphasize lay activity and worldly effort. Second, the only American scholar with both indisputable credentials and significant sympathy, Charles Lanman, did not forcefully and publicly refute negativist interpretations. If he had, for example, taken to delivering frequent fiery lectures or to writing judicious newspaper editorials on the subject, the situation might have been slightly different. In fact, the treatment of Buddhism in the press was part of the problem. The sensationalized stories about eccentric American converts and exotic Asian spokespersons did not help. Consider, for instance, the front-page headline and the contents of an article about Ida E. Russell's interest in Buddhism published in the *San Francisco Examiner:* "BUDDHA SHRINE WORSHIPPED IN HOUSE OF MYSTERY." This story and the subsequent accounts of her esoteric views and those of the "religious cult" that occupied her mansion in San Francisco portrayed Russell and the tradition she professed as, among other things, passive. The author of this piece suggested that "Mother Russell" and her "colony of devotees" retreated to the "seclusion" of her large home in order to seek "absolute tranquility." They were, the headline on a subsequent page read, "trying to reach higher life by living away from the world." This "head of [a] strange band of votaries," an occult seeker who had studied with Soyen Shaku, was presented as an idiosyncratic, world-denouncing cult leader. Buddhism appeared hopelessly quietistic. There were few Asian teachers in America to correct mistaken views that arose in this and other accounts, and that was another problem that Buddhist defenders had to confront.[27]

A final difficulty had something to do with the situation in contemporary Buddhist nations and not only the sensationalist coverage in the press, the inertia of negativist interpretations, the paucity of texts and teachers, or the arrogance of Anglo-Saxon Victorian Protestants. If contemporary Buddhist nations were any indication, critics argued, the religion did not seem to lead to vigorous economies, developed cultures, powerful governments, or just societies. Right for the wrong reasons, they had a point. But they took the thread of truth in their claims and blanketed Buddhism with condemnations. In Buddhist nations in which Western imperialistic influence had been great, they credited the Christian West for any positive developments. Where they found no significant economic, social, and political "progress," they blamed Buddhism. When Americans looked to the mountains and monasteries of Tibet to discern the wider influence of Buddhism, for instance, they could find little to recommend it. Also— unfortunately for those trying to establish Buddhism's superior social effects—the late nineteenth-century discussion occurred at a time when many Japanese were implicitly or explicitly acknowledging the inferiority of their economy, society, and culture and looking to the West for aid and examples. At the same time, late Ch'ing dynasty China also was experiencing, by almost any standards, a "real decline and stagnation in many aspects of Chinese life." Buddhist apologists tried, but it was difficult to evaluate these contemporary Asian nations in terms of Christian critics' standards and to reach an unqualified positive conclusion. In any case, there seemed to be little chance of converting to their position those who overflowed with confidence in Western technological superiority, faith in Protestant Christianity's finality, pride in Western economic vitality, and certainty about American democratic supremacy.[28]

Yet there was some help for those who wanted to find—or create—an optimistic and activistic Buddhism. In the preface to his popular poem, Edwin Arnold defied many other interpreters by announcing that this religion had in it "the eternity of a universal hope, the immortality of a boundless love, an indestructible element of faith in final good, and the proudest assertion ever made of human freedom." In a similar way, Rhys Davids proclaimed in his Hibbert Lectures for 1881 that Buddhism was "essentially a positive not a negative system." Dharmapala stressed "the constructive optimism" and fundamental "activism" of authentic Buddhism. "Buddhism," he claimed, "teaches an energetic life, to be active in doing good work all the time." His firm commitment to engagement with the world was encapsulated in the title he chose for himself, "Anagarika." This Pali term was one of the epithets of Buddhist monks, but it never served as a title. Dharmapala used the label to designate a new status between monk and layman. He took some of the vows traditionally reserved for monks—e.g., chastity—and wore the monk's robe. Yet he rejected the relative seclusion of the monastery for the life of political and social action. There were few defenses of Buddhism's activistic spirit by non-Buddhists except the almost universal acknowledgment of its tolerance. However, apologists could continue to appeal to the earlier scholarly interpretations of Buddha as a reformer, hold up Asian Buddhists like Dharmapala as models, and build on the widely accepted view that Buddhism's personal ethical code was sound.[29]

The activistic and optimistic character of Buddhism was proclaimed by Caucasian and Japanese Buddhists in San Francisco. In an obvious attempt to defend Buddhism against its critics, the Japanese editors of the *Light of Dharma* placed a passage from the Buddhist scriptures just beneath the description of the contents. It assured American readers that "the Dharma of the Tathagata does not require a man to go into homelessness or to resign the world." The secretary of the Dharma Sangha of Buddha, the Caucasian group connected with the Japanese mission, made a similar point. Kathleen Melrena McIntire told the readers of the *Light of Dharma* in an account of their founding and a call for new members that Buddhism, and the Dharma Sangha, appealed to "man's better nature." Using a term employed by Felix Adler's reform-minded religious group, she claimed that Buddhism provided its adherents with "the truest and most powerful instruments for ethical culture." In fact, McIntire suggested, activism was at the heart of the Buddhist group's purpose: it had been incorporated in the spring of 1900, she reported, in order to "found schools, hospitals, asylums and other institutions of any kind that would be helpful to mankind."[30]

This affirmation of activism and optimism also surfaced in the writings of sympathizers and adherents outside San Francisco. Olcott, the esoteric Buddhist who worked for religious and social reform in Ceylon and India, consciously rejected the usual claims. He pointed to Buddhism's fair treatment of women and its beliefs about the obligations of its adherents to the poor. He asserted that its moral precepts showed that it was an "active" and not a "passive" religion. Vetterling, the editor of the esoteric *Buddhist Ray*, rejected the reigning interpretations of Buddhism by suggesting that a true Buddhist is neither optimistic nor pessimistic, but, like the Buddha, rejects "the folly of the extremists" and follows the "middle path." Canavarro, who had longed to do "some noble, useful and sacrificing work," served as director of a convent and orphanage in Ceylon. She found in Buddhism, or brought to it, a theoretical foundation for social action. In her autobiography she defended Buddhism, and Oriental religions and cultures in general, against the charge of apathy and passivity by acknowledging that the people of the East are never hurried. This does not mean, however, that they are inactive. They simply "make haste slowly." Other Buddhist converts who worked in Asia—such as A. Christina Albers and Catherine Shearer—also apparently found in Buddhism grounds for their social concern.[31]

Edmunds, another esoteric, had some personal tendencies toward pessimism. One friend said that he had a "constitutional predisposition to maintain that whatever is, is wrong." In fact, Edmunds once confessed to his diary that he was considering suicide. When he wrote to his friend Lanman about his mood, Lanman reminded him that "the gracious Buddha taught and taught and taught the value of cheerfulness." Lanman even added a testimonial: he reported that Buddhism had helped him make "some progress in calmness of spirit and cheerfulness." Whether or not Lanman's missive cheered him up, Edmunds did not allow his personal proclivities to distort his public interpretations of Buddhism. (Although sometimes they found vague expression during the solitude of night: "A dream lately showed me a Buddhist temple in gloom, but a Christian one with access to the light of heaven!") On the other hand, Edmunds showed few personal proclivities toward passivity. And he explicitly defended Buddhism on this point. In a later article titled "Buddha as Reformer," Edmunds criticized one popular encyclopedia's interpretation of the tradition as quietistic. Buddhism did not lack "philanthropic" interests, as the entry had claimed. In fact, he reminded his readers, the Buddha had condemned slavery, weapons, butchery, and liquor and had advocated abolition, nonviolence, vegetarianism, and "prohibition." In this sense, the Buddha had anticipated American reform movements of the nineteenth century.[32]

The rationalist C. T. Strauss also rejected the usual negative characterizations. He pointed out that Buddhism avoids the extremes of optimism and pessimism and "teaches the truth that lies between them." In any case, he suggested, the tradition is certainly more optimistic than Christianity: "And a religion which teaches that one can make an end of suffering by one's efforts is certainly less pessimistic than one which teaches that one's salvation depends on the grace of a God, that only few are chosen and that all the rest are doomed to eternal damnation." Further, against those who asserted that Buddhism "paralyses energy," Strauss argued that its emphasis on compassion and "right endeavor" led Buddhism to promote "perseverance and zeal" and condemn "idleness and laziness."[33]

The Reverend Clarence Edgar Rice did not find this true of Buddhism in Japan. He had spent six years there, and he concluded that it failed the pragmatic test. Rice claimed, in an article entitled "Buddhism as I Have Seen It," that the central idea of Buddhism—that "life is essentially evil"— informs the behavior of its followers. In Japan, as elsewhere, it has led to "an apathy as regards life, a crushing fatalism." This attitude, in turn, has led to a series of moral defects and social injustices. The rationalist Buddhist Myra E. Withee responded directly to Rice's charges. She acknowledged some criticisms and deflected others. Yet even when she granted in principle that Japanese civilization had defects, she suggested that these had resulted from transgressions of Buddha's teachings or from the negative effects of Western imperialism. Further, Withee suggested that Christianity would fail a similar test. "Judging a religion by those who profess it," she asked, "how did Christianity appear at the time of Inquisition? How does it appear to-day, as exemplified by the conduct of a large percentage of its devotees? What would be the verdict of a Buddhist who should visit Christendom and judge Christianity by what he found in her cities, especially those that are, as many Christians declare, 'blots upon the earth?' " Withee then piled on the statistics: even in her city of 163,000 inhabitants (St. Paul), which was often considered a "model of purity" compared with other cities of its size or larger, one hundred and thirty Christian churches coexisted with three hundred licensed saloons, twenty-eight public houses of ill repute, and many daily criminal episodes. It is not fair to judge religions only by their influence on the moral character of societies. If we do, however, Buddhism will not lose. In fact, Withee proposed, Buddhism has a superior theoretical foundation for moral action and social justice. The doctrine of karma that "compels each to reap exactly what he sows" is a greater force in making people, and so societies, moral than is Christianity's doctrine of "the forgiveness of sins."[34]

Thomas B. Wilson also interpreted Buddhism as optimistic and activistic. In one article he concurred with Carus's assessment: "Buddhism is no pessimism. Buddhism, it is true, boldly and squarely faces the problem of evil, and recognizes the existence of evil; but it does so in order to show to mankind the way of escape. Buddhism does not preach annihilation, but salvation; it does not teach death, but life." Buddhism, Wilson implied, confirms the reigning confidence in the capacities of individuals and the course of history. Using the optimistic language of evolutionism, but modifying the usual notions of the *telos*, Wilson proclaimed that "every new civilization is another step toward Nirvana for the race." He also consistently presented Buddhism as activistic and this-worldly. "Buddhism," he asserted, "makes it a duty to work for better conditions of existence for human kind, right here in this world, leaving salvation to be the blossom and the fruit of such work." In an attack on contrary interpretations, Wilson suggested that all the great religious teachers had "sought the field of action." In particular, it is incompatible with Buddhist ethics "to quit the active currents of human progress, to hide . . . away in caves and forests." In an unusually clear example of assent to the dominant economic principles and forms, Wilson also presented Buddhism as compatible with capitalism and commerce. Followers have a right, even an obligation, to seek great wealth! Preaching the "Gospel of Wealth" proclaimed by prominent entrepreneurs of the Gilded Age, Wilson announced that Buddhism, and all religions, approved of the accumulation of great wealth as long as the individual distributed some to those in need. Wilson and other rationalist and esoteric apologists implied, then, that Buddhists were as American as social activists like William Lloyd Garrison, influential democrats like Andrew Jackson, incurable optimists like Walt Whitman, and aggressive business leaders like Andrew Carnegie.[35]

It might seem at first glance that romantics—and others with strong mystical impulses, clear aesthetic tendencies, or significant interest in Schopenhauer's philosophy—might embrace Buddhism's alleged pessimism and passivity without reserve. It might be expected that Wilson, Lum, and Lodge, who were drawn to Schopenhauer's thought, might welcome the gloomy, world-denying religion criticized by many in the public conversation. Or those who inclined toward mysticism, aestheticism, and the "feminine" aspects of Buddhism and Asian cultures—Fenollosa, Adams, Lodge, and Bigelow—might be expected to maintain the negative perceptions. After all, they celebrated "the silence of Nirwana's glory" and the "feminine" passivity of the East. Some rejected economic activity—temporarily or permanently—to pursue art and Buddhism (e.g., Bigelow and Lodge).[36]

These expectations are fulfilled to some extent, but the perspectives of these New England intellectuals, as Jackson Lears has noticed, actually seem to have been more ambivalent. For example, it is difficult to find affirmations of activism and optimism in Lodge's poetic tribute to nirvana in which—he told Bigelow in a letter—he had tried to capture the experience of the silent "monotone" he had approached during an hour of Buddhist meditation. And few such affirmations appear in his other brooding poems of spiritual quest. Yet Lodge turned away from his ambivalent pursuit of oceanic withdrawal long enough to be "swept up in the romantic activism of the 1890s." Although these commitments found little place in his poetic treatments of Buddhism, Lodge embraced the dominant ideals of activism, masculinity, and strenuousness by, for example, serving as a naval cadet in the Spanish-American War. Lodge's friend and mentor, Bigelow, seems to stand convicted of interpreting Buddhism as ascetic and world-denying, but the progressivism of Bigelow's evolutionary framework and the optimism in his view of human nature make his perspective more complex than a simple and unqualified rejection of activism and optimism. In a letter to Phillips Brooks, Bigelow implied that the Buddha had a high estimate of human nature. Bigelow claimed that all great thinkers, including the Buddha, had proclaimed that "the Kingdom of God is within you." In other words, he suggested that Buddhism affirmed the reigning optimism about the value, even sacredness, of the individual.[37]

Bigelow's friend, Fenollosa, offered an even more sweeping affirmation of Western values. He confessed that "however much I may sympathize with past civilizations of the East, I am in this incarnation a man of Western race, and bound to do my part towards the development of Western civilization." Even when he linked "feminine" qualities with Asia and Buddhism, Fenollosa was not advocating an unqualified acceptance of passivity. As his poem "East and West" indicates, what he really hoped for was a future synthesis of the active masculine West with the passive feminine East. From such a future union, which Fenollosa predicted with a confidence that mirrored the attitude of many of his Protestant contemporaries, a higher civilization and religion would emerge. Cleverly turning some of the Christian critics' complaints against them, in another poem he even explicitly suggested that the Buddhist hope of rebirth and emphasis on worldly "service" provide a more clearly activistic, and affirmative teaching. The Buddhist version of "immortality" provides a conception "so real, so rich, so tender to all our efforts/so different from the vague blank hope of my fathers!" Life-affirming Buddhism speaks of continued activity in future lives; while nihilistic, pessimistic, quietistic Christianity seeks only eternal rest in heaven: " 'Come unto me, ye laborers, and I will give you rest!'/Yet rest!—rest, cessation, nothingness! Is this the last burden of Religion's chant?/Is Creation all a failure?" Buddhists, Fenollosa announced, answer a decisive no!: "We kiss our loved ones, shoulder our burdens, and stride off, whistling./We ask no Christ to promise us a bed-ridden heaven."[38]

Even those who expressed appreciation for Schopenhauer's thought also affirmed Victorian convictions and attitudes. As I have indicated, Wilson clearly did so. Although there seems to have been a limited acceptance of passivity and pessimism in his life and work, so did Lum. The rationalist Lum was drawn to Schopenhauer's thought and lured by a humanistic mysticism. His niece described him as "a pessimist of the darkest hue" because he believed, with most Buddhists, that consciousness necessarily brings suffering. Lum was suicidal; he clearly did not have the incurably optimistic temperament of Whitman. He did not sacralize the ordinary or embrace all that is. In fact, Lum referred to his own perspective at times as "Schopenhauerismus" or "philosophic pessimism." Further, if we looked only at the passages in his writings that affirm no-self and look forward to the "absolute rest" of nirvana, it would be easy to conclude that Lum's Buddhism was both pessimistic and passive.[39]

Yet Lum also clearly expressed a commitment to optimism and activism. He was sustained in his continuing efforts at reform, for example, by a lofty view of humanity. Lum possessed that deep faith in the natural capacities of persons that is characteristic of most libertarians and anarchists and that was shared by most participants in Victorian culture. He called for the development of increasing freedom in all areas of human life because he believed that this would lead inevitably to the moral perfection of the race. The application of "the Law of Equal Freedom" to religion, politics, society, and economy would lead to "the normal evolution of sympathetic natures." It would stimulate the development of "an emancipated people living in the mutual bonds of peace and fraternity." Further, in his interpretation of Buddhism, he emphasized its compatibility with activism. The Buddha was a social and religious reformer who expressed egalitarian principles in his acceptance of women into the religious order and in his challenge of the Indian caste system. Applying pragmatic criteria and leaning on the authority of mid-Victorian interpretations, Lum described the "markedly beneficial" social effects of Buddhism. He stressed Buddhism's fundamental optimism about humans and argued that its "cardinal idea of the perfectibility of man" was the basis for a personal and social ethic. It had led, for example, to a tolerant spirit and a low crime rate. Buddhism could pass "the test of history." So even when American advocates spoke of the pervasiveness of suffering or welcomed mystical or aesthetic interpretations of Buddhism, they seemed to agree with their contemporary critics and mid-Victorian predecessors about the sort of religiousness that best suited their age.[40]

THE LIMITS OF CULTURAL DISSENT AND
THE LIMITS OF BUDDHIST SUCCESS

Buddhism attracted interest in late-Victorian America for a variety of reasons. It had a number of things going for it. It was received at a time when many had grown dissatisfied with traditional religious answers and in a nation that constitutionally protected the right to seek resolution of one's spiritual crisis in unconventional faiths. At the same time, apologists managed to convince many that this Asian religion might be able to answer their spiritual needs: it seemed more scientific and tolerant. Also, several American apologists—Carus stands out—were especially informed and articulate. A few Asian teachers—Dharmapala had the most influence—

had enough magnetism and passion to attract followers. Yet Buddhism's success as a movement was limited by several factors. Few texts, as I indicated, were translated. Few authoritative Asian teachers permanently resided in the United States; and the specifically Buddhist institutions—the American Maha Bodhi Society and Dharma Sangha of Buddha—were small, weak, and disorganized. The prospects for nurturing strong institutional affiliations or socializing a second generation of followers, therefore, were dim.

In retrospect, this ineffective institutionalization seems predictable. Both temperamental and intellectual factors played a role. Those who were independent—even combative—enough to risk censure by challenging inherited beliefs were not likely to easily, quickly, or fully embrace a new tradition. Those who were infuriated by the intolerant attitudes and dismissive policies of Christianity and other religions were unlikely to join any other institution. Many—and not just rationalists—mistrusted all institutionalized forms of religion. Esoterics, who were committed to the ancient hidden wisdom found at the core of many exoteric traditions, also seemed to be poor candidates for unqualified allegiance to Buddhism, or any single religion. Sympathizers might affiliate with groups that allowed great doctrinal and practical latitude, such as the Theosophical or Ethical Culture Societies. But Buddhism—at least as it had been practiced in Asia—would have restricted individual freedom and required intellectual compromises. Perhaps, then, Buddhism could have been no more successful as a movement.

Yet if Buddhism could have been even more effective in inspiring exclusive allegiance or fostering enduring institutions, it was its perceived discontinuity that doomed it to having less impact than the volatile religious context otherwise might have allowed. As I suggested in the previous chapter, successful new religious movements must have a significant degree of continuity with the conventional faiths and the dominant culture. There cannot be too much tension with the religious and cultural environment. In fact, there seem to have been limits to dissent in Victorian America, and few—including those sympathetic to Buddhism—ventured beyond those limits. Both critics' denunciations and apologists' refutations point to similar commitments. They delineate the cultural boundaries. If the public conversation about Buddhism is any indication, optimism and activism were fundamental to Victorian religious culture. And—although this might seem odd—they often were as difficult to denounce as theism and individualism. It would seem that ideas about a personal creator and a substantial self would be more incontrovertible. But, as I have suggested, the shifting intellectual currents of late-Victorian America carried a number of intellectuals toward agnostic views of ultimate reality and nonsubstantialist views of selfhood. On these issues there were grounds, even precedents, for proudly proclaiming dissent. It was not the same with activism and optimism. In many ways, for late-Victorians, it was more acceptable to be atheistic than apathetic. "Whether a God exist," William James proclaimed in 1891, "or whether no God exist, in yon blue heaven above us bent, we form at any rate an ethical republic here below."[41]

Many Buddhist apologists took a similar stand. Whether there is a personal creator or a substantial self, there still can be an attractive founder, a noble ethics, a Protestant spirit, a "God-idea," a blissful "afterlife," and a self-reliant tone. Most of all, there still *must* be optimism and activism. With few exceptions, Buddhist apologists stood united with American critics, travelers, and scholars in implicitly or explicitly affirming the high capacities of persons, the progressive development of history, and the role of religion in stimulating effective economic, political, and social activity. Almost all participants in Victorian culture and contributors to the public discourse about Buddhism agreed: whatever else true religion was, it was optimistic and activistic. In many ways, then, nineteenth-century Euro-American Buddhist sympathizers had more in common with their mainline Protestant contemporaries than with nineteenth-century Asian-American or twentieth-century Caucasian Buddhists. In their affirmation of the dominant culture, Victorian sympathizers and adherents resembled Henry Ward Beecher and Lyman Abbott more than Jack Kerouac and Gary Snyder.

Yet the connection between Buddhism and countercultural values—in particular pessimism and passivity—seems to have limited its appeal for those who otherwise might have been drawn to it. It also diminished the intensity of the commitment among many who already were attracted. This point was explicitly acknowledged in an article from a Pennsylvania newspaper that was reprinted in the *Buddhist Ray*. The article gave an account of a local lecture on Buddhism. The speaker suggested that "if it were not for a consistent and thorough going pessimism, every religion and every philosophy must yield the palm to Buddhism." And although Warren Felt Evans managed to overcome this difficulty enough to say some nice things about Buddhism, the religion's association with gloominess also severely limited its attractiveness for many who shared the bubbling optimism of the New Thought movement. To offer a final example, Carus's inability to embrace Buddhism fully seems to have been related not only to his worries about sectarianism but also to his discomfort with Buddhism's passivity. Confirming the opinions of many Western scholars and Christian critics, he admitted its quietistic tendencies. "The main advantage of Christianity over Buddhism," he wrote, "consists in the activity which it inspires. Buddhism has to a great extent (with the exception, perhaps, of some Japanese sects) favored a passive attitude in life."[42]

Most sympathetic contributors to the public discourse managed to discover—or construct—an optimistic and activistic Buddhism; yet the force of contrary interpretations finally proved too difficult to overcome for many others. Perhaps numerous Asian teachers, dense internal networks, accurate textual translations, inclinations toward affiliation, and strong native institutions might have inspired more firm and enduring loyalties. But without dislodging the widely accepted view of Buddhism as pessimistic and passive, it seems unlikely that those sympathizers who failed to embrace it fully or exclusively could have intensified their commitment. It seems unlikely that significantly larger numbers of the spiritually disillusioned could have found the tradition intellectually compatible and emotionally satisfying. Despite the efforts of a number of public advocates, most information that Americans readers and audiences received portrayed Buddhism as incompatible with the most cherished of Victorian beliefs and values. Finally, then, although a few thousand identified with the religion and thousands more felt some attraction, most disillusioned Victorians felt that they had to look elsewhere for aid in resolving their religious crisis. Yet if Buddhism did not achieve the success as a movement that, for example, Mormonism finally enjoyed, apologists had not failed either. By the time interest waned and the discussion quieted in the years preceding the First World War, Buddhism had created more of a stir than early Victorian interpreters ever might have imagined.

POSTSCRIPT

Buddhism in America after 1912

In 1921, Dharmapala looked back nostalgically on the late-Victorian interest in Buddhism in a letter to Mary Carus written two years after her influential husband had died. "At one time there was some kind of activity in certain parts of the U.S. where some people took interest in Buddhism; but I see none of that now." He hoped—but it was not to be—that "perhaps again through the Open Court we might revive the American Maha Bodhi Society of which your late husband was President." A wistful and pensive Dharmapala concluded this letter by reflecting on the cycles of existence: "Life continues and we are born again under changed conditions with a new set of skhandas. They are the same and not the same. No individual lives permanently nor is he annihilated. He appears in a new garb." Though more research is needed before firm conclusions are reached, it seems that the same might be said of Buddhism in twentieth-century America. It has been both the same and not the same.[1]

There were, first of all, some significant differences. In an essay published in 1913, the philosopher George Santayana felt the rumblings of a religious and cultural shift. "The present age is a critical one and interesting to live in," he wrote. "The civilization characteristic of Christendom has not disappeared, yet another civilization has begun to take its place." Christianity, of course, would not be displaced. Protestantism did not suddenly or completely lose its cultural power. But it was about 1912 or 1913 that Victorian culture began to lose its dominance in the cities. The Modernist culture—or really the variety of cultures, subcultures, and countercultures—that took its place was less overtly and fully Anglo-Saxon Protestant. A mainline Protestant establishment continued to exert significant influence through the 1950s, but the traditional claims about its moral guardianship and cultural responsibility seemed more self-conscious and less convincing. Even after the 1960s, Protestantism remained the majority faith, but a pulsing pluralism had set in.[2]

All this, and other developments, changed the character of the conversation about Buddhism and the nature of sympathetic responses to the tradition. Some of the beliefs and values that had played so prominent a role in the earlier debate had lost some of their persuasive power. Surveys into the 1990s continued to show that an overwhelming majority of Americans reported belief in God. Yet belief in a personal creator, at least among intellectuals, seemed somewhat less firm as the natural and behavioral sciences continued to erode traditional views. At the same time, processive, nonsubstantialist views of the universe and the self were advanced by natural scientists and philosophers and given expression in, for example, Modernist fiction and painting. The most significant change, however, was that Victorian optimism now seemed to many dangerous at worst and naive at best. The experience of the First World War, among other things, convinced a number of intellectuals that Victorians had overestimated human inclinations and misjudged history's course. Nyogen Sensaki, the Japanese Rinzai Zen master who died in 1958, felt that Americans' "optimism" prepared them well to receive Buddhist teachings. There might be some truth in this observation. A tempered and modified optimism survived among some. And a surge of confidence, even a renewal of the sense of America's destiny, was felt for two decades after World War II. Yet the situation had changed significantly. The atrocities of the death camps, and the American battles in Korea and Vietnam, made unqualified optimism about human propensities and history's progress more difficult to espouse.[3]

Soldiers directly encountered Buddhism in those wars in Asia, and Americans at home continued to have contact with those of Asian descent. But the encounters, as in the previous century, were not always benevolent. Asian-American Buddhists continued to suffer restrictions and persecutions. The immigration act of 1924 limited the annual quota of immigrants from any country to 2 percent of the number of individuals born in that country and resident in the United States in 1890. This totally excluded the Japanese. Buddhist temples, however, still continued to be built on the West Coast after 1924—for example, in San Diego, Oxnard, and Gardena. Despite the restrictions and the humiliations of internment during the Second World War, Pure Land Buddhism adapted to the new cultural context and survived into the postwar era. Since the immigration act of 1965 eliminated the national origins quota system, more Asian Buddhists have come to the United States.[4]

Asian teachers who arrived before and after 1965 provided Asian Americans from a variety of Buddhist nations and sects with opportunities to practice their inherited faith in their adopted land. Some of these teachers also helped to make the postwar interest among Caucasians possible. Sensaki, who had landed in California in 1905, did not begin to teach Zen until years later. But by the 1920s he had established permanent institutions—in San Francisco in 1928 and in Los Angeles in 1929. Until the surge of interest after 1950 or so, however, it was D. T. Suzuki who was as influential as any. In 1921 he founded *The Eastern Buddhist*. In an interesting coincidence, he also sent Mary Carus a letter in that same year—the year that Dharmapala's had arrived—requesting her help. Like Dharmapala, he asked for Carus's aid in promoting Buddhism. Suzuki hoped that Open Court Publishing Company might circulate a collection of essays on Zen he was writing. Open Court did not publish that collection, but it appeared in English several years later. With its publication, Suzuki began to exert his considerable influence in the West.[5]

This lay follower extended his influence even further when he returned to America for eight years during the 1950s, and other Asian Buddhist authorities from Zen and other sects arrived in the following decades. Unlike in the Victorian period, then, Caucasian sympathizers and adherents in the second half of the twentieth century could find institutions to support their interest and teachers to nurture their development. This had an effect on the nature of Buddhist conversions and the sources of its appeal. The lure of an alien "intellectual landscape" and the desire for a more intellectually satisfying worldview seems to have been more relevant to nineteenth-century Buddhist interest. One recent study of contemporary conversions to Asian meditation groups suggested that intellectual factors, while relatively important, were not decisive. Another more impressionistic study listed eleven overlapping sources of Buddhism's appeal for Americans of the 1970s. Some of these—"the intellectual, scientific appeal," "the need for a wise and benevolent authority figure," and "the appeal of pageantry, symbolism, and the esoteric"—also seem relevant to late-Victorians. Others do not fit as well. For example, the psychologist responsible for the study hypothesized that the single most significant motive for joining Buddhist groups was the desire to find relief from physical and psychological suffering through practices such as chanting and meditation. Similarly, R. E. Gussman and S. D. Berkowitz found that contemporary Americans turned to Asian meditation groups to a large extent "to enrich and extend experience through often difficult and exacting forms of religious practice." Nineteenth-century sympathizers had less access to Buddhist teachers and institutions, and far fewer had the opportunity to engage in sustained practice. The psychological and physical benefits derived from regular meditation and other practices, then, seem to have been important only to the most dedicated and privileged of Victorians. A century later, Caucasian followers would be drawn by experiences unavailable to most of their Victorian counterparts.[6]

American Buddhists—those associated with Zen, Tibetan, and Theravadin groups, for example—have consciously and unconsciously transformed traditions. American Buddhist communities, for instance, seem more egalitarian than most of their Asian models: female and lay followers play a more significant role. At the same time, however, twentieth-century sympathizers and adherents seem more willing to dissent from the beliefs of Judeo-Christian tradition and the values of the popular culture. The extreme examples of this inclination—the Beats and the hippies—are well known. But many others who did not "drop out" found Buddhism's alleged countercultural impulses attractive. From the 1950s through the 1970s, many who were disillusioned with American nationalism and militarism sought partial identification—in dress, diet, music, and religion—with exotic cultures. Less confident about American "civilization," capitalist "advance," and technological "progress," some welcomed—to use Jack Kerouac's term—the "lunacy" of Zen masters and, even, the passivity of Buddhism.[7]

But dissensus should not be overemphasized, and continuities with the earlier period should not be overlooked. In fact, some who participated in the late-Victorian conversation lived on into the next period, and a few—like Strauss and Edmunds—continued to write about Buddhism. A handful survived in the imaginations of twentieth-century American readers. Unable to shake the impression even after death, William Sturgis Bigelow was portrayed as idiosyncratic and iconoclastic in an article titled "Bohemian and Buddhist" that appeared in *Atlantic Monthly* in 1936. Although this was somewhat less crucial for its appeal, twentieth-century sympathizers also continued to note Buddhism's compatibility with science and tolerance. L. Adams Beck (1862–1939) took this stand in an article for *Atlantic* in 1926. With the horrors of the First World War still fresh in many readers' minds, Beck also could apply the pragmatic test to Christian civilizations and pronounce it a failure: " 'By their fruits ye shall know them,' said your Prophet; and to your fruits I am content to appeal. Irony of ironies! It is the nations taught by Christ who have come to us to teach us by sword and fire that Right in this world is powerless unless it be supported by Might." Like some of his late-Victorian predecessors, Beck also noted the compatibilities between the doctrine of no-self and scientific conclusions. "Science," he claimed, "is unraveling the constituents of personality, on the very lines of the Buddha's teachings more than two millenniums ago."[8]

At the same time, Christian interlocutors continued to struggle with some elements of Buddhism's distinctiveness, and a range of interpreters still used the language of enchantment and even the rhetoric of negation. One account of Japanese Buddhists in New York City published in *Newsweek* in 1947 opened this way: "Before the gilt and teakwood altar a thin thread of incense-burning smoke curled from a jar-shaped burner. Between two tall candles were symbolic offerings of rice and apples. Worshippers sat quietly on benches and chairs. A priest in embroidered robes, with a string of beads in one hand and a padded stick in the other, struck a bowl-like gong. A sonorous bass note echoed against yellow plaster walls." This report concluded by listing Buddhism's differences: "Unlike Christian services, Buddhist services have no prayers, since

Buddhists never ask for anything. Nor do they recognize miracles, divine beings, or any supernatural powers of intervention in man's affairs."[9]

Every indication suggests that this journalist was trying to be fair to Buddhism. Some Protestants, like the psychologist and philosopher James Bisset Pratt (1875–1944), also tried. Pratt's announced goal in one book was to "enable the reader to understand a little how it feels to be a Buddhist." D. T. Suzuki, among others, thought that Pratt had succeeded. Yet Christian critics sometimes still pointed to Buddhism's nihilism, pessimism, and passivity. In fact, a number of Protestant theologians between the world wars used Buddhism as the "other" over against which to define their world-transforming Christianity. Reinhold Niebuhr, for instance, relied on the classifications of religions offered by Nathan Söderblom and John Oman to distinguish between mystical and mythical religions. Western forms of idealistic monism—as in Plato and Hegel—did not share these characteristics, but the dualistic mysticisms of Asia were pessimistic and passive. Buddhism, which Niebuhr viewed as Christianity's "only serious competition," exhibited these gloomy, world-rejecting tendencies most clearly. "In Buddhism," he explained, "the various tendencies of these types of dualistic pantheism are driven to their logical conclusion and ultimate salvation is conceived as life in a state of quasi-existence, a state in which life and consciousness have been stripped of all that is finite, but also of all that is dynamic or meaningful." Repeating the criticisms of an earlier generation, Niebuhr complained that Buddhists seek only "escape from the temporal world" and "destruction of individual personality." To Niebuhr and others committed to individual rights and social activism, this was particularly reprehensible and repellant.[10]

Some late twentieth-century Asian and American Buddhists, like Masao Abe, have accepted some of these Western criticisms and sought to transform Buddhism—and Christianity—through interreligious encounter. Many Buddhists also have continued to argue that the religion has been misunderstood. Contemporary Buddhist scholars and apologists, for instance, have pointed to the theoretical foundations for activism in Theravada and Mahayana traditions. The same happened earlier in the century. Dwight Goddard, the American Protestant missionary turned Buddhist apologist, explicitly rejected most of the standard negative interpretations. He was drawn to Buddhist asceticism and monasticism and, so, was less troubled by the "passive" elements that others had condemned. Still, he argued that Zen encourages "cheerful industry." He also claimed that Buddhism is neither pessimistic nor nihilistic. He even denied that it is atheistic. Buddhism, Goddard suggested, allows for an optimistic attitude, a blissful afterlife, and a God-idea. Goddard's life and work paralleled late-Victorians' in other ways too. For example, like Carus, he compiled a very popular *Buddhist Bible* that has been reprinted many times since it first appeared in 1932. Goddard also evidenced syncretistic impulses, stressed parallels between the founders' lives and teachings, and even discussed— at length—the claims about Buddhist influence on the Christ. In these ways, and others, the twentieth-century conversation and converts recalled earlier patterns and continued earlier developments.[11]

TABLE 1

**Analysis of the "List of Subscription, Contribution, and Exchange"
for *The Light of Dharma*, 1901–1907**

I. United States and Foreign

Category of Listing	Country	
	U.S.	Foreign
Subscriptions (Paying sub-scribers)	101	24
Contributions (Persons/institutions sent the maga-zine without charge)	48	65
Exchanges (Periodicals that sent their own publication in exchange for a copy of *LD*)	31	5

Total Persons Listed: 204
Total Institutions Listed: 99

II. United States and Its Possessions

Total Persons and In-stitutions Listed with Ad-dresses in U.S. and Its Pos-sessions	199
Gender of Subscribers	60% male (61/101) 40% female (40/101)
Ethnicity of Subscribers	97% non-Asians (98/101) 3% Asian descent (3/101)
Urban vs. Rural Subscribers	65% urban

TABLE 1

(Continued)

Urban Areas with Largest Number of Subscriptions, Contributions, and Exchanges	San Francisco (43); New York City (32); Boston (21); Chicago (15); Philadelphia (12); Honolulu (5).
States and Possessions Represented	California (67); New York (35); Massachusetts (23); Illinois (15); Pennsylvania (14); Hawaii (8); Oregon (4); Connecticut (4); Maine (4); Minnesota (3); Missouri (3); Kansas (2); Puerto Rico (2); Washington (2); South Dakota (2). States with one mention each: Colorado; Louisiana; Maryland; Michigan; Nebraska; Nevada; New Hampshire; Ohio; Tennessee; Texas; Vermont.

Source: "List of the Subscription, Contribution, and Exchange. The Light of Dharma." Notebook, ms., Archives of the Buddhist Churches of America, San Francisco.

TABLE 2

Typology of Euro-American Buddhist Sympathizers and Adherents in the United States, 1875–1912

I. The Esoteric or Occult Type

Intellectual and Cultural Sources: Neoplatonism, Theosophy, Mesmerism, Spiritualism, Swedenborgianism.

Institutional Expressions: Theosophical Society, Maha Bodhi Society (during the 1890s), and most members of the Dharma Sangha of Buddha.

Exemplars: 1. Philangi Dasa (Herman Carl Vetterling); 2. Henry Steel Olcott; 3. Sister Sanghamitta (Marie deSouza Canavarro).

Characterization: Interest in "hidden" or occult beliefs and practices. Metaphysical and cosmological focus. Most spiritually eclectic before, during, and after their attraction to Buddhism. Despite possible theoretical affinity between this type and Tantric traditions in Tibet and Japan, a large number of esoterics focused on Theravada Buddhism.

Elective Affinities: Highest proportion of women. Most ethnically diverse and socially marginal. Predominantly urban but more likely to be found in rural areas than other types.

II. The Rationalistic Type

Intellectual and Cultural Sources: "The Skeptical Enlightenment," Deism, the Rationalist stream in British and American Unitarianism, Auguste Comte's positivism, and Herbert Spencer's evolutionism.

TABLE 2

(Continued)

Institutional Expressions: No clear institutional embodiment. Found among some members of the Free Religious Association, Ethical Culture Society, Maha Bodhi Society, and Dharma Sangha of Buddha. Also expressed in the pages of radical religious and political magazines (e.g., *The Index, The Radical Review, Open Court*).

Exemplars: 1. Dyer Daniel Lum; 2. Paul Carus; 3. Thomas B. Wilson.

Characterization: Focus on rational-discursive means of attaining religious truth and meaning. Anthropological and ethical focus. Interest primarily, though not exclusively, in Theravada Buddhism.

Elective Affinities: Like romantics, high level of education and high proportion of professionals. Even more likely than esoterics to hold radical political and economic views.

III. The Romantic or Exotic-Culture Type

Intellectual and Cultural Sources: Romanticism; increased contact with Asian nations with significant Buddhist followings such as Japan and Tibet and with Asian Buddhists made possible by technological, political, cultural, economic, and social developments.

Institutional Expressions: No clear institutional embodiment. Sometimes formal links with traditional Buddhist institutions in Asia. The Japanese Collections at the Boston Museum of Fine Arts.

Exemplars: 1. Ernest Fenollosa; 2. Lafcadio Hearn; 3. William Sturgis Bigelow.

Characterization: Focus on aesthetic avenues to religious meaning. Commitment to Buddhism as part of immersion in and attachment to an exotic Buddhist culture as a whole—art, architecture, drama, music, customs, rituals, literature, and language as well as religion. Literary and artistic emphasis. Tended to focus on Japan and Tibet and forms of Buddhism found there.

Elective Affinities: Along with rationalists, the best educated. More likely to be from the elite of major urban centers. Least likely to be found in rural areas and to hold radical political or economic views.

Notes

INTRODUCTION

1. Ezra Stiles, *The United States Elevated to Glory and Honour* . . . , 2nd ed. (1783; Worcester: Isaiah Thomas, 1785), 139. Hannah Adams, *An Alphabetical Compendium of the Various Sects* . . . (Boston: B. Edes, 1784). In an interesting twist, Adams used Stiles's election sermon as a source for her knowledge of Buddhism. In another twist, Stiles later played another role in expanding Adams's knowledge of "idolatry" by recommending that she read the journal of the Asiatik Society. See Ezra Stiles to Hannah Adams, 12 June 1794, The Hannah Adams Papers, New England Historic Genealogical Society, Boston, Massachusetts. The unofficial beginning of academic Sinology can be dated from 1814 when Abel Remusat (1788–1832) was installed in the first European chair of "langues et littératures chinoises et tartares-mandchoues" at the Collège de France. The first academic instruction in classical Indian languages also began in the same year with the establishment of a chair in Sanskrit at the same institution. The best overview of developments in America before the 1840s is Carl Jackson, *The Oriental Religions and American Thought* (Westport, Conn.: Greenwood, 1981), 3–43. On American Oriental tales in the late eighteenth and nineteenth century see Mukhtar Isani, "The Oriental Tale in America through 1865: A Study in American Fiction," Ph.D. diss., Princeton University, 1962. See also David S. Reynolds, *Faith in Fiction: The Emergence of Religious Literature in America* (Cambridge: Harvard University Press, 1981), 9–68.

2. "A Review of the Eighteenth Century," *Monthly Anthology* 2 (May 1805): 226. [Joseph Tuckerman], "On the Causes by Which Unitarians Have Been Withheld from Exertions in the Cause of Foreign Missions," *Christian Examiner* 1 (May–June 1824): 183. David Benedict, *History of All Religions: As Divided into Paganism, Mahometism, Judaism, and Christianity* (Providence: John Miller, 1824) 1–51, 359. John S. Pancake, ed., *Thomas Jefferson: Revolutionary Philosopher: A Selection of Writings* (Woodbury, N.J.: Barron's, 1976), 326, 334.

3. Ralph L. Rusk, ed., *The Letters of Ralph Waldo Emerson* (New York: Columbia University Press, 1939), 3: 179.

4. Paul Carus, "Hinduism Different from Buddhism," *Open Court* 20 (Apr. 1906): 253.

5. On the emergence of Buddha as historical figure and religious founder see Philip C. Almond, "The Buddha in the West: From Myth to History," *Religion* 16 (Oct. 1986): 305–22. J. W. deJong, "A Brief History of Buddhist Studies in Europe and America," *The Eastern Buddhist* 7 (May 1974): 55–106; 7 (Oct. 1974): 49–82. Eugène Burnouf and Christian Lassen, *Essai sur le pali* (Paris: Dondey-Dupré, 1826). Eugène Burnouf, *L'Introduction à l'histoire du buddhisme indien* (Paris: Imprimerie royale, 1844). Burnouf was only one of the founders of Buddhist studies. For information on the others see Guy Welbon, *The Buddhist Nirvana and Its Western Interpreters* (Chicago: University of Chicago Press, 1968), 23–50.

6. Edward E. Salisbury, "Memoir on the History of Buddhism," *Journal of the American Oriental Society* 1 (1843–49): 81–135. Salisbury was a member of the Center Church, on New Haven Green, from 1840 to 1872. He served as a deacon there from 1849 to 1862. In 1872, he transferred his affiliation to the church in Yale College. For evidence of his piety see Edward Elbridge Salisbury, "The Influence of the Spirit of Christianity on the Discovery of Truth," n.d., Salisbury Family Papers,

168 Notes to pages xxxi – xxxiii

Sterling Memorial Library, Yale University, New Haven. See also his journals and sermons: Edward Elbridge Salisbury, "Mathew 26:36–44," "II Timothy 3:6," "I John 4:18," n.d., Salisbury Family Papers. [Elizabeth Palmer Peabody, trans.], "The Preaching of the Buddha," *The Dial* 4 (Jan. 1844): 391–401. See also Wendell Piez, "Anonymous Was a Woman—Again," *Tricycle: The Buddhist Review* 3 (Fall 1993): 10–11.

7. I have borrowed the phrase "community of discourse" from the historian David Hollinger—although I focus less on intellectual elites than Hollinger's formulation of this notion suggests. See David Hollinger, "Historians and the Discourse of Intellectuals," in *New Directions in American Intellectual History*, ed. John Higham and Paul K. Conkin (Baltimore: The Johns Hopkins University Press, 1979), 42–63. This "community," for my purposes, includes any person who contributed to the public conversation and not only those contributors who had the greatest knowledge about the topic. My approach to the historical analysis of beliefs and values has been informed by traditions in interpretive sociology, social history, women's studies, Anglo-American philosophy, and cultural anthropology. Several pieces about method in intellectual and cultural history have clarified my thinking—including William J. Bousma, "Intellectual History in the 1980s: From History of Ideas to History of Meaning," in *The New History: The 1980s and Beyond*, ed. Theodore K. Rabb and Robert I. Rotberg (Princeton: Princeton University Press, 1982), 279–91 and Bernard S. Cohn, "Anthropology and History: Toward a Reapproachment," in *New History*, ed. Rabb and Rotberg, 227–52. The other methodological essays in *New Directions in American Intellectual History* also have been useful.

8. For an English translation of William's travel narrative see Manuel Komroff, *Contemporaries of Marco Polo . . .* (New York: Boni and Liveright, 1928), 53–209. The staged debate is recounted on pages 171–82. William of Rubruck also is known as William of Ruysbroek, Ruysbrock, or Rubruquis. Henri deLubac, *La Rencontre du bouddhisme et de l'occident* (Paris: Aubier, Editions montaigne, 1952). Notto R. Thelle, *Buddhism and Christianity in Japan: From Conflict to Dialogue* (Honolulu: University of Hawaii Press, 1987). Christopher Clausen, "Victorian Buddhism and the Origins of Comparative Religion," *Religion* 5 (1973): 1–15. Vijitha Rajapakse, "Buddhism in Huxley's Evolution and Ethics: A Note on a Victorian Evaluation and Its Comparativist Dimension," *Philosophy East and West* 35 (July 1985): 295–304. Philip C. Almond, *The British Discovery of Buddhism* (New York: Cambridge University Press, 1988). T. Christmas Humphreys, *The Development of Buddhism in England* (London: The Buddhist Lodge, 1937). Ian P. Oliver, *Buddhism in Britain* (London: Rider, 1979). Jackson, *Oriental Religions and American Thought*, 141–56. Louise H. Hunter, *Buddhism in Hawaii: Its Impact on a Yankee Community* (Honolulu: University of Hawaii Press, 1971). Tetsuden Kashima, *Buddhism in America: The Social Organization of an Ethnic Religious Organization* (Westport, Conn.: Greenwood, 1977). William Charles Rust, "The Shin Sect of Buddhism in America," Ph.D. diss., University of Southern California, 1951. Isao Horinouchi, "Americanized Buddhism: A Sociological Analysis of a Protestantized Japanese Religion," Ph.D. diss., University of California, Davis, 1973. Emma McCloy Layman, *Buddhism in America* (Chicago: Nelson-Hall, 1976). Charles S. Prebish, *American Buddhism* (North Scituate, Mass.: Duxbury, 1979). Rick Fields, *How the Swans Came to the Lake: A Narrative History of Buddhism in America*, rev. ed. (Boston: Shambhala, 1986). For other relevant sources see the bibliography.

9. R. Laurence Moore, *In Search of White Crows: Spiritualism, Parapsychology, and American Culture* (New York: Oxford University Press, 1977). Catherine L. Albanese, *Corresponding Motion: Transcendental Religion and the New America* (Philadelphia: Temple University Press, 1977). Stephen Gottschalk, *The Emergence of*

Christian Science in American Religious Life (Berkeley: University of California Press, 1973). Klaus J. Hansen, *Mormonism and the American Experience* (Chicago: University of Chicago Press, 1981). Rodney Stark has made the same point about cultural continuity. See "How New Religions Succeed: A Theoretical Model," in *The Future of New Religious Movements*, ed. David G. Bromley and Phillip E. Hammond (Macon, Ga.: Mercer University Press, 1987), 11–29.

10. On the transition to China see Erik Zürcher, *The Buddhist Conquest of China* (Leiden: Brill, 1959). On Confucian "activism," and Taoist "quietism," see Richard Mather, "The Controversy over Conformity and Naturalness During the Six Dynasties," *History of Religions* 9 (Nov. and Feb. 1969–70): 160–79. For an analysis of Buddhism's role in the debate on activism and quietism in China see Richard Mather, "Vimilakirti and Gentry Buddhism," *History of Religions* 8 (Aug. 1968): 60–73. On Buddhist borrowing of Taoist terms, see Arthur E. Link, "The Taoist Antecedents of Tao-An's Prajna Ontology," *History of Religions* 9 (Nov. and Feb. 1969–70): 181–215. For an example of a Chinese Buddhist apologist emphasizing Confucian parallels see Sun Ch'o's (d. 370) *Clarification of the Way*: Arthur E. Link and Tim Lee, "Sun Ch'o's *Yü-Tao-Lun*: A Clarification of the Way," *Monumenta Serica* 25 (1966): 169–96.

11. Daniel Walker Howe, "Victorian Culture in America," in *Victorian America*, ed. Daniel Walker Howe (Philadelphia: University of Pennsylvania Press, 1976), 5.

12. There is a rich secondary literature on British and American Victorianism. One of the best attempts at characterization is Daniel Walker Howe's essay "Victorian Culture in America." My account relies on that fine essay in a number of ways. Howe notes, for example, the regional and denominational variations. "Presbygational" was a nickname contemporaries coined by combining "Presbyterian" and "Congregational." The continuities and discontinuities of southern Victorianism have been noted by Daniel Joseph Singal, *The War Within: From Victorian to Modernist Thought in the South, 1919–1945* (Chapel Hill: The University of North Carolina Press, 1982), 11–33. This characterization of the shifts in Victorian culture over time is suggested in Karen Halttunen, *Confidence Men and Painted Women: A Study of Middle-Class Victorian Culture in America, 1830–1870* (New Haven: Yale University Press, 1982). On distinct male and female spheres or cultures see Carroll Smith-Rosenberg, *Disorderly Conduct: Visions of Gender in Victorian America* (New York: Oxford University Press, 1985), 60. Compare William Buell Sprague's (1795–1876) varying advice to young men and young women: William B. Sprague, *Letters to Young Men, Founded on the History of Joseph* (Albany: Eratus H. Pease, 1845); William B. Sprague, *The Excellent Woman as Described in the Book of Proverbs* (Boston: Gould and Lincoln, 1851).

13. Alexis deTocqueville, *Democracy in America*, trans. Henry Reeve (1835–40; New York: Vintage, 1945), 2: 104. Belief in a personal creator and substantial self were so central to Victorianism that few scholars have felt the need to note their importance. There are some exceptions. In their attempts to define Modernist culture in America, some scholars have been led to recognize that a belief in an immutable and substantial self was a component of the culture that Modernism replaced. See Daniel Joseph Singal, "Towards a Definition of American Modernism," *American Quarterly* 39 (Spring 1987): 15. In a similar way, scholars who have traced nontraditional forms of thinking about God sometimes have felt compelled to note theism's pervasiveness. On nineteenth-century agnostic and atheistic thinking in the United States see James Turner, *Without God, Without Creed: The Origins of Unbelief in America* (Baltimore: Johns Hopkins University Press, 1985). Activism and optimism, although important, were slightly less obvious. So historians have consistently and explicitly linked Victorian culture with these two clusters of beliefs and values. For example, Walter E. Houghton associated British Victorianism with

"optimism" and "enthusiasm" (even "moral optimism"). Walter E. Houghton, *The Victorian Frame of Mind, 1830–1870* (New Haven: Yale University Press, 1957), 27–53; 263–304. Frank Thistlethwaite emphasized the connection between British and American activism in "The Anglo-American World of Humanitarian Endeavor," in *Ante-Bellum Reform*, ed. David Brion Davis (New York: Harper and Row, 1967), 63–81. Henry May argued that the Didactic Enlightenment—i.e., the Scottish philosophy of "Common Sense"—was assimilated by the official culture of the nineteenth century; and its influence was evident in that culture's emphasis on moral values and progress. Henry F. May, *The Enlightenment in America* (New York: Oxford University Press, 1976), 337–62. Scholars have discovered an emphasis on optimism in mainstream Protestantism and its leaders during the period. See William G. McLoughlin, *The Meaning of Henry Ward Beecher: An Essay on the Shifting Values of Mid-Victorian America, 1840–1870* (New York: Alfred A. Knopf, 1970). Frank Luther Mott suggested that a spirit of "optimism" characterized all the leading general magazines between 1850 and 1865. Mott, *A History of American Magazines*, 2: 27. Singal found "steadfast optimism," a "gospel of progress," "practicality," and "paternalistic benevolence" in Southern Victorianism. Singal, *The War Within*, 23–24. Finally, Howe identified "future-orientedness," "moral seriousness," and "didacticism" as part of Victorian culture in America. Confidently focused on the future, he suggested, Americans engaged in numerous efforts to moralize and reform. Howe, "Victorian Culture in America," 19–23.

1. "THE SEEMING ANOMALY OF BUDDHIST NEGATION"

1. James C[lement] Moffat, *A Comparative History of Religions* (New York: Dodd and Mead, 1871, 1873), 2: 230, 243, 235, 242, 240, 241.

2. On the opening of the conversation see the Introduction. On the rise of the university see Laurence R. Veysey, *The Emergence of the American University* (Chicago: University of Chicago Press, 1965). The Free Religious Association, the least well-known of these three groups, emerged out of both Unitarianism and Transcendentalism. The preamble to the constitution of the National Unitarian Conference (1865) defined the denomination as explicitly Christian. The more radical Unitarians, and others who already had left or never had belonged, formed the Free Religious Association two years later. Membership statistics are lacking, but the organization was never very large. Nonetheless, as I will show here and in subsequent chapters, its members played a disproportionately large role in the American conversation about Buddhism and other Asian religions. See Stow Persons, *Free Religion: An American Faith* (New Haven: Yale University Press, 1947).

3. The general magazines included *The North American Review* (1815–current), *The Atlantic Monthly* (1857–current), *Harper's New Monthly Magazine* (1850–current), *The Southern Literary Messenger* (1834–64), and *The Nation* (1865–current). Articles also appeared in mainline Protestant magazines such as *The Missionary Herald* (1821–1951), *The Methodist Quarterly Review* (1830–84), *The New Englander* (1843–92), *The Princeton Review* (1825–88), *The Baptist Quarterly* (1867–77), and *The Bibliotheca Sacra* (1843–current). A number of pieces were published in Unitarian, Universalist, Transcendentalist, and Free Religionist periodicals, such as *The Christian Examiner* (1824–69), *The Dial* (1840–44), *The Universalist Quarterly Review* (1844–91), *The Index* (1870–86), and *The Radical* (1865–72). Some of these periodicals, of course, appeared earlier or later under different titles. For example, *The Princeton Review* appeared as *Biblical Repertory* from 1825–71, as *Presbyterian Quarterly and Princeton Review* from 1872–77, and as *The New Princeton Review* from 1886–88.

4. Michael Cooper, ed., *They Came to Japan: An Anthology of European Reports on Japan, 1543–1640* (Berkeley: University of California Press, 1965), 315, 317, 322.

5. [James T. Dickinson], "The Hindoos," *Christian Examiner* 64 (Mar. 1858): 173–208; "The Chinese," *Christian Examiner* 65 (Sept. 1858): 177–205; "Asiatic Civilization," *Christian Examiner* 67 (July 1859): 1–31.

6. Thomas Wentworth Higginson, *Contemporaries* (Boston and New York: Houghton Mifflin, 1899), 131–32. Lydia Maria Child, *The Progress of Religious Ideas through Successive Ages* (New York: C. S. Francis; London, S. Low, 1855), 1: x.

7. Child's failure to acknowledge Adams's similar intentions is especially surprising since she had visited the older woman at least several times. In one of her *Letters from New York*, this one dated 15 May 1844, Child recounted carrying a bunch of fresh violets to the aged Miss Adams. She described Adams as "the simple-hearted old lady, so well remembered as the earliest writer among the women of New England." Apparently, Child forgot or—is it possible?—never read Adams's survey of the religions. Lydia Maria Child, *Letters from New York*, second series (New York: C. S. Francis; Boston: J. H. Francis, 1852), 131. Lydia Maria Child to Thomas Wentworth Higginson, 9 Sept. 1877, Thomas Wentworth Higginson Papers, Houghton Library, Harvard University, Cambridge, Mass.

8. Child, *Progress of Religious Ideas*, 2: 154; 1: 85–86. For Child's explicit account of the parallels between Buddhism and Christianity see *Progress of Religious Ideas*, 3: 434–37. Thomas Wentworth Higginson to Lydia Maria Child, 15 Nov. 1873, Autograph File, Houghton Library. In this letter Higginson expressed his gratitude: "Thank you cordially for the unexpected present—the autographs would make the books valuable, were there nothing else. I shall enjoy the fine eloquence of the Dhammapada all the more for your note."

9. Italics are Judson's. *Records of the Life, Character, and Achievements of Adoniram Judson* (New York: Edward H. Fletcher, 1854), 88–89. For Adoniram's brief overview of Burmese Buddhism see *Records of the Life*, 83–88. For further information—selected letters, journal entries, and biographical details—on Adoniram Judson see Francis Wayland, *A Memoir of the Life and Labors of the Rev. Adoniram Judson, D.D.*, 2 vols. (Boston: Phillips, Sampson, and Company; Cincinnati: Moore, Anderson, and Company, 1853). For autobiographical and biographical material on Ann Judson see James Davis Knowles, *Memoir of Mrs. Ann H. Judson, Late Missionary to Burmah* (Boston: Lincoln and Edmands, 1829). For her account of the early missions in Burma see Ann Judson, *An Account of the American Baptist Mission to the Burman Empire* . . . (London: J. Butterworth, 1823). Wayland, *Memoir of Adoniram Judson*, 56. Those missionaries in Buddhist nations included Judson, the Congregationalist turned Baptist, who arrived in Burma in 1814. It also included Daniel Poor (1789–1855), a Congregationalist missionary who arrived in Ceylon in 1816; Elijah Coleman Bridgman (1801–61), the first American missionary in China; and John Taylor Jones (1802–51), the first American missionary in Siam (1833). These and other missionaries who followed them contributed to the public conversation through their letters, lectures, articles, and books. For their reports, for example, see the pages of the *Missionary Herald* and *Chinese Repository*. Many missionaries served as "corresponding members" of the American Oriental Society, and they published reports in that organization's journal as well. See Francis Mason, "Hints on the Introduction of Buddhism into Burmah," *Journal of the American Oriental Society* 2 (1851): 334–36. Chester Bennett, "Life of Gaudama; A Translation from the Burmese Book Entitled *Ma-la-len-ga-ra wottoo*," *Journal of the American Oriental Society* 3 (1853): 1–164.

10. "A Peep at the 'Peraharra,' " *Harper's* 3 (Aug. 1851): 322–23; 326. See also [Joseph Dalton Hooker], "A Naturalist among the Himalayas" *Harper's* 9 (Oct. 1854): 604–17; "Sketches in the East Indies: Pulo Pinang" *Harper's* 11 (Aug. 1855): 324–35; "Commodore Perry's Expedition to Japan" *Harper's* 12 (May 1856): 733–54; "Pictures of the Japanese" *Harper's* 39 (Aug. 1869): 305–22; "A Visit to Bangkok"

Harper's 41 (Aug. 1870): 359–68, and "Land of the White Elephant" *Harper's* 48 (Feb. 1874): 378–89. Travel narratives that focused on Buddhist nations also were published in book form and collected in anthologies. See Henry Howe, ed., *Travels and Adventures of Celebrated Travellers* (Cincinnati: Henry Howe, 1853), 174–210, 355–72, 601–38.

11. These magazines included *The Princeton Review, The North American Review, The Christian Examiner, Christian World, The Methodist Quarterly Review, The Radical, The Atlantic Monthly, The Bibliotheca Sacra, The New Englander, The Index,* and *The Baptist Quarterly.* For one example of a report on the recent Buddhist scholarship see Dr. Mullens, "Buddhism—Its Literature, Origin, and Doctrine," *Christian World* 20 (Nov. 1869): 333–35. Eugène Burnouf, *L'Introduction à l'histoire du buddhisme indien* (Paris: Imprimerie Royale, 1844). R[obert] Spence Hardy, *Eastern Monachism* (London: Partridge and Oakey, 1850). R[obert] Spence Hardy, *A Manual of Buddhism in its Modern Development* (London: Partridge and Oakey, 1853). F[riedrich] Max Müller, "Buddhist Pilgrims [1857]," in *Chips from a German Workshop,* vol. 1 (1869; Chico: Scholars Press, 1985), 232–75. F[riedrich] Max Müller, "The Meaning of Nirvana [1857]," *Chips from a German Workshop,* vol. 1 (1869; Chico: Scholars Press, 1985), 276–87. Jules Barthélemy Saint-Hilaire, *Le Bouddha et sa religion* (1860; Paris: Didier, 1862).

12. For examples of early Catholic missionaries noticing Buddhist difference see Cooper, ed., *They Came to Japan,* 313, 317, 318. Burnouf might have qualified or rejected these interpretations if he had had the opportunity to complete the comparative study of Buddhist scriptures that he had planned, but it was he who gave this constellation of interpretations an aura of authority. Other influential European writers—Müller, Hardy, St. Hilaire, Albrecht Weber, and James d'Alwis—followed his lead. Burnouf, *L'Introduction à l'histoire du buddhisme indien,* 589–90. See Albrecht Weber, "Über den Buddhismus," *Indische Skizzen* (Berlin: Dummlers, 1857) and James d'Alwis, *Buddhist Nirvana: A Review of Max Müller's Dhammapada* (Colombo, Ceylon: William Skeen, Government Printer, 1871).

13. Arthur Schopenhauer, *The World as Will and Representation,* 2 vols., trans. E. F. J. Payne (1818; New York: Dover, 1969), 2: 169. On the association between Buddhism, Schopenhauer, and pessimism see "Schopenhauer and His Pessimism," *Methodist Quarterly Review* 28 (July 1876): 489, 508 and [Herman J. Warner], "The Last Phase of Atheism," *Christian Examiner* 78 (July 1865): 78–80.

14. The passage from Alexander is quoted in Welbon, *Buddhist Nirvana,* 19. [F. W. Holland], "Siam," *Christian Examiner* 66 (Mar. 1859): 237. On Buddha as a reformer see F. Max Müller, "Buddhism [1862]," *Chips from a German Workshop,* vol. 1 (1869; Chico: Scholars Press, 1985); Albrecht Weber, "Über den Buddhismus"; Karl Koeppen, *Die Religion des Buddha und ihre Enstehung* (Berlin: F. Schneider, 1857); and Phillipe Edouard Foucaux, *Doctrine des bouddhistes sur le nirvana* (Paris: Benjamin Duprat, 1864). The passage about Buddhism as a "civilizing influence" is from Müller, "Buddhist Pilgrims," 243. The passage from Weber is quoted in Welbon, *Buddhist Nirvana,* 65.

15. A Traveller, "Buddhism—Its Origin, Tenets, and Tendencies," *Southern Literary Messenger* 25 (Nov. 1857): 380. The passage from Ware is quoted in Daniel Walker Howe, *The Unitarian Conscience: Harvard Moral Philosophy, 1805–1861* (1970; Middletown, Conn.: Wesleyan University Press, 1988), 96. Edwin Scott Gaustad, *Dissent in American Religion* (Chicago: Chicago University Press, 1973), 42.

16. J. B. Syme, ed., *The Mourner's Friend; Or, Sighs of Sympathy for Those Who Sorrow* (Worcester: S. A. Howland, 1852), 28. On the Victorian cult of mourning see Halttunen, *Confidence Men and Painted Women,* 124–52.

17. Philip Schaff, *America: A Sketch of Its Political, Social, and Religious Character,* ed. Perry Miller (1855; Cambridge: Harvard University Press, 1961), 88, 94, 95. Others besides Schaff, of course, testified to the pervasiveness and significance of

these two values in American Victorianism. See O. D., "On the Signs and Prospects of the Age," *Christian Examiner* 36 (Jan. 1844): 22. This piece argued that Unitarians and their Trinitarian opponents were united in their common affirmation of "reform" and "progress."

18. Ernest Lee Tuveson, *Redeemer Nation: The Idea of America's Millennial Role* (Chicago: Chicago University Press, 1968). The phrase "cosmic optimism" is found in George M. Fredrickson, *The Inner Civil War: Northern Intellectuals and the Crisis of the Union* (New York: Harper and Row, 1965), 7. The speeches by Lincoln and Bushnell are reprinted in Conrad Cherry, ed., *God's New Israel: Religious Interpretations of American Destiny* (Englewood Cliffs, N.J.: Prentice-Hall, 1971), 195–96, 197–209. Samuel Johnson, "American Religion," *The Radical* (Jan. 1867): 257. Henry Ward Beecher, "The Tendencies of American Progress," in *The Original Plymouth Pulpit: Sermons of Henry Ward Beecher . . .* (Boston and Chicago: Pilgrim Press, 1871), 5: 218. Beecher preached this sermon on 24 Nov. 1870.

19. William Ellery Channing, "The Moral Argument against Calvinism," in *William Ellery Channing: Selected Writings*, ed. David Robinson (1820; New York: Paulist Press, 1985), 103–21.

20. Sprague, *The Excellent Woman*, 59.

21. Robert T. Handy, ed., *Religion in the American Experience: The Pluralistic Style* (New York: Harper and Row, 1972), 85–89.

22. [Anne Tuttle Bullard], *The Wife for a Missionary* (Cincinnati: Truman, Smith, and Co., 1834), 64–65, 73, 150, 9, 151. See also [Anne Tuttle Bullard], *The Reformation: A True Tale of the Sixteenth Century* (Boston: Massachusetts Sabbath School Society, 1832). On Calvinist fiction see Reynolds, *Faith in Fiction*, 73–95. Stowe's means of exhorting her readers to reforming action were typically Victorian: she appealed to sentiment and domesticity. "And you, mothers of America," Stowe wrote, "—you who have learned, by the cradles of your own children, to love and feel for all mankind . . . —I beseech you, pity the mother who has all your affections, and not one legal right to protect, guide, or educate, the child of her bosom!" Harriet Beecher Stowe, *Uncle Tom's Cabin; Or, Life among the Lowly* (1852; New York: Penguin, 1981), 629, 623. Colleen McDannell, *The Christian Home in Victorian America, 1840–1900*, Religion in North America Series (Bloomington: Indiana University Press, 1986), 22. On Cole see John Dillenberger, *The Visual Arts and Christianity in America: From the Colonial Period to the Present* (New York: Crossroad, 1989), 97–103. On the didactic function of fashion in this period see Halttunen, *Confidence Men and Painted Women*, 158.

23. [Edward Hungerford], "Buddhism and Christianity," *The New Englander* 33 (Apr. 1874): 278–79. [Herman J. Warner], "The Last Phase of Atheism," *Christian Examiner* 78 (July 1865): 86. American interpreters had expressed a vague sense of Buddhism's singularity before 1858. Hannah Adams, relying on a European interpretive tradition, had claimed that one Chinese sect of Buddhism "teaches a philosophical atheism," denies immortality of the soul, "acknowledges no other god than the *void* or *nothing*," and "makes the supreme happiness of mankind to consist in a *total inaction*, an *entire insensibility*, and a *perfect quietude.*" Adams, *Alphabetical Compendium*, 56. For one text in that European interpretive tradition that Adams drew on see P. [Jean Baptiste] DuHalde, *The General History of China . . .* (London: John Watts, 1736), 3: 38. See also Salisbury, "Memoir," 86. A Traveller, "Buddhism—Its Origin, Tenets, and Tendencies," 381. A Traveller, "Buddhist Superstition," *Southern Literary Messenger* 25 (Oct. 1857): 257–78. "Buddhism," *The New Englander* 3 (Apr. 1845): 182–83. To see the differences in interpretation between the earlier and later periods compare the treatment of Buddhism in Moffat's survey cited above with another influential Protestant survey of the religions by Charles Augustus Goodrich (1790–1862). Charles Augustus Goodrich, *A Pictorial*

and Descriptive View of All Religions . . . (Hartford: A. C. Goodman, 1854), 4–5, 492. The first edition of Goodrich's work appeared as Charles Augustus Goodrich, *Religious Ceremonies and Customs; Or, the Forms of Worship Practiced by the Several Nations of the Known World* (Hartford: Hutchison and Dwier, 1832) and was based on Bernard Picart, *Cérémonies et coutumes religieuses de tous les peuples du monde* . . . (Amsterdam: J. F. Bernard, 1728–43).

24. [J. K. Wight?], "Buddhism in India and China," *Princeton Review* 31 (July 1859): 391. "The Sanskrit Language," *Methodist Quarterly Review* 19 (July 1867): 362. R. H. Graves, "Three Systems of Belief in China," *Baptist Quarterly* 6 (1872): 412. Müller, "Buddhist Pilgrims," 243.

25. Müller, "Buddhist Pilgrims," 243–44.

26. Müller, "Buddhism," 230–31.

27. Quoted in Welbon, *The Buddhist Nirvana*, 198. Edwin Arnold, the influential British interpreter, used this argument in the later period. In his popular poem about the Buddha's life he declared that "a third of mankind [note that the proportion changed] would never have been brought to believe in blank abstractions, or in Nothingness as the issue and ground of Being." Edwin Arnold, *The Light of Asia; Or the Great Renunciation; Being the Life and Teaching of Gautama* (1879; Wheaton, Ill.: Theosophical Publishing House, 1969), viii.

28. Wight, "Buddhism in India and China," 415. See also David C. Scudder, "A Sketch of Hindu Philosophy: Article II," *Bibliotheca Sacra* 18 (July 1861): 578. On Pure Land see [L. W. Pilcher?] "Gautama and Lao Tzu," *Methodist Quarterly Review* 28 (Oct. 1876): 653. Philip Schaff, "Rise and Progress of Monasticism: Origin of Christian Monasticism: Comparison with Other Forms of Asceticism," *Bibliotheca Sacra* 22 (Apr. 1864): 386. Graves, "Three Systems of Belief in China," 412. For examples of interpreters who acknowledged the Buddha's lofty moral principles and effective reform efforts see Warner, "The Last Phase of Atheism," Scudder, "A Sketch of Hindu Philosophy," and Hungerford, "Buddhism and Christianity." On Buddha as a reformer and Buddhism as the "Protestantism of India" see Scudder, "Sketch of Hindu Philosophy," 581, and Graves, "Three Systems of Belief in China," 413.

29. For further information on the Oriental explorations of these liberals and radicals see Jackson, *The Oriental Religions and American Thought*, 103–40.

30. Ahlstrom and Carey make the point about Clarke's influence in Sydney E. Ahlstrom and Jonathan S. Carey, ed., *An American Reformation: A Documentary History of Unitarian Christianity* (Middletown, Conn.: Wesleyan University Press, 1985), 292. James Freeman Clarke to ? ["My Dear Sir"], 9 Jan. 1846, New York Historical Society, New York City. James Freeman Clarke, *Autobiography, Diary, and Correspondence*, ed. Edward Everett Hale (Boston and New York: Houghton, Mifflin, and Company, 1891), 226. James Freeman Clarke, "Buddhism; Or, the Protestantism of the East," *Atlantic Monthly* 23 (June 1869): 713–28. James Freeman Clarke, *Ten Great Religions* (Boston: James R. Osgood, 1871), 166.

31. William M. Bryant, review of *The Indian Saint; Or, Buddha and Buddhism*, by Charles deBerard Mills *The Western* 3 (Aug. 1877): 503. Charles D. B. Mills, *The Indian Saint; Or, Buddha and Buddhism* (Northampton, Mass.: Journal and Free Press, 1876), 65–66. Felix Adler, "A Prophet of the People," *Atlantic Monthly* 37 (June 1876): 683–84.

32. William Rounseville Alger, *The Poetry of the East* (Boston: Whittemore, Niles, and Hall, 1856). William R. Alger, "The Brahmanic and Buddhist Doctrine of a Future Life," *North American Review* 86 (Apr. 1858): 456–58, 462. See also the book in which he reprinted this piece on Hinduism and Buddhism: William R. Alger, *A Critical History of the Doctrine of the Future Life* (1859; Philadelphia: Childs, 1864).

33. Thomas Wentworth Higginson, *The Results of Spiritualism: A Discourse Deliv-*

ered at Dodsworth Hall, Sunday, March 6, 1859 (New York: St. Munson, [1859]), 5, 21. This pamphlet is found in the Thomas Wentworth Higginson Papers, Thomas Wentworth Higginson Miscellaneous Pamphlets, no. 36. Mary Thacher Higginson, *Letters and Journals of Thomas Wentworth Higginson, 1846–1906* (Boston and New York: Houghton Mifflin, 1921), 347–48. [Thérèse (deSolms) Blanc], *A Typical American: Thomas Wentworth Higginson*, trans. E. M. Waller (London and New York: Howard Wilford Bell, 1902). For examples of his continuing commitment to these beliefs and values see his autobiography, *Cheerful Yesterdays*, in which he emphasized the positive turns in his life and the steady progress of history. He also continued to actively engage public issues when he protested United States intervention in the Philippines. Thomas Wentworth Higginson, *Cheerful Yesterdays* (Boston and New York: Houghton, Mifflin, and Company, 1898). See also . . . *Mass Meetings of Protest against the Suppression of Truth about the Philippines, Faneuil Hall, Thursday, March 19, 3 and 8 pm: Addresses by the Hon. George S. Boutwell, The Hon. Charles S. Hamlin, Col. T. W. Higginson . . .* (Boston: 1903). This pamphlet can be found in the Thomas Wentworth Higginson Papers.

34. Thomas Wentworth Higginson, "The Sympathy of Religions," *The Radical* 8 (Feb. 1871): 1–23. Thomas Wentworth Higginson, "The Character of Buddha," *Index* 3 (16 Mar. 1872): 81–83. Thomas Wentworth Higginson, "The Buddhist Path of Virtue," *Radical* 8 (June 1871): 62.

35. T[homas] W[entworth] H[igginson], rev. of *Oriental Religions and Their Relation to Universal Religion*, vol. 1, by Samuel Johnson, *The Index* 3 (9 Nov. 1872): 361. Samuel Johnson, *Oriental Religions and Their Relation to Universal Religion*, 3 vols. (Boston: Houghton, Mifflin, and Company, 1872, 1877, 1885). Emerson's description of Johnson, and Johnson's account of his own stand, are quoted in Roger C. Mueller, "Samuel Johnson, American Transcendentalist: A Short Biography," *Essex Institute Historical Collections* 115 (Jan. 1979): 9. Johnson urged his radical friends not to form an official body. Their present troubles, he argued, were a result of organizations. After they ignored his advice, Johnson did have some loose connections with the Free Religious Association. A few of his sermons and letters to the editor were published in its official organ, the *Index;* and he delivered a few addresses under the auspices of the organization. On his connection to the FRA see Mueller, "Samuel Johnson," 39–40. Samuel Johnson, *Oriental Religions*, 1: 2.

36. Johnson, *Oriental Religions*, 2: 759. Johnson, *Oriental Religions*, 2: 757; 1: 611.

37. Samuel Johnson, *Lectures, Essays, and Sermons* (Boston: Houghton, Mifflin, and Company, 1883), 353. "Samuel Johnson," *Atlantic Monthly* 51 (June 1883): 850.

38. Mueller, "Samuel Johnson," 25. Samuel Johnson to Wendell Phillips, 14 May 1869, Houghton Library. Johnson, *Lectures, Essays, and Sermons*, 387.

39. E[rnest] J[ohn] Eitel, rev. of *Oriental Religions and Their Relation to Universal Religion*, by Samuel Johnson, reprinted in Samuel Johnson, *Lectures, Essays, and Sermons*, 463. This review by Eitel, who served the London Missionary Society and produced a Sanskrit-Chinese dictionary, originally appeared in the *China Review* in 1882. See E. J. Eitel, *Handbook for the Student of Chinese Buddhism* (Hong Kong and Shanghai: Lane, Crawford, and Company, 1870). Daniel Dyer Lum, "Buddhism Notwithstanding: An Attempt to Interpret Buddhism from a Buddhist Standpoint," *Index* 29 (29 Apr. 1875; 6 May 1875): 195–96; 206–8.

40. John Ogden Gordon, "The Buddhist and Christian Ideas of Hell," *The Presbyterian Quarterly and Princeton Review* 4 (Jan. 1875): 43, 38, 45, 41.

41. Higginson, "The Character of Buddha," 83. This lecture was the ninth in a series of eleven "Sunday Afternoon Lectures" that he delivered in Horticultural Hall under the auspices of the Free Religious Association.

42. Hungerford, "Buddhism and Christianity," 268.

2. "SHALL WE ALL BECOME BUDDHISTS?"

1. The Shaker writer was Alonzo G. Hollister, and this passage is from a piece that was published in *The Shaker Manifesto* (13, 8, 97–100). It has been reprinted in Robely Edward Whitson, ed., *The Shakers: Two Centuries of Spiritual Reflection* (New York: Paulist Press, 1983), 320–22. William Davies, "The Religion of Gotama Buddha," *Atlantic Monthly* 74 (Sept. 1894): 335. Review of *Buddha's Tooth Worshipped by the Buddhists of Ceylon in the Pagoda called "Dalada-Maligawa" at Kandy*, American *Ecclesiastical Review*, n.s., 9 (Dec. 1898): 659–61. The reviewer might have been the Reverend Herman J. Heuser, the German-born priest of the archdiocese of Philadelphia who edited the *American Ecclesiastical Review* from its founding in 1889 until 1927. Heuser wrote over two thousand book reviews for this traditional Catholic magazine. On Heuser and this periodical see Charles H. Lippy, ed., *Religious Periodicals in the United States: Academic and Scholarly Journals* (Westport, Conn.: Greenwood, 1986), 21–25.

2. Paul Carus to Anagarika Dharmapala, 26 Aug. 1899, The Open Court Papers, Morris Library, Southern Illinois University, Carbondale. "Buddhism in America," *Maha Bodhi* 8 (Nov. 1899): 1. The *Maha Bodhi* story was reprinted in *Light of Dharma* 3 (Oct. 1903): 76. On the history of the Maha Bodhi Society see the articles in *Maha Bodhi Society of India: Diamond Jubilee Souvenir, 1891–1951* (Calcutta: Maha Bodhi Society of India, 1952). On Dharmapala, one of the most important figures in modern Sinhalese Buddhism, see Ananda Guruge, ed., *Return to Righteousness: A Collection of Speeches, Essays, and Letters of Anagarika Dharmapala* (Ceylon: The Government Press, 1965), and Bhikkhu Sangharakshita, *Anagarika Dharmapala: A Biographical Sketch* (Kandy: Buddhist Publication Society, 1964). See also Gananath Obeyesekere, "Personal Identity and Cultural Crisis: The Case of Anagarika Dharmapala of Sri Lanka," in *The Biographical Process: Studies in the History and Psychology of Religion*, ed. Frank E. Reynolds and Donald Capps (The Hague: Mouton, 1976), 221–52; George Bond, *The Buddhist Revival in Sri Lanka: Religious Tradition, Reinterpretation and Response*, Studies in Comparative Religion (Columbia: University of South Carolina Press, 1988), 53–61; and Richard F. Gombrich, *Theravada Buddhism: A Social History from Ancient Benares to Modern Colombo* (London and New York: Routledge and Kegan Paul, 1988), 188–91. As Obeyesekere noted, Dharmapala was registered, following the Sinhalese practice of placing the surname first, as "Hevavitaranalage Don David." He apparently assumed the name Anagarika Dharmapala in 1881. "Dharmapala" means "protector of the Dharma" or "defender of the faith." "Anagarika" was an innovation. See Gombrich, *Theravada Buddhism*, 76, 188, 192.

3. Alexander V. G. Allen, *Life and Letters of Phillips Brooks* (New York: E. P. Dutton, 1901), 2: 519. Bostonians continued to be interested in Buddhism after 1883, and Brooks continued to ponder the causes of their interest. See William Sturgis Bigelow to Phillips Brooks, 19 Aug. 1889, Houghton Library, Harvard University, Cambridge, Mass.; Phillips Brooks to William Sturgis Bigelow, 2 Sept. 1889, Houghton Library. Both letters are reprinted in Akiko Murakata, "Selected Letters of William Sturgis Bigelow" (Ph.D. diss., George Washington University, 1971), 82–86. The New Thought follower was Lilian Whiting. The passage from Whiting is quoted in Lawrence W. Chisolm, *Fenollosa: The Far East and American Culture* (New Haven: Yale University Press, 1963), 103. The passage from the *New York Journal* was quoted in Rick Fields, *How the Swans Came to the Lake*, 131. This excerpt appeared in the *Buddhist Ray* 6.5–6 (May-June 1893): 4. And Fields apparently took this passage from that Buddhist magazine. I have been unable to locate the original newspaper article.

4. Thomas B. Wilson, "Buddhism in America," *Light of Dharma* 2 (June 1902): 1.

The reference to a "vogue" is found in Jackson, *Oriental Religions,* 141: "Once taken up, a Buddhist vogue swept the country, leading to a general discussion of the relative merits of Buddhism and Christianity." Another scholar, Joseph Kitagawa, also suggested that there was "rather widespread interest in Indian religion and Buddhism among the American reading public in the latter half of the nineteenth century" although he avoided calling it a "vogue." Joseph Kitagawa, "Buddhism in America, with Special Reference to Zen," *Japanese Religions* 5 (July 1967): 41.

5. For example, Percival Lowell, *The Soul of the Far East* (Boston: Houghton Mifflin, 1888). Ernest Francisco Fenollosa, "Chinese and Japanese Traits," *Atlantic Monthly* 69 (June 1892): 769–74. For interesting analyses of the cultural and religious interaction between Japan and America during this period see Robert A. Rosenstone, *Mirror in the Shrine: American Encounters with Meijii Japan* (Cambridge, Mass.: Harvard University Press, 1988) and Notto R. Thelle, *Buddhism and Christianity in Japan: From Conflict to Dialogue, 1854–1899* (Honolulu: University of Hawaii Press, 1987). See also Jackson, *Oriental Religions,* 201–41.

6. Edwin Arnold, *The Light of Asia; Or, the Great Renunciation; Being the Life and Teaching of Gautama* (1879; Wheaton, Illinois: Theosophical Publishing House, 1969). Jackson, *Oriental Religions,* 143. Brooks Wright, *Interpreter of Buddhism to the West: Sir Edwin Arnold* (New York: Bookman Associates, 1957), 75. For other bestsellers of the period see Appendix A, "Overall Best Sellers in the United States" and Appendix B, "Best Sellers" in Frank Luther Mott, *Golden Multitudes: The Story of Best Sellers in the United States* (New York: Macmillan, 1947), 303–29 and "Chronological Index of Books Discussed in the Text" in James D. Hart, *The Popular Book: A History of America's Literary Taste* (New York: Oxford University Press, 1950), 301–12. Helena P. Blavatsky, "The Light of Asia," *The Theosophist* 1 (Oct. 1879): 20–25. John Gmeiner, "The Light of Asia and the Light of the World," *Catholic World* 42 (Oct. 1885): 1–9. For two examples of the reviews by New England intellectuals see Oliver Wendell Holmes, "The Light of Asia," *International Review* 7 (Oct. 1879): 345–72 and [Francis Ellingwood Abbot], "The Light of Asia," *The Index* 11 (22 Apr. 1880): 198.

7. S[amuel] H[enry] Kellogg, *The Light of Asia and the Light of the World: A Comparison of the Legend, the Doctrine, and the Ethics of the Buddha with the Story, the Doctrine, and the Ethics of Christ* (London: Macmillan, 1885), 1. Wright, *Interpreter of Buddhism,* 143–46.

8. DeJong has dated the rise of the second period of Buddhist studies from 1877, when many Pali texts were edited. It might be dated a few years later. Either way, around this time the sophistication of European scholarship increased. DeJong, "Brief History of Buddhist Studies," 76–77. Henry C. Warren, *Buddhism in Translations* (1896; New York: Atheneum, 1979).

9. As far as I know, no comprehensive study of Protestant missionary interpretations of Buddhism has yet appeared. There are a number of volumes on intercultural interaction and American Protestant foreign missions that contain some information but do not focus on Buddhism. See those works listed in the Bibliography.

10. *Pansil* is an abbreviation of *Pancha Sila,* the five moral precepts. These are the five basic rules that all Theravadin Buddhists promise to observe. The phrase "taking *pansil*" also is used to refer to the recitation on Buddhist occasions of the triple invocation of the Buddha and the Three Refuges as well as *pansil* proper. Henry Steel Olcott, *Old Diary Leaves,* 2: 167–69. Henry S. Olcott, *The Buddhist Catechism,* 44th ed. (1881; Talent, Oregon: Eastern School Press, 1983). For a historical overview of the Theosophical Society see Bruce F. Campbell, *Ancient Wisdom Revisited: A History of the Theosophical Movement* (Berkeley: University of California Press, 1980).

11. There were many accounts of the Parliament and many collections of the

papers published between 1893 and 1895. Of these, John Henry Barrows's collection is the best. John Henry Barrows, ed., *The World's Parliament of Religions,* 2 vols. (Chicago: The Parliament Publishing Co., 1893). The parliament has received less scholarly attention than it deserves. Kenten Druyvesteyn and Richard Seager have written dissertations on the topic. Kenten Druyvesteyn, "The World's Parliament of Religions" (Ph.D. diss., University of Chicago, 1976). Richard H. Seager, "The World's Parliament of Religions, Chicago, Illinois, 1893" (Ph.D. diss., Harvard University, 1987). Clay Lancaster's book is of limited aid to the historian. Clay Lancaster, *The Incredible World's Parliament of Religions at the Chicago Columbian Exposition of 1893: A Comparative and Critical Study* (Fontwell, Sussex: Centaur Press, 1987). But several article-length studies offer some help. See Joseph Kitagawa, "The 1893 World's Parliament of Religions and Its Legacy," The Eleventh John Nuveen Lecture (Chicago: University of Chicago Divinity School, 1983); Donald H. Bishop, "Religious Confrontation: A Case Study: The 1893 Parliament of Religions," *Numen* 16 (Apr. 1969): 63–76; Larry Fader, "Zen in the West: Historical and Philosophical Implications of the 1893 Chicago World's Parliament of Religions," *The Eastern Buddhist,* n.s., 15 (Spring 1982): 122–45; Jackson, *Oriental Religions,* 243–61. Maha Bodhi Society, *Maha Bodhi Society,* 77; 84. Soyen Shaku, *Sermons of a Buddhist Abbott* (LaSalle, Ill.: Open Court, 1906). There had been "representatives" of the Maha Bodhi Society in the United States for several years before Dharmapala's 1897 visit: *Maha Bodhi,* the journal of the Society, listed C. T. Strauss as its representative in New York and Philangi Dasa as its representative in California. Dharmapala had personal influence on, for example, Marie deSouza Canavarro and Mary Foster. For further information on his influence see the accounts of these and other Buddhist followers in this chapter and the next.

12. There has been very little attention given to these two magazines. On the *Buddhist Ray* see Paul Carter, *The Spiritual Crisis of the Gilded Age* (Dekalb: Northern Illinois University Press, 1971), 206–7 and Fields, *How the Swans Came to the Lake,* 130–32. Both periodicals are mentioned in a brief account of "Theosophical Periodicals" in Mott, *History of Magazines: 1885–1905,* 287. The information on recipients of the *Light of Dharma* is found in "List of the Subscription, Contribution, and Exchange, The Light of Dharma, May 19, 1904" (notebook, Archives of the Buddhist Churches of America, San Francisco). The eminent scholars who received the *Light of Dharma* included Professors E. W. Hopkins of Yale, George Foot Moore of Harvard, G. S. Goodspeed of the University of Chicago, and Morris Jastrow of the University of Pennsylvania. My analysis is based on a survey of fifty magazines published during the period between 1844 and 1912. All claims in this section are based on articles published between 1879 and 1912. Most of the magazines mentioned below are described in either Mott, *History of Magazines* or Lippy, *Religious Periodicals of the United States.*

13. H. P. Blavatsky, "New York Buddhists," *Theosophist* 2 (Apr. 1881): 152–53. Henry C. Warren, "On the So-Called Chain of Causation of the Buddhists," *Journal of the American Oriental Society* 16 (1893): xxvii–xxx. Arthur Onken Lovejoy, "The Buddhistic Technical Terms Upadana and Upadisesa," *Journal of the American Oriental Society* 19 (July-Dec. 1898): 126–36. E. Washburn Hopkins, "The Buddhistic Rule against Eating Meat," *Journal of the American Oriental Society* 27 (July-Dec. 1906): 455–64. Despite these articles and others, the pages of the Oriental Society's journal still did not devote a great deal of attention to Buddhism—even at the peak of American interest. For example, none of the forty-seven papers that were listed as having been read at the annual meeting in 1898 focused on Buddhism. *Journal of the American Oriental Society* 19 (1898). William Davies, "The Religion of Gotama Buddha," *Atlantic Monthly* 74 (Sept. 1894): 334–40. D[avid] Brainerd [*sic*] Spooner,

"Welcoming the Buddha's Most Holy Bones," *Overland Monthly* 37 (Jan. 1901): 585–92.

14. Paul Carus to Soyen Shaku, 26 Jan. 1896, Open Court Papers. [Paul Carus, ed.], "A Controversy on Buddhism," *Open Court* 11 (Jan. 1897): 43–58. Anagarika Dharmapala, "Is There More Than One Buddhism?: A Reply to the Rev. Dr. Ellinwood," *Open Court* 11 (Feb. 1897): 82–84. The first editor of *Open Court*, Benjamin F. Underwood, described its heritage and purpose in the first volume: "The leading object of *The Open Court* is to continue the work of *The Index*, that is, to establish religion on the basis of Science and in connection therewith it will present the Monistic philosophy. . . . [It] will aim to substitute for unquestioning credulity intelligent inquiry, for blind faith rational religious views, for unreasoning bigotry a liberal spirit, for sectarianism a broad and generous humanitarianism." *Open Court* 1 (21 July 1887): 325. See also Mott, *History of Magazines*, 5: 302. For another example of an article in the radical and liberal journals see George R. Matthews, "Notes on Buddhism at Home," *Unitarian Review* 36 (Sept. 1891): 185–93.

15. *Biblical World* was a nonsectarian journal that focused on biblical scholarship, but it was clearly associated with mainline Protestantism. J. Wesley Johnston, "Christ and Buddha: Resemblances and Contrasts," *Methodist Review* 80 (Jan.–Feb. 1898): 32–40. M. L. Gordon, "Buddhism's Best Gospel," *Andover Review* 6 (Oct. 1886): 395–403. M. L. Gordon, "The Buddhisms of Japan," *Andover Review* 5 (Mar. 1886): 301–11.

16. John Gmeiner, "The Light of Asia and the Light of the World," *Catholic World* 42 (Oct. 1885): 1–9. R. M. Ryan, "More Light on 'The Light of Asia,' " *Catholic World* 61 (Aug. 1895): 677–87. R. M. Ryan, "The Lustre of 'The Light of Asia,' " *Catholic World* 61 (Sept. 1895): 809–26. J. S. Geisler, "Buddha and His Doctrine," *American Catholic Quarterly Review* 22 (Oct. 1897): 857–75. Merwin-Marie Snell, "Parseeism and Buddhism," *Catholic World* 46 (Jan. 1888): 451–57. For an example of Snell's lack of sympathy for non-Catholic religions see his *One Hundred Theses on the Foundations of Human Knowledge* (Washington, D.C.: published by the author, 1891), 34, 40.

17. F. Max Müller, "Buddhist Charity," *North American Review* 140 (Mar. 1885): 221–36. T. W. Rhys Davids, "Buddhism," *North American Review* 171 (Oct. 1900): 517–27.

18. Not all Chinese were on the West Coast. For a study of the Chinese brought to the South, especially Louisiana, as replacements for the emancipated slaves see Lucy M. Cohen, *Chinese in the Post–Civil War South* (Baton Rouge: Louisiana State University Press, 1984). The Korean immigration lasted only a short time because the Japanese government blocked it in order to deprive Hawaii's plantation owners of scab workers. On Korean immigration to Hawaii see Wayne Patterson, *The Korean Frontier in America: Immigration to Hawaii, 1896–1910* (Honolulu: University of Hawaii Press, 1988). On K. Y. Kira see Maha Bodhi Society, *Maha Bodhi Society*, 87. That first Japanese Buddhist missionary to Hawaii was Soryu Kagahi, who arrived on 2 March 1889. On Buddhism in Hawaii see Louise H. Hunter, *Buddhism in Hawaii: Its Impact on a Yankee Community* (Honolulu: University of Hawaii Press, 1971).

19. Frederick J. Masters, "Pagan Temples in San Francisco," *The Californian* 2 (Nov. 1892): 727–41. For an account of American interpretations of Chinese religion and culture found in another important West Coast magazine see Limin Chu, "The Images of China and the Chinese in the *Overland Monthly*, 1868–1875; 1883–1935" (Ph.D. diss., Duke University, 1965). See also Stuart Creigton Miller, *The Unwelcome Immigrant: The American Image of the Chinese 1785–1882* (Berkeley: University of California Press, 1969) and Harold Isaacs, *Scratches on Our Minds: American Views of India and China* (1958; Armonk, New York: M. E. Sharpe, 1980), 63–238. Miller

focuses on the earlier period, but his work still offers insights into late nineteenth-century interpretations.

20. The Chinese started arriving in significant numbers during the 1850s. In 1852 alone 200,000 arrived. There were approximately 150,000 just as the anti-Chinese sentiment reached its peak around 1882. That was the year, of course, that the Chinese Exclusion Act was passed. Even after several years of net loss in the Chinese population, there were still over 100,000 Chinese-Americans recorded in the 1890 census. All subsequent references to census figures in this and later chapters are taken from U.S. Census Office, *Report on Statistics of Churches in the United States at the Eleventh Census: 1890* (Washington, D.C.: Government Printing Office, 1894) and U.S. Bureau of the Census, *Religious Bodies: 1906*, parts 1 and 2 (Washington, D.C.: Government Printing Office, 1910). Since the 1890 and the 1906 census listed only the number of "temples" reported (forty-seven in 1890 and sixty-two in 1906), it is difficult to gauge the number of individuals who could be labeled, or would have labeled themselves, Buddhist. To confuse the matter further, the figures for the number of temples are misleading because some of them were in private residences and businesses (U.S. Bureau of the Census, *Religious Bodies: 1906*, 2:177). Yet given the number of Chinese in the United States and the likelihood that Buddhism was the central tradition for a fairly high percentage of them, it is safe to say that there were tens of thousands. Depending on the criteria used for identification, there might have been as few as ten thousand and as many as seventy thousand at any time. Lewis Lancaster has offered similar estimates and highlighted the significance of the lack of leadership in the decline of vitality in the Chinese-American Buddhist community in a brief but provocative article. Lewis Lancaster, "Buddhism in the United States: The Untold and Unfinished Story," *International Buddhist Forum Quarterly* (Sept. 1977): 26–29. The relative lack of religious leadership and organization among Chinese Americans as compared with Japanese Americans is evident, for example, in the census statistics. In 1906, there was only one Chinese religious official in the United States, while there were fourteen Japanese Pure Land priests (U.S. Bureau of the Census, *Religious Bodies: 1906*, 2: 175). As far as I know, no full-length survey of Chinese-American religious life has yet appeared, so information must be gathered from a variety of primary and secondary sources. Overviews of Chinese-American history usually contain a brief account of religion. For example, see Shih-shan Henry Tsai, *The Chinese Experience in America* (Bloomington: Indiana University Press, 1986), 42–45.

21. Although Japan allowed trade earlier, the Japanese were not permitted to emigrate to the West until 1884. According to the census figures, the Japanese population in the United States increased from 55 in 1870 to 2,039 in 1890 and to 24,327 in 1900. In 1906 there were more than 25,000 Japanese in the United States and approximately 10,500 in San Francisco alone.

22. The role of Christian missionary activity in the sending of Japanese Buddhist leaders is explored in William Charles Rust, "The Shin Sect of Buddhism in America," (Ph.D. diss., University of Southern California, 1951), 141. *Hompa Hongwanji* is an abbreviation of *Hongwanji-Ha Hongwanji*, which means literally school of the temple of the original vow (of Amida Buddha). It refers to one of the ten subdenominations of *Jodo-Shin-shu* in Japan, and the Buddhist Churches of America is affiliated with this subdenomination of Pure Land Buddhism. *Jodo-Shin-shu* or True Pure Land Buddhism is a form of Mahayana Buddhism that traces its lineage to a Kamakura period Buddhist, Shinran (1173–1263). It centers on devotion to Amida Buddha, the enlightened being who presides over the Pure Land in the West. With proper devotion and conduct the adherent can expect to be reborn into this Western paradise; and there it is easy to practice Buddhism and, finally, attain enlightenment. The point about the regional origins of Japanese immigrants is

made in Tetsuden Kashima, *Buddhism in America: The Social Organization of an Ethnic Religious Organization* (Westport, Conn.: Greenwood, 1977), 13. The historical details about the early years of Japanese Pure Land in America are taken from a variety of published and unpublished sources. Besides the works listed above see also Buddhist Churches of America, *Buddhist Churches of America: Seventy Five Year History, 1899–1974*, (Chicago: Nobart, 1974), 1: 43–52; Isao Horinouchi, "Americanized Buddhism: A Sociological Analysis of a Protestantized Japanese Religion" (Ph.D. diss., University of California, Davis, 1973).

23. The phrase "ultimate aliens" is used in George Fredrickson and Dale T. Knobel, "A History of Discrimination," in *Prejudice, A Series of Selections from the Harvard Encyclopedia of American Ethnic Groups* (Cambridge, Mass.: Harvard University Press, 1982), 52. On Japanese-American assimilation and Caucasian attitudes toward these immigrants see Yuji Ichioka, *Issei: The World of the First Generation Japanese Immigrants, 1885–1924* (New York: The Free Press, 1988), especially 176–243. Ichioka, *Issei*, 187–89. Sidney L. Gulick, *American Democracy and Asiatic Citizenship* (New York: Charles Scribners, 1918), 216.

24. Ichioka, *Issei*, 191, 185.

25. Kashima, *Buddhism in America*, 17. E. Snodgrass, "Buddhism and Christianity," *Missionary Review of the World* 16 (July 1893): 656. Evidence of Americanization is noted in all the works on Japanese Buddhism in America listed above, but it is the focus of the dissertation by Horinouchi. Japanese Buddhist priests consistently were given the title "Reverend" in the pages of the *Light of Dharma*. On the first Buddhist Sunday School see Rust, "The Shin Sect of Buddhism in America," 146. On religious architecture see Horinouchi, "Americanized Buddhism," 115–16; 382–85. "Onward Buddhist Soldiers" is discussed in Hunter, *Buddhism in Hawaii*, 131.

26. S. Sonoda to Paul Carus, 14 Nov.[?] 1899, Open Court Papers. K. Hori to Paul Carus, 2 Oct. 1903, Open Court Papers. See also S. Sonoda to Paul Carus, 12 May 1900, Open Court Papers; K. Nishijima to Albert J. Edmunds, 10 May 1902, Albert J. Edmunds Papers, Historical Society of Pennsylvania, Philadelphia.

27. S. Sonoda to Paul Carus, 14 Nov.[?] 1899, Open Court Papers. Skesaburo Nagao, *The Outline of Buddhism* (San Francisco: San Francisco Buddhist Mission, 1900). On the interactions with Caucasians see Rust, "The Shin Sect of Buddhism in America," 143–45. *Nisshi* (Daily records), four notebooks in Japanese, variously titled, 1902–3, 1904, 1908, 1909 (Archives, Buddhist Churches of America). Further information about the Dharma Sangha of Buddha can be found in the pages of the *Light of Dharma*. See "The Dharma-Sangher [sic] of Buddha," *Light of Dharma* 1 (Apr. 1901): 20; "A Joyful Occasion," *Light of Dharma* 1 (Aug. 1901): 26–28; "New Activity Shown by the American Branch of Association," *Light of Dharma* 4 (Oct. 1905): 131–32. S. Sonoda to Paul Carus, 12 May 1900, Open Court Papers. Entries in the San Francisco city directories describe Hayes as an author and composer who taught singing at a conservatory in the area.

28. K. Nishijima to Dharmapala, 20 Apr. 1901, printed in *Maha Bodhi* 10 (Aug. 1901): 48–49. Rust, "The Shin Sect of Buddhism in America," 143–44. A "great crowd" of Caucasians and Japanese also assembled at the dedication of the Buddhist Temple in Sacramento. The notice about this event in the *Maha Bodhi* also claimed that since the San Francisco "congregation" was not formally incorporated, this was "the first incorporated place of worship of the followers of Buddha in America." "The Buddhist Church, Sacrament[o]," *Maha Bodhi* 10 (Feb. 1902): 92.

29. This formal ceremony was described in a number of American periodicals, for example the *Salt Lake Weekly* and the *Philadelphia Times;* and a few of those accounts were reprinted in *Maha Bodhi*. See "A Convert to Buddhism," *Maha Bodhi* 2 (Nov. 1893): 3 and "Buddhist Converts," *Maha Bodhi* 2 (Apr. 1894): 1–2. There is some biographical information about Strauss scattered throughout his correspond-

ence with Paul Carus (The Open Court Papers), in announcements and reviews in *Maha Bodhi*, and brief passages in secondary sources. See William Peiris, *The Western Contribution to Buddhism* (Delhi, India: Motilal Banarsidass, 1973), 239–40; Maha Bodhi Society, *Maha Bodhi Society*, 74, 78–79; Fields, *How the Swans Came to the Lake*, 129. The best and probably most reliable account is found in a letter from Carus to a Buddhist sympathizer in Philadelphia: Paul Carus to Albert J. Edmunds, 24 Aug. 1903, Albert J. Edmunds Papers. The few secondary sources that mention Strauss describe him as German American; but Carus, who corresponded with him fairly regularly, claimed that he was born in Switzerland.

30. Dyer D. Lum, "Buddhism Notwithstanding: An Attempt to Interpret Buddha from a Buddhist Standpoint," *The Index* 6 (29 Apr. 1875): 194–96; (6 May 1875): 206–8. On Lum's continuing affiliation with Buddhism see Voltairine deCleyre, "Dyer D. Lum," in *Selected Works of Voltairine deCleyre*, ed. Alexander Berkman (New York: Mother Earth, 1914), 289–90. Root claimed to have been "close upon the eve of [his] finishing this poem" when Edwin Arnold's similar *Light of Asia* appeared. E. D. Root, *Sakya Buddha: A Versified, Annotated Narrative of the Life and Teachings; With an Excursus Containing Citations from the Dhammapada, or Buddhist Canon* (New York: Charles P. Somerby, 1880): 16. The book also was in Emerson's library and was mentioned in Christy's account of Asian influences on the Transcendentalists. Christy, *Orient in American Transcendentalism*, 301. On the ceremony in Ceylon see Henry Steel Olcott, *Old Diary Leaves: The True History of the Theosophical Society*, 2d series (Madras, India: Theosophical Publishing House, 1900), 167–69. On the ceremony in Japan see Akiko Murakata, "Selected Letters of Dr. William Sturgis Bigelow" (Ph.D. diss., George Washington University, 1971), 7.

31. Hopkins, *Religions of India*, 562. See Gordon, "Buddhisms of Japan" and "Buddhism's Best Gospel."

32. [Herman Vetterling], "The Growth of Enlightenment," *Buddhist Ray* 6 (May–June 1893): 4, 1; "Bostonian 'Buddhists' and Tearful Theosophists," *Buddhist Ray* 2 (Mar. 1889): [17].

33. Almond, *British Discovery of Buddhism*, p. 147, n. 10. On Almond's aims see *British Discovery of Buddhism*, ix.

34. Philangi Dasa published passages from the writings of Davis in which he had discussed Buddhism; and, as he often did, the opinionated editor of the *Buddhist Ray* added comments and corrections where he thought he had missed the point. The passages by Davis were sympathetic to Buddhism, although not uncritical. Andrew Jackson Davis, "The Buddha," *Buddhist Ray* 4 (Jan.–Feb. 1891): 14–16. For Evans's sympathetic attitude toward Buddhism see his *Esoteric Christianity and Mental Therapies* (Boston: H. H. Carter and Karrick, 1886). See also Carl T. Jackson, "The New Thought Movement and the Nineteenth Century Discovery of Oriental Philosophy," *Journal of Popular Culture* 9 (Winter 1975): 526–28.

35. Wayland, ed., *Memoir of the Life and Labors of the Rev. Adoniram Judson*, 2: 110. Abby Ann Judson to Paul Carus, 2 Nov. 1894, The Open Court Papers.

36. Many of the tentative conclusions in this section are based on an analysis of those who subscribed to the *Light of Dharma*. "List of the Subscription, Contribution, and Exchange. The Light of Dharma. May 19, 1904." The information on Davis was provided by Student Records, Office of the Registrar, University of South Dakota, Vermillion, South Dakota. F. Graeme Davis to Rev. Nishijima, 27 Apr. 1901, reprinted in *Light of Dharma* 1 (June 1901): 28–29. B. Sumendhankara to S. Sonoda, 29 Jan. 1901, reprinted in *Light of Dharma* 1 (June 1901): 28.

37. Arba N. Waterman to Paul Carus, 2 May 1898, Open Court Papers.

38. Andrew Carnegie, *Autobiography of Andrew Carnegie* (Boston: Houghton Mifflin, 1920), 207. Alexander Russell to *San Francisco Chronicle*, Autobiographical Sketch, 23 Sept. 1911, California Historical Society, San Francisco. "Alexander

Russell, Figure in Civic Affairs, Is Dead," *San Francisco Chronicle*, 21 Dec. 1919. The obituary on Withee is found in the *St. Paul Pioneer Press*, 15 Dec. 1911. Withee's occupations are listed in the St. Paul city directories. On his contributions to benevolent activities of the Maha Bodhi Society see American Maha Bodhi Society, "Receipts for Indo-American Industrial Education Propaganda," [1 Apr. 1903], Open Court Papers. Clowe, who apparently did not know Carus at the time he wrote, complained about Carus's treatment of Buddhism in his *Gospel of Buddha* and suggested that he learn about the tradition from Sister Sanghamitta (Marie Canavarro). Clarence Clowe to Paul Carus, 17 June 1901, Open Court Papers. The names of Russell, Withee, and Clowe all appear on the subscription list of the *Light of Dharma*.

39. All the women named were subscribers to the *Light of Dharma*. According to the 1906 census, women constituted 72 percent of the 85,717 Christian Scientists; 63 percent of the 2,336 Theosophists; 55 percent of the 35,056 Spiritualists; and 62 percent of the 5,749,838 Methodists. Several other groups—including the Universalists and the Baha'is—had female membership of 60 percent or more. Among the Universalists, 33,346 of the 64,158 members were women; among the Baha'is, 842 of the 1,280 members were women.

40. There were about three hundred to four hundred copies of *Light of Dharma* circulated before 1904 since many of the institutions who received the magazine got multiple copies (usually 5), and starting in October of 1904 they added two hundred copies of each issue. These are conservative estimates based on the figures contained in the subscription list and information given in the pages of the magazine. According to the subscription list, Japanese Buddhist Churches on the Pacific Coast and in Hawaii received multiple copies of the magazine. At least nine university libraries were sent the magazine, including most of the major institutions of the time: Harvard, Yale, Columbia, Johns Hopkins, Pennsylvania, Stanford, and Berkeley. The magazine also had an exchange agreement with at least thirty-six other magazines and newspapers in the United States and abroad. On the circulation of *Open Court* see Mott, *American Magazines* 4: 302.

41. Henry Steel Olcott, *The Buddhist Catechism*. Paul Carus, ed., *The Gospel of Buddha* (1894; Tucson: Omen, 1972).

42. "Golden Gate Lodge," *Light of Dharma* 2 (Aug. 1902): 112. According to census figures for 1906, toward the end of the peak of Buddhist interest, there were 2,336 Theosophists; 2,040 members of the Ethical Culture Societies; and 35,056 Spiritualists. The percentage of Buddhist sympathizers in these groups would be greatest by far among the Theosophists, especially during the years in which that organization focused on Buddhism more than Hinduism (approximately 1881 to 1907). No one has yet uncovered firm statistics for American members of the Maha Bodhi Society or those connected with Pure Land temples. But the numbers were probably never very high. The Dharma Sangha of Buddha, the Caucasian Buddhist group associated with the mission in San Francisco, might have had no more than twenty-five members.

43. Veysey, *Emergence of the American University*, 281. There had been reports of Buddhist interest at Harvard's traditional rival several years earlier. Two Nichiren Buddhists from Japan were studying philosophy at Yale, and they began preaching about the intellectual advantages of the tradition on that campus. One report suggested that they created "some sensation" there, and "some American professors and students sympathize with the declaration, though there is of course opposition." See "Buddhism in Yale University in America," *Maha Bodhi* 11 (Oct. 1902): 104.

44. Olcott, *Old Diary Leaves*, 4: 113. On the overestimation of membership and disproportionate influence of the Unification Church, and other new religious

movements, see J. Milton Yinger, *Countercultures: The Promise and Peril of a World Turned Upside Down* (New York: The Free Press, 1982), 233.

3. ESOTERICS, RATIONALISTS, AND ROMANTICS

1. Jeanie Drake, "Under the Bodhi Tree," *Catholic World* 52 (Jan. 1891): 570, 573.
2. Drake, "Bodhi Tree," 577, 579.
3. C. T. Strauss to Paul Carus, 9 July 1896, Open Court Papers.
4. Weber used ideal types in a variety of his works. For one of the most helpful theoretical discussions of types see Max Weber, " 'Objectivity' in the Social Sciences and Social Policy," in *Methodology in the Social Sciences,* trans. Edward A. Shils and Henry A. Finch (New York: Free Press, 1949), 49–112. See also Max Weber, *Economy and Society,* ed. Guenther Roth and Claus Wittich (Berkeley: University of California Press, 1978), 1: 4–7, 20–22. For critical discussions of Weber's ideal type theory see Alexander Von Shelting, "Max Webers Wissenshaftslehre," in *Max Weber's Ideal Type Theory,* ed. Rolf E. Rogers (New York: Philosophical Library, 1969), 45–55; J.W.N. Watkins, "Ideal Types and Historical Explanation," in *The Philosophy of Social Explanation,* ed. Alan Ryan (Oxford: Oxford University Press, 1973), 82–104; Alfred Schutz, "Problems in Interpretive Sociology," in *Philosophy of Social Explanation,* ed. Ryan, 203–19; and Susan Hekman, *Weber: The Ideal Type and Contemporary Social Theory* (Notre Dame, Ind.: University of Notre Dame Press, 1983). For a discussion of the variety of types that Weber used in his work see Hekman, *Weber,* 38–60.
5. Of course, it might have some usefulness for studying other groups, cultures, and periods. One scholar already has used a modified version of my typology as I had outlined it in my dissertation to interpret the range of perspectives among American Baha'is around the turn of the century. See Robert Harold Stockman, "The Baha'i Faith and American Protestantism" (Th.D. diss., Harvard Divinity School, 1990), 51–88.
6. Weber employed the notion of "elective affinities" in a number of his books and articles. One good example can be found in his *Sociology of Religion,* which was first published in 1922 as part of his *Wirtschaft und Gesellschaft.* See Weber, *Economy and Society,* 1: 468–518.
7. Howard Kerr and Charles L. Crow, Introduction, *The Occult in America: New Historical Perspectives,* ed. Howard Kerr and Charles L. Crow (Urbana: University of Illinois Press, 1983), 16. Robert Galbreath, "Explaining Modern Occultism," in *Occult in America,* ed. Kerr and Crow, 18–19.
8. This confession comes from an excerpt from the *Detroit Tribune* which Philangi Dasa published in the *Buddhist Ray* without citation or comment. See Vetterling, "Growth of Enlightenment," 4. The San Francisco city directory listed Stoddard's occupation as "medium." On the medium as an instance of "female professionalism" see Moore, *In Search of White Crows,* 102–29. H. P. Blavatsky, *The Key to Theosophy* . . . (London: The Theosophical Publishing Company; New York: W. Q. Judge, 1889), 12–15. William H. Galvani, "Buddhism and Theosophy," *Maha Bodhi Society* 5 (May-June 1896): 8.
9. Guruge, ed., *Return to Righteousness: A Collection of Speeches, Essays, and Letters of Anagarika Dharmapala,* 685, 687. On Olcott's titles see Maha Bodhi Society, *Maha Bodhi Society,* 69. Efforts by members of the Maha Bodhi Society to distinguish the Theravada Buddhism of their group from the esoteric blend of teachings of the Theosophical Society actually started even before the turn of the century. For example, in an 1896 piece an unidentified author asserted that "Buddha had no esoteric teachings" and "the lower sciences of astrology, palmistry, and other

superstitions are foreign to Buddhism." See "Esoteric and Exoteric Buddhism," *Maha Bodhi* 4 (Feb. 1896): 79.

10. Henry Steel Olcott, "Col. Olcott's Address at the Buddhist Mission," *Light of Dharma* 1 (Apr. 1901): 9–13. K. Nishijima to [Dharmapala], 20 Apr. 1901, reprinted as "Buddhism in America," in *Maha Bodhi* 10 (Aug. 1901): 48–49. D. T. Suzuki, "Individual Immortality," *Light of Dharma* 3 (Oct. 1903): 67–72.

11. On Foster, a wealthy Theosophist from Honolulu who provided significant financial support for the Maha Bodhi Society see Maha Bodhi Society, *Maha Bodhi Society*, 77, 101, 137. On Shearer see "Miss C. Shearer," *Maha Bodhi* 15 (Sept. 1907): 140. Notes by the Japanese priests in San Francisco indicate that Shearer was responsible for "introducing" a number of Americans to Buddhism and for recommending their Buddhist magazine. See "List of Subscription, Contribution, and Exchange. The Light of Dharma, May 19, 1904." Before the turn of the century she also had worked for Buddhism in Ceylon. Later, after studying in Japan, she was asked to establish a Buddhist school for girls in Burma. On those plans see Marie Canavarro to Paul Carus, 24 Oct. 1909, Open Court Papers. See also the other correspondence by and about her in that collection. Farmer, the spiritually eclectic founder of the Monslavat School for Comparative Study of Religion, contributed to the Maha Bodhi Society, subscribed to the *Light of Dharma*, and indirectly promoted Buddhism by inviting Dharmapala to lecture at the conferences held at Greenacre, her farm in Eliot, Maine. She seems to have been more drawn by New Thought, Vedanta Hinduism, and Baha'i. Yet she and many other women of the period combined concern for the occult with interest in Buddhism. For biographical information see *Who Was Who in America, 1897–1942*, s.v. "Farmer, Sarah." For her understanding of New Thought see Sarah J. Farmer, "The Abundant Life," *Mind* 5 (Dec. 1899): 212–17. For her view of Greenacre see Sarah J. Farmer, "The Purpose of Greenacre," *Mind* 5 (Oct. 1899): 6–9. On women and alternative religions see Mary Farrell Bednarowski, "Outside the Mainstream: Women's Religion and Women Religious Leaders in Nineteenth Century America," *Journal of the American Academy of Religion* 48 (June 1980): 207–31.

12. Marie Canavarro to Paul Carus, 22 Dec. 1900, Open Court Papers. Marie Canavarro to Paul Carus, 28 May 1901, Open Court Papers. Martin E. Marty, "The Occult Establishment," *Social Research* 37 (Summer 1970): 212–30. Johnson was a subscriber to the *Light of Dharma* who wrote, edited, and translated Platonist and Neoplatonist works. He edited two relatively obscure periodicals, *The Platonist* (1881–88) and *Bibliotheca Platonica* (1889–90), and his "esoteric" interests were revealed in some of his articles for the former. For example, along with his interpretations of Plato's writings and translations of Platonic and Neoplatonic works, Johnson authored pieces like "The Magnetic Mysteries," *Platonist* 2 (1884): 131–32; "Notes on the Kabbalah," *Platonist* 3 (1887): 91–101; and "The Taro," *Platonist* 2 (1884): 126–28.

13. Olcott, Old Diary Leaves, 4: 99. On Anna Brown see Albert J. Edmunds, Diary 11, 14–15 Jan. 1907, 18 Mar. 1907, Albert J. Edmunds Papers. Edmunds reported that Brown was "a Blavatsky Theosophist" who spent two years in Ceylon and India (c. 1904–6), but he was unimpressed by the level of understanding she brought back with her.

14. [D.] Teitaro Suzuki, rev. of *Christianity Reconstructed* [formerly *Catechism for a Young Christian*], by Albert J. Edmunds, *The Eastern Buddhist* 2 (Nov. 1922): 92. On the "voices" see Albert J. Edmunds, Diary 11, 22 Nov. 1906, Albert J. Edmunds Papers. On telepathy see Albert J. Edmunds, Diary 11, 14 July 1906, Albert J. Edmunds Papers. See also Albert J. Edmunds, "Has Swedenborg's 'Lost Word' Been Found?" *Journal of the American Society for Psychical Research* 7 (May 1913): 257–71; Albert J. Edmunds, "F.W.H. Meyers, Swedenborg, and Buddha," *Pro-*

ceedings of the American Society for Psychical Research 8 (Aug. 1914): 253–85. For Edmunds's account of how he got Suzuki interested in Swedenborg after a week with him in LaSalle, Illinois, see Albert J. Edmunds, Diary 10, 18 July 1903, Albert J. Edmunds Papers. The interest endured: Suzuki went on to translate Swedenborg's works into Japanese.

15. Helena Petrovna Blavatsky, *Posthumous Memoirs of Helena Petrovna Blavatsky. Dictated from the Spirit-World, upon the Typewriter, Independent of All Human Contact, under the Supervision of G.W.N. Yost* . . . (Boston: J. M. Wade, 1896). "A Sacred Buddha in Wood," *Light of Dharma* 2 (Aug. 1903): 109–10. Joseph M. Wade, "The One Life-Necessary Action," *Light of Dharma* 2 (1902): 24–25. See also "Joseph M. Wade, Publisher, Friend of Japan, Student of the Occult," *Boston Evening Transcript*, 23 Jan. 1905, 16. Paul Carus to His Excellency Count Canavarro, 19 March 1912, Open Court Papers. On Albers see "A Biographical Sketch," *Open Court* 19 (Oct. 1905): 637–38. For an example of her correspondence with Carus see this fourteen-page letter from the headquarters of the Maha Bodhi Society in Calcutta: A. C. Albers to Paul Carus, 23 Oct. 1901, Open Court Papers. For an example of her religious poetry see A. Christina Albers, "Reincarnation," *Light of Dharma* 2 (Apr. 1902): 19–20.

16. On Olcott's life and thought see Howard Murphet, *Hammer on the Mountain: The Life of Henry Steel Olcott (1832–1907)* (Wheaton, Ill.: The Theosophical Publishing House, 1972), and Stephen Prothero, "Henry Steel Olcott (1832–1907) and the Construction of 'Protestant Buddhism' " (Ph.D. diss., Harvard University, 1990). See also passages or sections on him in these and other works on Asian and alternative religions in America: Campbell, *Ancient Wisdom Revisited*, 6–8, 20–29, 34–35, 76–86, 96–100, 103–11, 113–18; Ellwood, *Alternative Altars*, 104–35; Jackson, *Oriental Religions and American Thought*, 157–77. The best published sources of information about Olcott are probably his own multivolume reflections on the history of the Theosophical Society *(Old Diary Leaves)* and the contemporary notices and articles in Theosophical and Buddhist periodicals like the *Theosophist* and *Maha Bodhi*.

17. Olcott, *Old Diary Leaves*, 1: 1–9, 1: 113–46.

18. Olcott, *Old Diary Leaves*, 2: 298–303; 3: 351–52; 4: 106–15; 4: 402–8. Olcott, *Buddhist Catechism*, 344, 38, 380.

19. I fixed the date of her death (and birth) by consulting the index to California death certificates that is housed in the California State Library in Sacramento. The other facts about her life have been patched together from references in her autobiography *(Insight into the Far East)*, her correspondence with Paul Carus (Open Court Papers) and 'Abdu'l Bahá, the Master of the Baha'i faith (Baha'i National Archives), and the brief contemporary accounts published in magazines and news-papers. Of these, the most reliable seem to be "Funeral Will Be Held for Author," *Glendale News Press*, 27 July 1933, 8; Ella Wheeler Wilcox, "Women in the Orient," *New York Journal*, 20 Nov. 1901, editorial page; and "Countess Canavarro's First Lecture in Calcutta," *Maha Bodhi* 8 (May 1899): 5–6. See also Paul Carus, "Sister Sanghamitta," *Open Court* 15 (Apr. 1901): 251–52; Paul Carus, "A Modern Instance of World Renunciation," *Open Court* 2 (Feb. 1899): 111–17; "Sister Sanghamitta the Buddhist Nun," *Light of Dharma* 1 (Apr. 1901): 21; Sister Sanghamitta [Marie Cana-varro], "Peace and Blessings," Letter from Sister Sanghamitta to Rev. M. Mizuki, 12 May 1901, reprinted in *Light of Dharma* 1 (June 1901): 88–90; "True till Death," *Maha Bodhi* 7 (Apr. 1899): 114–15. Canavarro, *Insight into the Far East*, 13.

20. For one description of the ceremony see the piece included in an 1897 issue of the *New York Journal*, which was subsequently reprinted in *Maha Bodhi*: "A Unique Ceremony in America," *Maha Bodhi* 6 (Nov. 1897): 55–56.

21. On the causes of her leaving Ceylon see Marie Canavarro to Paul Carus, 22

Nov. 1899, Open Court Papers. Paul Carus to Count Canavarro, 19 March 1912, Open Court Papers. There is abundant evidence of Canavarro's work for the Maha Bodhi Society, in Asia and America. For her work in Asia see Marie Canavarro to Paul Carus, 20 Mar. 1899, Open Court Papers. For her work in America, where she served as one of its ten directors and helped nurture groups in Chicago and New York, see Marie Canavarro to Paul Carus, 3 Oct. 1901, Open Court Papers.

22. On her continuing interest in Buddhism see Marie Canavarro to Paul Carus, 24 Oct. 1909, Open Court Papers. She presented four lectures on Buddhism at Greenacre in 1901, and her correspondence suggests that she returned in subsequent summers. On her subsequent lectures there see Kenneth Walter Cameron, ed., *Transcendentalists in Transition: . . . the Greenacre Summer Conferences and the Mosalvat School (1894–1909) . . .* (Hartford Transcendental Books, 1980), 125, 163. On her involvement with Baha'i see Marzieh Gail, Foreword, *The Master in 'Akká*, by Myron H. Phelps (1903; Los Angeles: Kalimat Press, 1985). On Greenacre see Robert P. Richardson, "The Rise and Fall of the Parliament of Religions at Greenacre," *Open Court* 46 (Mar. 1931): 129–66. See also Charles Mason Remey, "Reminiscences of the Summer School Greenacre Eliot, Maine," 1949, National Baha'i Archives.

23. For example see two of Canavarro's published lectures: Sister Sanghamitta, "Nirvana," *Light of Dharma* 1 (Dec. 1901): 22–24; 1 (Feb. 1902): 19–21; 2 (Apr. 1902): 25–26; 2 (Aug. 1902): 88–90 and Sister Sanghamitta, "The Ethics of Buddhism; Or, The Eightfold Path," *Light of Dharma* 1 (June 1901): 10–14. On the dispute about Canavarro's hearing of "voices" see Dr. Carter to Paul Carus, 14 Aug. 1908, Open Court Papers. For a sympathetic portrayal of the occult in her fiction see Marie deS[ouza] Canavarro, *The Broken Vase* (Boston: Christopher, 1933), 108.

24. On Vetterling's religious education and ordination see Edw. C. Mitchell, "An Opportunity," *New Jerusalem Messenger* 24 (Jan-June 1873): 58. On this and other matters of his biography see Horace B. Blackmer, Biographical Note about Vetterling from an Account by Mr. Whittemore, 30 Sept. 1950, Library, Swedenborg School of Religion, Newton, Massachusetts. On the scandal see "Sad If True: A Serious Charge against the Rev. Mr. Vetterling," *Detroit Post and Tribune*, 7 July 1881. Membership records housed at the Theosophical Society in Pasadena, California, indicate that Vetterling joined the Society on 27 July 1884, while he was living in St. Paul, Minnesota. There are a few brief references in the literature to this paradigmatic esoteric Buddhist, but these accounts contain very little biographical information and no analysis of his writings. See Paul Carter, *The Spiritual Crisis of the Gilded Age* (DeKalb: Northern Illinois University Press, 1971), 206–7; Fields, *How the Swans Came to the Lake*, 130–32. I found his dates of birth and death, and a few other important biographical facts, in San Jose Public Library, *Authors of Santa Clara County*, n.p., n.d. [after Feb. 1954].

25. The odd reference to his occupation as "farmer" appears in Polk-Husted Directory Company, *San Jose City and Santa Clara County Directory* (San Jose: Mercury Publishing Company, 1910), 609. He apparently turned to farming later in life, at least part time. Philangi Dasa, *Swedenborg the Buddhist; Or, The Higher Swedenborgianism: Its Secrets and Thibetan Origin* (Los Angeles: The Buddhistic Swedenborgian Brotherhood, 1887), 3, 3–4, 10, 12, 54, 94.

26. "A 'Theosophical' Attack on the New Church," rev. of *Swedenborg the Buddhist*, by Philangi Dasa, *New Church Life* (Feb. 1888): 24–25. James L. Foulds, "Swedenborg and Buddhism," rev. of *Swedenborg the Buddhist*, by Philangi Dasa, *New Church Magazine* [London] 11 (1892): 12–17. [Vetterling], *Swedenborg the Buddhist*, 322.

27. [Vetterling], *Swedenborg the Buddhist*, 322. [Vetterling], "Prospectus," *Buddhist Ray* 1 (Jan. 1888): 1.

28. Paul Carus to T. B. Wakeman, 12 Feb. 1896, Open Court Papers. The "Skeptical Enlightenment," to use Henry May's term, had special significance for rationalists. See May, *Enlightenment in America*, 105–49. On "supernatural rationalism" see Conrad Wright, *The Liberal Christians: Essays on American Unitarian History* (Boston: Unitarian Universalist Association, 1970), 1–21. On the Enlightenment and Deism in the United States see May, *Enlightenment in America;* Adolf E. Koch, *Religion of the American Enlightenment* (1933; New York: Crowell, 1968), 74–113; and David Lundberg and Henry F. May, "The Enlightened Reader in America," *American Quarterly* 28 (Summer 1976): 262–71. On the influence of the Scottish Common Sense philosophy see Sydney E. Ahlstrom, "The Scottish Philosophy and American Theology," *Church History* 24 (Sept. 1955): 257–72.

29. Robert Green Ingersoll to Paul Carus, 29 June 1895, Open Court Papers.

30. Felix Adler, *The Religion of Duty* (New York: McClure, Philips, 1905).

31. One fine magazine that Adler coedited was founded on a broader base than just Ethical Culture, *The International Journal of Ethics*. It was "devoted to the Advancement of Ethical Knowledge and Practice." Like other periodicals associated with Ethical Culture, it published pieces that focused on Buddhism and many others that mentioned it in passing. See the sophisticated piece by the professor at Johns Hopkins, Maurice Bloomfield, "The Essentials of Buddhist Doctrine and Ethics," *International Journal of Ethics* 2 (Apr. 1892): 313–26. See also Tokiwo Yokoi, "The Ethical Life and Conceptions of the Japanese," *International Journal of Ethics* 6 (Jan. 1896): 182–204; George William Knox, "Religion and Ethics," *International Journal of Ethics* 12 (Apr. 1902): 305–7; C. H. Toy, "The Religious Element in Ethical Codes," *International Journal of Ethics* 1 (Apr. 1891): 307. On Adler's discourse see Albert J. Edmunds, Diary 10, 6 Mar. 1904, Albert J. Edmunds Papers. On Edmunds's lectures, the first of which was "The Sacred Books of Buddhism and Their Ethical Teachings," see Albert J. Edmunds, Diary 10, 19 Oct. 1903, Albert J. Edmunds Papers. "The Buddhists of Brooklyn," *Maha Bodhi* 6 (Oct. 1897): 42. This 1897 account is from an unidentified American newspaper of the period, probably in the New York area. The letter from the corresponding secretary of the Brooklyn Ethical Association to Dharmapala in which Mr. Moore thanked Dharmapala for speaking to their group was also published in the same periodical: Henry Hoyt Moore to H. Dharmapala, *Maha Bodhi* 5 (Apr. 1897): 95. On Moore's and Janes's links with the school for comparative religion in Maine see Cameron, *Transcendentalists in Transition*, 123. "Death of Dr. Lewis G. Janes," *Light of Dharma* 1 (Oct. 1901): 30. "Dr. Lewis G. Janes," *Maha Bodhi* 10 (Nov. 1901): 61–62.

32. Moncure Conway, "The Theist's Problems and Tasks," *Radical* 10 (June 1872): 423. See also Moncure Conway, *The Sacred Anthology: A Book of Ethnical Scriptures* (New York: Henry Holt and Co., 1874). Conway's response is recorded in Moncure Conway, *My Pilgrimage to the Wise Men of the East* (Boston: Houghton, Mifflin, 1906), 133. On his journey to Ceylon see Conway, *Pilgrimage;* Moncure Daniel Conway, *Autobiography, Memories, and Experiences* (Boston and New York: Houghton, Mifflin, 1904), 1: 143; 2: 328, 329. See also Mary Elizabeth Burtis, *Moncure Conway, 1832–1907* (New Brunswick, N.J.: Rutgers University Press, 1952), 193, 220. *Woman's Who's Who of America, 1914–1915*, s.v. "Moore, Eleanor M. Hiestand." "List of the Subscription, Contribution, and Exchange. The Light of Dharma." [Eleanor M. Hiestand Moore], "The Ethical Side of the Material," *Light of Dharma* 3 (Oct. 1903): 76–79. Strauss's occupation at the time of conversion was identified in a piece from the *Philadelphia Times* that was reprinted in the "Notes and News" section of the *Maha Bodhi:* "Buddhist Converts," *Maha Bodhi* 2 (Apr. 1894): 1–2. On his association with the Ethical Culture Society see "Remarkable Religious Researches of C. T. Strauss, of New York," *Maha Bodhi* 2 (Nov. 1893): 6. The best

source of information about Strauss is the correspondence by, to, and about him in the Open Court Papers. Strauss, *The Buddha and His Doctrine,* 104–5, 93–117.

33. For biographical information on Lum see *Biographical Dictionary of the American Left,* s.v. "Lum, Dyer," and the article by his niece and fellow anarchist Voltairine deCleyre (1866–1912): Voltairine deCleyre, "Dyer D. Lum," in *Selected Works of Voltairine deCleyre,* ed. Alexander Berkman (New York: Mother Earth, 1915), 284–96. The author of the introduction to her *Selected Works,* Hippolyte Havel, suggested that Lum was Voltairine's "teacher, her confidant, and comrade"; but if their correspondence is any indication, their relationship was even more intense and intimate than that. In fact, the more than seventy letters between them that have survived are another helpful source of information about Lum's last years and his thought (Houghton Library, Harvard University, Cambridge). See also Dyer D. Lum, "Autobiographical P. S.," 13 May 1892, The Joseph Ishill Collection, University of Florida, Gainesville. Two essays at the Houghton Library show his sense of humor and irony and help fill out our understanding of his philosophical position: "Jottings" and "The One and the All." On his problems with alcohol see, for example, Dyer Lum to Voltairine deCleyre, 25 Sept. 1887, Houghton Library. The author of the entry on Lum in the *Biographical Dictionary of the American Left,* Bernard K. Johnpoll, suggests that he was also addicted to opium in his last year.

34. As far as I can tell, the only scholar of American religious thought even to mention Lum is Carl Jackson, who devoted a paragraph to Lum's lecture, "Buddhism Notwithstanding": Jackson, *Oriental Religions,* 106. The modest amount of attention that Lum has received in the secondary literature has been almost exclusively from students of the American political left. See Bruce C. Nelson, *Beyond the Martyrs: A Social History of Chicago's Anarchists, 1870–1900* (New Brunswick and London: Rutgers University Press, 1988), 214, 217; William O. Reichert, *Partisans of Freedom: A Study in American Anarchism* (Bowling Green, Ohio: Bowling Green Popular Press, 1976), 236–44; James Martin, *Man against the State: The Expositors of Individualist Anarchism in America, 1827–1908* (Colorado Springs: Ralph Myles, 1970), 259–61. On his anarchist defense of the Mormons see John S. McCormick, "An Anarchist Defends the Mormons: The Case of Dyer D. Lum," *Utah Historical Quarterly* 44 (Spring 1976): 156–69. On his "critical" nature see Dyer Lum to Voltairine deCleyre, n.d. (folder 1), Houghton Library. On his reading of Comte see Dyer Lum to Voltairine deCleyre, 14 Sept. 1890, Houghton Library.

35. Lum, "Buddhism Notwithstanding," 208. Dyer Lum, "The Basis of Morals: A Posthumous Paper of an Anarchist Philosopher," *The Monist* 7 (July 1897): 554–70. Lum, "Buddhism Notwithstanding," 195.

36. Dyer D. Lum, "Nirvana," *The Radical Review* (Aug. 1877): 260–62. DeCleyre, "Dyer D. Lum," 289–90.

37. For biographical information on Carus see *Dictionary of American Biography,* s.v. "Carus, Paul" and James Francis Sheridan, "Paul Carus: A Study of the Thought and Work of the Editor of the Open Court Publishing Company" (Ph.D. diss., University of Illinois, 1957). See also the several pieces relating to him in the September 1919 issue of the magazine he edited, *Open Court.* Carus's massive correspondence, now collected in the Open Court Papers, contains revealing information. For analyses of his thought see William H. Hay, "Paul Carus: A Case-Study of Philosophy on the Frontier," *Journal of the History of Ideas* 17 (Oct. 1956): 498–510; Donald H. Meyer, "Paul Carus and the Religion of Science," *American Quarterly* 14 (Winter 1962): 597–607; Carl T. Jackson, "The Meeting of East and West: The Case of Paul Carus," *Journal of the History of Ideas* 29 (Jan.-Mar. 1968): 73–92. There is also information in Fader, "Zen in the West."

38. Marie Canavarro to Paul Carus, 3 Jan. 1899, Open Court Papers.

39. Paul Carus to Charles E. Hooper, 21 Aug. 1899, Open Court Papers. Paul Carus, "Religion and Science," *Open Court* 1 (1877–78): 405–7. Paul Carus, *The Religion of Science* (Chicago: Open Court, 1893). For an example of his rationalist interpretation of Buddhism see Paul Carus, *The Dharma; Or, the Religion of Enlightenment* (Chicago: Open Court, 1897).

40. For a good summary of Haeckel's position see Ernest Haeckel, *The Monistic Alliance: Theses for the Organization of Monism* (St. Louis: Bund der Freien Gemeinden und Freidenker-Vereine von Nord Amerika, 1904). On monism, and Carus's version of it, see Sheridan, "Paul Carus," 7–18, 32–62.

41. Theodore Parker, "The Transient and the Permanent in Christianity," in *Three Prophets of Religious Liberalism: Channing, Emerson, and Parker,* by Conrad Wright (Boston: Unitarian Universalist Association, 1983), 113–49. Carus, *Gospel of Buddha,* viii, vi, viii, x, viii.

42. For evidence of Carus's influence on Wilson see Wilson, "Buddhism in America," 3; Thomas B. Wilson, "The Great Teachers," *Light of Dharma* 2 (1902): 9–10. I could find no mention of Thomas B. Wilson in biographical dictionaries, local histories, newspaper indexes, or library catalogs in the San Francisco Bay area. Or, more precisely, I have been unable to discern with certainty which of the several men with that common name who appear in the records, if any, was the person who wrote about Buddhism. Wilson's name also does not appear in indexes to manuscript collections or in the indexes to collections elsewhere which contain material on Buddhist sympathizers. On Wilson's editing of the *Overland Monthly* see Mott, *History of Magazines,* 2: 402.

43. *Nisshi,* Archives, Buddhist Churches of America. His lecture was reprinted: Thomas B. Wilson, "The Philosophy of Pain," *Light of Dharma* 1 (Aug. 1901): 16–21.

44. An anonymous piece about Buddhism that was included in one of the issues of the *Overland Monthly* by Wilson was signed "By a Liberal Religionist." This article was almost certainly written by Wilson since the language, style, and content mirror that of the pieces written by Thomas B. Wilson for the *Light of Dharma.* Also, one review of that issue that appeared in the *San Francisco Call* on May 7 indicated that Wilson had contributed several pieces; yet only one included his name. By a Liberal Religionist, "Concerning Buddhism," *Overland Monthly* 45 (May 1905): 387–89. Wilson, "Buddhism in America," 3. Thomas B. Wilson, "Buddhism-Rationalism," *Light of Dharma* 2 (June 1902): 46–49. Wilson, "Buddhism in America," 2, 4. Carus, *Dharma,* 45–46.

45. Wilson, "Buddhism in America," 2–3.

46. Thomas B. Wilson, "The String of Life," *Light of Dharma* 1 (Dec. 1901): 12. [Wilson], "Concerning Buddhism," 387. Wilson, "Great Teachers," 7. Ernest Fenollosa to Isabella Stuart Gardner, n.d. [c. 1897], Fenway Court Museum. The passage from this letter by Fenollosa is quoted in Chisolm, *Fenollosa,* 104.

47. Gabriel Weisberg et. al., *Japonisme: Japanese Influence on French Art, 1854–1910* (Cleveland: Cleveland Museum of Art, [1975]). Society for the Study of Japonisme, *Japonisme in Art: An International Symposium* (Tokyo: Committee for the Year 2001, 1980). Siegfried Wickmann, *Japonismus: Ostasien-Europa: Begegnungen in der Kunst des 19. und 20. Jahrhunderts* (Herrshing: Schuler, 1980). Clay Lancaster, *The Japanese Influence in America* (New York: Walton H. Rawls, 1963).

48. Of course, I am oversimplifying the characterizations of Brooks, Lears, and other historians but the prevailing picture is very similar to the one I draw here. Van Wyck Brooks, "Fenollosa and His Circle," in *Fenollosa and His Circle: With Other Essays in Biography* (New York: Dutton, 1962), 1–68. Lears, *No Place of Grace,* 225–41. Ernest Fenollosa, "Studies of Buddhism," Notebook, 27 June 1885, Houghton Library. Bigelow, *Buddhism and Immortality.*

49. The passage from LaFarge is quoted in Jackson, *Oriental Religions and Amer-*

ican Thought, 214. The passage about Adams's "unconversion" is quoted in the same source, p. 212. Henry Adams, "Buddha and Brahma," *The Yale Review* 5 (Oct. 1915): 82–89. This poem was written in 1895. Adams's letter to Bigelow is quoted in Vern Wagner, "The Lotus of Henry Adams," *New England Quarterly* 27 (Mar. 1954): 86. It was Wagner, in this article, who emphasized the centrality of Buddhism for Adams's work.

50. For Mary McNeil Fenollosa's brief account of their study under Keiyen Ajari see Mary Fenollosa, Preface, *Epochs of Chinese and Japanese Art*, by Ernest F. Fenollosa (1912; New York: Dover, 1963), 1: xx. Akiko Murakata suggested that her interest amounted to a conversion: see Akiko Murakata, "Ernest F. Fenollosa's 'Ode on Reincarnation,' " *Harvard Library Bulletin* 21 (1973): 51. One entry in a biographical dictionary describes Mary Fenollosa's religious affiliation as Christian Science. See *Who Was Who Among North American Authors, 1921–1939*, s.v. "Fenollosa, Mary." She, like some others, might have had dual affiliation. Mary McNeil Fenollosa, "The Path of Prayer," in *Out of the Nest: A Flight of Verses* (Boston: Little, Brown, and Company, 1899), 47–48.

51. Ernest F. Fenollosa, "Chinese and Japanese Traits." Ernest F. Fenollosa, *East and West: The Discovery of America and Other Poems* (New York: Crowell, 1893). Ernest F. Fenollosa, *Epochs of Chinese and Japanese Art*. For evidence of his attraction to Japanese culture see Fenollosa, *East and West*, 39–55. Chisolm's biography of Fenollosa is excellent so there is no need to reconstruct his life and work here as fully as is necessary with some of the other more obscure exemplars. For other references to the secondary literature on Fenollosa see the bibliographical note in Chisolm's book (257–70). That work also contains a guide to the relevant manuscript sources and a list of Fenollosa's published works (270–76).

52. Mary Fenollosa, Preface, *Epochs of Chinese and Japanese Art*, xv. For evidence of his deep interest in Buddhist-inspired art see Ernest F. Fenollosa, Notebooks, 3 Aug. 1884, Houghton Library. See also Ernest F. Fenollosa, "Sketch Book," Notes and Sketches Made in Japan, 22 July [1884–85?], Houghton Library. Chisolm, *Fenollosa*, 109.

53. No biography has appeared yet, but there are entries on Bigelow in several biographical dictionaries and brief discussions of his Buddhist interests in several secondary sources. The best single source of information is Murakata, "Selected Letters of Dr. William Sturgis Bigelow." See also Mrs. Winthrop [Margaret] Chanler, *Autumn in the Valley* (Boston: Little, Brown, 1936), 23–34; W. T. Councilman, "William Sturgis Bigelow (1850–1926)," in *Later Years of the Saturday Club, 1870–1920*, ed. M. A. DeWolfe Howe (Boston and New York: Houghton Mifflin, 1927), 265–69; and Frederick Cheever Shattuck, "William Sturgis Bigelow," *Proceedings of the Massachusetts Historical Society* 40 (Oct. 1926-June 1927): 15–19. One of his cousins destroyed Bigelow's papers at his death, but a substantial amount of his correspondence has survived. For a list of his correspondence and where the letters are held see Murakata's dissertation (515–28).

54. Bigelow used the term "sacraments" to describe these ceremonies of the Tendai and Shingon sects in William Sturgis Bigelow, "Prefatory Note to 'On the Method of Practicing Concentration and Contemplation' by Chi Ki, Translated by Okakura Kakuzo," *Harvard Theological Review* 16 (Apr. 1923): 110. In the *Bodhisattvasila* [Bodhisattva Discipline] ceremony Bigelow committed himself to the path of compassion and wisdom and linked himself with the lineage of those who previously perfected the Bodhisattva path. The "Certificate of Bodhisattvasila according to the Tendai Sect" is dated 14 August, the twenty-first year of the Meiji (1888), and is stamped with the official seal of the Hieizan monastery. The folio folder that contains these three documents contains accompanying translations. The inscription on the "Certificate of *Bodhisattvasila* reads: "Inasmuch as the Buddhist disciple

[Bigelow] had a pure faith in the *Triratna* (Three Jewels) before receiving *Bodhisatt-vakarama* (the spiritual momentum of a Bodhisattva), he succeeds to this wonderful *Bodhisattvasila* of the Tendai sect. Through the merit of this pure *Sila* [discipline] and through the help of the Buddha, may he be reborn in the peaceful Pure Land, and may his place therein be soon attained" ("Certificate from the Hieizan Monastery for the Study of Buddhism," 14 Aug. 1888, Massachusetts Historical Society). The *Bodhisattvasila* is a Mahayana *sila* based on the precepts of the *Bommokyo*. The latter is an important Mahayana sutra dealing with monastic discipline *(vinaya)* and containing the ten major and forty-eight minor precepts of Mahayana Buddhism. On the *Bodhisattvasila* see Matsunaga and Matsunaga, *Foundation of Japanese Buddhism,* 1: 47–48, 121, 148, 265; 2: 322. On his intention to become a Buddhist priest see "Personal Letter about Dr. William Sturgis Bigelow (1850–1926) from John E. Lodge to Frederick Cheever Shattuck," *Proceedings of the Massachusetts Historical Society* 75 (Jan.-Dec. 1963): 109.

55. On Fenollosa's continuing interest in Emerson see William Sturgis Bigelow to E. S. Morse, 3 Sept. 1883, which is reprinted in Murakata, "Selected Letters," 61. According to Bigelow, Fenollosa was reading Emerson in Japan in 1883. William Sturgis Bigelow to Phillips Brooks, 19 Aug. 1889, Houghton Library. (That letter is also reprinted in Murakata, "Selected Letters," 82–86.) Murakata, "Selected Letters," 10–11, 20–24. *Encyclopedia of Japan,* s.v. "Bigelow, William Sturgis."

56. Chanler, *Autumn in the Valley,* 24. On Bigelow's "muted response" to aesthetic components in Buddhism see Chisolm, *Fenollosa,* 109. William Sturgis Bigelow, "Fragmentary Notes on Buddhism, Taken Jan. 30 and 31, 1922, Being Dr. Bigelow's Answers to Questions and Also Comments on Keien [Sakurai] Ajari's Lectures," Houghton Library.

57. There is a good deal of secondary literature about Hearn. See, for example, Beongchen Yu, *An Ape of Gods: The Art and Thought of Lafcadio Hearn* (Detroit: Wayne State University Press, 1964). For a very helpful tribute that focuses on his Japanese and Buddhist interests see K. K. Kawakami, "Yakumo Koizumi: The Interpreter of Japan," *Open Court* 20 (Oct. 1906): 624–32. The best sources of information are the collections of letters: Elizabeth Bisland, ed., *The Japanese Letters of Lafcadio Hearn,* 2 vols. (Boston and New York: Houghton Mifflin, 1910) and Elizabeth Bisland, ed., *The Life and Letters of Lafcadio Hearn,* 2 vols. (Boston and New York: Houghton Mifflin, 1906).

58. Bisland, ed., *Life and Letters,* 2: 409. The passage about his inability to adopt a faith is quoted in Jackson, *Oriental Religions and American Thought,* 233. Lafcadio Hearn, "The Higher Buddhism," in *The Buddhist Writings of Lafcadio Hearn,* ed. Kenneth Rexroth (Santa Barbara: Ross-Erikson, 1977), 277–97.

59. For Hearn's assessment of esoterics see Bisland, ed., *Life and Letters,* 1: 265, 400–401. For rationalist themes in Hearn see Bisland, ed., *Life and Letters,* 2: 131–32, 2: 146–47.

60. Murakata, "Selected Letters," 212. The passage about the wisdom of Tibet is found in William Sturgis Bigelow to Henry Cabot Lodge, 30 Sept. 1883, Henry Cabot Lodge Papers, Massachusetts Historical Society. The letter also is included in Murakata, "Selected Letters," 64–69.

61. Murakata offered this interpretation in "Selected Letters," 57–58. The meeting and Roosevelt's reaction are recorded in a letter from T. R. to Henry Cabot Lodge after meeting Bigelow in Paris in 1887, and it is quoted in Murakata, "Selected Letters," xiv-xv. Roosevelt found Bigelow "charming," and apparently he was not too disturbed by his friend's religious stance since in 1912 he even encouraged Bigelow to write a book on Buddhism (Murakata, "Selected Letters," xxii). On their friendship see Akiko Murakata, "Theodore Roosevelt and William Sturgis Bigelow: The Story of a Friendship," *Harvard Library Bulletin* 23 (Jan. 1975): 90–108. Bigelow, *Buddhism and Immortality,* 62.

62. Moore, "The Ethical Side," 77. Albert J. Edmunds, Diary 11, 30 May 1907, 1 June 1907, Albert J. Edmunds Papers. The New Church minister denied his request: "Letter from Worcester, saying that I cannot join the church on any lower footing than acceptance of the official creed. So I am an outcast forever." Albert J. Edmunds, Diary 11, 3 June 1907, Albert J. Edmunds Papers. Canavarro, "The Ethics of Buddhism," 11. Canavarro, "Nirvana," 22.

4. "WALKING IN FAIRYLAND"

1. This description of Boston in the 1890s was offered by Van Wyck Brooks in *New England: Indian Summer, 1865–1915* (Cleveland and New York: World Publishing Company, 1940), 414. Bigelow to Phillips Brooks, 19 Aug. 1889, The Philips Brooks Papers, Houghton Library. (Also printed in Murakata, "Selected Letters," 82–86.) Mrs. Winthrop [Margaret] Chanler, *Autumn in the Valley* (Boston: Little, Brown, 1936), 25.

2. The revealing and interesting details of the burial of Bigelow's ashes have found their way into a few accounts including *Encyclopedia of Japan*, s.v. "Bigelow, William Sturgis"; Fields, *Swans*, 163; Lears, *No Place of Grace*, 234. The best source of information about Bigelow's wishes is "Personal Letter about Dr. William Sturgis Bigelow (1850–1926) from John E. Lodge to Frederick Cheever Shattuck," *Proceedings of the Massachusetts Historical Society* 75 (Jan.-Dec. 1963): 108–9. On all other matters pertaining to his death, see Murakata, "Selected Letters." Morris Carter, *Isabella Stewart Gardner and Fenway Court* (Boston and New York: Houghton Mifflin, 1930), 59. Quoted in Murakata, "Selected Letters," 6. John F. Fulton, *Harvey Cushing: A Biography* (Springfield, Ill.: Charles C. Thomas, 1946), 495. Quoted in Murakata, "Selected Letters," 20.

3. Murakata, "Selected Letters," 8. William Sturgis Bigelow to Naobayashi Keien, 10 June 1921, Homyoin, Otsu, Japan. Also printed in Murakata, "Selected Letters," 495–500.

4. For further information on F. Graeme Davis see chapter 2. Ellinwood, *Oriental Religions*, 156.

5. Italics mine. Clarence Edgar Rice, "Buddhism as I Have Seen It," *The Arena* 27 (May 1902): 479. For my working definitions of society, politics, economy, and culture, see the Introduction.

6. Alan Trachtenberg, *The Incorporation of America: Culture and Society in the Gilded Age* (New York: Hill and Wang, 1982), 5.

7. Mark Twain and Charles Dudley Warner, *The Gilded Age: A Tale of Today* (1873–74; Indianapolis: Bobbs-Merrill, 1972).

8. The Civic Club, *A Directory of the Charitable, Social Improvement, Educational, and Religious Associations and Churches of Philadelphia*, 2nd ed. (Philadelphia: The Civic Club, 1903): 478–81, 546. The best source of information on the Vegetarian Society is its magazine, *Food, Home, and Garden*. On the Philadelphia Bible-Christian Church see that magazine and Albert J. Edmunds, "The Vegetarian Church: 1817–1941," ms., Society Miscellaneous Collection, Historical Society of Pennsylvania. See also "Men and Things," newspaper clipping from *The Philadelphia Evening Bulletin*, 16 Mar. 1923, Society Miscellaneous Collection, Pennsylvania Historical Society. The "Vegetarian Church," also active at the height of Buddhist interest in the late nineteenth century, had twelve members when this article appeared in 1923. Schaff, the church historian, had read about this church in a German work at mid-century, but he found the idea—that they lived "on water and vegetable food!"—so unbelievable that he cited it as another example of European exaggeration about American religion. Schaff, *America*, 104–5.

9. For Carus's claim that he had received many manuscripts on "the Anti-Vivisection question" see Carus to Mrs. Fairchild-Allen, 26 July 1897, Open Court

Papers. For his personal disagreement with the movement see Carus to C. L. Doll, 8 June 1897, Open Court Papers. For his rejection of Galvani's piece see Carus to William H. Galvani, 3 Oct. 1893, Open Court Papers.

10. On Galvani's plans see "Oregon Colonization," *Food, Home, and Garden* 3 (Dec. 1891): 153. William H. Galvani, "The Hog," *Food, Home, and Garden* 3 (July-Aug. 1891): 84. Examples of articles by Buddhist sympathizers in Buddhist magazines include William H. Galvani, "Heirs of Immortality," *Buddhist Ray* 6 (Mar.-Apr. 1893): 13; Joseph M. Wade, "The One Life-Necessary Action," *Light of Dharma* 2 (1902): 24–25. Herman Vetterling, "Why Buddhism?" *Buddhist Ray* 1 (Jan. 1888): 1. On Vetterling's donation of $50,000 see San Jose Public Library, *Authors of Santa Clara County*, (n.p., n.d. [after Feb. 1954]), 101.

11. Charles T. Strauss was listed as a member of the Vegetarian Society. See "Vegetarian Society of America: Cash Received Since Last Issue," *Food, Home, and Garden* 3 (Mar. 1891). Strauss's request for information about a Vegetarian Society or restaurant in New York City was published with the editor's response: "Society Movements," *Food, Home, and Garden* 3 (Feb. 1891): 29. Albert J. Edmunds, Diary 11, 25 May 1906, Albert J. Edmunds Papers. Edmunds, Diary 10, 2 Dec. 1900 and 12 Dec. 1902, Albert J. Edmunds Papers. For Edmunds's justification of vegetarianism and temperance in Christian terms see Albert J. Edmunds, "Food in the Light of Scripture," *Food, Home, and Garden* 3 (July-Aug. 1891): 88–89.

12. Laura C[arter] Holloway, *The Buddhist Diet Book* (New York: Funk and Wagnalls, 1886). Laura C. Holloway, *The Ladies of the White House* ([1869]; New York: United States Publishing Co, 1870; San Francisco: H. H. Bancroft, 1870). For biographical information on Langford, best known by her first husband's name (Holloway), see The Laura Carter Holloway Langford Papers, The Edward Deming Andrews Memorial Shaker Collection, The Henry Francis duPont Winterthur Museum, Winterthur, Delaware and the guide to that collection, E. Richard McKinstry, *The Edward Deming Andrews Memorial Shaker Collection* (New York and London: Garland, 1987): 292–94. Especially helpful are the newspaper clippings collected in her "Scrapbook." "Vegetarianism Among the Shakers," *Food, Home, and Garden* 1 (Oct. 1889): 79. Anna White to Laura Langford, 13 Nov. 1901, Langford Papers.

13. *San Francisco Post*, 11 Dec. 1886. See also *New York Star*, 13 Dec. 1886; *Newark Advertiser*, 6 Dec. 1886. These and many other reviews of her book can be found in the Langford Papers. *Denver Times*, 8 Dec. 1886. *Indianapolis Journal*, 6 Dec. 1886.

14. Robert H. Wiebe, *The Search for Order, 1877–1920* (New York: Hill and Wang, 1967), 114. San Jose Public Library, *Authors*, 101.

15. Edmunds, Diary 8, 26 Nov. 1885; Diary 8, 29 Nov. 1885; Diary 10, 7 Oct. 1902, Albert J. Edmunds Papers.

16. The biographical details here are taken from several accounts including *Biographical Dictionary of the American Left*, s.v. "Lum, Dyer Daniel" and McCormick, "Anarchist Defends the Mormons," 156–60. For other biographical sources see the note about Lum in chapter 3. His history of the Haymarket riot and trial was published as *A Concise History of the Great Trial of the Chicago Anarchists in 1886* (Chicago: Socialistic Publishing Company, [1886]).

17. Dyer D. Lum, "Why I Am a Social Revolutionist," *Twentieth Century* 5 (30 Oct. 1890): 5–6. Dyer D. Lum, *The Social Problems of Today; Or, the Mormon Question in Its Economic Aspects* (Port Jarvis, N.Y.: D. D. Lum, 1886); *The Economics of Anarchy* (New York: Twentieth Century, [1890]); *The Philosophy of Trade Unions* (New York: American Federation of Labor, 1892). The latter greatly influenced the American Federation of Labor, and was reprinted by that organization for many years afterward.

18. On the emergence of this "cult" see Barbara Welter, "The Cult of True Womanhood, 1820–1860," *American Quarterly* 18 (1966): 151–74. Smith-Rosenberg,

Disorderly Conduct, 13. Elizabeth Cady Stanton, "Has Christianity Benefitted Woman?" *North American Review* 140 (May 1885): 390–91. Edmunds, Diary 11, 21 Jan. 1906, Albert J. Edmunds Papers.

19. For missionary interpretations of Buddhism as unegalitarian see M. L. Gordon, *An American Missionary in Japan* (Boston and New York: Houghton Mifflin, 1900): 173–85; Helen Barrett Montgomery, *Western Women in Eastern Lands* (New York: Macmillan, 1910), 47, 68. For scholarly interpretations of Buddhism as unegalitarian see Warren, *Buddhism in Translations*, 392 and E. Washburn Hopkins, *The Religions of India*, Handbooks on the History of Religion, no. 1 (Boston: Ginn, 1895): 310. For a more egalitarian interpretation see Rhys Davids, *Buddhism*, 71–75. There is a growing scholarly literature about the images of women in Buddhist literature and the status of women in Buddhist institutions and nations. For example, see the early study by I. B. Horner and the more recent work of Diana Paul: I. B. Horner, *Women Under Primitive Buddhism* (London: George Routledge, 1930); Diana Paul, *The Buddhist Feminine Ideal*, The AAR Dissertation Series (Missoula, Mont.: Scholars Press, 1980); Diana Paul, *Women in Buddhism: Images of the Feminine in the Mahayana Tradition* (1979; Berkeley: University of California Press, 1980).

20. Vetterling, "Why Buddhism," 1. Lum, "Buddhism Notwithstanding," 206. Withee, "Is Buddhism to Blame?" 459–60. Strauss, *Buddha*, 105–7. *Woman's Who's Who of America*, s.v. "Moore, Eleanor M. Hiestand."

21. Canavarro, "Extracts from an Address," Thorton Chase Papers, National Baha'i Archives, Wilmette, Ill. Canavarro, *Insight*, 8. Canavarro to Paul Carus, 28 May [1897], Open Court Papers. She did not seem to regret her radical decision, however. This passage continues: "*thinking* I was making a great sacrifice, and now I find how puny [?] that all is in comparison to what I have found." P[aul] C[arus], "Sister Sanghamitta," 251.

22. Canavarro to Paul Carus, 24 October 1909, Open Court Papers. Canavarro to Paul Carus, 7 May 1902, Open Court Papers. Canavarro to Paul Carus, 1 June 1902, Open Court Papers. Canavarro also confessed to the Master of the Baha'i faith that she had been secretly "married" to Phelps. Both Carus and he strongly advised her to change her living arrangement. See Canavarro to 'Abdul'l-Bahá, n.d., Thorton Chase Papers. Canavarro told Carus that she could not reveal many of the details of the split with Phelps since "they could not be written." She did reveal, in the letter of 24 October 1909, that Phelps had "quit her" two years earlier (1907) "on the most absurd grounds imaginable." On Phelps see also *Dictionary of North American Authors*, s.v. "Phelps, Myron Henry." Canavarro's rejection of the institution of marriage seems especially interesting since she was married at least twice more before she died. See "Funeral Will Be Held for Author," *Glendale News Press*, 27 July 1933.

23. Ann Braude, *Radical Spirits: Spiritualism and Women's Rights in Nineteenth-Century America* (Boston: Beacon Press, 1989). Mary Farrell Bednarowski, "Women in Occult America," in Kerr and Crow, *The Occult in America*, 181–82; 183–87.

24. Canavarro, *Insight*, 15.

25. Bigelow to Rt. Rev. Kanrio Naobayashi, 16 July 1895, Homyoin Temple, Otsu, Japan. (Reprinted in Murakata, "Selected Letters," 122–27.) On Mary Foster's relation to Dharmapala see Maha Bodhi Society, *Maha Bodhi Society of India*, 133–44. Lears, *No Place of Grace*, 229. For Canavarro's version of some of the accusations that she had an "eccentric and sensational disposition" see Canavarro to Paul Carus, 28 May 1901, Open Court Papers. For Canavarro's confession that her behavior in Asia "may have seemed a little erratic," see Canavarro to Paul Carus, 14 July 1900, Open Court Papers.

26. The psychological and sociological literature on conversion is rich and voluminous. For a lucid overview of these theories, and the developmental theory

discussed below, see Robert S. Ellwood and Harry B. Partin, *Religious and Spiritual Groups in Modern America,* 2d ed. (Englewood Cliffs, N.J.: Prentice Hall, 1988): 266–91. See also Brock Kilbourne and James T. Richardson, "Paradigm Conflict, Types of Conversion, and Conversion Theories," *Sociological Analysis* 50 (1988): 1–21.

27. J. Gordon Melton and Robert L. Moore, *The Cult Experience: Responding to the New Religious Pluralism* (New York: The Pilgrim Press, 1982).

28. For an example of an "interactionist theory" see Anson D. Shupe, Jr., *Six Perspectives on New Religions* (New York: Edwin Mellen, 1981). Many cultural anthropologists and interpretive sociologists, of course, view religion in this way, and other scholars have interpreted conversion as a change of frameworks of meaning or universes of discourse. See David Snow and Richard Machalek, "The Convert as a Social Type," in *Sociological Theory,* ed. R. Collins (San Francisco: Jossey-Bass, 1983). David Snow and Richard Machalek, "The Sociology of Conversion," *Annual Review of Sociology* 10 (1984): 167–90. See also the helpful corrective to the Snow and Machalek model in Clifford L. Staples and Armand L. Mauss, "Conversion or Commitment?: A Reassesment of the Snow and Machalek Approach to the Study of Conversion," *Journal for the Scientific Study of Religion* 26 (1987): 133–47.

29. John Lofland and Rodney Stark, "Becoming a World-Saver: A Theory of Conversion to a Deviant Perspective," *American Sociological Review* 30 (Dec. 1965): 862–75. John Lofland, " 'Becoming a World-Saver' Revisited," *American Behavioral Scientist* 20 (July/Aug. 1977): 805–18. In the latter piece, Lofland suggested that students of alternative religions consider "how people go about converting themselves." And recently activist theories have gained in prominence. See R. Straus, "Changing Oneself: Seekers and the Creative Transformation of Life Experience," in *Doing Social Life,* ed. J. Lofland (New York: John Wiley, 1976), 252–72. J. T. Richardson, "The Active vs. the Passive Convert: Paradigm Conflict in Conversion/ Recruitment Research," *Journal for the Scientific Study of Religion* 24 (1985): 163–79. Lorne Dawson, "Self-Affirmation, Freedom, and Rationality: Theoretically Elaborating 'Active' Conversions," *Journal for the Scientific Study of Religion* 29 (June 1990): 141–63.

30. Sheridan, "Paul Carus," 2–4. Soyen Shaku, untitled account of Carus and his *Gospel of Buddha,* Open Court Papers. Edmunds, Diary 10, 23 Apr. 1903, Albert J. Edmunds Papers.

31. Carus to W. Henry Green, 21 Sept. 1899, Open Court Papers.

32. Clifford Geertz, *The Interpretation of Cultures* (New York: Basic Books, 1973), 90. J. Milton Yinger, *Countercultures* (New York: The Free Press, 1982), 8. For analysis of the European cultural ferment see, for example, H. Stuart Hughes, *Consciousness and Society: The Reorientation of European Social Thought, 1890–1930* (New York: Knopf, 1958); Fritz Richard Stern, *The Politics of Cultural Despair* (Garden City, N.Y.: Doubleday, 1965); Carl E. Schorske, *Fin-de-Siècle Vienna: Politics and Culture* (New York: Knopf, 1980); and Eugen Weber, *France, Fin de Siècle* (Cambridge, Mass.: Harvard University Press). On the American side, see John Higham, "The Reorientation of American Culture in the 1890s," *Writing American History* (Bloomington: Indiana University Press, 1970), 73–102; Henry F. May, *The End of American Innocence* (1959; New York: Oxford University Press, 1979); Stanley Coben, "The Assault on Victorianism in the Twentieth Century," in *Victorian America,* ed. Daniel Walker Howe (Philadelphia: University of Pennsylvania Press, 1976), 160–81; and Lears, *No Place of Grace.*

33. A number of historians have described this "spiritual crisis." Arthur Schlesinger, Sr., was one of the first. Arthur M. Schlesinger, Sr., "A Critical Period in American Religion, 1875–1900," *Proceedings of the Massachusetts Historical Society* 64 (1930–32): 523–46. See also Francis Weisenburger, *Ordeal of Faith: The Crisis of*

Church-Going America, 1865–1900 (New York: Philosophical Library, 1959); Paul A. Carter, *The Spiritual Crisis of the Gilded Age* (Dekalb: Northern Illinois University Press, 1971); D. H. Meyer, "American Intellectuals and the Victorian Crisis of Faith," in *Victorian America*, 59–77; and James Turner, *Without God, Without Creed: The Origins of Unbelief in America* (Baltimore: Johns Hopkins University Press, 1985). Several scholars have noted the role that the Victorian spiritual crisis played in turning Western intellectuals away from Christianity and toward Asian religions. For a brief but helpful discussion of British developments see Christopher Clausen, "Victorian Buddhism and the Origins of Comparative Religion," *Religion* 5 (1973): 3–7. On the American side see Joseph Kitagawa, "Buddhism in America, with Special Reference to Zen," *Japanese Religions* 5 (July 1967): 41; Jackson, *Oriental Religions*, 152–53. Octavius Brooks Frothingham, "The Religion of Humanity," *The Radical* 10 (Apr. 1872): 241.

34. Myron H. Goodwin, "Theological Ruins," *Twentieth Century* 8 (24 Mar. 1892): 2.

35. Adams, *Alphabetical Compendium*, lxxxiii. In fact, William Hutchison has argued that the uniqueness and finality of Christianity was "the central religious problem" for Protestant liberals of the 1890s. William R. Hutchison, *The Modernist Impulse in American Protestantism* (New York: Oxford University Press, 1976): 129, 111–44.

36. Italics mine. C. H. Currier, "Buddhism in America," letter to the editor of *The Boston Herald*, 16 Aug. 1899, *Journal of the Maha Bodhi Society* 8 (Dec. 1899): 71. Carus to C. H. Currier, 24 Aug. 1899, Open Court Papers. To give another example, Carus granted permission to K. Ohara to translate his Buddhist story, *Karma*, into Japanese and Chinese on the condition that he use the profits to spread Buddhism. See Carus to K. Ohara, 30 Jan. 1896, Open Court Papers.

37. Wilson, "Buddhism in America," 1.

38. Bigelow to Naobayashi Kanryo Ajari, 21 Oct. 1902, Homyoin, Otsu, Japan. (Reprinted in Murakata, "Selected Letters," 210–12.) Lears has offered a persuasive account of the appeal of medievalism and Catholicism for Lodge and other late nineteenth-century American intellectuals: Lears, *No Place of Grace*, 238, 141–215. Bruce Kuklick, *The Rise of American Philosophy: Cambridge, Massachusetts, 1860–1930* (New Haven: Yale University Press, 1977), xxi. One historian of Baha'i in America, for example, has suggested that it was continuity with the Christian tradition, especially Baha'is' claim to be a fulfillment of biblical prophecy, that was central to its appeal between 1892 and 1900. Robert H. Stockman, *The Baha'i Faith in America: Origins, 1892–1900*, vol. 1 (Wilmette, Ill.: Baha'i Publishing Trust, 1985). See also Stockman, "Baha'i Faith and American Protestantism."

39. Warren, *Buddhism in Translations*, 283–84. Vetterling, "Growth of Enlightenment," 4. Strauss, *Buddha*, 73. For a very helpful analysis of the sources of the nineteenth-century interest in Buddhism that focuses on Europe, and especially on disillusioned British intellectuals, see Clausen, "Victorian Buddhism and the Origins of Comparative Religion," 4–7. His account of the five sources of Buddhism's appeal for British intellectuals also points to some of the reasons nineteenth-century Americans were drawn to the tradition.

40. Moore, *Religious Outsiders*.

41. Clark, "Primitive Buddhism," 200.

42. That there was hostility toward those outside the boundaries of Anglo-Protestant Victorian culture has been well documented by historians. Many studies of particular religious and ethnic groups have appeared—too many to mention here. The standard study of Anglo-Protestant hostility toward immigrants is still John Higham, *Strangers in the Land: Patterns of American Nativism, 1860–1925* (1955; New York: Atheneum, 1968). See also George M. Fredrickson and Dale T. Knobel,

"The History of Discrimination," in *Prejudice*, selections from the *Harvard Encyclopedia of American Ethnic Groups* (Cambridge, Mass.: Harvard University Press, 1982), 30–87. The secondary literature about American foreign missions, foreign policy, and world's fairs also provides many illuminating examples of nineteenth-century Anglo-Protestant hostility toward, or at least anxiety about, "alien" religions, races, and cultures. For example see Hutchison, *Errand* and Robert W. Rydel, *All the World's a Fair: Visions of Empire at American International Expositions, 1876–1916* (Chicago: University of Chicago Press, 1984).

43. For one recent study of colonial religious diversity see Richard W. Pointer, *Protestant Pluralism and the New York Experience: A Study of Eighteenth-Century Religious Diversity*, Religion in North America Series (Bloomington and Indianapolis: Indiana University Press, 1988).

44. Olcott noted the role of this discovery in shaping Western perceptions: Olcott, *Buddhist Catechism*, 77. Asoka's *Dharma-lipi* (records of morality) had to be rediscovered and translated in the nineteenth century because Prakrit, the language of the stone inscriptions, had ceased to be the spoken dialect of the people. The first modern account of the inscriptions (1756) was by Father Joseph Tieffentaller, a Jesuit missionary and noted geographer, but it was not until 1837 that the Asoka script was deciphered by James Prinsep. After that time the inscriptions were rediscovered, published, and interpreted. N. A. Nikam and Richard McKeon, eds., *The Edicts of Asoka* (Chicago: University of Chicago Press, 1959), 1–3, 51–52. See also Kanlinga Edict II in Nikam and McKeon, *Edicts of Asoka*, 53–54. While he was in India, Phillips Brooks, who also was committed to tolerance, made a pilgrimage to see these inscriptions. See Allen, ed., *Life and Letters*, 2: 518.

45. Fenollosa, *East and West*, 3–55. Bisland, ed., *Life and Letters*, 2: 311, 131–33. Bigelow, "Fragmentary Notes." Bigelow to Naobayashi Keien Ajari, 20 Dec. 1902, Homyoin, Otsu, Japan. (Also reprinted in Murakata, "Selected Letters," 215–16.) A few of the most informed among the American Christian critics, such as M. L. Gordon, reminded Buddhist advocates of the Nichiren sect's "violent spirit against other sects." Gordon, "The Buddhisms of Japan," 306. For Nichiren's (1222–82) advocacy of coercive subjugation *(shakubuku)* see his "Treatise on the Establishment of the Orthodox Teaching and the Peace of the Nation" *(Rissho Ankokuron)* in Laurel Rasplica Rodd, *Nichiren: Selected Writings*, Asian Studies at Hawaii, no. 26 (Honolulu: University of Hawaii Press, 1980), 59–81, especially 72–73. Although many scholars and believers have felt that Nichiren was being un-Buddhist, Nichiren himself thought his policy was continuous with the Buddhist tradition; and he even quoted Buddhist scriptures to support it.

46. Carus to Theodore F. Seward, 11 Apr. 1899, Open Court Papers.

47. Carus to Clarence Clowe, 22 June 1901, Open Court Papers. Carus to Anagarika H. Dharmapala, 22 June 1897, Open Court Papers.

48. Carus, *Gospel of Buddha*, ix–x. Carus to Anagarika H. Dharmapala, 26 Feb. 1896, Open Court Papers.

49. Lum, "Buddhism Notwithstanding," 207. C. T. Strauss, "The Future of Artificial Languages," *Monist* 18 (Oct. 1908): 609–19. Strauss, who favored Bolak not Esperanto, was refuting an editorial by Carus. Carus did not believe an artificial international language was feasible. Carus, the editor, included his own reply at the end of Strauss's piece. On Strauss's interest in this artificial language see the exchange between him and Carus about the article. [Paul Carus] to C. T. Strauss, 7 May 1908, Open Court Papers. C. T. Strauss to Paul Carus, 4 Sept. 1908, Open Court Papers. Strauss, *Buddha*, 107–8.

50. Campbell, *Ancient Wisdom Revisited*, 36–37.

51. Vetterling, "Why Buddhism?" 1. Olcott, *Buddhist Catechism*, 74–77.

52. Edmunds, Diary 8, 5 Jan. 1891; Diary 11, 26 Jan. 1907; Diary 11, 21 Apr. 1906; Diary 10, 7 June 1904, Albert J. Edmunds Papers. For Lanman's offer of this position see Charles R. Lanman to Albert J. Edmunds, 20 Nov. 1903, Albert J. Edmunds Papers. See also Edmunds, Diary #10, 27 Nov. 1903, Albert J. Edmunds Papers.

53. Canavarro, *Insight*, 15. Canavarro, "Extracts from an Address," Thorton Chase Papers. Canavarro, *Insight*, 186–87. Swami Paramananda, *Principles and Purpose of Vedanta*, 9th ed. (Cohasset, Mass.: The Vendanta Centre, 1937), 33.

54. Carus to Albert Réville, 5 Aug. 1899, Open Court Papers. Carus to Anagarika H. Dharmapala, 26 Feb. 1896, Open Court Papers.

55. For a discussion of Buddhism and "God" in the late-Victorian period see the following chapter.

56. The passage from Arnold is quoted in Carter, *Spiritual Crisis*, 221. William Peiris, *Edwin Arnold: A Brief Account of His Life and Contribution to Buddhism* (Kandy, Ceylon: Buddhist Publication Society, 1970), 69–70. Dharmapala's speech in Oakland was reprinted and given a misleading title: "Mr. H. Dharmapala at the Parliament of Religions, Chicago," *Maha Bodhi* 2 (Nov. 1893): 2. Reverend Shuye Sonoda sent Carus a handwritten copy of his first public lecture on Buddhism and a copy of the local newspaper's account of the event in which Sonoda quoted Carus on the compatibility of Buddhism with science. S. Sonoda to Paul Carus. 14 [Sept.] 1899, Open Court Papers. "Dharma-Sangher [sic] of Buddha," *Light of Dharma* 1 (Apr. 1901): 20–21.

57. Lum, "Buddhism Notwithstanding," 208. Wilson, "Buddhism in America." [Moore], "The Ethical Side of the Material," *Light of Dharma* 3 (Oct. 1903): 77.

58. Carus, "Religion and Science," *Open Court* 1 (1877–78): 405–7. Paul Carus, *The Religion of Science* (Chicago: Open Court, 1893): v. Carus, *Christian Critics*, 309. Carus, *The Dharma*, 45–46.

59. Carus to May Cline, 30 Sept. 1897, Open Court Papers. Carus, *Religion of Science*, iv. On Carus's interest in purifying religion in terms of "scientific" principles see also Carus to Anagarika H. Dharmapala, 26 Feb. 1896, Open Court Papers; Sheridan, "Paul Carus," 77–88.

60. Bisland, *Life and Letters*, 2: 235.

61. Bisland, *Japanese Letters*, 56, 413. Bisland, *Life and Letters*, 2: 338–39.

62. Bisland, *Japanese Letters*, 56. Bisland, *Life and Letters*, 1: 400. Hearn, "Higher Buddhism," 281, 280.

63. See for example Bigelow, *Buddhism and Immortality*, 49, 55, 61, 65, 69. Bigelow, *Buddhism and Immortality*, 71, 69–71.

64. Kerr and Crow, *Occult in America*, 5. Ellwood, *Alternative Altars*, 84–87. Italics mine. A. Marques, *The Human Aura* (San Francisco: Office of *Mercury*, 1896): v. Later, Marques was an esoteric Buddhist sympathizer and a subscriber to the *Light of Dharma*. On appeals to "science" and "empirical evidence" by nonmainstream groups, see R. Laurence Moore, "The Occult Connection? Mormonism, Christian Science, and Spiritualism," in *Occult in America*, ed. Kerr and Crow, 135–61; Sydney E. Ahlstrom, *A Religious History of the American People* (New Haven: Yale University Press, 1972): 1020, n. 1; Kerr and Crow, *Occult in America*, 4; Campbell, *Ancient Wisdom Revisited*, 17.

65. See for example Sinnett, "Preface to the Annotated Edition," *Esoteric Buddhism*, ix–xv. Canavarro, *Insight*, 14–15. Canavarro, "Nirvana," 22.

66. Edmunds, Diary 11, 25 Jan. 1906, Albert J. Edmunds Papers. Edmunds, "F.W.H. Meyers, Swedenborg, and Buddha," 261. Edmunds, Diary 11, 14 July 1906, Albert J. Edmunds Papers.

67. Albert J. Edmunds, "A Sunday Noon in the Thirtieth Century," World-

Religion Christmas and Birthday Cards, no. 2 (Philadelphia: Innes and Sons, 1913). Edmunds, "Meyers, Swedenborg, and Buddha," 278.

68. Olcott, *Old Diary Leaves*, 2d Series, 116. Olcott, *Buddhist Catechism*, 84–85.

5. STROLLING DOWN MAIN STREET

1. Emphasis mine. Paul Carus to F. S. Ryman, 15 Sept. 1897, Open Court Papers. John Quincy Adams Ward, *Henry Ward Beecher*, 1891, The Metropolitan Museum of Art, Rogers Fund, 1917.

2. Rodney Stark, "How New Religions Succeed: A Theoretical Model," in *The Future of New Religious Movements*, ed. David G. Bromley and Phillip E. Hammond (Macon, Ga.: Mercer University Press, 1987), 13. Mark Twain, "Christian Science," *North American Review* 175 (Dec. 1902): 761.

3. Twain, "Christian Science," 757.

4. Hutchison, *Modernist Impulse*, 86–87. William Newton Clarke, *An Outline of Christian Theology* (Cambridge, Mass.: J. Wilson, 1894). For views of other faiths as they were expressed by Barrows, one of the leaders of the Parliament, see Barrows, *Parliament of Religions*, 75, 183–84. For his acknowledgment that the Parliament bore a "Christian imprint" see Barrows, *Parliament of Religions*, 37. On American cultural, religious, and racial supremacy at the Parliament and other world's fairs between 1876 and 1916 see Rydell, *All the World's a Fair*, especially 38–71.

5. Henry Ward Beecher, "Progress of Thought in the Church," *North American Review* 135 (Aug. 1882): 112. Bryant, "Buddhism and Christianity," 380. See Newman Smyth, *The Religious Feeling* (New York: Scribner, Armstrong, & Co., 1877); Henry Ward Beecher, *Evolution and Religion*, 2 vols. (New York: Fords, Howard, and Hulbert, 1885); James McCosh, *The Religious Aspect of Evolution*, The Bedell Lectures, 1887 (New York: G. P. Putnam's, 1888); Lyman Abbott, *The Evolution of Christianity* (Boston: Houghton, Mifflin, 1892) and *The Theology of an Evolutionist* (Boston: Houghton, Mifflin, 1897). The useful distinction between evangelical and liberal modernists is taken from Kenneth Cauthen's study, *The Impact of American Religious Liberalism* (New York: Harper and Row, 1962).

6. Paul Carus to Julius Nelson, 3 Aug. 1897, Open Court Papers. Marsden, *Fundamentalism and American Culture*, 7. Theodore Dwight Bozeman, *Protestants in an Age of Science: The Baconian Ideal and Antebellum Religious Thought* (Chapel Hill: University of North Carolina Press, 1977).

7. See James Freeman Clarke, "Affinities of Buddhism and Christianity," *North American Review* 136 (May 1883): 467–77; W. L. Courtney, "Socrates, Buddha, and Christ," *North American Review* 140 (Jan. 1885): 63–77; James T[hompson] Bixby, "Buddhism in the New Testament," *The Arena* 3 (Apr. 1891): 555–66; Bryant, "Buddhism and Christianity"; F. F. Ellinwood, "Buddhism and Christianity—A Crusade Which Must Be Met," *The Missionary Review of the World* 14 (Feb. 1891): 108–17; Albert J. Edmunds, "Gospel Parallels from Pali Texts," *Open Court* 16 (Sept. 1902): 559–61; Gmeiner, "The Light of Asia and the Light of the World." See also Ellinwood, *Oriental Religions and Christianity*, 140–78; Aiken, *The Dhamma of Gotama the Buddha and the Gospel of Jesus the Christ*; and Edmunds, *Buddhist and Christian Gospels*. For a brief discussion of this debate see Jackson, *Oriental Religions*, 146–50. I also profited from an unpublished paper by J. Gordon Melton on the topic: "The American Buddhist Apologetic against Christianity, 1880–1940," Buddhism in America Group, "Buddhism and Christianity: Toward the Human Future," Berkeley, 10–15 Aug. 1987.

8. Paul Carus to Professor and Mrs. Burkitt, 14 Jan. 1911, Open Court Papers. Samuel Kellogg, "The Legend of the Buddha and the Life of Christ," *Bibliotheca*

Sacra 39 (July 1882): 458–97. Kellogg, *The Light of Asia and the Light of the World*. Felix Oswald, "The Secret of the East: Buddha and His Galilean Successor," *Index* 14 (22 Mar. 1883): 448. See also Felix Oswald, "Was Christ a Buddhist?" *Arena* 3 (Jan. 1891): 193–201. See some of the replies: James T. Bixby, "Buddhism in the New Testament" and Snell, "Was Christ a Buddhist?" See also two pieces by Charles Schroder: "What is Buddhism?" *Arena* 5 (Jan. 1892): 217–27 and "Buddhism and Christianity," *Arena* 5 (Mar. 1892): 458–63. Another article, very sympathetic to Buddhism, appeared later in the same magazine: Annie Elizabeth Cheney, "Mahayana Buddhism in Japan," *Arena* 16 (Aug. 1896): 439–44. Hopkins, *History of Religions*, 194–95. Albert Schweitzer, *The Quest of the Historical Jesus*, trans. W. Montgomery (1906; New York: Macmillan, 1968), 291.

9. Geisler, "Buddha and His Doctrine," 860.

10. Regis Evariste Huc, *Travels in Tartary, Thibet, and China During the Years 1844, 1845, 1846*, 2 vols. (New York: Appleton, 1852). This account was read and/or cited by a number of the American participants in the discussion about Buddhism, including Thoreau, Emerson, and Clarke. See Christy, *The Orient in American Transcendentalism*, 319. Huc's book was advertised in the pages of *Open Court* in the June 1904 issue, with the usual testimonials, because Open Court Publishing Company had issued an edition of the two-volume work. Fernand Grénard, *Tibet: The Country and Its Inhabitants*, trans. A. Teixeira de Mattos (London: Hutchison and Co., 1904). Lydia Maria Child, "Resemblances between the Buddhist and Roman Catholic Religions," *Atlantic Monthly* 26 (Dec. 1870): 660.

11. See George L. Mason, "Buddhism and Romanism," *Missionary Review of the World* 14 (Sept. 1891): 658–61. Gmeiner, "The Light of Asia and the Light of the World"; Ryan, "More Light on the Light of Asia"; Geisler, "Buddha and His Doctrine"; Snell, "Was Christ a Buddhist?"; and Aiken, *The Dhamma of Gotama the Buddha and the Gospel of Jesus the Christ*. Merwin-Marie Snell, "Evangelical Buddhism," *Biblical World* 7 (Jan.-June 1896): 182–88. Darley Dale, "Tibetan Buddhism and Catholicity," *American Catholic Quarterly Review* 30 (Jan. 1905): 174–75.

12. Clarke, "Protestantism of the East," 715. See also Clarke, *Ten Great Religions*, 139–70. Müller, *Chips*, 1: 216. Rhys Davids, *Buddhism: Its History and Literature*, 147.

13. Bond, *Buddhist Revival in Sri Lanka*, 45–74. Gomrich, *Theravada Buddhism: A Social History from Ancient Benares to Modern Colombo*, 172–97. Christopher Clausen has astutely pointed out the way in which this interpretation of Buddhism as "Protestant" fed on anti-Catholic prejudices of British and Continental readers and made the Buddhist tradition seem more accessible to the disillusioned there. See Clausen, "Victorian Buddhism," 7. As I will show below, the appeal of Buddhism's noble founder, lofty ethics, and emphasis on self-reliance for British and Continental religious seekers that Clausen noted also had American parallels. See Clausen, "Victorian Buddhism," 5–6.

14. Quoted in Daniel L. Pals, *The Victorian "Lives" of Jesus*, Trinity University Monograph Series in Religion (San Antonio: Trinity University Press, 1982), 165. Albrecht Ritschl, *The Christian Doctrine of Justification and Reconciliation*, trans. H. R. Macintosh, et al. (Edinburgh: T. and T. Clark, 1900). William Adams Brown, *The Essence of Christianity* (New York: Scribner's, 1902). These developments in Protestant thought have been analyzed in a number of useful books and articles. See Hutchison, *The Modernist Impulse*, 111–44 and Claude Welch, *Protestant Thought in the Nineteenth Century*, 2: 1–30, 136–82, 212–65. This focus on the founder of Christianity also was linked with the search for "origins" that was characteristic of the study of religion in general during the late nineteenth and early twentieth century. On this see Morris Jastrow, *The Study of Religion*, Classics in Religious Studies (1901; Chico, Calif.: Scholars Press, 1981), 173–98; Louis Henry Jordan, *Comparative Religion: Its Genesis and Growth*, Reprints and Translations Series (1905;

Atlanta: Scholars Press, 1986); Mircea Eliade, *The Quest: History and Meaning in Religion* (Chicago: University of Chicago Press, 1969), 37–53.

15. Edmunds, *Buddhist and Christian Gospels*, 49. Hopkins, *Religions of India*, 325–26. Clausen, "Victorian Buddhism," 6.

16. Strauss, *Buddha and His Doctrine*, 73. Geisler, "Buddha and His Doctrine," 858.

17. Johnston, "Christ and Buddha," 39.

18. For Christian critics' agreement about Buddhism's rejection of theism see Clark, "Primitive Buddhism," 201 and Davies, "Religion of Gotama Buddha," 335.

19. Ryan, "More Light on 'The Light of Asia,' " 687. King, "Shall We Become Buddhists?" 68. In a very hostile account, the Reverend Frederick F. Kramer of Colorado Divinity School also said it was not a religion. See Frederick Kramer, "Jesus Christ and Gautama Buddha as Literary Critics," *Biblical World* 3 (Apr. 1894): 259.

20. Hopkins, *Religions of India*, 319–20, 336–37. Oldenberg, *Buddha*.

21. Welbon, *Buddhist Nirvana*, 194–247, 204–5. J. W. deJong has dated the rise of the second period in Buddhist Studies from 1877; but in a sense this stage of scholarship began in full only with the publication of Oldenberg's *Buddha* (1881) and Rhys Davids's *The Origin and Growth of Religion as Illustrated by Some Points in the History of Indian Buddhism* (1882). Welbon has suggested that "critical Buddhist Studies" came to "full maturity" with the publication of the former. And if awareness of the multivocality of the primary sources, sensitivity to the complexity of issues, and awareness of the diversity of "Buddhist" positions and traditions is any indication of "maturity," then Welbon is right. In some ways, this second stage continued until approximately 1942, as deJong has claimed. There were few stunning shifts in the field after World War I, especially in the United States where the influence of the older "Anglo-German" school continued to be felt after 1914. In this sense it is somewhat artificial to end the discussion of Buddhist Studies around World War I, as I do here. DeJong, "Brief History of Buddhist Studies," 76–77. Welbon, *Buddhist Nirvana*, 201. Kitagawa, "Buddhism in America," 43–44. Rhys Davids, *Buddhism: Its History and Literature*, 187–222.

22. Gordon, "Buddhisms of Japan." Gordon, "Buddhism's Best Gospel," 408.

23. Warren, *Buddhism*, 112–13, 284. Rhys Davids, *Buddhism: Its History and Literature*, 125, 143, 176, 180.

24. Conze, *Buddhism*, 38–43.

25. Edmunds, "The Psychic Elements in Buddhism," 1. Edmunds, "F.W.H. Myers, Swedenborg, and Buddha," 259, 279. Guruge, ed., *Return to Righteousness*, 81, 809.

26. On the origins of atheism and agnosticism in America see Turner, *Without God, Without Creed*. For one example of a rejection of a personal creator see Olcott, *Buddhist Catechism*, 45. Lodge, *Poems and Dramas*, 1: 81. See also Fenollosa, *East and West*, 55 and Moore, "Ethical Side of the Material," 77.

27. The Mahayana doctrine of the "Three Bodies" *(Trikaya)* of the Buddha suggests that the historical Buddha who appeared in the ordinary world of suffering was only one form *(Nirmanakaya)*. Siddhartha Gautama was a manifestation of the Body of Bliss *(Sambhogakaya)*—Buddha as a sort of celestial superhuman being. In turn this "body" was an emanation of the Body of Essence *(Dharmakaya)*, the ultimate or cosmic Buddha that pervades and grounds the whole universe. For one classic formulation see the selection from Asanga's *Ornament of Mahayana Sutras*, a versified compendium of Mahayana doctrine, in William Theodore de Bary, ed., *The Buddhist Tradition in India, China, and Japan* (New York: Vintage Books, 1972), 94–95. Carus, *Christian Critics*, 196–98.

28. Edmunds, *Buddhist and Christian Gospels*, 51.

29. "Suicide Club," *Dollar Weekly*, 28 Jan. 1893. "Bridgeton's Departure," unidentified newspaper clipping pasted in Edmunds's diary, 11 Feb. 1893, Diary 8, Albert J. Edmunds Papers.

30. For a sample of the articles on suicide in magazines see Henry Morselli, "Catholicism, Protestantism, and Suicide," *Popular Science Monthly* 20 (Dec. 1881): 220–25; William Mathews, "Civilization and Suicide," *North American Review* 152 (Apr. 1891): 470–84; and Frederick L. Hoffman, "Suicides and Modern Civilization," *Arena* 42 (May 1893): 680–95. On the conflicting attitudes toward suicide in Victorian Britain see Barbara T. Gates, *Victorian Suicide: Mad Crimes and Sad Histories* (Princeton: Princeton University Press, 1988). Edward Bellamy, *Looking Backward, 2000–1887* (1888; New York: Penguin, 1984), 78.

31. Hearn's response is quoted in Jackson, *Oriental Religions*, 236. Carus, *Christian Critics*, 308. As I noted below, Daniel Joseph Singal persuasively argued that the Modernist culture that became influential among intellectuals and others after World War I was associated with a dynamic, nonsubstantialist view of the self. In a sense, then, these sympathizers and adherents were early participants in the Modernist culture that was only beginning to emerge at the turn of century. Singal, "Towards a Definition of Modernism," 15.

32. Paul Carus to Dharmapala, 18 June 1897, Open Court Papers.

33. Edmunds, "F.W.H. Myers, Swedenborg, and Buddha," 278. Carus, *Christian Critics*, 128.

34. Akiko Murakata, "Ernest Fenollosa's 'Ode on Re-incarnation,' " *Harvard Library Bulletin* 21 (1973): 59, 60, 61.

35. Lears, *No Place of Grace*, 224. Fenollosa, *East and West*, 55.

36. DeCleyre, "Dyer D. Lum," 284. Lum, "Nirvana," 260. Dyer Lum, "The One and the All," ms., Houghton Library. Lum, "Nirvana," 261–62. Lum, "Basis of Morals," 559. Lum, "Nirvana," 262.

37. Canavarro, "Nirvana," 26.

38. Emerson, "Each and All" in *The Portable Emerson*, ed. Carl Bode and Malcom Cowley (New York: Penguin, 1981), 632.

39. For one of Luther's formulations of this concept see "An den christlichen Adel deutscher Nation von des christlichen Standes Besserung" in *Luthers Werke . . ., ed. Otto Clemen (1520; Berlin: Walter deGruyter, 1966–67): 1: 362–425. Ralph Waldo Emerson, "Self Reliance," in *The Portable Emerson*, 138–64. Ralph Waldo Emerson, "Address," delivered before the senior class in Divinity College, Cambridge, 15 July 1838, in *The Portable Emerson*, 72–91. Immanuel Kant, "Beantwortung der Frage: Was ist Aufklärung?" in *Was ist Aufklärung?: Aufsätze zur Geschichte und Philosophie* (1784; Göttingen: Vandenoek und Ruprecht, 1975), 55. As Lukes has noted, an affirmation of self-reliance was expressed in the thought of Thomas Aquinas and has been a part of the Catholic heritage as well: Aquinas announced in *Quaestiones disputatae de veritate* (qu. 17, art. 4) that "everyone is bound to examine his own actions in the light of the knowledge which he has from God." Steven Lukes, *Dictionary of the History of Ideas*, s.v., "Types of Individualism." On economic individualism see Trachtenberg, *Incorporation of America*, 5. Emerson, "Address," in *Portable Emerson*, 87.

40. Ellinwood, *Oriental Religions*, 154. Rhys Davids, *Buddhism: Its History and Literature*, 143, 176, 180. For another example of a Protestant interpretation of Buddhist self-reliance as selfishness see W. C. Dodd, "The Heart of Buddhism and the Heart of Christianity," *Missionary Review of the World* 16 (July 1893): 515.

41. Lears, *No Place of Grace*, 218–41. Bigelow, "Fragmentary Notes."

42. Olcott, *Buddhist Catechism*, 45. Vetterling, "Why Buddhism?" 1. Wilson, "Buddhism in America," 2. Strauss, *Buddha and His Doctrine*, 115.

6. OPTIMISM AND ACTIVISM

1. J. T. Gracey, "What Ails Buddhism?" *Homiletic Review* 23 (Jan. 1892): 27.

2. Henry Steele Commager, Foreword, *McGuffey's Sixth Eclectic Reader*, 1879 edition (New York: New American Library, 1962), xi. On popular religious fiction see Elmer F. Sudermann, "Religion in the Popular American Novel: 1870–1900," *Journal of Popular Culture* 9 (Spring 1976): 1003–9. Lewis Wallace, *Ben-Hur: A Tale of the Christ* (New York: Harper and Brothers, 1880).

3. Henry Ward Beecher, *Yale Lectures on Preaching* (New York: Fords, Howard, and Hulbert, 1887). George A. Gordon, *The New Epoch for Faith* (Boston: Houghton, Mifflin, 1901). Beecher, "Progress of Thought in the Church," 102. John Fiske, *The Destiny of Man Viewed in the Light of His Origin* (1884; Boston and New York: Houghton Mifflin, 1912), 118.

4. On the common rejection of Calvinist views among Spiritualists and members of other alternative groups see Moore, *White Crows*, 41. See also Judah, *History and Philosophy*, 13. James Freeman Clarke, "The Five Points of Calvinism and the Five Points of the New Theology," in *Vexed Questions in Theology: A Series of Essays* (Boston: George Ellis, 1886), 16–17.

5. James, "Is Life Worth Living?" 2–3. James, *Pragmatism*, 189–90. Higham, "The Reorientation of American Culture in the 1890s," 93. I am indebted to Higham's article for many of the insights in this discussion of pessimism in American culture during this period.

6. James, *Pragmatism*, 184–85. Carus also advocated "meliorism." See Paul Carus, "The Prophet of Pessimism," *Open Court* 11 (May 1897): 264. Richard T. Ely, *Social Aspects of Christianity* (New York: Thomas Crowell and Co., 1889), 77.

7. The lecture by the Reverend Elwood Worcester, rector of Emmanuel Protestant Episcopal Church in Boston, was reprinted in the *Philadelphia Inquirer*. Edmunds pasted the clipping in his diary: Diary 11, 2 Feb. 1908, Albert J. Edmunds Papers. James, "The Gospel of Relaxation," 247. James, "The Energies of Men," 218–19.

8. For an example of an emphasis on the lethargy of the 1870s and 1880s, see May, *Protestant Churches*, 39–87. Theodore Roosevelt, *The Strenuous Life: Essays and Addresses* (New York: The Century Company, 1900). Higham, "Reorientation." Richard Hofstadter outlined two conflicting "ethoses" in the Progressive Era—"the ethos of the boss-immigrant-machine complex and that of the reformer-individualist-Anglo-Saxon complex." And in a more recent article, John D. Buenker has argued that these two "ethoses" were actually "full-blown political cultures." See Richard Hofstadter, *The Age of Reform* (New York: Vintage, 1955), 186. John D. Buenker, "Sovereign Individuals and Organic Networks: Political Cultures in Conflict during the Progressive Era," *American Quarterly* 40 (June 1988): 187–204.

9. Hutchison, "The Americanness of the Social Gospel," 1–2. Hudson, "How American Is Religion in America?" Some Europeans were worried that the new expressions of activism in Western popular culture might threaten traditional values, and they sometimes equated "activism" with "Americanism." On this see Higham, "Reorientation," 85. Booker T. Washington, "The Religious Life of the Negro," *North American Review* 181 (July 1905): 22. Beecher, "Progress of Thought in the Church," 101.

10. Lyman Abbott, "What is Christianity?" *Arena* (1890): 46. Henry C. Potter and Charles W. Shields, "The Social Problem of Church Unity: The Report of Bishop Potter and Professor Shields," in "Present-Day Papers," ed. Charles W. Shields, *Century* 40 (Sept. 1890): 687. Charles M. Sheldon, *In His Steps; Or, What Would Jesus Do?* (1897; Chicago: John C. Winston Co., 1957), 254–59.

11. Edgbert C. Smyth, "The Theological Purpose of the Review," *Andover Review*

1 (Jan. 1884): 12. Judson Smith, "Protestant Foreign Missions: A Retrospect of the Nineteenth Century," *North American Review* 172 (Mar. 1901): 394. Protestant missionary activity also boomed in other Western nations during this period. On this development see the essays in Torben Christensen and William R. Hutchison, ed., *Missionary Ideologies in the Imperialist Era, 1880–1920* (Aarhus, Denmark: Aros Publishers; Cambridge, Mass.: Harvard Theological Review, 1984).

12. Hutchison, *Errand*, 92. Winthrop Hudson, "Protestant Clergy Debate the Nation's Vocation, 1898–1899," *Church History* 42 (Mar. 1973): 110–18. Lyman Abbott, "Can a Nation Have a Religion?" *Century* 41 (Dec. 1890): 275–81. Rockhill, "The Open Door." Varg, *Open Door Diplomat*. Wiebe, *Search for Order*, 224–55.

13. For an example of a Christian interpretation that praised the Buddha's reforming tendencies and moral teachings but condemned the tradition see Frank S[tockton] Dobbins, *Error's Chains: How Forged and Broken* (New York: Standard Publishing House, 1883), 500–502, 509–10, 518. Josiah Royce, "The Christian Doctrine of Life," *Hibbert Journal* 11 (1913): 476–78.

14. Rhys Davids, *Origin and Growth*, 90, 215. Oldenberg, *Buddha*, 1, 46, 50, 212–15.

15. Monier-Williams, *Buddhism*, 337–563.

16. Charles Rockwell Lanman, *A Sanskrit Reader, with Vocabulary and Notes* (Boston: Ginn and Co., 1912). Charles Rockwell Lanman, "A Statistical Count of Noun-Inflection in the Veda," *Journal of the American Oriental Society* 10 (1880): 325–601. Charles R. Lanman, "Henry Clarke Warren: An Obituary Notice," *Journal of the American Oriental Society* 20 (1899): 332, 334. Warren, *Buddhism in Translations*, 113, 284.

17. Hopkins, *Religions of India*, 320, 306–17. Hopkins also taught a generation of Yale students that Buddhism had a "profoundly pessimistic attitude to life." See Edward Washburn Hopkins, "Lectures on Buddhism," pp. 15–16, Hopkins Family Papers, Sterling Memorial Library, Yale University, New Haven.

18. Hopkins, *Origin and Evolution of Religion*, 269. Hopkins, *Religions of India*, 318, 307–19. Hopkins, *History of Religions*, 184–90. Hopkins, *Religions of India*, 567–71.

19. LaFarge, "An Artist's Letters from Japan," 574.

20. Rockhill, *Life of the Buddha*. Rockhill, "An American in Tibet," 3–4.

21. Ryan, "More Light on the 'Light of Asia,' " 687. Aiken, *Dhamma of Gotama*, 112. Dall, "The Buddha and the Christ," 244, 233. Bixby, "Buddhism in the New Testament," 556. See also Mathews, "Notes on Buddhism at Home."

22. Gordon, *American Missionary in Japan*, 117, 176.

23. Kellogg, *Handbook*, 111. Ellinwood, *Oriental Religions*, 156–57. King, "Shall We Become Buddhists?" 64. Constance F. Gordon Cumming, "Ningpo and the Buddhist Temples," *Century* 24 (Sept. 1882): 738.

24. Davies, "Religion of Gotama Buddha," 335. Bryant, "Buddhism and Christianity," 267, 366, 380–81, 368–69.

25. Paul Carus, "Americanism and Expansion," *Open Court* 13 (June 1899): 215–23. For evidence of Edmunds's interest in cycling see Diary 8, 6 July 1889 and 18 Jan. 1890, Albert J. Edmunds Papers. Dyer Lum to Joseph A. Labadie, 14 Aug. 1888, Joseph Ishill Papers, Houghton Library, Harvard University, Cambridge, Mass.

26. Carus, "Prophet of Pessimism," 263. For evidence of the enduring link between Buddhist teachings and Schopenhauer's philosophy see the long poem by Robert Buchanan: "The New Buddha," *North American Review* 140 (May 1885): 445–55.

27. It is not that Lanman never lectured on Buddhism. He did. And in one speech at the Bell Street Chapel in Providence, he emphasized Buddhism's tolerance and interpreted nirvana as "the extinction of lust, ill-will, and delusion." But

he seems to have left open the possibility that it also involved "total extinction," the newspaper account of his talk indicated. And if this account is accurate, he offered no defense against the criticisms of Buddhism as passive and pessimistic. Vetterling reprinted this newspaper account from the *Providence Journal* without citing title or date: Vetterling, "The Growth of Enlightenment," 5. "Buddha Shrine Worshiped in House of Mystery," *San Francisco Examiner*, 15 Sept. 1910. See also " 'House of Mystery' Threatened by Fire," *San Francisco Examiner*, 19 Nov. 1910. Before and after this date the Russells took in orphans, apparently six of them; and Ida Russell had proposed a plan for low-cost housing for the poor. The newspapers covered this too, but these examples of this-worldly concern were not included in the stories about her religious interests. See "Homes for the People: Opportunities for Philanthropy without Cost," *San Francisco Examiner* 27 May 1906 and "Alexander Russell Is Allowed $400 Month," *San Francisco Examiner*, 19 July 1918.

28. Charles O. Hucker, *China's Imperial Past: An Introduction to Chinese History and Culture* (Stanford: Stanford University Press, 1975), 384.

29. Arnold, *Life of Asia*, vii. Rhys Davids, *Origin and Growth*, 90. "The Constructive Optimism of Buddhism" was an article he published in *Maha Bodhi* in 1915 (vol. 23); it was reprinted in Guruge, ed., *Return to Righteousness*, 391–400. The quotation about activism is from a later piece of his also published in *Maha Bodhi* and reprinted later: see Guruge, ed., *Return to Righteousness*, 669. The significance of the title "Anagarika" has been noted by several scholars. See Gomrich, *Theravada Buddhism*, 188–94.

30. The passage was inserted beneath the table of contents of the *Light of Dharma* starting with the June 1902 issue. McIntire, "Report of Secretary," 28, 27. It should be noted, too, that the Maha Bodhi Society was involved in several "benevolent" activities, and American sympathizers supported these.

31. Olcott, *Buddhist Catechism*, 55, 53, 33. Vetterling, "Optimist, Buddhist, Pessimist," 1. Canavarro, *Insight*, 13, 70.

32. The assessment of his temperament was recorded in Edmunds, Diary 11, 22 Sept. 1906, Albert J. Edmunds Papers. On his contemplation of suicide see Edmunds, Diary 7, 16 June 1884, Albert J. Edmunds Papers. For Lanman's response to a later struggle with depression see Charles R. Lanman to Albert J. Edmunds, 20 Nov. 1903, Albert J. Edmunds Papers. His dream was reported in Edmunds, Diary 8, 28 Jan. 1891, Albert J. Edmunds Papers. Albert J. Edmunds, "Buddha as Reformer," *Buddhist Annual of Ceylon* 1 (1921): 13.

33. Strauss, *Buddha and His Doctrine*, 93, 94, 94–99.

34. Rice, "Buddhism as I Have Seen It," 481. Withee, "Is Buddhism to Blame,?" 461–62, 456–57, 462.

35. Wilson, "Buddhism in America," 4. Wilson, "Philosophy of Pain," 18. Wilson, "Sectarianism in Asia," 126. Wilson, "The Great Teachers," 7. Wilson, "The Duty of Wealth." Andrew Carnegie, "Wealth," *North American Review* 148 (June 1889): 653–64.

36. Wilson, "Philosophy of Pain." Adams, *Life of George Cabot Lodge*, 47–48, 58–59. Fenollosa, *East and West*, 55. Lodge, *Poems and Dramas*, 1: 80–81.

37. Adams, *Life of George Cabot Lodge*, 68–71. Lodge, *Poems and Dramas*. Lears, *No Place of Grace*, 239. Bigelow, "Fragmentary Notes," Houghton Library. Bigelow, *Buddhism and Immortality*. William Sturgis Bigelow to Phillips Brooks, 19 August 1889, The Phillips Brooks Papers.

38. Quoted in Fields, *How the Swans Came to the Lake*, 155. Fenollosa, *East and West*, 50–51, 48. Murakata, "Fenollosa's 'Ode on Re-incarnation,' " 59–61.

39. DeCleyre, "Dyer Lum," 290. Dyer Lum to Voltairine deCleyre, 14 Sept. 1890, The Joseph Ishill Papers. See also Lum, "Autobiographical P. S."

40. Lum, "Basis of Morals," 569–70. Lum, "Buddhism Notwithstanding," 206.

41. James, "The Moral Philosopher," 198.

42. Vetterling, "The Growth of Enlightenment," 4. The editor, Vetterling, included no author, title, or date for this excerpt from the *Wilkes-Barre Leader*. The speaker was identified as "Rabbi Joseph." Jackson, "New Thought," 526. Carus, *Christian Critics*, 6.

POSTSCRIPT

1. Anagarika Dharmapala to Mrs. Carus, 14 July 1921, Open Court Papers.

2. G. Santayana, *Winds of Doctrine: Studies in Contemporary Opinion* (1913; London and Toronto: J. M. Dent and Sons; New York: Charles Scribner's Sons, 1914), 1. On this cultural shift see Stanley Coben, "The Assault on Victorianism in the Twentieth Century," in *Victorian America*, ed. Howe, 160–81; May, *End of American Innocence*; Higham, "Reorientation of American Culture in the 1890s"; Singal, *The War Within*. On Modernist culture see Singal, "Towards a Definition of American Modernism" and Malcom Bradbury and James McFarlane, eds., *Modernism, 1890–1930* (Sussex: Harvester Press; New Jersey: Humanities Press, 1978). The introductory essay by the editors is especially helpful (pp. 19–55). On the Protestant establishment see William R. Hutchison, ed., *Between the Times: The Travail of the Protestant Establishment in America, 1900–1960* (Cambridge and New York: Cambridge University Press, 1989).

3. Eighty-eight percent of Americans polled reported that they never even entertained doubts about the existence of God. See George Gallup, Jr. and Jim Castelli, *The People's Religion: American Faith in the Nineties* (New York: Macmillan, 1989), 56. The quote from Sensaki is found in Prebish, *American Buddhism*, 7.

4. On Japanese Pure Land in twentieth-century America see Kashima, *Buddhism in America*.

5. On Sensaki see Prebish, *American Buddhism*, 6. D. T. Suzuki to Mrs. Carus, 15 July 1921, Open Court Papers. Suzuki reported in that letter that he was almost finished with the essays and that her husband, Paul, had seen earlier versions of the collection. D. T. Suzuki, *Essays in Zen Buddhism, First Series* (London: Luzac and Co., 1927).

6. R. E. Gussner and S. D. Berkowitz, "Scholars, Sects, and Sanghas, I: Recruitment to Asian-Based Meditation Groups in North America," *Sociological Analysis* 49 (1988): 136–70. Layman, *Buddhism in America*, 264–75. For one listing of Buddhist groups in America see Don Morreale, ed., *Buddhist America: Centers, Retreats, and Practices* (Santa Fe: John Muir Publications, 1988).

7. Jack Kerouac, *Dharma Bums* (1958; New York: Penguin Books, 1976), 97–98. A number of books and articles about women and Buddhism in America have appeared. For example see Sandy Boucher, *Turning the Wheel: American Women Creating the New Buddhism* (San Francisco: Harper and Row, 1988).

8. Strauss had been a public figure, had been a supporting member of Buddhist groups, and had translated a Buddhist catechism earlier; but it was only in 1922 that his major statement of the faith appeared *(Buddha and His Doctrine)*. His book was favorably reviewed in Buddhist circles. For example, review of *Buddhism and His Doctrine* by C. T. Strauss, *Maha Bodhi* 32 (July 1924): 362–63. This reviewer said that the book was the best account since Arnold's *Light of Asia*, Warren's *Buddhism in Translations*, and Carus's *Gospel of Buddha*. Strauss moved back to Europe in his later years: he was listed as the representative of the Maha Bodhi Society in Frankfurt in 1936, for example. See *Maha Bodhi* 44 (Sept. 1936). He also engaged in a lively debate among Buddhists about the proper relation to the nonhuman world. See C. T. Strauss, "Justifiable Killing," letter to the editor, *Maha Bodhi* 42 (Oct. 1934):

469–70; C. T. Strauss, letter to the editor, *Maha Bodhi* 42 (May-June 1934): 273–74. See also "Another Rejoinder to Mr. Strauss," *Maha Bodhi* 42 (Aug. 1934): 374. Mrs. Winthrop Chanler, "Bohemian and Buddhist," *Atlantic* 158 (Sept. 1938): 271–78. This piece on Bigelow was excerpted from his friend Chanler's forthcoming book, *Autumn in the Valley.* Beck, by my standards, was a Buddhist sympathizer. L. Adams Beck, "The Challenge: The Buddha and the Christ," *Atlantic* 137 (May 1926): 585–86, 590. For a similar application of a pragmatic test to the Christian West see the lectures by the Japanese scholar, Masaharu Anesaki: *The Religious and Social Problems of the Orient: Four Lectures Given at the University of California under the Auspices of the Earl Foundation, Pacific School of Religion* (New York: Macmillan, 1923).

9. "Buddha on Ninety-fourth Street," *Newsweek,* 9 June 1947, 82–83.

10. James Bissett Pratt, *Pilgrimage of Buddhism and A Buddhist Pilgrimage* (New York: Macmillan, 1928), viii. D. T. Suzuki, "Comprehending Zen Buddhism," in *Self, Religion, and Metaphysics: Essays in Memory of James Bissett Pratt,* ed. Gerald E. Myers (New York: Macmillan, 1961), 122. Niebuhr's assessment of Buddhism as Christianity's only competitor was offered in a piece in 1937: Reinhold Niebuhr, "The Christian Church in a Secular Age," in *The Essential Reinhold Niebuhr: Selected Essays and Addresses,* ed. Robert McAfee Brown (New Haven: Yale University Press, 1986), 85. Reinhold Niebuhr, *An Interpretation of Christian Ethics* (1935; New York: Seabury, 1979), 43, 41.

11. "Buddhist-Christian Dialogue: Past, Present, and Future," Masao Abe and John Cobb interviewed by Bruce Long, *Buddhist-Christian Studies* 1 (1981): 21–25. Robert Thurman is one American Buddhist scholar and apologist who has stressed Buddhism's activism. See Robert A. F. Thurman, "Guidelines for Buddhist Social Activism Based on Nargarjuna's *Jewel Garland of Royal Counsels,*" *Eastern Buddhist,* n.s., 16 (Spring 1983): 19–51. Asian Buddhists have taken up similar themes. For example see S. Sivaraksa, *A Buddhist Vision for Renewing Society* (Bangkok: Tienwan Publishing House, 1986). Some American Buddhist groups have stressed this activistic impulse. The Buddhist Peace Fellowship, founded in 1978, publishes a newsletter from its national office in Berkeley. See for example Joanna Macy, "Dharma and Civil War: The Prospects for Peace in Sri Lanka," *Buddhist Peace Fellowship Newsletter* 8 (Autumn 1986): 1–5. Another group, Buddhists Concerned for Social Justice and World Peace, operates out of Zen communities in Ann Arbor and Toronto. See Samu Sunim, "An Appeal for Social Action," pamphlet, Buddhists Concerned for Social Justice and World Peace, 30 June 1987. Dwight Goddard, *A Buddhist Bible: The Favorite Scriptures of the Zen Sect . . .* (Thetford, Vt.: n.p., 1932), 11, 10. Dwight Goddard, *Was Jesus Influenced by Buddhism?* (Thetford, Vt.: Printed by Charles R. Cummings, 1927).

Select Bibliography

The following bibliography contains only the published and unpublished sources that were most relevant to the public discussion about Buddhism and most important in writing this book. It is not a complete record of all materials I have consulted or all works I have cited in the notes. Some sources of limited scope or relevance—for example, biographical material—have been listed in the notes but not here. Primary and secondary sources are separated. Under these two main headings the works are classified further according to topic—"The Conversation about Buddhism" and "Religion and Culture in Victorian America."

PRIMARY SOURCES

Manuscripts

Buddhist Churches of America, Archives, San Francisco.
> "List of the Subscription, Contribution, and Exchange. The Light of Dharma. May 19, 1904," Notebook
> "*Nisshi*" [Daily records], Four notebooks, variously titled: 1902–3, 1904, 1908, 1909

Henry Francis du Pont Winterthur Museum, Winterthur, Delaware.
> Laura Carter Holloway Langford Papers, The Edward Deming Andrews Memorial Shaker Collection

Historical Society of Pennsylvania, Philadelphia.
> Albert J. Edmunds Papers
>> Masaharu Anesaki, Letters
>> Edwin Arnold, Letters
>> Paul Carus, Letters
>> Charles Rockwell Lanman, Letters
>> D. T. Suzuki, Letters

Houghton Library, Harvard University, Cambridge.
> William Sturgis Bigelow, Letters
> The Phillips Brooks Papers
> Ernest Francisco Fenollosa, Letters and Notebooks
> Thomas Wentworth Higginson Papers
> Dyer Daniel Lum, Letters and Essays, Joseph Ishill Papers

Massachusetts Historical Society, Boston.
> William Sturgis Bigelow, Letters and Assorted Materials
> George Cabot Lodge Papers

Morris Library, Southern Illinois University, Carbondale.
> Open Court Publishing Company Papers
>> American Maha Bodhi Society, Assorted Materials
>> Marie deSouza Canavarro, Letters
>> Paul Carus, Letters and Assorted Materials
>> Anagarika Dharmapala, Letters
>> Soyen Shaku, Letters
>> C. T. Strauss, Letters
>> D. T. Suzuki, Letters

National Baha'i Archives, Wilmette, Illinois.
　　Marie deSouza Canavarro, Letters and Addresses, Thorton Chase. Papers
　　Charles Mason Remey, "Reminiscences of the Summer School Greenacre
　　Eliot, Maine"
Sterling Memorial Library, Yale University, New Haven.
　　Edward Elbridge Salisbury Family Papers
　　　　Edward Elbridge Salisbury, Letters, Sermons, Essays, and Journals
　　　　Edward Washburn Hopkins, Letters
　　Hopkins Family Papers
　　　　Edward Washburn Hopkins, Lectures and Journals
University of Florida, Rare Books and Manuscripts, Gainesville.
　　Dyer Daniel Lum, Letters, Autobiographical Account, and Essays, Joseph
　　Ishill Papers

The Conversation about Buddhism

[Abbot, Francis Ellingwood.] "The Light of Asia." *Index* 11 (22 Apr. 1880): 198.
Adams, Hannah. *An Alphabetical Compendium of the Various Sects. . . .* Boston: B.
　　Edes, 1784.
———. *A Dictionary of All Religions and Religious Denominations, Jewish, Heathen,*
　　Mahometan, and Christian. . . . 4th ed. Boston: Cummings and Hilliard, 1817.
Adams, Henry. "Buddha and Brahma." 1895. *Yale Review,* n.s. 5 (Oct. 1915): 82–89.
———. *The Life of George Cabot Lodge.* Boston and New York: Houghton Mifflin,
　　1911.
Adler, Felix. "A Prophet of the People." *Atlantic Monthly* 37 (June 1876): 674–89.
Aiken, Charles Francis. *The Dhamma of Gotama the Buddha and the Gospel of Jesus the*
　　Christ: A Critical Inquiry into the Alleged Relations of Buddhism with Primitive
　　Christianity. Boston: Marlier, 1900.
Albers, A. Christina. *The Gospel of Love.* 2d ed. Maha Bodhi Pamphlet Series, no. 26.
　　Calcutta: Maha Bodhi Society, [1949].
———. "Modern India." *Open Court* 19 (Oct. 1905): 588–603.
———. "The Path." *Light of Dharma* 1 (Dec. 1901): 21.
———. "Reincarnation." *Light of Dharma* 2 (Apr. 1902): 19–20.
Alger, William R[ounseville]. "The Brahmanic and Buddhist Doctrine of a Future
　　Life." *North American Review* 86 (Apr. 1858): 435–63.
———. *A Critical History of the Doctrine of a Future Life.* 1859. [4th ed.] Philadelphia:
　　Childs, 1864.
———. "The Lonely Character." *Buddhist Ray* 4 (Nov.–Dec. 1891): 5–12.
———. *Poetry of the East.* Boston: Wittemore, Niles, and Hall, 1856.
Anesaki, Masaharu. *The Religious and Social Problems of the Orient: Four Lectures Given*
　　at the University of California under the Auspices of the Earl Foundation, Pacific
　　School of Religion. New York: Macmillan, 1923.
Arnold, Edwin. *The Light of Asia; or, The Great Renunciation; Being the Life and Teaching*
　　of Gautama. 1879. Wheaton, Ill.: Theosophical Publishing House, 1969.
Barrows, John Henry, ed. *The World's Parliament of Religions.* 2 vols. Chicago: The
　　Parliament Publishing Co., 1893.
Barthélemy Saint-Hilaire, Jules. *Le Bouddha et sa religion.* 1860. Paris: Didier, 1862.
Benedict, David. *History of All Religions: As Divided into Paganism, Mahometism,*
　　Judaism, and Christianity. Providence: John Miller, 1824.
Bennett, Chester. "Life of Gaudama: A Translation from the Burmese Book Entitled
　　Ma-la-len-ga-ra wottoo." *Journal of the American Oriental Society* 3 (1853): 1–164.
Bigelow, William Sturgis. *Buddhism and Immortality.* The Ingersoll Lecture, 1908.
　　Boston: Houghton Mifflin; Cambridge: Riverside Press, 1908.

————. "A Prefatory Note to 'On the Method of Practicing Concentration and Contemplation' by Chi Ki. Translated by Okakura Kakuzo." *Harvard Theological Review* 16 (Apr. 1923): 109–17.

Bisland, Elizabeth, ed. *The Japanese Letters of Lafcadio Hearn.* Boston: Houghton Mifflin, 1910.

————. *The Life and Letters of Lafcadio Hearn.* 2 vols. Boston and New York: Houghton Mifflin, 1906.

Bixby, James T[hompson]. "Buddhism in the New Testament." *Arena* 3 (Apr. 1891): 555–66.

Blavatsky, Helena P. *Isis Unveiled: A Master-Key to the Mysteries of Ancient and Modern Science and Theology.* 2 vols. New York: J. W. Bouton, 1877.

————. *The Key to Theosophy.* . . . London: Theosophical Publishing Co.; New York: W. Q. Judge, 1889.

————. "The Light of Asia." *Theosophist* 1 (Oct. 1879): 20–25.

————. "New York Buddhists." *Theosophist* 2 (Apr. 1881): 152–53.

Bloomfied, Maurice. "The Essentials of Buddhist Doctrine and Ethics." *International Journal of Ethics* 2 (Apr. 1892): 313–26.

Bridgman, Elijah C. "Extracts from a Letter of Rev. Elijah C. Bridgman, Dated Canton, 5th of March, 1830." *Missionary Herald* 26 (Sept. 1830): 279–80.

Bryant, William M. "Buddhism and Christianity." *Andover Review* 2 (Sept. 1884): 255–68; (Oct. 1884): 365–81.

————. Review of *The Indian Saint; or Buddha and Buddhism,* by Charles de Berard Mills. *The Western,* n.s. 3 (Aug. 1877): 503.

Buchanan, Robert. "The New Buddha." *North American Review* 140 (May 1885): 445–55.

"Buddha Shrine Worshiped in House of Mystery." *San Francisco Examiner,* 15 Sept. 1910.

"Buddhism." *New Englander* 10 (Apr. 1845): 182–91.

"Buddhism in Yale University in America." *Maha Bodhi* 11 (Oct. 1902): 104.

"Buddhism." Review of *Buddhism in Translations,* by Henry Clarke Warren. *Outlook* 58 (29 Jan. 1898): 283–85.

"Buddhist Church of Sacrament[o]." *Maha Bodhi* 10 (Feb. 1902): 92.

"Buddhist Converts." *Maha Bodhi* 2 (Apr. 1894): 1–2.

"The Buddhists of Brooklyn." *Maha Bodhi* 6 (Oct. 1897): 42.

Burnouf, Eugène. *L'Introduction à l'histoire du buddhisme indien.* Paris: Imprimerie Royale, 1844.

————, and Christian Lassen. *Essai sur le pali.* Paris: Dondey-Dupré, 1826.

Canavarro, Marie deS[ouza]. *The Broken Vase.* Boston: Christopher, 1933.

————. [Sister Sanghamitta, pseud.]. "The Ethics of Buddhism; Or, The Eightfold Path." *Light of Dharma* 1 (June 1901): 10–14.

————. *Insight into the Far East.* Los Angeles: Wetzel, n.d. [1925].

————. [Sister Sanghamitta, pseud.]. "Nirvana." *Light of Dharma* 1 (Dec. 1901): 22–24; 1 (Feb. 1902): 19–21; 2 (Apr. 1902): 25–26; 2 (Aug. 1902): 88–90.

————. [Sister Sanghamitta, pseud.]. "Peace and Blessings." Letter from Sister Sanghamitta to Rev. M. Mizuki. 12 May 1901. *Light of Dharma* 1 (June 1901): 29.

Carus, Paul. "Americanism and Expansion." *Open Court* 13 (June 1899): 215–23.

————. *Buddhism and its Christian Critics.* Chicago: Open Court, 1897.

————. *The Dharma; Or, the Religion of Enlightenment.* Chicago: Open Court, 1898.

————. "Editorial Reply." Reply to M. L. Gordon, "Shall We Welcome Buddhist Missionaries to America?" *Open Court* 14 (May 1900): 303.

[————.] "Hinduism Different from Buddhism." *Open Court* 20 (Apr. 1906): 253–54.

[————.] "The Lay Church." *Open Court* 20 (Apr. 1906): 251–53.

[————.] "A Modern Instance of World Renunciation." *Open Court* 13 (Feb. 1899): 111–17.

[————.] "The Prophet of Pessimism." *Open Court* 11 (May 1897): 257–64.

————. "Religion and Science." *Open Court* 1 (1877–88): 405–7.

————. *The Religion of Science.* Chicago: Open Court, 1893.

C[arus], P[aul]. "Sister Sanghamitta." *Open Court* 15 (Apr. 1901): 251–52.

————. "Two Buddhist Songs." *Open Court* 19 (Jan. 1905): 49–50.

————, ed. *The Gospel of Buddha.* 1894. Tucson: Omen, 1972.

Cheney, Annie Elizabeth. "Mahayana Buddhism in Japan." *Arena* 16 (Aug. 1896): 439–44.

Child, Lydia Maria. "The Intermingling of Religions." *Atlantic Monthly* 28 (Oct. 1871): 385–95.

————. *The Progress of Religious Ideas through Successive Ages.* 3 vols. New York: Francis; London: S. Low, 1855.

————. "Resemblances between the Buddhist and Roman Catholic Religions." *Atlantic Monthly* 26 (Dec. 1870): 660–65.

Childers, Robert Caesar. *A Dictionary of the Pali Language.* London: Kegan Paul, Trench, Trubner, 1873.

Clark, N. G. "Primitive Buddhism." *Andover Review* 12 (Aug. 1889): 185–200.

Clarke, James Freeman. "Affinities of Buddhism and Christianity." *North American Review* 136 (May 1883): 467–77.

————. "Buddhism; Or, The Protestantism of the East." *Atlantic Monthly* 23 (June 1869): 713–28.

————. *Ten Great Religions.* Boston: James R. Osgood, 1871.

"Commodore Perry's Expedition to Japan." *Harper's New Monthly Magazine* 12 (May 1856): 733–54.

"A Controversy on Buddhism." *Open Court* 11 (Jan. 1897): 43–58.

"A Convert to Buddhism." *Maha Bodhi* 2 (Nov. 1893): 3.

Conway, Moncure. *My Pilgrimage to the Wise Men of the East.* Boston: Houghton Mifflin, 1906.

————. "The Theist's Problems and Tasks." *Radical* 10 (June 1872): 420–31.

————, ed. *The Sacred Anthology: A Book of Ethnical Scriptures.* New York: Henry Holt and Co., 1874.

Cooper, Michael, ed. *They Came to Japan: An Anthology of European Reports on Japan, 1543–1640.* Berkeley: University of California Press, 1965.

"Countess Canavarro's First Lecture in Calcutta." *Maha Bodhi* 8 (May 1899): 5–6.

Courtney, W. L. "Socrates, Buddha, and Christ." *North American Review* 140 (Jan. 1885): 63–77.

Cumming, Constance F. Gordon. "Ningpo and the Buddhist Temples." *Century* 24 (Sept. 1882): 726–39.

Currier, C. H. "Buddhism in America." Letter to editor of *Boston Herald.* 16 Aug. 1899. *Maha Bodhi* 8 (Dec. 1899): 71.

Dale, Darley. "Tibetan Buddhism and Catholicity." *American Catholic Quarterly Review* 30 (Jan. 1905): 167–75.

Dall, C[harles] H[enry] A[ppleton]. "The Buddha and the Christ." *Unitarian Review* 18 (Sept. 1882): 230–41.

d'Alwis, James. *Buddhist Nirvana: A Review of Max Müller's Dhammapada.* Colombo, Ceylon: William Skeen, Government Printer, 1871.

Davies, William. "The Religion of Gotama Buddha." *Atlantic Monthly* 74 (Sept. 1894): 334–40.

Davis, Andrew Jackson. "The Buddha." *Buddhist Ray* 4 (Jan.–Feb. 1891): 14–16.

Davis, F[rank] Graeme to Rev. Nishijima. 27 April 1901. *Light of Dharma* 1 (June 1901): 28–29.

deCleyre, Voltairine. "Dyer D. Lum." In *Selected Works of Voltairine deCleyre*, edited by Alexander Berkman, 284–96. New York: Mother Earth, 1914.

"Dharma-Sangher [*sic*] of Buddha." *Light of Dharma* 1 (Apr. 1901): 20.

Dharmapala, Anagarika [D. H. Hewavitarne]. "The Buddha Dharma." *Light of Dharma* 4 (July 1904): 183–86; 4 (Oct. 1904): 219–22.

———. "Is There More than One Buddhism?: In Reply to the Rev. Dr. Ellinwood." *Open Court* 11 (Feb. 1897): 82–84.

———. "The Life of the Tathagata Buddha." *Light of Dharma* 2 (Apr. 1902): 3–6.

———. *Return to Righteousness: A Collection of Speeches, Essays, and Letters of the Anagarika Dharmapala*. Edited by Ananda Guruge. Colombo, Ceylon: The Government Press, 1965.

———. "The World's Debt to Buddha." In *The World's Parliament of Religions*, edited by John Henry Barrows, 862–80. Chicago: The Parliament Publishing Co., 1893.

[Dickinson, James T.] "Asiatic Civilization." *Christian Examiner* 67 (July 1859): 1–31.

———. "The Chinese." *Christian Examiner* 65 (Sept. 1858): 177–205.

———. "The Hindoos." *Christian Examiner* 64 (Mar. 1858): 173–208.

Dobbins, Frank S., S. Wells Williams, and Isaac Hall. *Error's Chains: How Forged and Broken*. New York: Standard, 1883.

Dodd, W. C. "The Heart of Buddhism and the Heart of Christianity." *Missionary Review of the World*, n.s. 6 (July 1893): 515–17.

Drake, Jeanie. "Under the Bodhi Tree." *Catholic World* 52 (Jan. 1891): 570–86.

DuHalde, P. [Jean Baptise]. *The General History of China. . . .* London: John Watts, 1736.

Dunlap, S[amuel] F[ales]. *Vestiges of the Spirit-History of Man*. New York: D. Appleton, 1858.

Edmunds, Albert J. "Buddha as Reformer." *Buddhist Annual of Ceylon* 1 (1921): 13.

———. "Buddha's Last Meal and the Christian Eucharist: Their Preservation of Earlier Rites." *Open Court* 17 (Apr. 1903): 240–42.

———. *Buddhist and Christian Gospels Now First Compared from the Originals; Being Gospel Parallels from Pali Texts, reprinted with Additions*. 1902. 3d ed. Tokyo: The Yuhokwan Publishing House, 1905.

———. "F.W.H. Meyers, Swedenborg, and Buddha." *Proceedings of the American Society for Psychical Research* 8 (Aug. 1914): 253–85.

———. "Food in the Light of Scripture: Brief Hints to Students." *Food, Home, and Garden* 3 (July–Aug. 1891): 88–89.

———. "Gospel Parallels from Pali Texts." *Open Court* 16 (Sept. 1902): 559–61.

———. "Has Swedenborg's 'Lost Word' Been Found?" *Journal of the American Society for Psychical Research* 7 (May 1913): 257–71.

———. "The Psychic Elements in Buddhism." *Two Worlds* 42 (10 May 1929): 1–2.

———. "Recent Translations of Buddhist Writings." *Harvard Theological Review* 7 (Apr. 1914): 245–60.

[Ellinwood, Frank Field?] "Buddhism." In *The Encyclopedia of Missions*. 2d ed. New York and London: Funk and Wagnalls, 1904.

Ellinwood, F[rank] F[ield]. "Buddhism and Christianity—A Crusade Which Must Be Met." *Missionary Review of the World*, n.s. 4 (February 1891): 108–17.

———. *Oriental Religions and Christianity: A Course of Lectures Delivered on the Ely Foundation before the Students of Union Theological Seminary, New York, 1891*. New York: Charles Scribners, 1892.

———. To Soyen Shaku. In "A Controversy on Buddhism." *Open Court* 11 (Jan. 1897): 46–58.

"Esoteric and Exoteric Buddhism." *Maha Bodhi* 4 (Feb. 1896): 79.

Evans, W[arren] F[elt]. *Esoteric Christianity and Mental Therapeutics*. Boston: H. H. Carter and Karrick, 1886.

Fenollosa, Ernest Francisco. "Chinese and Japanese Traits." *Atlantic Monthly* 69 (June 1892): 769–74.

———. "Contemporary Japanese Art." *Century* 46 (1893): 577–81.

———. *East and West: The Discovery of America and Other Poems.* New York: Crowell, 1893.

———. "Ernest Fenollosa's 'Ode on Reincarnation.' " Edited by Akiko Murakata. *Harvard Library Bulletin* 21 (1973): 50–72.

———. *Epochs of Chinese and Japanese Art: An Outline History of East Asiatic Design.* Edited by Mary McNeil Fenollosa. 2 vols. London: Heinemann, 1912.

Fenollosa, Mary McNeil. *Out of the Nest: A Flight of Verses.* Boston: Little, Brown, and Company, 1899.

"First Temple of Buddha Installed on American Ground." *Light of Dharma* 1 (Dec. 1901): 3–6.

Foucaux, Phillippe Edouard. *Doctrine des bouddhistes sur le nirvana.* Paris: Benjamin Duprat, 1864.

Foulds, James L. "Swedenborg and Buddhism." Review of *Swedenborg the Buddhist,* by Philangi Dasa. *New Church Magazine* [London] 11 (1892): 12–17.

Gail, Marzieh. Foreword to *The Master in 'Akká,* by Myron H. Phelps. 1903. Los Angeles: Kalimat Press, 1985.

Galvani, William H. "An Able Review of the Caste System of India." *Light of Dharma* 4 (Apr. 1904): 154–58; 4 (July 1904): 187–88; 4 (Oct. 1904): 225–28.

———. "Buddhism and Theosophy." *Maha Bodhi* 5 (May–June 1896): 12–13.

———. "Heirs of Immortality." *Buddhist Ray* 6 (Mar.–Apr. 1893): 13.

———. "The Hog." *Food, Home, and Garden* 3 (July–Aug. 1891): 84.

———. "Oregon Colonization." *Food, Home, and Garden* 3 (Dec. 1891): 153.

Geisler, J. S. "Buddha and His Doctrine." *American Catholic Quarterly Review* 22 (Oct. 1897): 857–75.

Gmeiner, John. "The Light of Asia and the Light of the World." *Catholic World* 42 (Oct. 1885): 1–9.

Goodrich, Charles Augustus. *A Pictorial and Descriptive View of All Religions. . . .* 1832. Hartford: A. C. Goodman, 1854.

Gordon, John Ogden, "Buddhist and Christian Ideas of Hell." *Princeton Review,* n.s. 4 (1875): 38–45.

Gordon, M[arquis] L[afayette]. *An American Missionary in Japan.* 1892. Boston and New York: Houghton Mifflin and Company, 1900.

———. "Buddhism's Best Gospel." *Andover Review* 6 (Oct. 1886): 395–403.

———. "The Buddhisms of Japan." *Andover Review* 5 (March 1886): 301–11.

———. "Shall We Welcome Buddhist Missionaries to America?" *Open Court* 14 (May 1900): 301–3.

Gracey, J. T. "What Ails Buddhism?" *Homiletic Review* 23 (January 1892): 20–26.

Graves, R. H. "Three Systems of Belief in China." *Baptist Quarterly* 6 (1872): 408–42.

Grenard, Fernand. *Tibet: The Country and Its Inhabitants.* Translated by A. Teixeira de Mattos. London: Hutchison and Co., 1904.

Gross, Joseph B. *The Heathen Religion in Its Popular and Symbolical Development.* Boston: John P. Jewett, 1856.

Hardy, R[obert] Spence. *Eastern Monachism.* London: Partridge and Oakey, 1850.

———. *The Legends and Theories of the Buddhists. . . .* London: Williams and Norgate, 1866.

———. *A Manual of Buddhism in Its Modern Development.* London: Partridge and Oakey, 1853.

Hearn, Lafcadio. *Gleanings in Buddha-Fields: Studies of Hand and Soul in the Far East.* 1897. Tokyo: Tuttle, 1971.

———. "The Higher Buddhism." *The Buddhist Writings of Lafcadio Hearn.* Edited by Kenneth Rexroth, 277–97. Santa Barbara: Ross-Erikson, 1977.

Higginson, Thomas Wentworth. "The Buddhist Path of Virtue." *Radical* 8 (June 1871): 358–62.

――――. "The Character of Buddha." *Index* 3 (16 Mar. 1872): 81–83.

――――. *Cheerful Yesterdays*. Boston and New York: Houghton, Mifflin, 1898.

[――――]. "Johnson's 'Oriental Religions.' " *Index* 3 (Nov. 9, 1872): 361–62.

――――. "The Sympathy of Religions." *Radical* 8 (Feb. 1871): 1–23.

――――. "The Sympathy of Religions." In *The World's Parliament of Religions*, edited by John Henry Barrows, 780–84. Chicago: The Parliament Publishing Co., 1893.

[Holland, F. W.] "Siam." *Christian Examiner* 66 (Mar. 1859): 236–46.

Holmes, Oliver Wendell. "The Light of Asia." *International Review* 7 (Oct. 1879): 345–72.

[Hooker, Joseph Dalton.] "A Naturalist among the Himalayas." *Harper's New Monthly Magazine* 9 (Oct. 1854): 604–17.

Hopkins, E. Washburn. "The Buddhistic Rule against Eating Meat." *Journal of the American Oriental Society* 27 (July–Dec. 1906): 455–64.

――――. *The History of Religions*. New York: Macmillan, 1918.

[――――]. "In Memorium [E. E. Salisbury]." *Journal of the American Oriental Society* 22 (Jan.–July 1901): 1–6.

――――. *Origin and Evolution of Religion*. New Haven: Yale University Press, 1923.

――――. *The Religions of India*. Handbooks on the History of Religion, no. 1. Boston: Ginn, 1895.

Huc, Evariste Regis. *Travels in Tartary, Thibet, and China during the Years 1844, 1845, 1846*. 2 vols. New York: Appleton, 1852.

[Hungerford, Edward.] "Buddhism and Christianity." *New Englander* 33 (Apr. 1874): 268–86.

Janes, Lewis G. "Monsalvat School of Comparative Religion." *Mind* 5 (Oct. 1899): 10–14.

Johnson, Samuel. *Lectures, Essays, and Sermons*. Boston: Houghton Mifflin, 1883.

――――. *Oriental Religions and Their Relation to Universal Religion*. 3 vols. Boston: Houghton Mifflin, 1872, 1877, 1885.

Johnson, Thomas M[oore], trans. *Three Treatises of Plotinus*. Osceola, Mo.: The "Sun" Book and Job Printing Office, 1880.

Johnston, J. Wesley. "Christ and Buddha: Resemblances and Contrasts." *Methodist Review* 80 (Jan. 1898): 32–40.

"A Joyful Occasion." *Light of Dharma* 1 (Aug. 1901): 26–28.

Judson, Ann. *An Account of the American Baptist Mission to the Burman Empire; In a Series of Letters, Addressed to Gentlemen in London*. London: J. Butterworth, 1823.

Kellogg, S[amuel] H[enry]. *A Handbook of Comparative Religion*. Philadelphia: Westminster, 1899.

――――. "The Legend of the Buddha and the Life of Christ." *Bibliotheca Sacra* 39 (July 1882): 458–97.

――――. *The Light of Asia and the Light of the World: A Comparison of the Legend, the Doctrine, and the Ethics of the Buddha with the Story, the Doctrine, and the Ethics of Christ*. London: Macmillan, 1885.

King, Henry M. "Shall We Become Buddhists?" *Christian Literature* 14 (Nov. 1895): 61–68.

Koeppen, Karl Friedrich. *Die lamaische Hierarchie und Kirche*. Berlin: F. Schneider, 1859.

――――. *Die Religion des Buddha und ihre Entstehung*. Berlin: F. Schneider, 1857.

Kramer, Frederick F. "Jesus Christ and Gautama Buddha as Literary Critics." *Biblical World* 3 (Apr. 1894): 252–59.

LaFarge, John. "An Artist's Letters from Japan." *Century* 40 (Aug. 1890): 195–203; (Sept. 1890): 566–74; (Oct. 1890): 751–59; (Nov. 1890): 866–77.
———. *An Artist's Letters from Japan.* New York: The Century Co., 1897.
"Land of the White Elephant." *Harper's New Monthly Magazine* 48 (Feb. 1874): 378–89.
Langford, Laura Carter Holloway. *The Buddhist Diet Book.* New York: Funk and Wagnalls, 1886.
Lanman, C[harles] R. *A Sanskrit Reader, with Vocabulary and Notes.* Boston: Ginn and Co., 1884.
———. "Trustworthy Account of Buddha and His Teachings." *Light of Dharma* 4 (July 1904): 189–90.
Lillie, Arthur. *Buddhism in Christendom; Or, Jesus the Essene.* London: K. Paul, Trench, 1887.
Lodge, George Cabot. *Poems and Dramas of George Cabot Lodge.* 2 vols. Boston and New York: Houghton Mifflin, 1911.
Lovejoy, Arthur Onken. "The Buddhistic Technical Terms Upadana and Upadisesa." *Journal of the American Oriental Society* 19 (July–Dec. 1898): 126–36.
Lowell, Percival. *The Soul of the Far East.* Boston: Houghton Mifflin, 1888.
Lum, Dyer Daniel. "The Basis of Morals: A Posthumous Paper of an Anarchist Philosopher." *Monist* 7 (July 1897): 554–70.
———. "Be Thyself." *Twentieth Century* 9 (1 Sept. 1892): 7–9.
———. "Buddhism Notwithstanding: An Attempt to Interpret Buddha from a Buddhist Standpoint." *Index* 29 (Apr. 1875): 195–96; (6 May 1875): 206–8.
———. *A Concise History of the Great Trial of the Chicago Anarchists in 1886.* Chicago: Socialistic Publishing Company, [1886].
———. *The Economics of Anarchy: A Study of the Industrial Type.* New York: Twentieth Century, [1890].
———. "Nirvana." *Radical Review* (Aug. 1877): 260–62.
———. *The Philosophy of Trade Unions.* New York: American Federation of Labor, 1892.
———. *The Social Problems of Today; Or, the Mormon Question in its Economic Aspects.* Port Jarvis, N.Y.: D. D. Lum, 1886.
———. "Why I Am a Social Revolutionist." *Twentieth Century* 5 (30 Oct. 1890): 5–6.
Mason, Francis. "Hints on the Introduction of Buddhism into Burmah." *Journal of the American Oriental Society* 2 (1851): 334–36.
———. "Mulamuli; Or, the Buddhist Genesis of Eastern India from the Shan, through the Talaing and Burman." *Journal of the American Oriental Society* 4 (1854): 103–18.
———. *The Story of a Working Man's Life: With Sketches of Travel in Europe, Asia, Africa, and America, as Related by Himself.* New York: Oakley, Mason, and Company, 1870.
Mason, George L. "Buddhism and Romanism." *Missionary Review of the World,* n.s. 4 (Sept. 1891): 658–61.
Masters, Frederick J. "The Buddhist Hell." *Californian* 3 (Mar. 1893): 489–99.
———. "Pagan Temples in San Francisco." *Californian* 2 (Nov. 1892): 727–41.
Mathews, George R. "Notes on Buddhism at Home." *Unitarian Review* 36 (Sept. 1891): 185–93.
McIntire, K[athleen] M[elrena.] "Report of Secretary." *Light of Dharma* 1 (Aug. 1901): 26–28.
Mills, Charles D. B. *The Indian Saint: Or, Buddha and Buddhism.* Northampton, Mass.: Journal and Free Press, 1876.
Milner, Vincent L. *Religious Denominations of the World. . . .* Philadelphia: Bradley, Garretson, and Company, 1872.

Moffat, James C[lement.] *A Comparative History of Religions.* 2 vols. New York: Dodd and Mead, 1871–73.

Monier-Williams, Monier. *Buddhism, in Its Connexion with Brahmanism and Hinduism, and in Its Contrast with Christianity.* London: John Murray, 1889.

———. *The Holy Bible and the Sacred Books of the East.* London: Seeley, 1887.

Montgomery, Helen Barrett. *Western Women in Eastern Lands: An Outline Study of Fifty Years of Woman's Work in Foreign Missions.* New York: Macmillan, 1910.

Moore, Eleanor Hiestand. "Did Buddhism Exist in Pre-historic America?" *Light of Dharma* 4 (Apr. 1904): 137–42.

[———]. "The Ethical Side of the Material." *Light of Dharma* 3 (Oct. 1903): 76–79.

———. "Sir Edwin Arnold on Japanese Buddhism." *Light of Dharma* 5 (Apr. 1905): 14–16.

Moore, Henry Hoyt to H. Dharmapala. *Journal of the Maha Bodhi Society* 5 (Apr. 1897): 95.

Dr. Mullens. "Buddhism—Its Literature, Origin, and Doctrine." *Christian World* 20 (Nov. 1869): 333–35.

Müller, F[riedrich] Max. "Buddhism." 1862. In *Chips from a German Workshop.* Vol. 1. 1869. Chico, Calif.: Scholars Press, 1985.

———. "Buddhist Charity." *North American Review* 140 (March 1885): 221–36.

———. "Buddhist Pilgrims." 1857. In *Chips from a German Workshop.* Vol. 1. 1869. Chico, Calif.: Scholars Press, 1985.

———. "The Meaning of Nirvana." 1857. In *Chips from a German Workshop.* vol. 1. 1869. Chico, Calif.: Scholars Press, 1985.

———. *Selected Essays on Language, Mythology, and Religion.* 2 vols. London: Longmans, Green, 1881.

———, trans. *The Dhammapada.* The Sacred Books of the East. Oxford: The Clarendon Press, 1881.

Nagao, Skesaburo. *The Outline of Buddhism.* San Francisco: San Francisco Buddhist Mission, 1900.

Nakamura, Keijiro. "Japanese Buddhism: Its Philosophic and Doctrinal Teachings." *Arena* 27 (May 1902): 468–78.

"New Activity Shown by the American Branch of Association." *Light of Dharma* 4 (Oct. 1905): 131–32.

Nishijima, K. To [Dharmapala]. 20 April 1901. Reprinted as "Buddhism in America." *Maha Bodhi* 10 (Aug. 1901): 48–49.

Olcott, Henry S. *The Buddhist Catechism.* 1881. 44th ed. 1915. Talent, Oregon: Eastern School Press, 1983.

———. "Col. Olcott's Address at the Buddhist Mission." *Light of Dharma* 1 (Apr. 1901): 9–13.

———. *Old Diary Leaves: The True History of the Theosophical Society.* 6 vols. Madras, India: Theosophical Publishing House, 1895–1935.

Oldenberg, Hermann. *Buddha: His Life, His Doctrine, His Order.* Translated by William Hoey. London: Williams and Norgate, 1882.

———. *Buddha: Sein Leben, seine Lehre, seine Gemeinde.* 1881. Berlin: Verlag Von Wilhelm Hertz, 1890.

Oswald, Felix. "The Secret of the East: Buddha and His Galilean Successor." *The Index* 14 (22 Mar. 1883): 447–48.

———. "Was Christ a Buddhist?" *Arena* 3 (Jan. 1891): 193–201.

[Parsons, R.] "Buddhism and Christianity Compared." *American Catholic Quarterly Review* 13 (July 1888): 462–77.

"A Peep at Peraharra." *Harper's New Monthly Magazine* 3 (Aug. 1851): 322–26.

Phelps, Myron H. *Life and Teachings of Abbas Effendi: A Study of the Religion of the Babis, or Beha'is. . . .* New York: G. P. Putnam's, 1903.

————. "The Wisdom of India." *Mind* 15 (May–June 1905): 500–507.

"Pictures of the Japanese." *Harper's New Monthly Magazine* 39 (Aug. 1869): 305–22.

"Pictures of the Japanese—Institutions and Policy." *Harper's New Monthly Magazine* 28 (Jan. 1864): 167–83.

[Pilcher, L. W.?] "Gautama and Lao-Tzu." *Methodist Quarterly Review.* 4th series. 28 (Oct. 1876): 644–54.

Priestley, Joseph. *A Comparison of the Institutions of Moses with Those of the Hindoos and Other Nations.* Northumberland, Pa: A. Kennedy, 1799.

Review of *Buddha's Tooth Worshipped by the Buddhists of Ceylon in the Pagoda called "Dalada-Maligawa" at Kandy. American Ecclesiastical Review* 9 (Dec. 1898): 659–61.

Review of *Lectures on the Science of Religion; with a Paper on Buddhist Nihilism; and a Translation of the Dhammapada or "Path of Virtue,"* by Max Müller. *Bibliotheca Sacra* 29 (July 1872): 580–82.

Rhys Davids, T[homas] W[illiam]. "Buddhism." *North American Review* 171 (Oct. 1900): 517–27.

————. *Buddhism: Its History and Literature.* New York and London: G. P. Putnam's, 1896.

————. *Lectures on the Origin and Growth of Religion as Illustrated by Some Points in the History of Indian Buddhism.* The Hibbert Lectures, 1881. New York: G. P. Putnam's, 1882.

Rice, Clarence Edgar. "Buddhism as I Have Seen It." *Arena* 27 (May 1902): 479–86.

"The Right Reverend Soyen Shaku." *Light of Dharma* 5 (July 1905): 68–69.

Rockhill, William Woodville. "An American in Tibet: An Account of a Journey through an Unknown Land." *Century* 41 (Nov. 1890): 3–17; (Dec. 1890): 250–63; (Jan. 1891): 350–61; (Feb. 1891): 599–606; (Mar. 1891): 720–30.

————. *The Land of the Lamas: Notes of a Journey through China, Mongolia, and Tibet.* New York: The Century Co., 1891.

————. *The Life of the Buddha and the Early History of the Order.* London: Trubner, 1884.

————. "The Open Door." Delivered at the Nineteenth Annual Banquet of the Boston Merchants Association, Boston, 19 Feb. 1900. *Miscellaneous Papers.* N.p., n.d.: 43–47.

Root, E. D. *Sakya Buddha: A Versified, Annotated Narrative of the Life and Teachings; with an Excursus Containing Citations from the Dhammapada, or Buddhist Canon.* New York: Charles P. Somerby, 1880.

Royce, Josiah. "The Christian Doctrine of Life." *Hibbert Journal* 11 (1913): 473–96.

Rubruck, William of. "The Journal of Friar William of Rubruck, 1253–1255." In *Contemporaries of Marco Polo,* edited by Manuel Komroff, 53–209. New York: Boni and Liveright, 1928.

Ryan, R. M. "The Lustre of 'The Light of Asia.' " *Catholic World* 61 (Sept. 1895): 809–26.

————. "More Light on 'The Light of Asia.' " *Catholic World* 61 (Aug. 1895): 677–87.

"A Sacred Buddha in Wood." *Light of Dharma* 2 (Aug. 1903): 109–10.

Salisbury, Edward E. "M. Burnouf on the History of Buddhism in India." *Journal of the American Oriental Society* 1 (1843–49): 275–98.

————. "Memoir on the History of Buddhism." *Journal of the American Oriental Society* 1 (1843–49): 81–135.

"The Sanscrit Language." *Methodist Quarterly Review* 19 (July 1867): 353–69.

Schaff, Philip. "Rise and Progress of Monasticism: Origin of Christian Monasticism. Comparison with Other Forms of Asceticism." *Bibliotheca Sacra* 22 (Apr. 1864): 384–424.

"Schopenhauer and His Pessimism." *Methodist Quarterly Review*. 4th series. 28 (July 1876): 487–510.

Schopenhauer, Arthur. *The World as Will and Representation*. 2 vols. 1818. Translated by E.F.J. Payne. New York: Dover, 1969.

Schroder, Charles. "Buddhism and Christianity." *Arena* 5 (Mar. 1892): 458–63.

———. "What Is Buddhism?" *Arena* 5 (Jan. 1892): 217–27.

Scudder, David C[oit]. "A Sketch of Hindu Philosophy: Article I." *Bibliotheca Sacra* 18 (Oct. 1861): 673–724.

———. "A Sketch of Hindu Philosophy: Article II." *Bibliotheca Sacra* 18 (July 1861): 535–95.

Seydel, Rudolph. *Das Evangelium von Jesu in seinen Verhältnissen zu Buddha-sage und Buddha-lehre*. . . . Leipzig: Breitkopf und Härtel, 1882.

Sinnett, A. P. *Esoteric Buddhism*. 1883. Wheaton, Ill.: Theosophical Publishing House, 1972.

"Sister Sanghamitta the Buddhist Nun." *Light of Dharma* 1 (Apr. 1901): 21.

"Sketches in the East Indies: Pulo Pinang." *Harper's New Monthly Magazine* 11 (Aug. 1855): 324–35.

Snell, Merwin-Marie. "Evangelical Buddhism." *Biblical World* 7 (Jan.–June 1896): 182–88.

———. *Hints on the Study of the Sacred Books*. Baltimore: John Murphy and Co., 1887.

———. *One Hundred Theses on the Foundations of Human Knowledge*. Washington, D.C.: Merwin-Marie Snell, 1891.

———. "Parseeism and Buddhism." *Catholic World* 46 (Jan. 1888): 451–57.

———. "Was Christ a Buddhist?" *New Englander* 54 (May 1891): 448–63.

Snodgrass, E. "Buddhism and Christianity." *Missionary Review of the World*, n.s. 4 (Sept. 1891): 654–58.

Soyen, Shaku. "The Law of Cause and Effect as Taught by the Buddha." In *The World's Parliament of Religions*, edited by John Henry Barrows, 829–31. Chicago: Parliament Publishing Co., 1893.

———. *Sermons of a Buddhist Abbot*. La Salle, Ill.: Open Court, 1906.

Spooner, D[avid] Brainerd. "Welcoming the Buddha's Most Holy Bones." *Overland Monthly* 37 (Jan. 1901): 585–92.

Stiles, Ezra. *The United States Elevated to Glory and Honour: A Sermon Preached before His Excellency Jonathan Trumbull . . . and the General Assembly of the State of Connecticut Convened at Hartford, at the Anniversary Election: May 8, 1783*. 1783. 2d ed. Worcester, Mass.: Isaiah Thomas, 1785.

Strauss, C. T. *The Buddha and His Doctrine*. 1922. Port Washington, N.Y.: Kennikat Press, 1970.

———. "The Future of Artificial Languages." *Monist* 18 (Oct. 1908): 609–19.

———. "Justifiable Killing." Letter to the editor. *Maha Bodhi* 42 (Oct. 1934): 469–70.

Sumendhankara, B. to S. Sonoda. 29 Jan. 1901. *Light of Dharma* 1.2 (June 1901): 28.

Suzuki, Daisetsu T. *Butsuda no Fukuin*. A Japanese translation of *The Gospel of Buddha* by Paul Carus. Tokyo: Morie Shoten, 1895.

———. *Essays in Zen Buddhism: First Series*. London: Luzac and Co., 1927.

———. "The Essence of Buddhism." *Light of Dharma* 4 (Oct. 1905): 73–75.

———. "Individual Immortality." *Light of Dharma* 3 (Oct. 1903): 67–72.

———. "Mahayana Buddhism." *Light of Dharma* 2 (Aug. 1902): 79–81.

[———.] "Notes." *Eastern Buddhist* 2 (May–Aug. 1922): 92–94.

———. *Outlines of Mahayana Buddhism*. Chicago: Open Court Publishing Co., 1908.

———. Review of *Christianity Reconstructed*, by Albert J. Edmunds. *Eastern Buddhist* 2 (Nov. 1922): 92–94.

————. *Tengai to Jigoku*. A Japanese translation of *Heaven and Hell* by Emanuel Swedenborg. London: Swedenborg Society; Tokyo: Yurakusha, 1910.

————. "What Is Buddhism?" *Light of Dharma* 2 (Apr. 1902): 11–14.

"A 'Theosophical' Attack on the New Church." Review of *Swedenborg the Buddhist*, by Philangi Dasa. *New Church Life* (Feb. 1888): 24–25.

[Thoreau, Henry David], ed. "The Preaching of the Buddha." *Dial* 4 (Jan. 1844): 391–401.

Toy, C. H. "The Religious Element in Ethical Codes." *International Journal of Ethics* 1 (Apr. 1891): 289–311.

A Traveller. "Budhism—Its Origin, Tenets, and Tendencies." *Southern Literary Messenger* 25 (Nov. 1857): 380–89.

"True Till Death." *Maha Bodhi* 7 (Apr. 1899): 114–15.

"A Unique Ceremony in America." *Maha Bodhi* 6 (Nov. 1897): 55–56.

[Vetterling, Herman.] "Bostonian 'Buddhists' and Tearful Theosophists." *Buddhist Ray* 2 (Mar. 1889): [17].

[————.] "The Growth of Enlightenment." *Buddhist Ray* 6 (May–June 1893): [1]–6.

————. *The Illuminate of Görlitz; Or, Jacob Böhme's Life and Philosophy: A Comparative Study*. Leipzig: Markert and Peters, 1923.

[————.] "Optimist, Buddhist, Pessimist." *Buddhist Ray* 5 (Jan.–Feb. 1892): 1–2.

[————.] "Prospectus." *Buddhist Ray* 1 (Jan. 1888): 1.

————. [Philangi Dasa, pseud.]. *Swedenborg the Buddhist: Or, The Higher Swedenborgianism: Its Secrets and Thibetan Origin*. Los Angeles: The Buddhistic Swedenborgian Brotherhood, 1887.

[————.] "Why Buddhism?" *The Buddhist Ray* (Jan. 1888): 1.

"A Visit to Bangkok." *Harper's New Monthly Magazine* 41 (Aug. 1870): 359–68.

Von Bunsen, Ernest. *The Angel-Messiah of Buddhists, Essenes, and Christians*. London: Longmans, Green, 1880.

Wade, Joseph M. "The One Life-Necessary Action." *Light of Dharma* 2 (1902): 24–25.

[Warner, Herman J.] "The Last Phase of Atheism." *Christian Examiner* 78 (July 1865): 78–88.

Warren, Henry C. *Buddhism in Translations*. 1896. New York: Atheneum, 1979.

————. "On the So-Called Chain of Causation of the Buddhists." *Journal of the American Oriental Society* 16 (Apr. 1893): xxvii–xxx.

Weber, Albrecht. "Über den Buddhismus." *Indische Skizzen*. Berlin: Dummlers, 1857.

Webster, Noah. *An American Dictionary of the English Language. . . .* 2 vols. New York: S. Converse, 1828.

[Wight, J. K.?] "Buddhism in India and China." *Princeton Review* 31 (July 1859): 391–438.

Williams, S. Wells. *The Middle Kingdom: A Survey of the Geography, Government, Education. Social Life, Arts, Religion, & of the Chinese Empire. . . .* 2 vols. New York and London: Wiley and Putnam, 1848.

Wilson, Thomas B. "Buddhism in America." *Light of Dharma* 3 (Apr. 1903): 1–4.

————. "Buddhism-Rationalism." *Light of Dharma* 2 (June 1902): 46–50.

————? [By a Liberal Religionist]. "Concerning Buddhism." *Overland Monthly* 45 (May 1905): 387–89.

————. "The Duty of Wealth." *Light of Dharma* 1 (Oct. 1901): 7–10.

————. "The Great Teachers." *Light of Dharma* 2 (Apr. 1902): 7–10.

————. "The Philosophy of Pain." *Light of Dharma* 1 (Aug. 1901): 16–21.

————. "Sectarianism in Asia." *Light of Dharma* 2 (Oct. 1902): 124–26.

————. "The String of Life." *Light of Dharma* 1 (Dec. 1901): 12–15.

Withee, Myra E. "Is Buddhism to Blame?" *Mind* 10 (Sept. 1902): 456–62.

Yokoi, Tokiwo. "The Ethical and Political Problems of New Japan." *International Journal of Ethics* 7 (Jan. 1897): 169–80.
————. "The Ethical Life and Conceptions of the Japanese." *International Journal of Ethics* 6 (Jan. 1896): 182–204.

Religion and Culture in Victorian America

Abbott, Lyman. "Can a Nation Have a Religion?" *Century* 41 (Dec. 1890): 275–81.
————. *The Evolution of Christianity.* Boston: Houghton, Mifflin, 1892.
————. *The Theology of an Evolutionist.* Boston: Houghton, Mifflin, 1897.
————. "What Is Christianity?" *Arena* (1890): 36–46.
Adams, Brooks. *The Law of Civilization and Decay: An Essay.* London: S. Sonnenschein; New York: Macmillan, 1893.
Adler, Felix. *The Religion of Duty.* New York: McClure, Philips, 1905.
Ahlstrom, Sydney E., and Jonathan S. Carey, eds. *An American Reformation: A Documentary History of Unitarian Christianity.* Middletown, Conn.: Wesleyan University Press, 1985.
Allen, Alexander V. G., ed. *Life and Letters of Phillips Brooks.* New York: E. P. Dutton, 1901.
Beecher, Henry Ward. *Evolution and Religion.* 2 vols. New York: Fords, Howard, and Hulbert, 1885.
————. "Progress of Thought in the Church." *North American Review* 135 (Aug. 1882): 99–117.
————. "The Tendencies of American Progress." In *The Original Plymouth Pulpit: Sermons of Henry Ward Beecher . . . from Stenographic Reports by T. J. Ellinwood,* 203–19. Vol. 5. Boston: The Pilgrim Press, 1871.
————. *Yale Lectures on Preaching.* New York: Fords, Howard, and Hulbert, 1887.
Bellamy, Edward. *Looking Backward, 2000–1887.* 1888. New York: Penguin, 1984.
Brown, William Adams. *The Essence of Christianity.* New York: Scribner's, 1902.
[Bullard, Anne Tuttle.] *The Wife for a Missionary.* Cincinnati: Truman, Smith, and Company, 1834.
Carnegie, Andrew. *The Autobiography of Andrew Carnegie.* Boston: Houghton Mifflin, 1920.
————. "Wealth." *North American Review* 148 (June 1889): 653–64.
Channing, William Ellery. "The Moral Argument against Calvinism." 1820. In *William Ellery Channing: Selected Writings,* edited by David Robinson, 103–21. New York: Paulist, 1985.
Cherry, Conrad, ed. *God's New Israel: Religious Interpretations of American Destiny.* Englewood Cliffs, N.J.: Prentice-Hall, 1971.
Child, Lydia Maria. *An Appeal in Favor of That Class of Americans Called Africans.* Boston: Allen and Ticknor, 1833.
Clarke, James Freeman. "The Five Points of Calvinism and the Five Points of the New Theology." In *Vexed Questions in Theology: A Series of Essays,* 9–18. Boston: George Ellis, 1886.
Clarke, William Newton. *An Outline of Christian Theology.* Cambridge, Mass.: J. Wilson, 1894.
Commager, Henry Steele, ed. *The Era of Reform, 1830–1860.* Princeton, N.J.: D. Van Nostrand, 1960.
Cross, Robert D., ed. *The Church and the City, 1865–1910.* Indianapolis and New York: Bobbs-Merrill, 1967.
deTocqueville, Alexis. *Democracy in America.* 2 vols. 1835–40. Translated by Henry Reeve. New York: Vintage, 1945.

Ely, Richard T. *Social Aspects of Christianity and Other Essays.* New York: Thomas Y. Crowell, 1889.

Emerson, Ralph Waldo. "Address." Delivered before the senior class in Divinity College, Cambridge, Sunday evening, 15 July 1838. In *The Portable Emerson*, edited by Carl Bode, 72–91. New York: Penguin, 1981.

———. "Each and All." In *The Portable Emerson*, edited by Carl Bode, 631–32. New York: Penguin, 1981.

———. "Self Reliance." In *The Portable Emerson*, edited by Carl Bode, 138–64. New York: Penguin, 1981.

Farmer, Sarah J. "The Abundant Life." *Mind* 5 (Dec. 1899): 212–17.

———. "The Purpose of Greenacre." *Mind* 5 (Oct. 1899): 6–9.

Fiske, John. *The Destiny of Man Viewed in the Light of His Origin.* 1884. Boston and New York: Houghton Mifflin Co., 1912.

Flower, B[enjamin] O[range.] *The New Time: A Plea for the Union of the Moral Forces for Practical Progress.* Boston: Arena Publishing Co., 1894.

Frothingham, Octavius Brooks. "The Religion of Humanity." *Radical* 10 (Apr. 1872): 241–72.

———. *Transcendentalism in New England: A History.* 1876. Philadelphia: University of Pennsylvania Press, 1972.

George, Henry. *Progress and Poverty.* San Francisco: W. M. Hinton, 1879.

Gladden, Washington. "The Church." In *Social Facts and Forces: The Factory, the Labor Union, the Corporation, the Railway, the City, the Church,* 192–227. New York and London: G. P. Putnam's, 1897.

Goodwin, Myron H. "Theological Ruins." *Twentieth Century* 8 (24 Mar. 1892): 2.

Gordon, George A[ngier]. *The New Epoch for Faith.* Boston: Houghton, Mifflin, 1901.

Haeckel, Ernest. *The Monistic Alliance: Theses for the Organization of Monism.* St. Louis: Bund der Freien Gemeinden und Freidenker-Vereine von Nord Amerika, 1904.

Handy, Robert T., ed. *Religion in the American Experience: The Pluralistic Style.* New York: Harper and Row, 1972.

Henderson, C[harles] R[ichmond]. *The Social Spirit in America.* Meadville, Penn.: Flood and Vincent; New York: The Chautauqua-Century Press, 1897.

Herron, George D[avis]. *The Christian State: A Political Vision of Christ.* New York: Thomas Y. Crowell, 1895.

Hoffman, Frederick L. "Suicides and Modern Civilization." *Arena* (May 1893): 680–95.

Hofstadter, Richard, and Wilson Smith, ed. *American Higher Education: A Documentary History.* 2 vols. Chicago: University of Chicago Press, 1961.

James, William. "The Energies of Men." In *Essays on Faith and Morals: William James,* edited by Ralph Barton Perry, 216–37. Cleveland: Meridian, 1962.

———. "The Gospel of Relaxation." In *Essays on Faith and Morals: William James,* edited by Ralph Barton Perry, 238–58. Cleveland: Meridian, 1962.

———. "Is Life Worth Living?" In *Essays on Faith and Morals: William James,* edited by Ralph Barton Perry, 1–31. Cleveland: Meridian, 1962.

———. "The Moral Philosopher and the Moral Life." In *Essays on Faith and Morals: William James,* edited by Ralph Barton Perry, 184–215. Cleveland: Meridian, 1962.

———. *Pragmatism and Four Essays from the Meaning of Truth.* 1907, 1909. Cleveland: Meridian, 1955.

———. *The Varieties of Religious Experience.* 1902. New York: Penguin, 1982.

Jastrow, Morris. *The Study of Religion.* 1901. Classics in Religious Studies. Chico, Calif.: Scholars Press, 1981.

Johnson, Samuel. "American Religion." *Radical* (Jan. 1867): 257–73.

Lyman, Benjamin Smith. *Vegetarian Diet and Dishes*. Philadelphia: Ferris and Leach, 1917.

Marques, S. D. *The Human Aura: A Study*. San Francisco: Office of Mercury, 1896.

Mathews, William. "Civilization and Suicide." *North American Review* 152 (Apr. 1891): 470–84.

McCosh, James. *The Religious Aspect of Evolution*. The Bedell Lectures, 1887. New York: G. P. Putnam's, 1888.

McGuffey, William Holmes. *Sixth Eclectic Reader*. 1879 edition. New York: New American Library, 1962.

Miller, Perry, ed. *American Thought: Civil War to World War I*. New York: Holt, Rinehart, and Winston, 1954.

Morselli, Henry. "Catholicism, Protestantism, and Suicide." *Popular Science Monthly* 20 (Dec. 1881): 220–25.

Mott, John R. *The Evangelization of the World in This Generation*. New York: Student Volunteer Movement, 1905.

O. D. "On the Signs and Prospects of the Age." *Christian Examiner* 36 (Jan. 1844): 7–23.

"Organization of the Vegetarian Society of America." *Food, Home, and Garden* 1 (Feb. 1889): 8.

Perry, Ralph Barton, ed. *Essays on Faith and Morals: William James*. Cleveland: Meridian, 1962.

[Phelps, Elizabeth Steward.] *Allendale's Choice, A Village Chronicle*. Milwaukee: The Young Churchman Co., 1895.

Potter, Henry C., and Charles W. Shields. "The Social Problem of Church Unity: The Report of Bishop Potter and Professor Shields." In "Present-Day Papers." Contributed by the Sociological Group, edited by Charles W. Shields, *Century* 40 (Sept. 1890): 687–97.

"A Review of the Eighteenth Century." *Monthly Anthology* 2 (May 1805): 223–28.

Ritschl, Albrecht. *The Christian Doctrine of Justification and Reconciliation*. Translated by H. R. Mackintosh and others. Edinburgh: T. and T. Clark, 1900.

Roe, Edward Payson. *Works*. 19 vols. New York: Collier, 1900.

Roosevelt, Theodore. *The Strenuous Life: Essays and Addresses*. New York: The Century Company, 1900.

Rusk, Ralph L., ed. *The Letters of Ralph Waldo Emerson*. New York: Columbia University Press, 1939.

Santayana, G. "The Intellectual Temper of the Age." In *Winds of Doctrine: Studies in Contemporary Opinion*, 1–24. London and Toronto: J. M. Dent and Sons; New York: Charles Scribner's Sons, 1913.

Schaff, Philip. *America: A Sketch of Its Political, Social, and Religious Character*. 1855. Reprint. Cambridge, Mass.: Harvard University Press, 1961.

Schweitzer, Albert. *The Quest of the Historical Jesus*. 1906. Translated by W. Montgomery. New York: Macmillan, 1968.

Smith, Judson. "Protestant Foreign Missions; A Retrospect of the Nineteenth Century." *North American Review* 172 (Mar. 1901): 394–402.

Smyth, Egbert C. "The Theological Purpose of the Review." *Andover Review* 1 (Jan. 1884): 1–13.

Smyth, Newman. *The Religious Feeling*. New York: Scribner, Armstrong, Co., 1877.

Snow, Louis Franklin. *The College Curriculum in the United States*. New York: Teachers College, Columbia University, 1907.

Spencer, Herbert. *First Principles*. 1862. Philadelphia: David McKay, 1880.

Sprague, William B. *The Excellent Woman as Described in the Book of Proverbs*. Boston: Gould and Lincoln, 1851.

————. *Letters to Young Men, Founded on the History of Joseph.* Albany: Erastus H. Pease, 1845.

Stanton, Elizabeth Cady. "Has Christianity Benefitted Woman?" *North American Review* 140 (May 1885): 389–99.

Stowe, Harriet Beecher. *Uncle Tom's Cabin; Or, Life among the Lowly.* 1852. New York: Penguin, 1981.

Strong, Josiah. *Our Country: Its Possible Future and Present Crisis.* 1885. Revised ed. New York: Baker and Taylor, 1891.

"Suicide Club." *Dollar Weekly,* 28 Jan. 1893.

"The Sure Triumph of Christianity." *Methodist Quarterly Review.* 4th series. 19 (Oct. 1867): 532–40.

Syme, J. B., ed. *The Mourner's Friend; Or, Sighs of Sympathy for Those Who Sorrow.* Worcester: S. A. Howland, 1852.

"To the Public." *Massachusetts Quarterly Review* 1 (Dec. 1847): 1–7.

[Tuckerman, Joseph.] "On the Causes by Which Unitarians Have Been Withheld from Exertions in the Cause of Foreign Missions." *Christian Examiner* 1 (May–June 1824): 182–96.

Twain, Mark [Samuel Langhorne Clemens]. "Christian Science." *North American Review* 175 (Dec. 1902): 756–68; 176 (Jan. 1903): 1–9; 176 (Feb. 1903): 173–84; 176 (Apr. 1903): 505–17.

————. *A Connecticut Yankee in King Arthur's Court.* New York: C. L. Webster, 1889.

————, and Charles Dudley Warner. *The Gilded Age: A Tale of Today.* 1873–74. Indianapolis: Bobbs-Merrill, 1972.

"The 'Vegetarian Church' and the *Tribune.*" *Food, Home, and Garden* 3 (Jan. 1891): 5–6.

Wallace, Lewis. *Ben-Hur, A Tale of Christ.* New York: Harper and Brothers, 1880.

Washington, Booker T. "The Religious Life of the Negro." *North American Review* 181 (July 1905): 20–23.

SECONDARY SOURCES

The Conversation about Buddhism

Abe, Masao, ed. *A Zen Life: D. T. Suzuki Remembered.* New York and Tokyo: Weatherhill, 1986.

Ahlstrom, Sydney E. *The American Encounter with World Religions.* Beloit, Wis.: Beloit College, 1962.

Almond, Philip C. "The Buddha in the West: From Myth to History." *Religion* 16 (Oct. 1986): 305–22.

————. *The British Discovery of Buddhism.* New York: Cambridge University Press, 1988.

Benz, Ernst. "Buddhist Influences outside Asia." In *Buddhism in the Modern World,* edited by Heinrich Doumoulin and John C. Maraldo, 305–22. New York: Collier, 1976.

Bishop, Donald H. "Religious Confrontation: A Case Study: The 1893 Parliament of Religions." *Numen* 16 (Apr. 1969): 63–76.

Bond, George. *The Buddhist Revival in Sri Lanka: Religious Tradition, Reinterpretation and Response.* Columbia: University of South Carolina Press, 1988.

Brooks, Van Wyck. "Fenollosa and His Circle." In *Fenollosa and His Circle: With Other Essays in Biography,* 1–68. New York: Dutton, 1962.

Buddhist Churches of America. *Buddhist Churches of America: Seventy-Five Year History, 1899–1974.* 2 vols. Chicago: Nobart, 1974.

Cameron, Kenneth Walter, ed. *Transcendentalists in Transition: Popularization of*

Emerson, Thoreau and the Concord School of Philosophy in the Greenacre Summer Conferences and the Monsalvat School (1894–1909): The Roles of Charles Malloy and Franklin Benjamin Sanborn before the Triumph of the Baha'i Movement in Eliot, Maine. Hartford: Transcendental Books, 1980.

Campbell, Bruce F. *Ancient Wisdom Revisited: A History of the Theosophical Movement.* Berkeley: University of California Press, 1980.

Carter, Paul A. *The Spiritual Crisis of the Gilded Age.* Dekalb: Northern Illinois University Press, 1971.

Chanler, Mrs. Winthrop [Margaret]. "Buddhism in Boston." In *Autumn in the Valley.* Boston: Little, Brown, and Co., 1936.

———. "Bohemian and Buddhist." *Atlantic Monthly* 158 (Sept. 1938): 271–78.

Chisolm, Lawrence W. *Fenollosa: The Far East and American Culture.* New Haven: Yale University Press, 1963.

Christy, Arthur E., ed. *The Asian Legacy and American Life.* New York: John Day, 1942.

———. *The Orient in American Transcendentalism: A Study of Emerson, Thoreau, and Alcott.* New York: Columbia University Press, 1932.

Clausen, Christopher. "Victorian Buddhism and the Origins of Comparative Religion." *Religion* 5 (1973): 1–15.

Conze, Edward. *Buddhism: Its Essence and Development.* 1951. New York: Harper and Row, 1975.

Councilman, W. T. "William Sturgis Bigelow (1850–1926)." In *Later Years of the Saturday Club, 1870–1920,* edited by M. A. DeWolfe Howe, 265–69. Boston and New York: Houghton Mifflin, 1927.

Crowley, John W. "Eden off Nantucket: W. S. Bigelow and 'Tuckanuck.' " *Essex Institute Historical Collections* 109 (Jan. 1973): 1–8.

deJong, J. W. "A Brief History of Buddhist Studies in Europe and America." *Eastern Buddhist,* n.s. 7 (May 1974): 55–106; 7 (Oct. 1974): 49–82.

deLubac, Henri. *La Recontre du bouddhisme et de l'occident.* Paris: Aubier, Editions montaigne, 1952.

Druyvesteyn, Kenten. "The World's Parliament of Religions." Ph.D diss., University of Chicago, 1976.

Dutt, Nalinaksha. "The Maha Bodhi Society: Its History and Influence." In *Maha Bodhi Society of India: Diamond Jubilee Souvenir, 1891–1951,* 66–132. Calcutta: Maha Bodhi Society of India, 1952.

Earhart, H. Byron. *Japanese Religion: Unity and Diversity.* 3d ed. Belmont, Calif.: Wadsworth, 1982.

Ellwood, Robert. *Alternative Altars: Unconventional and Eastern Spirituality in America.* Chicago History of American Religion Series. Chicago: University of Chicago Press, 1979.

Fader, Larry A. "Zen in the West: Historical and Philosophical Implications of the 1893 Chicago World's Parliament of Religions." *The Eastern Buddhist,* n.s. 15 (Spring 1982): 122–45.

Fields, Rick. *How the Swans Came to the Lake: A Narrative History of Buddhism in America.* Rev. ed. Boston: Shambhala, 1986.

Giardot, N. J. "Chinese Religion: History of Study." In *Encyclopedia of Religion,* 16 vols., edited by Mircea Eliade. New York: Macmillan, 1987.

Gombrich, Richard F. *Theravada Buddhism: A Social History from Ancient Benares to Modern Colombo.* London and New York: Routledge and Kegan Paul, 1988.

Hanayama, Shinsho. *Bibliography on Buddhism.* Tokyo: Hoduseido Press, 1961.

Handy, Robert T. *A Christian America: Protestant Hopes and Historical Realities.* 2d ed. New York: Oxford University Press, 1984.

Havel, Hippolyte. Introduction. *Selected Works of Voltairine deCleyre,* edited by Alexander Berkman. New York: Mother Earth, 1914.

Hay, William H. "Paul Carus: A Case-Study of Philosophy on the Frontier." *Journal of the History of Ideas* 17 (Oct. 1956): 498–510.

Horinouchi, Isao. "Americanized Buddhism: A Sociological Analysis of a Protestantized Japanese Religion." Ph.D. diss., University of California, Davis, 1973.

Horner, I. B. *Women under Primitive Buddhism.* London: George Routledge, 1930.

Hucker, Charles O. *China's Imperial Past: An Introduction to Chinese History and Culture.* Stanford: Stanford University Press, 1975.

Humphreys, T. Christmas. *The Development of Buddhism in England.* London: The Buddhist Lodge, 1937.

——. *Sixty Years of Buddhism in England.* London: The Buddhist Society, 1968.

Hunter, Louise H. *Buddhism in Hawaii: Its Impact on a Yankee Community.* Honolulu: University of Hawaii Press, 1971.

Isani, Mukhtar. "The Oriental Tale in America through 1865: A Study in American Fiction." Ph.D. diss., Princeton University, 1962.

Ichioka, Yuji. *The Issei: The World of the First Generation Japanese Immigrants, 1885–1924.* New York: Free Press, 1988.

Jackson, Carl T. "The Influence of Asia upon American Thought: A Bibliographical Essay." *American Studies International* 22 (Apr. 1984): 3–31.

——. "The Meeting of East and West: The Case of Paul Carus." *Journal of the History of Ideas* 29 (Jan.–Mar. 1968): 73–92.

——. "The New Thought Movement and the Nineteenth Century Discovery of Oriental Philosophy." *Journal of Popular Culture* 9 (Winter 1975): 523–48.

——. *The Oriental Religions and American Thought.* Westport, Conn.: Greenwood, 1981.

Jordon, Louis Henry. *Comparative Religion: Its Genesis and Growth.* 1905. Atlanta: Scholars Press, 1986.

Kashima, Tetsuden. *Buddhism in America: The Social Organization of an Ethnic Religious Organization.* Westport, Conn.: Greenwood, 1977.

Kitagawa, Joseph. "Buddhism in America, with Special Reference to Zen." *Japanese Religions* 5 (July 1967): 32–57.

——. "The 1893 World's Parliament of Religions and Its Legacy." The Eleventh John Nuveen Lecture. Chicago: University of Chicago Divinity School, 1983.

——. *Religion in Japanese History.* New York: Columbia University Press, 1966.

Lancaster, Clay. *The Japanese Influence in America.* New York: Walton H. Rawls, 1963.

Lancaster, Lewis. "Buddhism in the United States: The Untold and Unfinished Story." *International Buddhist Forum Quarterly* (Sept. 1977): 26–29.

Layman, Emma McCloy. *Buddhism in America.* Chicago: Nelson-Hall, 1976.

Lears, Jackson. *No Place of Grace: Antimodernism and the Transformation of American Culture, 1880–1920.* New York: Pantheon, 1981.

Maha Bodhi Society of India. *Maha Bodhi Society of India: Diamond Jubilee Souvenir, 1891–1951.* Calcutta: Maha Bodhi Society of India, 1952.

Malalgoda, Kitsiri. *Buddhism in Sinhalese Society, 1750–1900: A Study of Religious Revival and Change.* Berkeley: University of California Press, 1976.

Matsunaga, Daigan and Alicia Matsunaga. *Foundation of Japanese Buddhism.* 2 vols. Los Angeles: Buddhist Books International, 1974, 1976.

Meyer, Donald H. "Paul Carus and the Religion of Science." *American Quarterly* 14 (Winter 1962): 597–607.

Miller, Stuart Creighton. *The Unwelcome Immigrant: The American Image of the Chinese, 1785–1882.* Berkeley: University of California Press, 1969.

Mueller, Roger Chester. "The Orient in American Transcendental Periodicals (1835–1886)." Ph.D. diss., University of Minnesota, 1968.

———. "Samuel Johnson, American Transcendentalist: A Short Biography." *Essex Institute Historical Collections* 115 (Jan. 1979): 9–67.

———. "A Significant Buddhist Translation by Thoreau." *Thoreau Society Bulletin* (Winter 1977): 1–2.

Murakata, Akiko. "Selected Letters of Dr. William Sturgis Bigelow." Ph.D. diss., George Washington University, 1971.

———. "Theodore Roosevelt and William Sturgis Bigelow: The Story of a Friendship." *Harvard Library Bulletin* 23 (Jan. 1975): 90–108.

Murphet, Howard. *Hammer on the Mountain: The Life of Henry Steel Olcott (1832–1907).* Wheaton, Ill.: Theosophical Publishing House, 1972.

Nikam, N. A., and Richard McKeon, eds. and trans. *The Edicts of Asoka.* Chicago: University of Chicago Press, 1959.

Obeyesekere, Gananath. "Personal Identity and Cultural Crisis: The Case of Anagarika Dharmapala in Sri Lanka." In *The Biographical Process: Studies in the History and Psychology of Religion,* edited by Frank E. Reynolds and Donald Capps, 221–52. The Hague: Mouton, 1976.

Oliver, Ian P. *Buddhism in Britain.* London: Rider, 1979.

Paul, Diana. *The Buddhist Feminine Ideal.* AAR Dissertation Series. Missoula, Mont.: Scholars Press, 1980.

———. *Women in Buddhism: Images of the Feminine in the Mahayana Tradition.* 1979. Berkeley: University of California Press, 1985.

Peiris, William. *Edwin Arnold: Brief Account of His Life and Contribution to Buddhism.* Kandy, Ceylon: Buddhist Publication Society, 1970.

———. *The Western Contribution to Buddhism.* Delhi: Motilal Banarsidass, 1973.

"Personal Letter about Dr. William Sturgis Bigelow (1850–1926) from John E. Lodge to Frederick Cheever Shattuck." *Proceedings of the Massachusetts Historical Society* 75 (Jan.–Dec. 1963): 108–9.

Prebish, Charles S. *American Buddhism.* North Scituate, Mass.: Duxbury, 1979.

———. "Buddhist Studies American Style: A Shot in the Dark." *Religious Studies Review* 9 (1983): 323–30.

Prothero, Stephen. "Henry Steel Olcott (1832–1907) and the Construction of 'Protestant Buddhism.' " Ph.D. diss., Harvard University, 1990.

Rahula, Walpola. *History of Buddhism in Ceylon.* Colombo, Sri Lanka: M. D. Gunasena, 1956.

Rajapakse, Vijitha. "Buddhism in Huxley's *Evolution and Ethics:* A Note on a Victorian Evaluation and Its Comparativist Dimension." *Philosophy East and West* 35 (July 1985): 295–304.

Records of the Life, Character, and Achievements of Adoniram Judson. New York: Edward H. Fletcher, 1854.

Richardson, Robert P. "The Rise and Fall of the Parliament of Religions at Greenacre." *Open Court* 46 (Mar. 1931): 129–66.

Robinson, Richard H., and Willard L. Johnson. *The Buddhist Religion: A Historical Introduction.* 3d ed. Belmont, Calif.: Wadsworth, 1982.

Rosenstone, Robert A. *Mirror in the Shrine: American Encounters with Meiji Japan.* Cambridge, Mass.: Harvard University Press, 1988.

Rust, William Charles. "The Shin Sect of Buddhism in America." Ph.D. diss., University of Southern California, 1951.

Sangharakshita, Bikkhu. *Anagarika Dharmapala: A Biographical Sketch.* Kandy: Buddhist Publication Society, 1964.

Seager, Richard H. "The World's Parliament of Religions, Chicago, Illinois, 1893." Ph.D. diss., Harvard University, 1987.

Shattuck, [Frederick Cheever?]. "William Sturgis Bigelow." *Proceedings of the Massachusetts Historical Society* 40 (Oct. 1926–June 1927): 15–19.

Sheridan, James Francis. "Paul Carus: A Study of the Thought and Work of the Editor of the Open Court Publishing Company." Ph.D. diss., University of Illinois, 1957.

Spae, Joseph. "The Influence of Buddhism in Europe and America." In *Buddhism and Christianity,* edited by Claude Geffrè and Mariasusai Dhavamony, 118–23. New York: Seabury, 1979.

Swearer, Donald K. *Buddhism and Society in Southeast Asia.* Chambersburg, Pa.: Anima Books, 1981.

Takakusu, Junjiro. *The Essentials of Buddhist Philosophy.* 1947. Delhi: Motilal Banarsidass, 1975.

Thelle, Noto R. *Buddhism and Christianity in Japan: From Conflict to Dialogue.* Honolulu: University of Hawaii Press, 1987.

Tsai, Shih-shan Henry. *The Chinese Experience in America.* Bloomington: Indiana University Press, 1986.

Varg, Paul A. *Open Door Diplomat: The Life of W. W. Rockhill.* Urbana: University of Illinois Press, 1952.

Wagner, Vern. "The Lotus of Henry Adams." *New England Quarterly* 27 (Mar. 1954): 75–94.

Wayland, Francis. *A Memoir of the Life and Labors of Rev. Adoniram Judson, D.D.* 2 vols. Boston: Phillips, Sampson, and Company; Cincinnati: Moore, Anderson, and Company, 1853.

Welbon, Guy. *The Buddhist Nirvana and Its Western Interpreters.* Chicago: University of Chicago Press, 1968.

Wickremeratne, Ananda. *The Genesis of an Orientalist: Thomas William Rhys Davids in Sri Lanka.* Columbia, Mo.: South Asia Books, 1985.

Williams, George Hunston. "The Attitude of Liberals in New England toward Non-Christian Religions, 1784–1885." *Crane Review* 9 (Winter 1967): 59–89.

Wright, Brooks. *Interpreter of Buddhism to the West: Sir Edwin Arnold.* New York: Bookman Associates, 1957.

Yoo, Yushin. *Buddhism: A Subject Index to Periodical Articles in English, 1728–1971.* Metuchen, N. J.: Scarecrow Press, 1973.

Yu, Beongcheon. *An Ape of Gods: The Art and Thought of Lafcadio Hearn.* Detroit: Wayne State University Press, 1964.

———. *The Great Circle: American Writers and the Orient.* Detroit: Wayne State University Press, 1983.

Zürcher, Erik. *The Buddhist Conquest of China.* Leiden: Brill, 1959.

Religion and Culture in Victorian America

Aaron, Daniel. *Men of Good Hope: A Story of American Progressives.* New York: Oxford University Press, 1951.

Ahlstrom, Sydney E. *A Religious History of the American People.* New Haven: Yale University Press, 1972.

———. "The Scottish Philosophy and American Theology." *Church History* 24 (Sept. 1955): 257–72.

Albanese, Catherine L. *Corresponding Motion: Transcendental Religion and the New America.* Philadelphia: Temple University Press, 1977.

Baird, Robert. *Religion in America.* 1856. New York: Harper and Row, 1970.

Bednarowski, Mary Farrell. "Outside the Mainstream: Women's Religion and Women Religious Leaders in Nineteenth Century America." *Journal of the American Academy of Religion* 48 (June 1980): 207–31.

———. "Women in Occult America." In *The Occult in America*, edited by Howard Kerr and Charles L. Crow, 177–95. Urbana: University of Illinois Press, 1983.

Bellah, Robert N., et al. *Habits of the Heart: Individualism and Commitment in American Life*. Berkeley: University of California Press, 1985.

Bloch, Ruth. *Visionary Republic: Millennial Themes in American Thought, 1756–1800*. New York: Cambridge University Press, 1985.

Bousma, William J. "Intellectual History in the 1980s: From History of Ideas to History of Meaning." In *The New History: The 1980s and Beyond*, edited by Theodore Rabb and Robert I. Rotberg, 279–91. Princeton: Princeton University Press, 1982.

Bowden, Henry Warner. *Church History in the Age of Science: Historiographical Patterns in the United States, 1876–1918*. Chapel Hill: University of North Carolina Press, 1971.

———. *Dictionary of American Religious Biography*. Westport, Conn.: Greenwood, 1977.

Bozeman, Theodore Dwight. *Protestants in an Age of Science: The Baconian Ideal and Antebellum Religious Thought*. Chapel Hill: University of North Carolina Press, 1977.

Braude, Ann. *Radical Spirits: Spiritualism and Women's Rights in Nineteenth-Century America*. Boston: Beacon, 1989.

Brooks, Van Wyck. *New England: Indian Summer, 1865–1915*. Cleveland and New York: World Publishing Company, 1940.

Brown, Jerry Wayne. *The Rise of Biblical Criticism in America, 1800–1870: The New England Scholars*. Middletown, Conn.: Wesleyan University Press, 1969.

Buenker, John D. "Sovereign Individuals and Organic Networks: Political Cultures in Conflict During the Progressive Era." *American Quarterly* 40 (June 1988): 187–204.

Burr, Nelson R. *A Critical Bibliography of Religion in America*. 2 vols. Princeton: Princeton University Press, 1961.

Cauthen, Kenneth. *The Impact of American Religious Liberalism*. New York: Harper and Row, 1962.

Christensen, Torben, and William R. Hutchison, eds. *Missionary Ideologies in the Imperialist Era: 1880–1920*. Aarhus, Denmark: Aros Publishers; Cambridge, Mass.: Harvard Theological Review, 1984.

Coben, Stanley. "The Assault on Victorianism in the Twentieth Century." In *Victorian America*, edited by Daniel Walker Howe, 160–81. Philadelphia: University of Pennsylvania Press, 1976.

Cohn, Bernard S. "Anthropology and History in the 1980s." In *The New History*, edited by Theodore K. Rabb and Robert I. Rotberg, 227–52. Princeton: Princeton University Press, 1981.

David, Brion Davis, ed. *Ante-Bellum Reform*. New York, Evanston, and London: Harper and Row, 1967.

Dawson, Lorne. "Self-Affirmation, Freedom, and Rationality: Theoretically Elaborating 'Active' Conversions." *Journal for the Scientific Study of Religion* 29 (June 1990): 141–63.

Dictionary of American Biography. 20 vols. New York: Charles Scribner's Sons, 1928–36.

Dillenberger, John. *The Visual Arts and Christianity in America: From the Colonial Period to the Present*. Expanded ed. New York: Crossroad, 1989.

Douglas, Ann. *The Feminization of American Culture*. New York: Avon, 1977.

Dresser, Horatio W. *A History of the New Thought Movement*. New York: Thomas Y. Crowell, 1919.

Eliade, Mircea. *The Quest: History and Meaning in Religion.* Chicago: University of Chicago Press, 1969.

Ellwood, Robert, and Harry B. Partin. *Religious and Spiritual Groups in Modern America.* 2d ed. Englewood Cliffs, N.J.: Prentice-Hall, 1988.

The Encyclopedia of Missions. 2d ed. New York: Funk and Wagnalls, 1904.

Fredrickson, George M. *The Inner Civil War: Northern Intellectuals and the Crisis of the Union.* New York: Harper and Row, 1965.

————, and Dale T. Knobel. "A History of Discrimination." In *Prejudice. Selections from the Harvard Encyclopedia of American Ethnic Groups,* 30–87. Cambridge, Mass.: Harvard University Press, 1982.

Frei, Hans. *The Eclipse of Biblical Narrative: A Study in Eighteenth and Nineteenth Century Hermeneutics.* New Haven: Yale University Press, 1974.

Galbreath, Robert. "Explaining Modern Occultism." In *The Occult in America,* edited by Howard Kerr and Charles L. Crow, 11–37. Urbana: University of Illinois Press, 1983.

Gates, Barbara T. *Victorian Suicide: Mad Crimes and Sad Histories.* Princeton: Princeton University Press, 1988.

Gaustad, Edwin Scott. *Dissent in American Religion.* Chicago: University of Chicago Press, 1973.

Geertz, Clifford. *The Interpretation of Cultures.* New York: Basic Books, 1973.

————. *Local Knowledge: Further Essays in Interpretive Anthropology.* New York: Basic Books, 1983.

Gottschalk, Stephen. *The Emergence of Christian Science in American Religious Life.* Berkeley: University of California Press, 1973.

Halttunen, Karen. *Confidence Men and Painted Women: A Study of Middle Class Culture in America, 1830–1870.* New Haven and London: Yale University Press, 1982.

Hansen, Klaus J. *Mormonism and the American Experience.* Chicago History of American Religion Series. Chicago: University of Chicago Press, 1981.

Hart, James D. *The Popular Book: A History of America's Literary Taste.* New York: Oxford University Press, 1950.

Hekman, Susan J. *Weber, The Ideal Type, and Contemporary Social Theory.* Notre Dame, Ind.: Notre Dame University Press, 1983.

Hennesey, James. *American Catholics: A History of the Roman Catholic Community in the United States.* New York: Oxford University Press, 1981.

Higham, John. *From Boundlessness to Consolidation: The Transformation of American Culture, 1848–1860.* Ann Arbor: William L. Clements Library, 1969.

————. "Hanging Together: Divergent Unities in American History." *Journal of American History* 41 (June 1974): 5–28.

————. "The Reorientation of American Culture in the 1890s." In *Writing American History,* 73–102. Bloomington: Indiana University Press, 1970.

————. *Strangers in the Land: Patterns of American Nativism, 1860–1925.* 1955. New York: Atheneum, 1968.

————, and Paul K. Conkin, ed. *New Directions in American Intellectual History.* Baltimore: Johns Hopkins University Press, 1979.

Hofstadter, Richard. *The Age of Reform.* New York: Vintage, 1955.

Hollinger, David. "Historians and the Discourse of Intellectuals." In *New Directions in American Intellectual History,* edited by John Higham and Paul K. Conkin, 42–63. Baltimore: Johns Hopkins University Press, 1979.

Houghton, Walter E. *The Victorian Frame of Mind, 1830–1870.* New Haven: Yale University Press, 1957.

Howe, Daniel Walker. "At Morning Blest and Golden-Browed." In *A Stream of*

Light: A Short History of American Unitarian History, edited by Conrad Wright, 33–61. Boston: Unitarian Universalist Association, 1970.

―――. *The Unitarian Conscience: Harvard Moral Philosophy, 1805–1861.* 1970. Middletown, Conn.: Wesleyan University Press, 1988.

―――. "Victorian Culture in America." In *Victorian America,* edited by Daniel Walker Howe, 3–28. Philadelphia: University of Pennsylvania Press, 1976.

―――, ed. *Victorian America.* Philadelphia: University of Pennsylvania, 1976.

Hudson, Winthrop. "How American is Religion in America?" In *Reinterpretation in American Church History,* edited by Jerald C. Brauer. Chicago: University of Chicago Press, 1968.

―――. "Protestant Clergy Debate the Nation's Vocation, 1898–1899." *Church History* 42 (Mar. 1973): 110–18.

Hughes, H. Stuart. *Consciousness and Society: The Re-Orientation of European Social Thought, 1890–1930.* New York: Knopf, 1958.

Hutchison, William R. "The Americanness of the Social Gospel: An Inquiry in Comparative History." *Church History* 44 (Sept. 1975): 1–15.

―――. *Errand to the World: American Protestant Thought and Foreign Missions.* Chicago: University of Chicago Press, 1987.

―――. *The Modernist Impulse in American Protestantism.* New York: Oxford University Press, 1976.

Judah, J. Stillson. *The History and Philosophy of the Metaphysical Movements in America.* Philadelphia: Westminster, 1967.

Kerr, Howard, and Charles L. Crow, eds. *The Occult in America: New Historical Perspectives.* Urbana: University of Illinois Press, 1983.

Koch, G. Adolf. *Religion of the American Enlightenment.* 1933. New York: Crowell, 1968.

Kuklick, Bruce. *The Rise of American Philosophy: Cambridge, Massachusetts, 1860–1930.* New Haven: Yale University Press, 1977.

Lippy, Charles H., ed. *Religious Periodicals of the United States: Academic and Scholarly Journals.* Westport, Conn.: Greenwood, 1986.

Lofland, John. " 'Becoming a World-Saver' Revisited." *American Behavioral Scientist* 20 (July/Aug. 1977): 805–18.

―――, and Rodney Stark. "Becoming a World-Saver: A Theory of Conversion to a Deviant Perspective." *American Sociological Review* 30 (Dec. 1965): 862–75.

Lukes, Steven. "Types of Individualism." In *Dictionary of the History of Ideas,* 5 vols., edited by Phillip P. Wiener. New York: Scribner, 1968–74.

Marsden, George M. *Fundamentalism and American Culture: The Shaping of Twentieth-Century Evangelicalism, 1870–1925.* New York: Oxford University Press, 1980.

Marty, Martin E. "The Occult Establishment." *Social Research* 37 (Summer 1970): 212–30.

May, Henry F. *The End of American Innocence: The First Years of Our Own Time, 1912–1917.* 1959. New York: Oxford University Press, 1979.

―――. *The Enlightenment in America.* Oxford: Oxford University Press, 1976.

―――. *Protestant Churches and Industrial America.* New York: Harper and Brothers, 1949.

McDannell, Colleen. *The Christian Home in Victorian America, 1840–1900.* Religion in North America Series. Bloomington: Indiana University Press, 1986.

McLoughlin, William G. *The Meaning of Henry Ward Beecher: An Essay on the Shifting Values of Mid-Victorian America, 1840–1870.* New York: Alfred A. Knopf, 1970.

———. *Revivals, Awakenings, and Reform*. Chicago History of American Religion Series. Chicago: University of Chicago Press, 1978.

Meyer, D. H. "American Intellectuals and the Victorian Crisis of Faith." In *Victorian America*, edited by Daniel Walker Howe, 59–77. Philadelphia: University of Pennsylvania Press, 1976.

Moore, R. Laurence. *In Search of White Crows: Spiritualism, Parapsychology, and American Culture*. New York: Oxford University Press, 1977.

———. "The Occult Connection?: Mormonism, Christian Science, and Spiritualism." In *The Occult in America*, edited by Howard Kerr and Charles L. Crow, 135–61. Urbana and Chicago: University of Illinois Press, 1983.

———. *Religious Outsiders and the Making of Americans*. New York: Oxford University Press, 1986.

Mott, Frank Luther. *Golden Multitudes: The Story of Best Sellers in the United States*. New York: Macmillan, 1947.

———. *A History of American Magazines*. 5 vols. Cambridge, Mass.: Harvard University Press, 1938–68.

The National Cyclopædia of American Biography. New York: James T. White, 1893–1919.

Pals, Daniel L. *The Victorian "Lives" of Jesus*. Trinity University Monograph Series in Religion. San Antonio: Trinity University Press, 1982.

Persons, Stow. *Free Religion: An American Faith*. New Haven: Yale University Press, 1947.

Rabb, Theodore K. and Robert I. Rotberg, eds. *The New History: The 1980s and Beyond*. Princeton: Princeton University Press, 1982.

Reynolds, David S. *Faith in Fiction: The Emergence of Religious Literature in America*. Cambridge, Mass.: Harvard University Press, 1981.

Richardson, J. T. "The Active vs. the Passive Convert: Paradigm Conflict in Conversion/Recruitment Research." *Journal for the Scientific Study of Religion* 24 (1985): 165–79.

Rose, Anne C. *Transcendentalism as a Social Movement, 1830–1850*. New Haven: Yale University Press, 1981.

Rudolf, Frederick. *Curriculum: A History of the American Undergraduate Course of Study Since 1636*. San Francisco: Jossey-Bass, 1977.

Ruether, Rosemary Radford, and Rosemary Skinner Keller, eds. *Women and Religion in America: The Nineteenth Century: A Documentary History*. Vol. 1. San Francisco: Harper and Row, 1981.

Rydell, Robert W. *All the World's a Fair: Visions of Empire at American International Expositions, 1876–1916*. Chicago: University of Chicago Press, 1984.

Schlesinger, Arthur M., Sr. *The American as Reformer*. 1950. New York: Atheneum, 1968.

———. "A Critical Period in American Religion, 1875–1900." *Proceedings of the Massachusetts Historical Society* 64 (1930–32): 523–46. Reprinted in *Religion in American History: Interpretive Essays*, edited by John M. Mulder and John F. Wilson, 302–17. Englewood Cliffs, N.J.: Prentice-Hall, 1978.

Schorske, Carl E. *Fin-de-Siècle Vienna: Politics and Culture*. New York: Knopf, 1980.

Schutz, Alfred. "Problems in Interpretive Sociology." In *The Philosophy of Social Explanation*, edited by Alan Ryan, 203–19. Oxford: Oxford University Press, 1973.

Shils, Edward. *Center and Periphery: Essays in Macrosociology*. Chicago: University of Chicago Press, 1975.

Shupe, Anson D., Jr. *Six Perspectives on New Religions*. New York: Edwin Mellen, 1981.

Select Bibliography   233

Singal, Daniel Joseph. "Towards a Definition of American Modernism." *American
    Quarterly* 39 (Spring 1987): 7–26.
————. *The War Within: From Victorian to Modernist Thought in the South, 1919–1945.*
    Chapel Hill: University of North Carolina Press, 1982.
Smith-Rosenberg, Carroll. *Disorderly Conduct: Visions of Gender in Victorian America.*
    New York: Oxford University Press, 1985.
Snow, David, and Richard Machalek. "The Convert as a Social Type." In *Sociological
    Theory,* edited by R. Collins. San Francisco: Jossey-Bass, 1983.
————. "The Sociology of Conversion." *Annual Review of Sociology* 10 (1984): 167–90.
Staples, Clifford L., and Armand L. Mauss. "Conversion or Commitment?: A
    Reassessment of the Snow and Machalek Approach to the Study of Conver-
    sion." *Journal for the Scientific Study of Religion* 26 (1987): 133–47.
Stark, Rodney. "How New Religions Succeed: A Theoretical Model." In *The Future
    of New Religious Movements,* edited by David G. Bromley and Phillip E.
    Hammond, 11–29. Macon, Georgia: Mercer University Press, 1987.
Stern, Fritz Richard. *The Politics of Cultural Despair: A Study of the Rise of the Germanic
    Ideology.* Garden City, New York: Doubleday, 1965.
Stocking, George W., Jr. *Victorian Anthropology.* New York: Free Press, 1987.
Stockman, Robert H. "The Baha'i Faith and American Protestantism." Th.D. diss.,
    Harvard Divinity School, 1990.
————. *The Baha'i Faith in America: Origins, 1892–1900.* Vol. 1. Wilmette, Ill.: Baha'i
    Publishing Trust, 1985.
Straus, R. "Changing Oneself: Seekers and the Creative Transformation of Life
    Experience." In *Doing Social Life,* edited by John Lofland, 252–72. New York:
    John Wiley, 1976.
Sudermann, Elmer F. "Religion in the Popular American Novel, 1870–1900." *Journal
    of Popular Culture* 9 (Spring 1976): 1003–9.
Thomas, John L. "Romantic Reform in America." In *Ante-Bellum Reform,* edited by
    David Brion Davis. New York: Harper and Row, 1967.
Trachtenberg, Alan. *The Incorporation of America: Culture and Society in the Gilded Age.*
    New York: Hill and Wang, 1982.
Troeltsch, Ernst. *Protestantism and Progress: The Significance of Protestantism for the
    Rise of the Modern World.* 1912. Fortress Texts in Modern Theology. Phi-
    ladelphia: Fortress, 1986.
Turner, James. *Without God, Without Creed: The Origins of Unbelief in America.* Balti-
    more: Johns Hopkins University Press, 1985.
Turner, Victor. *Dramas, Fields, and Metaphors: Symbolic Action in Human Society.*
    Ithaca: Cornell University Press, 1974.
Tuveson, Ernest Lee. *Redeemer Nation: The Idea of America's Millennial Role.* Chicago:
    University of Chicago Press, 1968.
U.S. Bureau of the Census. *Religious Bodies: 1906.* Parts 1 and 2. Washington, D.C.:
    Government Printing Office, 1910.
U.S. Census Office. *Report on Statistics of Churches in the United States at the Eleventh
    Census: 1890.* Washington, D.C.: Government Printing Office, 1894.
Veysey, Laurence R. *The Emergence of the American University.* Chicago: University of
    Chicago Press, 1965.
————. "The Plural Organized Worlds of the Humanities." In *The Organization of
    Knowledge in Modern America, 1860–1920,* edited by Alexandra Oleson and
    John Voss, 51–106. Baltimore: Johns Hopkins University Press, 1979.
Von Shelting, Alexander. "Max Webers Wissenschaftslehre." Translated by Rolf E.
    Rogers. In *Max Weber's Ideal Type Theory,* edited by Rolf E. Rogers, 45–55.
    New York: Philosophical Library, 1969.

Walker, Robert H. "The Reform Frontier and the American Character." *Journal of American and Canadian Studies* 1 (Spring 1988): 1–11.

———. *The Reform Spirit in America*. New York: Putnam, 1976.

Watkins, J.W.N. "Ideal Types and Historical Explanation." In *The Philosophy of Social Explanation*, edited by Alan Ryan, 82–104. Oxford: Oxford University Press, 1973.

Weber, Eugen. *France, Fin de Siècle*. Cambridge, Mass.: Harvard University Press, 1986.

Weber, Max. *Economy and Society*. Edited by Guenther Roth and Claus Wittich. 2 vols. Berkeley: University of California Press, 1978.

———. *From Max Weber: Essays in Sociology*. Edited and translated by H. H. Gerth and C. Wright Mills. New York: Oxford University Press, 1946.

———. " 'Objectivity' in Social Sciences and Social Policy." *Methodology in the Social Sciences*. Translated by Edward A. Shils and Henry A. Finch, 49–112. New York: Free Press, 1949.

Weisenberger, Francis P. *Ordeal of Faith: The Crisis of Church-Going America, 1865–1900*. New York: Philosophical Library, 1959.

Welch, Claude. *Protestant Thought in the Nineteenth Century*. 2 vols. New Haven: Yale University Press, 1972, 1985.

Welter, Barbara. "The Cult of True Womanhood, 1820–1860." *American Quarterly* 18 (1966): 151–74.

Wiebe, Robert H. *The Search for Order, 1877–1920*. New York: Hill and Wang, 1967.

Wright, Conrad. *The Liberal Christians: Essays on American Unitarian History*. Boston: Unitarian Universalist Association, 1970.

———, ed. *A Stream of Light: A Short History of American Unitarianism*. Boston: Unitarian Universalist Association, 1975.

———, ed. *Three Prophets of Religious Liberalism: Channing, Emerson, and Parker*. 1961. Boston: Unitarian Universalist Association, 1983.

Yinger, J. Milton. *Countercultures: The Promise and Peril of a World Turned Upside Down*. New York: The Free Press, 1982.

Ziff, Larzer. *The American 1890s: Life and Times of a Lost Generation*. Lincoln and London: University of Nebraska Press, 1966.

Index